THE LOST HISTORY OF ROMAN THEATRE

The Lost History of Roman Theatre

T. P. Wiseman

PRINCETON UNIVERSITY PRESS
PRINCETON & OXFORD

Published by Princeton University Press
41 William Street, Princeton, New Jersey 08540
99 Banbury Road, Oxford OX2 6JX

press.princeton.edu

GPSR Authorized Representative: Easy Access System Europe - Mustamäe tee 50, 10621 Tallinn, Estonia, gpsr.requests@easproject.com

ISBN 9780691273235
ISBN (e-book) 9780691275840
Library of Congress Control Number: 2025938689

British Library Cataloging-in-Publication Data is available

Editorial: Ben Tate and Josh Drake
Production Editorial: Natalie Baan
Jacket Design: Karl Spurzem
Production: Danielle Amatucci
Publicity: Charlotte Coyne and William Pagdatoon
Copyeditor: Tash Siddiqui

Jacket image: ArchaiOptix / Wikimedia Commons

This book has been composed in Miller

Printed in the United States of America

10 9 8 7 6 5 4 3 2 1

For Rhinthon and Menippus, in Elysium

CONTENTS

PREFACE

WHAT'S 'LOST' about it? With thirty-six play-texts surviving more or less complete,[1] and a substantial number of theatre buildings still standing largely intact,[2] the subject ought to be pretty well understood.

In fact, there are enormous gaps in our knowledge. The civilisation we call 'classical antiquity' lasted a very long period of time: say fourteen hundred years, from the first Mediterranean city-states to the Lombard invasion of Italy (fig. 1).

The way those city-states honoured their gods and entertained their people, the two main aims of theatre in the ancient world,[3] did not remain static over all that time, and only a few privileged periods in that huge chronological range are adequately illuminated by the surviving texts of 'classical literature'.

The play-texts that happen to have been preserved give us a wonderful insight into Athenian theatre in the fifth and fourth centuries BC and Roman theatre in the second; but what about all the other times? Two recent scholars emphasise the problem: 'Historians of Roman theatre must, as one of the invariable conditions of their discipline, continually confront the unrepresentative nature, chronologically speaking, of our textual sources.'[4] Yes, we have the texts of Plautus, Terence and Seneca, but 'the rest, textually speaking, is silence, apart from a few fragments and passing references by ancient authors'.[5]

Well, it isn't quite that bad. The multifarious texts that survive from classical antiquity do provide plenty of relevant information, and the 'silence' may just be a result of scholars choosing not to grapple with the interpretative problems that make the scattered and haphazard textual material so difficult to use. This book has been written in the belief that a

1. Twenty comedies by Plautus, six comedies by Terence, nine tragedies by Seneca, one historical drama wrongly attributed to Seneca.

2. See the plates and figures at the end of Sear 2006.

3. Theatre belonged at the *ludi publici* in honour of the gods: see for instance Cicero *De legibus* 2.22 (*popularem laetitiam . . . cum diuum honore iungunto*), Livy 6.42.13 (*honoris deum immortalium causa*), Valerius Maximus 2.4.1 (*cultus deorum*).

4. Beacham and Denard 2023, 65; unimpressed by the literature, they brilliantly exploit the non-textual evidence of wall-paintings and architecture.

5. Beacham and Denard 2023, 65–6.

	700	Homer? Hesiod?
Roman Forum created		
	600	
		Aesop? Stesichorus
Tarquins expelled c. 507		Thespis
	500	Epicharmus
Secession of the *plebs* 494		Aeschylus
		Sophocles, Herodotus, Antiochus
	400	Aristophanes, Euripides, Thucydides
		Plato
		Aristotle
Roman conquest of Italy	**300**	Menander
She-wolf statue group 296		Rhinthon, Menippus
First Roman drama texts c. 240		Livius Andronicus, Naevius
	200	Plautus, Fabius Pictor
'Bacchanalia' abolished 186		Ennius, Terence, Pacuvius
Ti. Gracchus murdered 133		Lucilius
	100	Accius
Caesar murdered 44		Varro, Cicero, Laberius
	BC	Virgil, Horace, Livy
Augustus' principate 27 BC–AD 14		Dionysius, Ovid, Phaedrus
	AD	Velleius, Seneca, Persius
		Petronius, Quintilian, Silius
	100	Juvenal, Suetonius, Plutarch
		Tacitus
		Aulus Gellius
	200	Tertullian
	300	
Constantinople founded 324		
		Evanthius
	400	Diomedes, Jerome, Augustine
Rome sacked by Visigoths 410		Servius, Macrobius
Last western emperor 475–6		
Pope Gelasius 492–6	**500**	
		John Lydus
Justinian's reconquest of Italy		
Lombard invasions	**600**	
	700	

FIGURE 1. Timeline, 700 BC–AD 700. *Left:* selected historical events. *Right:* selected authors. Fourteen centuries are represented: another thirteen would take us to our own time.

historian should at least try to make sense of what the ancient sources say. It is, in effect, an attempt to break the silence.

The first chapter asks a fundamental question, 'when did Roman theatre begin?', and by testing what Cicero says on the subject against new archaeological evidence for archaic Rome, offers a very unexpected answer. Cicero himself never wrote for the stage, but the sheer volume of his surviving works makes his adult lifetime by far the best-attested period in Roman history, and chapter 2 discusses the passages in his letters, speeches and treatises that enable us to gain some insight into the theatre world of his time. In contrast, chapter 3 deals mainly with texts from late antiquity that claim to describe categories of theatrical performance existing at much earlier periods; by close reading of what they say it is possible to form an impression of the authorities they depended on, particularly works by Varro and Suetonius that have not survived to our time. The same late sources are exploited in chapter 4 to demonstrate that *satura* ('satire') was a performance genre, and not, as is usually assumed, merely a form of literature to be read in books.

The omnipresence of 'theatre' in Roman culture is variously exemplified in chapters 5 and 6, focusing respectively on the religious and political life of the late republic, and in chapters 7 and 8, which reveal Livy's use of contemporary stage performances to add dramatic effect to his own narratives of the early history of Rome. The 'theatre games', *ludi scaenici*, were also of interest to a later historian, the senator Velleius Paterculus (chapter 9), and even more urgently to his humbler contemporary Phaedrus, whose fables provide neglected evidence for the experience of theatre in the time of the emperor Tiberius (chapter 10). A century later Suetonius wrote extensively on the subject in a work now lost; a lengthy quotation from it—in a text three centuries later still—shows how he explained the hugely popular dance-drama called 'all-mime' (*pantomimus*) that had come into being in the time of Augustus (chapter 11). The final textual evidence discussed (chapter 12) is a polemic from the Christian Rome of the late fifth century AD about the 'street theatre' of the Lupercalia.

The aim of these twelve studies is to do justice to the complexities of the evidence, in the hope of achieving a more nuanced picture of the Romans' wide experience of theatre than the play-texts of Plautus, Terence and Seneca—wonderful though they are—can offer on their own.

The history of Roman theatre is not the same as the history of Roman drama as a literary genre. That began after 240 BC, with the preserved texts of tragedies and comedies by Lucius Livius Andronicus and his younger contemporary Gnaeus Naevius. As the known titles are enough to show, they were plays in the Greek manner:

Livius, tragedies: *Achilles, Aegisthus, Aiax mastigophorus, Andromeda, Danae, Equus Troianus, Hermiona, Tereus, Teucer.*
Naevius, tragedies: *Andromacha, Danae, Equus Troianus, Hector proficiscens, Hesiona, Iphigenia, Lycurgus.*
Naevius, comedies: e.g. *Acontizomenus, Agrypnuntes, Colax, Demetrius, Dolus, Glaucoma, Gymnasticus, Lampadio, Stalagmus, Stigmatias, Technicus, Triphallus.*

Was that a sudden decision to adopt an alien cultural form, as some have thought, or just an aspect of an already hellenised Roman culture?

It is one of the main arguments of this book that the latter option is not only historically possible, thanks to recent advances in the archaeological understanding of archaic Rome, but also historically necessary, in order to make sense of the visual evidence of artworks from the fourth century BC and of contemporary Greek perceptions of Rome as, in some sense, a Greek city. However, the Romans themselves reacted against that idea in the 180s BC, and most surviving Latin literature was written by authors who had little notion of it. That is what makes the enquiry so demanding.

The other main argument of the book is that tragedy and comedy in the traditional Athenian style were only one part of Roman theatre experience. Three of the chapters feature plays by known authors, but Decimus Laberius' *Anna Peranna* (chapter 5) was a *mimus*, essentially a variety show, and the serious dramas of Lucius Accius on Tullia (chapter 7) and of Cassius Parmensis on Brutus (chapter 8) dealt not with the themes of Attic tragedy but with events from the history of Rome itself. Phaedrus (chapter 10) wrote fables in the style of Aesop, but still regarded himself as a theatre performer if only he could get the chance, and those who did get the chance included animal impressionists and pipe-players flying over the stage by crane. The 'all-mime' dance-drama spectacle (chapter 11) was summed up by an enthusiast in the second century AD as 'the pipe, the flute, the foot-clappers, the clash of cymbals, the fine voice of an actor, the combined voice of singers'.[6] Somehow, we have to find room for all of that.

It can't be done in a systematic way because the evidence is so fragmented, and in fact this book was not composed in a systematic way.

6. Lucian *Saltatio* 68: αὐλόν, σύριγγα, ποδῶν κτύπον, κυμβάλου ψόφον, ὑποκριτοῦ εὐφωνίαν, ᾀδόντων ὁμοφωνίαν.

Most of the chapters started off as attempts to solve particular puzzles in Roman social or political history, and it was the way theatre, in one form or another, seemed to be involved in the likely solutions that prompted the idea of putting the studies together. What was planned as an introduction to the collection eventually came out as chapters 1–4.

So the following chapters are reprinted, with major or minor editing, from previous publications, with my thanks to the copyright-holders for permission:

Chapter 5: 'Anna and the *Plebs*: A Synthesis of Primary Evidence', in Gwynaeth McIntyre and Sarah McCallum (eds), *Uncovering Anna Perenna: A Focused Study of Roman Myth and Culture* (London: Bloomsbury Academic, 2019), 1–16.

Chapter 6: Part of 'Politics and the People: What Counts as Evidence?', *Bulletin of the Institute of Classical Studies* 60 (2017), 16–33.

Chapter 7: 'Tullia and the Furies', in K. Stebnicka and M. Węcowski (eds), *Studies in Honour of Adam Ziółkowski on the Occasion of His 70th Birthday*, vol. 2, *Palamedes* 15 ([2022], 2025).

Chapter 8: Extended version of 'A Puzzle in Livy', *Greece and Rome* 56 (2009), 203–10.

Chapter 9: 'Velleius and the Games', in Eleanor Cowan (ed.), *Velleius Paterculus: Making History* (Swansea: Classical Press of Wales, 2011), 279–86.

Chapter 11: 'Suetonius and the Origin of Pantomime', in Tristan Power and Roy K. Gibson (eds), *Suetonius the Biographer: Studies in Roman Lives* (Oxford: Oxford University Press, 2014), 256–72.

Chapters 1, 2, 3, 4, 10 and 12 are previously unpublished.

I am very grateful to the Princeton University Press's anonymous referees for their very helpful comments. Unless otherwise stated, all translations are mine.

THE LOST HISTORY OF ROMAN THEATRE

CHAPTER ONE

Rome and the Greek World

FIRST THERE were the Greeks, then there were the Romans. That is how theatre history usually begins, as in the first sentence of the first chapter of *The Cambridge Companion to Greek and Roman Theatre*:

> Greek and Latin literature and drama have been central and formative components of the Western cultural tradition ever since the Middle Ages; and modern conceptions of theatre in general, as of 'tragedy' and 'comedy' as particular dramatic forms, are indelibly shaped by the specific performance modes that evolved during the sixth to fourth centuries BC in Athens and during the third to first centuries BC in Rome.[1]

The separate chronologies are a factual datum: Aeschylus and Aristophanes in Greek wrote long before Plautus and Terence in Latin.

But surviving play-texts are not the only source of information. By taking account of a wider range of evidence, including the material record of archaic Rome (incomparably better understood now than it was fifty years ago), we may discover that '*first* there were the Greeks, *then* there were the Romans' is not, after all, a self-evident truth.

1.1. The orthodox version

Greek drama supposedly began with Thespis, who was evidently active in Athens in the years between 560 and 520 BC.[2] Roman drama supposedly began three centuries later with Lucius Livius ('Livius Andronicus'),[3]

1. Griffith 2007, 13. For a much more nuanced view see now Fulkerson and Tatum 2024, 6–14 and 41–58.

2. Marmor Parium *FGrH* 239 F43 (between 540 and 520 BC); Plutarch *Solon* 29.4-30.1; Diogenes Laertius 1.59-60 (c. 560 BC); *Suda* Θ 282 (535–532 BC). For the chronological problems see West 1989, Wright 2016, 1–12.

3. Cf. Aulus Gellius 6.7.11 (*L. Liuius*), 1.9.5 (*Liuii Andronici*); Goldberg 1995, 28–30.

whose debut is dated to 240 BC. Cicero provides that date, and he does so more than once, with some emphasis. The information comes in two passages from dialogues written in 46 and 45 BC:

> Greece used to surpass us in learning and in all types of literature. It was easy to win against no opposition, because while poets were the earliest authors in Greece, and Homer and Hesiod lived before Rome was founded and Archilochus during the reign of Romulus, we Romans were late-comers to poetry. It was in about the 510th year from the foundation of the city that Livius produced a play in the consulship of Gaius Claudius, Caecus' son, and Marcus Tuditanus, the year before Ennius was born.[4]

> Livius' plays aren't worth reading twice. This Livius was the first to produce a play—it was in the consulship of Gaius Claudius, Caecus' son, and Marcus Tuditanus, the year before Ennius was born, in the 514th year from the foundation of the city, as Atticus here says, and I follow him.[5]

What better authority could we hope for? But even Cicero has to be read carefully.

We need to ask why he was so insistent about the date,[6] and why he had to explain how he knew it: following Atticus, he had discovered the information 'in old documents'.[7] It evidently wasn't common knowledge, and he went on to apologise for this uncharacteristic historical pedantry.[8] Since

4. Cicero *Tusculan Disputations* 1.3: *doctrina Graecia nos et omni litterarum genere superabat, in quo erat facile uincere non repugnantes. nam cum apud Graecos antiquissimum e doctis genus sit poetarum, si quidem Homerus fuit et Hesiodus ante Romam conditam, Archilochus regnante Romulo, serius poeticam nos accepimus. annis fere CCCCCX post Romam conditam Liuius fabulam dedit C. Claudio Caeci filio M. Tuditano consulibus, anno ante natum Ennium.*

5. Cicero *Brutus* 71-2 = Atticus *FRHist* 33 F6: *Liuianae fabulae non satis dignae quae iterum legantur. atqui hic Liuius primus fabulam C. Claudio Caeci filio et M. Tuditano consulibus docuit anno ipso ante quam natus est Ennius, post Romam conditam autem quartodecimo et quingentensimo, ut hic ait, quem nos sequimur.* The inconsistent *ab urbe condita* dates may be the result of textual corruption, or just Cicero's use of two different chronological systems (cf. Wiseman 2009, 95–6). The 'foundation' of Rome was of course a legendary story, not a historical event.

6. He mentions it again at *De senectute* 50, where the elder Cato refers to Livius' play produced 'six years before I was born, when [C. Claudius] Cento and [M. Sempronius] Tuditanus were consuls'; cf. Fulkerson and Tatum 2024, 7 ('a surprising and suspicious exactitude').

7. Cicero *Brutus* 72: *et Atticus scribit et nos in antiquis commentariis inuenimus.* That evidence disproved a rival version that put Livius' work a generation later (details and discussion in Oakley 1998, 61–3).

8. Cicero *Brutus* 73: 'put the blame on Atticus—he's fired me with enthusiasm for chasing up the lives and times of eminent men'.

Livius' play was produced at the *ludi Romani*, which were the responsibility of the curule aediles,[9] the documents that dated it were no doubt in the aediles' archive on the Capitol.[10]

What Cicero found there was the name and date of the first *known* Roman poet and playwright. What he inferred from it, that 'Romans were late-comers to poetry', depended on the assumption that there had been no unrecorded poets and playwrights before 240 BC. But absence of evidence is not in itself evidence of absence, and he may have been wrong to assume that. It is perfectly possible that the innovation in 240 BC was not poetry and drama as such, but the recording of playwrights' names in an annual archive of the public games.[11]

Cicero's contrast with 'Greece' (*Graecia*) requires equally careful handling. No doubt he shared our modern assumption that 'Greek' and 'Roman' were always mutually exclusive concepts. In fact, they were not. Livius Andronicus himself was a Greek, from Taras in south Italy, enslaved when his city fell to the Romans in 272 BC.[12] At that time Rome itself could be thought of as a Greek city,[13] founded by Achaeans blown off course on their return from Troy (as Aristotle believed), or by exiles from the Arcadian town of Pallantion (as in Stesichorus' 'lyric epic' *Geryoneis*, written in the sixth century BC).[14]

9. Cassiodorus *Chronica* 316 Mommsen = *MGH Chronica minora* 2.128: *his consulibus* ['239 BC'] *ludis Romanis primum tragoedia et comoedia a Lucio Liuio ad scaenam data.* Responsibility: Livy 6.42.12-14 (with Wiseman 2008, 169–70), Dio Cassius 37.8.1 (Caesar as curule aedile).

10. Mentioned by Polybius 3.26.1: Rome's treaties with Carthage were 'preserved even now on bronze tablets beside the temple of Jupiter Capitolinus in the treasury of the aediles'.

11. As suggested in Wiseman 2015, 45–7. *Contra* Feeney 2016, who takes Cicero as documenting 'one of the strangest and most unlikely events in Mediterranean history' (4), 'the reform in the year 240 of the great annual festival of the Roman state, the *Ludi Romani*, to allow for the staging of a Latin play translated from a Greek original' (60); he assumes that previously the Roman *ludi scaenici* had featured merely 'improvisatory medley' or 'slapstick farce' (105–6).

12. Cicero *Brutus* 72-3 (misdated by Accius); cf. Suetonius *De grammaticis* 1.2 (*semigraecus*).

13. Heraclides Ponticus fr. 102 Wehrli (Plutarch *Camillus* 22.2): πόλιν Ἑλληνίδα Ῥώμην. For *Roma* as ῥώμη, see Lycophron 1233, Plutarch *Romulus* 1.1; sometimes explained as translated from an earlier Latin *Valentia* (Solinus 1.1, Festus 328L = Hyperochos of Kyme *BNJ* 576 F3, Servius on Virgil *Aeneid* 1.273 = Ateius Praetextatus fr. 14 Funaioli).

14. Aristotle fr. 609 Rose (Dionysius of Halicarnassus *Roman Antiquities* 1.72.3-4); Stesichorus *Geryoneis* fr. 21 (Pausanias 8.3.2) with Usener 1913, 330, Davies and Finglass 2014, 290.

In the mid-second century BC a distinguished senator called Gaius Acilius wrote a history of Rome in which the Greek ritual at the archaic altar of Hercules (*ara maxima*) was taken as proof that Rome was a Greek foundation.[15] He could equally well have used the rituals for Saturn (Kronos) or for Ceres (Demeter), both cults established in the late sixth or early fifth centuries BC and conducted, as three separate and well-informed sources attest, 'in the Greek manner'.[16]

By Cicero's time, however, Rome was believed to be of Trojan origin. According to the poets, Romulus was the son of Aeneas' daughter;[17] the historians, constrained by the supposed chronology, used not only the tale of Aeneas' voyage from Troy to Italy but also the elaborate quasi-history devised by Fabius Pictor in the late third century BC, in which fifteen generations of Aeneas' descendants ruled at 'Alba Longa' before the birth of Romulus.[18] Of course it was a fictional narrative (to be more precise, a combination of two fictional narratives), but its acceptance by the first century BC as the canonical account of the origin of Rome is itself a historical fact of some importance.[19] Thanks largely to Livy and Virgil, in modern times it has come to be treated as 'the' Roman foundation-legend; but it was only one story out of many,[20] with no resemblance to anything like historical reality.

15. Strabo 5.3.3 C230 = Acilius *FRHist* 7 F7: καὶ ὅ γ' Ἀκύλιος, ὁ τῶν Ῥωμαίων συγγραφεύς, τοῦτο τίθεται σημεῖον τοῦ Ἑλληνικὸν εἶναι κτίσμα τὴν Ῥώμην, τὸ παρ' αὐτοῖς τὴν πάτριον θυσίαν Ἑλληνικὴν εἶναι τῷ Ἡρακλεῖ. For Acilius see Cicero *De officiis* 3.115 (*qui Graece scripsit historiam*), Plutarch *Cato maior* 22.4 (ἀνὴρ ἐπιφανής).

16. Cato *Orationes* 77 Malcovati (*Graeco ritu fiebantur Saturnalia*), Cicero *Pro Balbo* 55 (*sacra Cereris . . . adsumpta de Graecia et per Graecas curata sunt semper sacerdotes*); cf. Dionysius of Halicarnassus *Roman Antiquities* 1.40.5 (*ara maxima* sacrifice ἔθεσιν Ἑλληνικοῖς), 6.1.4 (altar of Kronos established at Rome by Herakles Ἑλληνικοῖς ἔθεσιν).

17. Servius *auctus* on Virgil *Aeneid* 1.273: *Naeuius et Ennius Aeneae ex filia nepotem Romulum conditorem urbis tradunt.*

18. Fabius Pictor *FRHist* 1 F1-6, with Wiseman 2024, 29–30; for the fiction of 'Alba Longa' as a city see Grandazzi 2008, 179–514.

19. Lucretius 1.1 (Romans as *Aeneadae*), cf. Caesar *ap.* Suetonius *Diuus Iulius* 6.1 (*a Venere Iulii, cuius gentis familia est nostra*); the supposed descent of the patrician Iulii from Jupiter, via Venus and her son the Trojan prince Aeneas, will have helped to establish the story (Wiseman 2019, 77–81).

20. For the variety of competing 'origin of Rome' stories see Dionysius of Halicarnassus *Roman Antiquities* 1.72.1 (ἀμφισβητήσεως δὲ πολλῆς οὔσης καὶ περὶ τοῦ χρόνου τῆς κτίσεως καὶ περὶ τῶν οἰκιστῶν τῆς πόλεως), Plutarch *Romulus* 1.1 (τὸ μέγα τῆς Ῥώμης ὄνομα . . . ἀφ' ὅτου καὶ δι' ἣν αἰτίαν τῇ πόλει γέγονεν, οὐχ ὡμολόγηται παρὰ τοῖς συγγραφεῦσιν), Servius *auctus* on Virgil *Aeneid* 1.273 (*sed de origine et conditore urbis diuersa a diuersis traduntur*), Servius on Virgil *Aeneid* 7.678 (*de auctoribus conditarum urbium dissensio inuenitur, adeo ut ne urbis quidem Romae origo possit diligenter agnosci*). See Wiseman 1995, 160–68 for a collection of surviving examples.

Another quasi-historical datum accepted as axiomatic by Romans in Cicero's time was the belief that their ancestors had made the republic great from a very humble beginning.[21] The *paupertas* of early Rome was a source of pride and an article of faith,[22] unshaken even by the counter-evidence of surviving architecture:

> The temple as it stands was built many years later, because in the times of the kings all religious buildings were on a small scale.[23]

We don't know which particular temple Marcus Varro was referring to here; what matters is the reason he gave for his belief, which archaeology has now thoroughly disproved. Some religious buildings in the time of the kings and the first years of the republic were on a very substantial scale indeed.

The grandest of them was the temple of Jupiter Optimus Maximus on the Capitol, built by Tarquin and dedicated immediately after his expulsion, but at least six others were constructed in the late sixth and early fifth centuries BC.[24] Discussing the scale of their remains, a leading authority on early Roman architecture comes to this very striking conclusion:

> With its excess of temples—from modest to monumental to colossal—and its houses to rival any in the region, Rome appears to have been unparalleled by any contemporaneous city on the whole of the Italic Peninsula.[25]

For the Capitoline temple at least, the closest parallels were in Sicily, Athens and Ionia. The sheer size and number of the Roman building projects, not only in the time of Tarquin but for decades after his expulsion, imply

21. See for instance Cicero *Pro Caelio* 39 (*eos qui haec ex minimis tanta fecerunt*), Sallust *Catiline* 51.42 (*qui ex paruis opibus tantum imperium fecere*) and 52.19 (*rem publicam ex parua magnam fecisse*); cf. Suetonius *Diuus Augustus* 31.5 (*qui imperium p.R. ex minimo maximum reddidissent*).

22. See for instance Varro *De uita populi Romani* frr. 3 and 6 Pittà (Nonius 63L, 239L), Sallust *Catiline* 53.4, Livy pref. 11.

23. Varro *De uita populi Romani* fr. 8 Pittà (Nonius 792L): *haec aedis quae nunc est multis annis post facta sit, namque omnia regiis temporibus delubra parua facta*. For the context see Wiseman 2016, cxiv–v.

24. Wiseman 2024, 11–14: to Matuta (Leukothea) and Fortuna (Tyche), exact date uncertain; to Saturn (Kronos), c. 498 BC; to Mercury (Hermes), 495; to Ceres, Liber and Libera (Demeter, Dionysus and Kore), 493; and to Castor and Pollux (the Dioskouroi), 484. For the general reliability of the transmitted dates see Cornell 2014, 253–4.

25. Hopkins 2016, 173; details in Hopkins 2016, 66–125 ('on a new scale', 550–500 BC), 126–52 ('continuity of splendor', 500–450 BC).

that the city had both the ambition and the resources to undertake grand projects and pay for the necessary imported expertise.[26]

Not only that: each temple implied a commitment to a cult, with sacrifices and appropriate annual festivals. Previously financed at the king's expense, after the expulsion of Tarquin they became a public responsibility, with public officials (*aediles*) appointed to guarantee the upkeep of the buildings and the funding of the public 'games'.[27] And that is why the archaeological evidence is so important for our subject: whenever it was that 'Roman theatre' began, those games were where it happened.

1.2. A different perspective

There is thus a fundamental mismatch between what the Romans of Cicero's generation believed and what archaeology has now revealed: the beginning of the Roman republic was characterised not by poverty and frugality but by wealth and public display.

A generation after Cicero, when Livy's history of Rome came to report an event in 364 BC that involved theatre games (*ludi scaenici*), his lengthy account of 'small beginnings' depended on the same moralising mindset.[28] He treated stage performance as a complete novelty, unconnected with the Greek theatre tradition flourishing at that time, of which he evidently assumed the Romans could have known nothing.[29] A quite different perspective, however, was offered by one of Livy's contemporaries.

Dionysius of Halicarnassus' detailed history of early Rome was written in the years between 30 and 7 BC.[30] His aim was to show that Rome had been a Greek city from the very beginning,[31] and he was unaffected by any Roman prejudice in favour of virtuous frugality. On the contrary,

26. See Winter 2009, 580–81 and Hopkins 2016, 110–16, detecting the work of 'east Greek' experts. Two names happen to be known: Damophilos and Gorgasos, the terracotta modellers who decorated the new temple of Ceres, Liber and Libera (Pliny *Natural History* 35.154, quoting an archaic inscription).

27. As spelt out by Cicero as aedile-elect (*In Verrem* 2.5.36): *habeo rationem quid a populo Romano acceperim: mihi ludos sanctissimos . . . faciundos, mihi sacrarum aedium procurationem . . . commissam.*

28. Livy 7.2.4 and 13 (*parua principia*), 7.3.1 (*ludorum primum initium*); cf. pref. 4 on Rome itself, *ab exiguis profecta initiis*. The passage is analysed in section 3.1 below.

29. Livy 7.2.3 (*noua res*), with Oakley 1998, 54 ('he manages to avoid mentioning Greek drama throughout the digression').

30. Dionysius of Halicarnassus *Roman Antiquities* 1.8.2 (from the origins down to 265 BC), cf. 1.3.4 and 1.7.2 for the time of composition.

31. Dionysius of Halicarnassus *Roman Antiquities* 1.5.1 (Ἕλληνας τε αὐτοὺς ὄντας ἐπιδείξειν), 1.79.1 (Ἕλλαδα πόλιν), 7.70–73.

in his account of the first years of the republic he refers several times to the Romans' great expenditure on sacrifices and sacred festivals.[32] That certainly makes good sense in the light of the archaeological evidence. But how could Dionysius, a Greek rhetorician only newly resident in Rome, know better than the Romans themselves what the early republic was like?

The answer may be that Dionysius had better sources. Having decided to make the origin and early history of Rome his subject, he naturally turned first to the Greek historians who might be able to provide information.[33] Right at the beginning of his account he cited 'Antiochus of Syracuse, a very early historian, in his work on the settlement of Italy', even quoting verbatim what look like the opening words:

> Antiochus son of Xenophanes put together this written account of Italy from the most reliable and intelligible of the ancient stories.[34]

Writing in the late fifth century BC, and certainly aware of Rome,[35] Antiochus was a very valuable source—'not just any historian', as Dionysius put it, 'and not a recent one either'.[36]

It is a remarkable fact that the only authors known to have used 'Antiochus on Italy' are Dionysius himself and Strabo of Amaseia, another Greek historian working in Rome at the time.[37] Furthermore—and it's unlikely to be a coincidence—Dionysius and Strabo are the only authors to give a

32. Dionysius of Halicarnassus *Roman Antiquities* 5.36.4 (θυσίας ἀπέδοσαν τοῖς θεοῖς ἀπὸ χρημάτων πολλῶν, 506 BC), 6.1.4 (δημοτελεῖς ἀναδειχθῆναι . . . ἑορτάς τε καὶ θυσίας, 497 BC), 6.10.1 (θυσίας τε μεγάλας ἀπὸ πολλῶν ἐπιτελέσειν χρημάτων καὶ ἀγῶνας καταστήσεσθαι πολυτελεῖς, 496 BC), 6.13.4 (θυσίαι τε πολυτελεῖς, 496 BC), 6.17.2 (ἀγῶνάς τε καὶ θυσίας τοῖς θεοῖς ἀπὸ τετταράκοντα ταλάντων, 496 BC). Cf. Cornell 2014, 254: 'the archaeological evidence confirms the general prosperity and sophistication of Rome in the sixth century'.

33. Dionysius of Halicarnassus *Roman Antiquities* 1.6.1: Hieronymus of Cardia, Timaeus, Antigonus, Polybius, Silenus 'and countless others'.

34. Dionysius of Halicarnassus *Roman Antiquities* 1.12.3: Ἀντίοχος δὲ ὁ Συρακούσιος, συγγραφεὺς πάνυ ἀρχαῖος, ἐν Ἰταλίας οἰκισμῷ . . . εἰπὼν ὧδε· Ἀντίοχος Ξενοφάνεος τάδε συνέγραψε περὶ Ἰταλίης ἐκ τῶν ἀρχαίων λόγων τὰ πιστότατα καὶ σαφέστατα. See Pearson 1987, 11–18 on Antiochus; his importance as a source for Dionysius was already noted by Pais 1908, 233–4.

35. Diodorus Siculus 12.71.2 (Antiochus' history of Sicily stopped at 424–3 BC); Antiochus *BNJ* 555 F6 = Dionysius of Halicarnassus *Roman Antiquities* 1.73.4-5 (ἄνδρα φυγάδα ἐκ Ῥώμης).

36. Dionysius of Halicarnassus *Roman Antiquities* 1.73.4: οὐ τῶν ἐπιτυχόντων τις οὐδὲ νέων συγγραφεύς.

37. Strabo 6.1.4 C254 (Ἀντίοχος ἐν τῷ περὶ τῆς Ἰταλίας συγγράμματι); Antiochus *BNJ* 555 F2 and 4-6 (from Dionysius), F3a and 7-13 (from Strabo). The natural inference is that a rare copy survived in the 'Greek library' on the Palatine (Suetonius *Diuus Augustus* 29.3, Houston 2014, 220–22) or one of the other libraries of Augustan Rome.

circumstantial account of the careers in Italy of Demaratus of Corinth and his son. Here is Dionysius on the subject:

> The Corinthian Demaratus, of the family of the Bacchiadae, sailed to Italy in his own ship with his own cargo, which he sold in the Tyrrhenian cities, at that time the most flourishing in Italy. Having gained great profit from it, he no longer wanted to visit any other market but continued to work the same sea, carrying Greek cargo to the Tyrrhenians and Tyrrhenian cargo to Greece, and thus became the possessor of very great wealth.
>
> But when Corinth was gripped by civil strife and the tyranny of Cypselus rose against the Bacchiadae [c. 657 BC], Demaratus thought it unsafe to live under a tyranny as a rich man belonging to the oligarchic family, so he collected together as much of his property as he could and sailed away from Corinth. He had many good friends among the Tyrrhenians as a result of his close association with them, especially at Tarquinii, then a large and prosperous city, so he built a house there and married a lady of distinguished family.[38]

And here is Strabo, who merges the story with the Roman 'seven kings' tradition:[39]

> Corinth was ruled by the Bacchiadae, a rich, extensive and aristocratic family, who held power there for nearly two hundred years and exploited the city's trade without opposition. Cypselus overthrew them and seized power. . . . Demaratus, one of the previously ruling family, escaping from the political upheaval, took so much wealth from his home city to Tyrrhenia that he himself became ruler of the city that received him [Tarquinii], and his son was even made king of the Romans.
>
> Demaratus arrived from Corinth with a multitude of people,[40] was received by the Tarquinians and married a lady of the place by whom he had a son called Lucumo. A friend of Ancus Marcius, king of Rome, Lucumo became king himself and changed his name to Lucius Tarquinius Priscus.[41] Like his father before him, he too

38. Dionysius of Halicarnassus *Roman Antiquities* 3.46.3-5; see also Polybius 6.11a.10, Cicero *De republica* 2.34, Livy 1.34.1-10, Zonaras 7.8.

39. Strabo 8.6.20 C378 and 5.2.2 C219-20. See Wiseman 2024, 29–30 on the Roman tradition, evidently created by Fabius Pictor.

40. λαὸν ἄγων ἐκ Κορίνθου: not colonists, as assumed by Biffi 1988, 33.

41. The *cognomen* is an obvious anachronism: he only needed to be called *Priscus* ('the former') when he had to be distinguished in retrospect from the later king Tarquinius, his son or grandson. Similarly, 'Ancus Marcius' may well have been an invention of the late third century BC (Wiseman 2008, 314–17).

embellished Tyrrhenia,[42] the father by the great supply of artisans he had brought with him from Corinth, the son by means of resources from Rome.[43]

I think it is a reasonable supposition that this narrative was first put on record by Antiochus in the fifth century BC in Syracuse, a Corinthian colony itself founded by one of the wealthy Bacchiadae.[44]

Modern historians are reluctant to believe in Lucumo son of Demaratus as a real historical figure, but it seems to me that such doubts are unnecessary.[45] Even the later Roman tradition knew things about 'Lucius Tarquinius Priscus' that were not integral to the factitious narrative of the seven kings, and may therefore derive from some earlier and more authentic source. First, he created a public market-place surrounded by workshops;[46] second, he marked out a space for horse-racing, and provided wooden stands for spectators;[47] third (and most important for the lost history of Roman theatre), he founded the annual festival, known as

42. ἐκόσμησε τὴν Τυρρηνίαν: for the nature of the embellishment see for instance Blakeway 1935, 147–9, Winter 2009, 578–80. The Greek term 'Tyrrhenia' meant west central Italy in general, not just Etruria: according to Hesiod (*Theogony* 1011–16) it was ruled by 'Latinos, excellent and strong', son of Odysseus and Circe and eponym of the Latins.

43. ὁ μὲν εὐπορίᾳ δημιουργῶν τῶν συνακολουθησάντων οἴκοθεν, ὁ δὲ παῖς ἐκ τῆς Ῥώμης ἀφορμαῖς: for the artisans cf. Pliny *Natural History* 35.16 (Ecphantus of Corinth, pioneer painter), 35.152 (terracotta modellers Eucheir, Diopus and Eugrammus); the Roman resources may have been the clay-beds now known to have existed in the stream valley between the Palatine and the Capitol (Ammerman et al. 2008, Winter et al. 2009).

44. Archias: Thucydides 6.3.2, Strabo 6.2.4 C269 (emphasising the consequent wealth of Syracuse).

45. See for instance Cornell 1995, 124 ('a secondary extension of the tradition'), Forsythe 2005, 101 ('probably not historical'); but it is hard to imagine any motive for its invention, and the assumption that Greek sources about Corinth 'are unlikely to have been interested in Rome' (Cornell) is essentially a *petitio principii*. For Lucumo's historical context see now Bradley 2020, 74, 118–19.

46. Livy 1.35.10 (*circa forum priuatis aedificanda diuisa sunt loca; porticus tabernaeque facta*), Dionysius of Halicarnassus *Roman Antiquities* 3.67.4-5 (τήν τε ἀγοράν . . . ἐκόσμησεν ἐργαστηρίοις τε καὶ παστάσι περιλαβών); see Hopkins 2016, 27–34 for the probable creation of the Roman Forum in the seventh century BC, Ampolo 2013, 268–70 for the introduction of tiled roofs at that time as an index of Rome becoming an urban society.

47. Livy 1.35.8-9 (*tum primum circo qui nunc maximus dicitur designatus locus est. loca diuisa . . . fori appellati; spectauere furcis duodenos ab terra spectacula alta sustinentibus pedes*), Dionysius of Halicarnassus *Roman Antiquities* 3.68.1 (κατεσκευάσε δὲ καὶ τὸν μέγιστον τῶν ἱπποδρόμων . . . ποιήσας περὶ αὐτὸν καθέδρας . . . ἐπ' ἰκρίοις, δοκῶν ξυλίναις σκηναῖς ὑποκειμένων).

'great games' because of the great expense involved, that later became the *ludi Romani*.[48] Contradicting the 'poverty of early Rome' tradition as they do, such items are unlikely to have been invented from nothing.

In fact, the vast wealth Demaratus brought from Corinth is a recurring theme in Dionysius' ongoing narrative.[49] Lucumo inherited it, took it with him to Rome, and used it to establish his position there;[50] the younger Tarquin insisted that his own inheritance of it entitled him to rule;[51] he demanded its restoration when he and his family were expelled from Rome,[52] but the Romans declared it forfeit because of his tyranny.[53] If that narrative was well founded, perhaps reported by Antiochus of Syracuse less than a century after the final events, it would account for how the newly free Roman state could afford those temples and those expensive festivals.

So yes: surprising as it seems, Dionysius of Halicarnassus did have better information about early Rome than either Cicero or Livy. And unlike their romantic idea of virtuous poverty, it is wholly consistent with the material evidence for prosperity and architectural splendour that has emerged in the last fifty years.

48. Cicero *De republica* 2.36 (*primum ludos maximos, qui Romani dicti sunt, fecisse accepimus*); Eutropius 1.6.1 (*circum Romae aedificauit, ludos magnos instituit qui ad nostram memoriam permanent*), *De uiris illustribus* 6.8 (*circum maximum aedificauit, ludos magnos instituit*). Expense: ps.Asconius 217 Stangl: *Romani ludi sub regibus instituti sunt magnique appellati, quod magnis impensibus dati.*

49. Dionysius of Halicarnassus *Roman Antiquities* 3.46.3-4 (πολλῶν χρημάτων κύριος . . . πολλὰ κεκτημένος); cf. Cicero *De republica* 2.34 (*fortunis facile ciuitatis suae principem . . . fugisse cum magna pecunia dicitur*), *Tusculan Disputations* 5.109 (*fugit Tarquinios Corintho et ibi suas fortunas constituit*).

50. Dionysius of Halicarnassus *Roman Antiquities* 3.47.1-2 (τὸν πατρικὸν πλοῦτον μέγαν ὄντα . . . τά τε χρήματα πάντα συσκευασάμενος), 3.48.1 (πᾶσαν τὴν πατρικὴν οὐσίαν ἐπαγόμενος), 3.48.44 (χρημάτων μεταδόσει); cf. Livy 1.34.1 (*uir impiger ac diuitiis potens*), 1.34.4 (*omnium heredi bonorum*), 1.34.11 (*Romanis conspicuum eum nouitas diuitiaeque faciebant*).

51. Dionysius of Halicarnassus *Roman Antiquities* 4.31.1 (προσήκει μοι . . . μὴ μόνον τῶν χρημάτων ἀλλὰ καὶ τῆς βασιλείας αὐτοῦ κληρονομεῖν), 4.31.3 (ἅμα τοῖς χρήμασι καὶ τὴν βασιλείαν ἀποδεδωκέναι), 4.37.3 (σὺν τοῖς χρήμασι καὶ τὴν ἀρχήν).

52. Dionysius of Halicarnassus *Roman Antiquities* 5.5.2 (τὴν οὐσίαν ἣν ὁ πάππος αὐτοῦ πρότερον ἐκέκτητο), 5.21.1-2 (τὰς οὐσίας ἀνακομισάμενος ἃς ἀφῃρέθησαν), 5.31.3 (χρήματα . . . ἅπαντα ὅσα Ταρκύνιός τε ὁ πρεσβύτατος κατέλιπε); cf. Livy 2.3.5-6 (*bona repetentes*), 2.4.3 (*reddenda bona*), 2.19.10 (*ob erepta bona*).

53. Dionysius of Halicarnassus *Roman Antiquities* 5.5.3 (κατέχειν τὰ χρήματα συνεβούλευσε τιμωρίας τε χάριν ἀνθ' ὧν οἱ τύραννοι τὸ κοινὸν ἠδίκησαν), 5.32.2 (ἐκ τῶν κοινῶν τοῖς τυράννοις μηδὲν ἀποδιδόναι); cf. Livy 2.5.1-3 (*de bonis regiis*), 2.34.4 (*pro bonis Tarquiniorum*).

1.3. The right conditions

The notion of Rome as a Greek city,[54] apparently so paradoxical, turns out to be perfectly credible. There is no reason to think that Rome had any kind of urban identity before the arrival, some time in the second half of the seventh century BC, of wealthy Lucumo, son of Corinthian Demaratus, who created an *agora* and a *hippodromos* (the Forum and the Circus Maximus) and set up the 'great games' that would bring honour to the city.[55]

At this point we need to remember that a *hippodromos* was not restricted to horse- or chariot-racing, or athletics. What went on there on all the days of the year when such elaborate set-piece events were *not* happening? Our best evidence happens to come from a Greek city in the second century AD, where Dio 'Chrysostom' in one of his moral sermons was urging his audience not to be distracted by the bustle of everyday life. This is the illustration he chose:

> I've seen it myself just now, walking through the *hippodromos*—lots of people doing different things in the same place, someone playing the pipes, someone dancing, someone juggling, someone reciting a poem, someone singing, someone telling a story or a myth, and not one of them prevented anyone from concentrating on doing their own thing.[56]

We should think of a *hippodromos*—including that of Lucumo at Rome—as a sort of fairground, suitable for all kinds of public performance.

Lucumo may also have set up the cult of Herakles, from whom his family, the Bacchiadae, traced their descent.[57] The foundation story of the *ara maxima* was that the hero himself was present in Rome with the cattle of Geryon, and built the altar when he learned of his future deification from the prophetess Themis, mother of Evander.[58] That tale evidently goes back to the *Geryoneis* of the Sicilian poet Stesichorus in the

54. See nn. 13–16, and cf. Cornell 1995, 151–72 on 'the myth of Etruscan Rome': the Tarquins were a Corinthian dynasty, not (as is often said) an Etruscan one.

55. See nn. 46–8, and cf. Pindar *Nemean Odes* 9.12 (ἄμφαινε κυδαίνων πόλιν) for the aim and effect of a king's newly founded games.

56. Dio Chrysostom *Oratio* 20.10: ἤδη δέ ποτε εἶδον ἐγὼ διὰ τοῦ ἱπποδρόμου βαδίζων πολλοὺς ἐν τῷ αὐτῷ ἀνθρώπους ἄλλο τι πράττοντας, τὸν μὲν αὐλοῦντα, τὸν δὲ ὀρχούμενον, τὸν δὲ θαῦμα ἀποδιδόμενον, τὸν δὲ ποιήμα ἀναγιγνώσκοντα, τὸν δὲ ᾄδοντα, τὸν δὲ ἱστορίαν τινὰ ἢ μῦθον διηγούμενον· καὶ οὐδὲ εἷς τούτων οὐδένα ἐκώλυσε προσέχειν αὐτῷ καὶ τὸ προκείμενον πράττειν.

57. Thucydides 6.3.2, Diodorus Siculus 7.9.4-6.

58. Dionysius of Halicarnassus *Roman Antiquities* 1.40.2-6, cf. 1.31.1 and 3; Livy 1.7.9-14 (mother not named); Strabo 5.3.3 C230 (mother Nikostrate); Ovid *Fasti* 1.497-500 and 583-4, cf. Virgil *Aeneid* 8.339-41 (mother Carmentis).

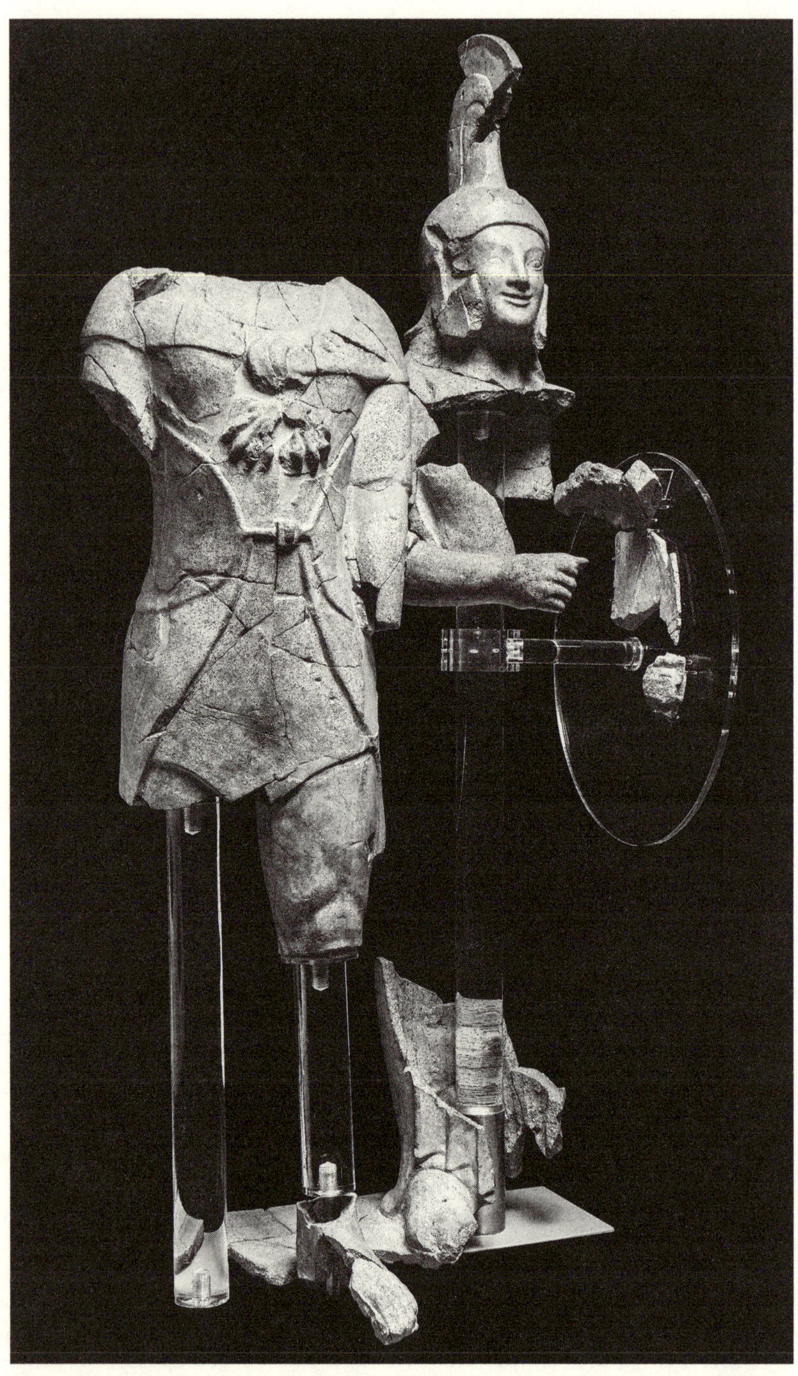

FIGURE 2. *Akroterion* statue group of Herakles and Pallas Athene from the rebuilt archaic temple at S. Omobono, c. 530 BC: Rome, Musei Capitolini, Palazzo dei Conservatori: Archivio Fotografico dei Musei Capitolini. © Roma, Sovrintendenza Capitolina ai Beni Culturali.

mid-sixth century BC,[59] a narrative demonstrably familiar to the Romans and their neighbours at just that time. At Rome and Satricum in Latium, and at Caere and Veii in south Etruria, artists in the east-Greek style were commissioned to create terracotta statues (*akroteria*, to stand on the roofs of temples) showing Pallas Athene escorting the newly deified Herakles to Olympus (fig. 2).[60] The hero was shown wearing the lionskin, a detail introduced into the story by Stesichorus himself.[61]

Stesichorus could have presented his *Geryoneis* at any or all of those Latin and south-Etruscan centres,[62] no doubt flattering his hosts each time with a reference to Herakles stopping there on his epic cattle-drive back to Argos. It was a sung narrative, a kitharode's 'lyric epic', of the kind Thespis in Athens, at just this time, was developing into 'drama', with performers in costume singing or speaking the roles.[63] In that context it is important to remember that festivals like the games founded by Lucumo were 'outreach' events, attracting spectators and competitors from far afield.[64] A famous example a couple of generations earlier was the kitharode Arion of Lesbos, who worked in Corinth but undertook a very profitable tour of the festivals of Sicily and Italy.[65] Since performers from many parts of the Greek world might meet at such events, we may suspect that Thespis' innovation soon became widely known.

It was certainly known and practised in Sicily, where, we are told, 'Epicharmus together with Phormus invented comedy in Syracuse', thus challenging even Athens for historic precedence as the origin of drama.[66]

59. Stesichorus *Geryoneis* fr. 21 (Pausanias 8.3.2) with Usener 1913, 330, Davies and Finglass 2014, 290.

60. Lulof 2000, Winter 2009, 377–80 (Veii and Rome), 466–7 (Satricum and Caere), 501–2 (Veii).

61. Athenaeus 12.512f-513a, quoting Megaclides (fourth century BC).

62. Cf. Herodotus 1.167.2 for games at Caere ('Agylla'), ordered by Delphi about 530 BC.

63. See n. 2; Herington 1985, esp. 19–20 (Stesichorus), 97–8 (Thespis); West 2015 ('lyric epic').

64. See for instance Fabius Pictor *FRHist* 1 F15 (Dionysius of Halicarnassus *Roman Antiquities* 7.72.1 and 73.4) on the *ludi Romani*: ἵνα φανερὰ γίνοιτο τοῖς ξένοις . . . ἐπιδείξεις τοῖς εἰς θέαν <u>συνεληλυθόσιν</u>). So too the games in the Romulus story: Dionysius of Halicarnassus *Roman Antiquities* 2.30.3-4 (περιήγγελλεν εἰς τὰς ἔγγιστα πόλεις καλῶν τοὺς βουλομένους ἀγορᾶς τε μεταλαμβάνειν καὶ ἀγώνων . . . <u>συνελθόντων</u> δὲ πολλῶν ξένων εἰς τῆν ἑορτὴν), Plutarch *Romulus* 14.4 (ἀγῶνα καὶ θέαν ἐκ καταγγελίας ἐπετέλει πανηγυρικήν· καὶ πολλοὶ μὲν ἄνθρωποι <u>συνῆλθον</u>).

65. Herodotus 1.24.1 (section 4.5 below); one would expect him to have performed at games newly founded by a Corinthian ruler.

66. *Suda* E 2766 (Ἐπίχαρμος . . . εὗρε τὴν κωμῳδίαν ἐν Συρακούσαις ἅμα Φόρμῳ); Aristotle *Poetics* 1448a33-4 (Ἐπίχαρμος ὁ ποιητὴς πολλῷ πρότερος ὢν Χιωνίδου καὶ Μάγνητος), 1449b5-9 (τὸ δὲ μύθους ποιεῖν [Ἐπίχαρμος καὶ Φόρμις] τὸ μὲν ἐξ ἀρχῆς ἐκ Σικελίας ἦλθε). For

Nothing is known of Phormus (or Phormis), but Epicharmus had attended the teachings of Pythagoras,[67] so his career as a dramatist probably began in the last two decades of the sixth century BC. He was evidently familiar with Rome: he knew that Pythagoras had been enrolled as an honorary citizen there, presumably after the expulsion of Tarquin,[68] and must have been aware that the games at Rome offered opportunities for people like himself.

Epicharmus' work, contemporary with the earliest Athenian satyr-plays, was itself in some sense satyric.[69] Certainly he was known for his association with Dionysus and the satyrs,[70] and it must be significant that satyrs were regularly portrayed in terracotta on public buildings in Sicily at just this time.[71] It is equally significant, though much less often noticed, that that architectural fashion was followed elsewhere only in Latium and at Rome (fig. 3).[72]

A Sicily–Rome connection in this period is implied also in Dionysius' account of the confiscation by the Romans of the ancestral wealth of the Bacchiadae after the expulsion of Tarquin.[73] How they used it is explained in his elaborate narrative of the great battle at Lake Regillus in 496 BC that finally freed Rome from the threat of the exiled Tarquin. He presents the Roman commander encouraging his troops:

> Postumius praised their enthusiasm, and vowed to the gods that if the battle had a good and fortunate outcome, he would provide sacrifices

---

theatre in 'west Greece' (Sicily and south Italy) see Bosher 2012, Csapo and Wilson 2020, 276–428.

67. Iamblichus *Vita Pythagorica* 266, Diogenes Laertius 8.78; other evidence that dates him to the 480s BC is not incompatible, since he lived to the age of ninety.

68. Plutarch *Numa* 8.9: Πυθαγόραν Ῥωμαῖοι τῇ πολιτείᾳ προσέγραψαν, ὡς ἱστόρηκεν Ἐπίχαρμος ὁ κωμικὸς ἔν τινι λόγῳ πρὸς Ἀντήνορα γεγραμμένῳ, παλαιὸς ἀνὴρ καὶ τῆς Πυθαγορικῆς διατριβῆς μετεσχηκώς. There is no reason to doubt the authenticity of the reference (Wiseman 2024, 10–11); for Romans among Pythagoras' disciples see Diogenes Laertius 8.14, Iamblichus *Vita Pythagorica* 241, Porphyry *Vita Pythagorae* 22.

69. Shaw 2014, 56–77; for Athens see *Suda* Π 2230 = *TrGF* 4 T1 ('499–6 BC'), with O'Sullivan and Collard 2013, 22–8.

70. *Anthologia Palatina* 7.82 (κεκορυθμένον ἀνέρα Βάκχῳ | καὶ σατύροις), cf. Theocritus *Anthologia Palatina* 9.600.

71. Marconi 2006, 81–7, Shaw 2014, 71–3; cf. Csapo and Wilson 2020, 364 on 'the (almost exclusively) Sicilian practice of attaching silen antefixes to temples'.

72. E.g. Satricum: Cristofani 1990, 243–4 (9.6.71-2). Rome: Cristofani 1990, 63 (3.4.1, Forum), 69 (3.6.1, Capitol), 91 (4.1.4, Palatine), 254 (10.1.4, Esquiline). See Marconi 2006, 84 ('l'antefissa silenica viene introdotta contemporaneamente, alla fine del VI secolo, sia in Sicilia, che in Italia Centrale'), Wiseman 2024, 14–17 and section 4.5 below.

73. See nn. 52–3: probably derived from a Syracusan source (Antiochus).

FIGURE 3. (a) Terracotta antefix from Satricum, 500–490 BC. Rome, Villa Giulia (foto n. 4559): © Museo Nazionale Etrusco di Villa Giulia, Archivio fotografico. (b) Terracotta antefix from the Roman Forum, 500–490 BC. Rome, ParCo_Archivio-Moderno-Fotografico_Foro-Romano-Palatino_Basilica-Giulia_Antefissa-a-testa-di-Sileno_Bruno-Angeli_Inv.1916_1. By permission of the Ministero della Cultura—Parco Archeologico del Colosseo.

> at great expense and establish lavishly funded games to be held every year by the Roman People.[74]

And after the victory the same commander pays the vow:

> Having set aside one tenth of the booty, he put on games and sacrifices to the gods and let the contract at forty talents for temples to Demeter, Dionysus and Kore.[75]

Demeter and Kore were the patron goddesses of Sicily.[76]

In Latin the three divinities were Ceres, Liber and Libera, with Demeter's daughter (Kore, 'the virgin') given the same 'speaking name' as Dionysus himself: Liber and Libera from *libertas*, gods of a free city.[77] Their joint temple was a magnificent one, dedicated in 493 BC next to the Circus Maximus where the games were held.[78] Were dramatic performances presented there, as they were in Sicily? Given the circumstantial evidence, there is no obvious reason to rule it out.

1.4. The god of drama

The Romans' choice of divinities, in a state newly freed from tyranny, could hardly be a random one. Demeter and Kore were the *Thesmophoroi*, guardians of the rule of law;[79] at Rome they guaranteed the *sacrosanctitas* of plebeian magistrates,[80] and their temple was where the plebeian aediles preserved the texts of *plebiscita*, and later *senatus consulta* too.[81] We should expect the choice of Dionysus (Liber) to be no less significant.

74. Dionysius of Halicarnassus *Roman Antiquities* 6.10.1: καὶ ὁ Ποστόμιος ἐπαινέσας τὸ πρόθυμον αὐτῶν καὶ τοῖς θεοῖς εὐξάμενος, ἐὰν εὐτυχὲς καὶ καλὸν τέλος ἀκολουθήσῃ τῇ μάχῃ, θυσίας τε μεγάλας ἀπὸ πολλῶν ἐπιτελέσειν χρημάτων καὶ ἀγῶνας καταστήσεσθαι πολυτελεῖς, οὓς ἄξει ὁ Ῥωμαίων δῆμος ἀνὰ πᾶν ἔτος, ἀπέλυσεν ἐπὶ τὰς τάξεις.

75. Dionysius of Halicarnassus *Roman Antiquities* 6.17.2: ἀπὸ δὲ τῶν λαφύρων ἐξελόμενος τὰς δεκάτας ἀγῶνάς τε καὶ θυσίας τοῖς θεοῖς ἀπὸ τετταράκοντα ταλάντων ἐποίει καὶ ναῶν κατασκευὰς ἐξεμίσθωσε Δήμητρι καὶ Διονύσῳ καὶ Κόρῃ κατ' εὐχήν.

76. Diodorus Siculus 5.2.3-5.3, Cicero *In Verrem* 2.4.106; see Kowalzig 2008 for their relevance to drama.

77. Servius on Virgil *Aeneid* 4.638, Wiseman 2008, 84–5; Dionysus is first attested as *Leiber* on a fourth-century BC *cista* (*ILLRP* 1198, Wiseman 2008, 87, fig. 17).

78. Dionysius of Halicarnassus *Roman Antiquities* 6.94.3 (τὸν νεὼν τῆς τε Δήμητρος καὶ Διονύσου καὶ Κόρης . . . ὅς ἐστιν ἐπὶ τοῖς τέρμασι τοῦ μεγίστου τῶν ἱπποδρόμων), Tacitus *Annals* 2.49.1; cf. Cicero *In Verrem* 2.4.108 (*pulcherrimum et magnificentissimum templum*).

79. Aristophanes *Thesmophoriazusae* 297-8 (τοῖν Θεσμοφόροιν τῇ Δήμητρι καὶ τῇ Κόρῃ), cf. Pindar fr. 37 Bergk (Kore), Diodorus Siculus 5.5.2 (Demeter).

80. Livy 3.55.7, Dionysius of Halicarnassus *Roman Antiquities* 6.89.3, 10.42.4; cf. Cicero *In Verrem* 2.4.108 for the need to placate Ceres (Demeter) after the murder of Tiberius Gracchus.

81. Livy 3.55.13 (*Scta*), Pomponius *Digest* 1.2.2.21.

His Roman name was a calque of Dionysus *Eleuthereus*,[82] the god of the main Athenian dramatic festival, the City Dionysia. His Roman festival, the *Liberalia*, which took place on 17 March each year,[83] certainly featured theatre games in the third century BC,[84] and for all we know may have done so from the start. Once it is recognised that Cicero's date of 240 BC is not, after all, a *terminus post quem*, the origin of Roman theatre can be conjecturally placed wherever contemporary evidence suggests an appropriate context.

Dramatic festivals were an expensive enterprise. At Syracuse they were funded by the 'tyrant' Hiero, who even brought Aeschylus from Athens to work in Sicily.[85] The Athenian democracy solved the financial problem by the 'liturgy' system, which required wealthy citizens to take turns funding specific public expenses, including the *choregia* to pay for the festivals.[86] At Rome, the windfall asset of the Tarquins' confiscated wealth wouldn't last for ever, and the constant warfare against newly aggressive neighbouring peoples must have been a drain on public resources throughout the fifth century BC.[87] Nevertheless, public buildings were still being constructed, and surviving antefix fragments are enough to show that satyrs were still a familiar part of the city's visual ambience.[88]

The financial problem was addressed in 367 BC, when the long political conflict between plebeians and patricians was finally resolved: a significant part of that historic compromise was the institution of 'curule aediles', as a way of channelling patrician wealth to the general benefit by subsidising expensive games.[89]

It is at this chronological point that our sources for Rome are at their most baffling. On the one hand, two contemporary Greek philosophers (each with an interest in the history of drama) took it for granted that

82. Alexander Polyhistor *BNJ* 273 F109 (Plutarch *Quaestiones Romanae* 104 = *Moralia* 289a): ἀπὸ τοῦ παρ' Ἐλευθερὰς τῆς Βοιωτίας Ἐλευθερέως Διονύσου προσαγορευομένου.

83. Degrassi 1963, 6 (*Fasti Antiates*), with Wiseman 2004, 63–5 for the significance of the date.

84. Festus (Paulus) 103L (*quae apud Graecos dicuntur* Διονύσια), citing Naevius ('*ludis Liberalibus*'). Later discontinued, presumably in the crackdown on '*Bacchanalia*' in 186 BC (Livy 39.8-18), Liber's games were absorbed into the *ludi Ceriales* (Ovid *Fasti* 3.783-6).

85. Probably in 471–468 BC: Anon. *uita Aeschyli* 8-10 = *TrGF* 5 T1; Herington 1967, Kowalzig 2008, Shaw 2014, 65–7, Csapo and Wilson 2020, 355–64 (also for Aeschylus' second Sicilian sojourn, at Gela in 458–456 BC). For a possible earlier visit by Phrynichus see Anon. *De comoedia* 32 = *TrGF* 3 T6; Csapo and Wilson 2020, 345–6.

86. Full details in Wilson 2000.

87. Details in Cornell 1995, 304–9.

88. Hopkins 2022, 660–3, fig. 3: two examples dated mid to late fifth century BC.

89. Livy 6.42.12-14, 7.1.1-2; Wiseman 1995, 134–6. For the expectation of generous subsidies see for instance Plutarch *Sulla* 5.1, *Caesar* 5.5.

Rome was a Greek city;[90] on the other hand, writing more than three hundred years later about an event in 364 BC, Livy chose to describe at length what he saw as the humble beginnings of the Roman theatre games, pointedly avoiding any hint of Greek influence.[91] It is good historical method to give greater weight to contemporary evidence, and in this case the material record gives us every reason to do so.

From the late fifth century BC to the end of the fourth, the cultural world of southern and central Italy is spectacularly illustrated by the red-figure vase-painters of Apulia, Lucania, Campania and Etruria, and the bronze-engravers of Etruria and Latium.[92] Dionysus, with his satyrs and maenads, is a ubiquitous presence in the iconography,[93] not least in his role as the god of drama. Intensive recent work on the vase-paintings has revealed widespread familiarity with the plots of Athenian tragedy, comedy and satyr-play.[94] And although Rome and her Latin neighbours had no local red-figure potters, they did have bronze-engravers working in an iconographically identical artistic tradition.[95]

Pottery survives, if only in fragments; bronze gets melted down and used for something else. By a fortunate chance, however, it seems that in the fourth century BC the Latin city of Praeneste (modern Palestrina), unlike Rome, still allowed the burial of precious objects with the dead.[96] That was what brought about the fortuitous preservation of the engraved bronze caskets that are now known as 'Praenestine *cistae*' (*ciste prenestine*) from the fact that the vast majority of surviving examples were discovered by plundering the cemeteries there.[97] The most famous of them, signed 'made

90. Aristotle and Heraclides Ponticus (n. 13); see Diogenes Laertius 5.88 for Heraclides' works περὶ τῶν τριῶν τραγῳδοποιῶν and περὶ ποιητικῆς καὶ τῶν ποιητῶν.

91. Livy 7.2.2-13 (nn. 28–9).

92. Painted pottery: Beazley 1947 (Etruria), Trendall 1987 and 1989 (South Italy and Sicily). Engraved bronzes: Beazley 1949 (Etruria), Battaglia and Emiliozzi 1979 and 1990 (Latium).

93. An authoritative judgement on the south-Italian vase-paintings—'Dionysos, in his triple capacity of god of wine, drama and the mysteries, appears more often than any of the other divinities' (Trendall 1989, 256)—applies equally across the whole range of the material.

94. Well summarised in Hart 2010; see especially Taplin 2007 (tragedy), Taplin and Wyles 2010 (satyr-play), Taplin 2020 (comedy). The iconography was not restricted to the Greek-speaking areas of the far south (Wiseman 2015, 29–36).

95. Battaglia and Emiliozzi 1979 and 1990, Pairault Massa 1992, 139–75, Menichetti 1995, Wiseman 2004, 87–114, Coarelli 2010, 207–29.

96. For Rome, cf. Cicero *De legibus* 2.22 and 59 on discouraging conspicuous expense at funerals.

97. Coarelli 2011, 200, rightly insisting that Praenestine provenance proves nothing about where they were made.

in Rome' by Novius Plautius,[98] is decorated around the cylindrical body of the casket with a Dionysiac version of an episode from the voyage of the Argonauts (the binding of Amykos, king of the Bebrykes), a story treated on the stage by Epicharmus in Syracuse and Sophocles in Athens.[99]

Even more significant for the argument of this chapter is a *cista* acquired by the Barberini family in the nineteenth century, which was engraved with a scene of Iphigeneia about to be sacrificed at Aulis, the theme of Euripides' classic tragedy (fig. 4).[100] This artefact didn't just represent a mythological story: it represented the *performance* of a mythological story, with music and dance. More even than that, it represented *theatre*, with Artemis taking part in the action through a window in the stage set (fig. 5).

Such windows are well illustrated on a near-contemporary red-figure vase-painting made either in Sicily or at Paestum in Lucania, about 180 miles south-east of Rome (fig. 6),[101] showing a stage performance in honour of Dionysus, presumably at his festival. The naked girl on stage, inspected by characters in the drama, is a feature of Athenian 'Old Comedy';[102] so too is the cross-talk between characters at windows, described by Aristophanes as typically comedic.[103]

The engraver of the bronze *cista* chose not to make his scene so specifically theatrical. There are no masks here, the plot is not comedy but tragedy (or tragic burlesque), and the naked young woman is part of the drama itself, even playing the heroine. The window alone, however, is enough to evoke a stage performance. Together, these two artworks imply a Dionysiac theatre tradition in fourth-century BC Italy that presupposed

98. Battaglia and Emiliozzi 1990, 211–25, no. 68 (Rome, Villa Giulia inv. 24787), *ILLRP* 1197 (*Nouios Plautios med Romai fecid* | *Dindia Macolnia filea dedit*); Wiseman 2004, 89–97, Coarelli 2011, 207–18.

99. Scholiast to Apollonius Rhodius 2.98 (Ἀπολλώνιος μὲν ἐμφαίνει ὡς ἀνῃρημένον τὸν Ἄμυκον, Ἐπίχαρμος δὲ καῖ Πείσανδρός φασιν ὅτι ἔδησεν αὐτὸν ὁ Πολυδεύκης); Athenaeus 3.94e, 9.400b (Sophocles); see Shaw 2014, 61–2, evidently unaware of the evidence of the *cista*.

100. Battaglia and Emiliozzi 1990, 273–7, Menichetti 1995, 65–7, Wiseman 2015, 33 and 38–9, fig. 14.

101. From the 'important group of vases which provides a direct link between Sicilian and the first truly Paestan vases from the workshop of Asteas' (Trendall 1987, 42, cf. Trendall 1989, 198–9 and 251); for windows in theatrical scenes (including fig. 7 here) see Green 1995, 109–10 and plate 10; Todisco 2020, 156, fig. 52; 161, fig. 62; 162, fig. 64.

102. As for instance at Aristophanes *Wasps* 1341-80, *Peace* 868-86, *Thesmophoriazusae* 1172-1201; dancing girls also at *Acharnians* 1091-3 and 1199-1221.

103. Aristophanes *Ecclesiazusae* 889 (produced in 393 BC): ἔχει τερπνόν τε καὶ κωμῳδικόν.

FIGURE 4. 'Unrolled' engraving on a cylindrical 'Praenestine' *cista*, fourth century BC: Rome, Villa Giulia (inv. 13141). Battaglia and Emiliozzi 1990, no. 82: drawing by M. Tibuzzi, reproduced by permission of the Istituto di Studi sul Mediterraneo Antico (CNR, Rome).
Left to right: (1) unidentified male figure, with horse and hunting dog; (2) grieving male figure, perhaps Achilles, Iphigeneia's promised bridegroom; (3) Iphigeneia disrobing; (4) Calchas, with the stag that caused Artemis' anger; (5) sacrificial attendant (*uictimarius*), with hunting dog; (6) Artemis or Clytemnestra watching through the window; (7) Agamemnon; (8) unidentified male figure with staff and sword-belt (Orestes?); (9) dancing satyr, with owl behind; (10) piping satyr seated on rocks; (11) naked young woman with mirror, her jewellery (ear-rings, necklace, bracelets) matching that of Iphigeneia.
For the satyr's hand-gesture (χεὶρ σιμή, Athenaeus 14.630a), matching that of the dancing satyr in fig. 3(a) above, see Wiseman 2008, 104–8.

'Greek drama' in all three of its forms, comic, tragic and satyric, and was certainly not confined to Greek-speaking communities.[104] On the contrary: the same iconography of satyrs, dancing girls and stories from Greek

104. Paestum, once the Greek city of Poseidonia (a colony of Sybaris), had been taken over by 'barbarian' Lucanians about 410 BC (Aristoxenus *ap.* Athenaeus 14.632a, Strabo 5.4.13 C251), half a century before the vase-paintings with the theatre scenes were produced there. On a Campanian red-figure jug of about 350–340 BC a comic actor playing Xanthias was identified in Oscan retrograde script (Taplin 1993, 40–41 and 94, British Museum inv. F 233).

drama is found right across southern and central Italy, from Apulia to Etruscan Clusium.[105]

Cicero and Livy, to whom we owe the 'orthodox version' of the origin of Roman drama, were either unaware of all this or unwilling to believe it. In 186 BC the Senate had declared Dionysiac rites (*Bacchanalia*) un-Roman and unacceptable, and that was still the official line when Cicero and Livy were writing.[106] Greek authors, however, had no such inhibitions, and once again Dionysius of Halicarnassus provides a valuable corrective. One of the proofs for his contention that Rome had been a Greek city from the very beginning was the presence of Dionysiac elements (satyrs and *silenoi*) at the *ludi Romani*, as attested by Fabius Pictor, the earliest of the Roman historians, at the end of the third century BC.[107]

It was probably a contemporary of Fabius' great-grandparents who commissioned the artist to engrave her bronze jewellery-box with a naked girl acting Iphigeneia at Aulis, and satyrs playing the music and dancing along (fig. 4).

105. For examples see Wiseman 2008, 107–8 (figs 34–5) and 112–13 (figs 37–8).

106. Livy 39.8-19, *ILLRP* 511; Cicero *De legibus* 2.37, Valerius Maximus 1.3.1, 6.3.7.

107. Dionysius of Halicarnassus *Roman Antiquities* 7.72.10-12, quoting Fabius Pictor *FRHist* 1 F15; see n. 31.

FIGURE 5. Reconstruction of a temporary theatre in fourth-century Italy, based on Paestan vase-paintings like the one in fig. 6. Beacham 2007, 213–14, fig. 18. Photo courtesy of Richard Beacham: © Martin Blazeby, King's 3D Visualisation Lab.

1.5. Mercury and the twins

What sort of performances took place on those *ad hoc* stage sets (fig. 5) at the Roman games in the fourth century BC? Contemporary red-figure pottery from Paestum may help us to imagine it (fig. 7).[108] This time, the comic scene is of 'Zeus on a love adventure, lighted on his way by Hermes'.[109]

Both gods were conspicuous in early Rome, Zeus (Jupiter) in Tarquin's great Capitoline temple, Hermes (Mercury) at one of the temples built after Tarquin's expulsion.[110] Hermes was born in Arcadia, and his cult at Rome was attributed to his son Euandros (Evander), the Arcadian

108. Trendall 1987, 124–5, plate 73a; Trendall 1989, 201–2, fig. 364; Hart 2010, 121, no. 58; Todisco 2020, 162, fig. 64.

109. Trendall 1989, 201; the woman is often identified as Alkmene (Alcumena in Plautus' *Amphitruo*), but Zeus's adulterous affairs were very numerous.

110. Livy 2.21.7, 2.27.5-6 (495 BC).

FIGURE 6. 'Kalyx-krater' of Sicilian or Paestan manufacture, 370–60 BC. Lipari, Museo Eoliano (inv. 927): by permission of the Department of Cultural Heritage and I.S. of the Sicilian Region—Archaeological Park of the Aeolian Islands, Luigi Bernabò Brea Museum—Lipari.
On a raised stage, to the left Dionysus sits holding a *thyrsus*, watching a naked girl acrobat perform; to the right are two actors in comic masks, one of them closely examining the girl; behind, two actors in female comic masks engage in dialogue from windows in the stage set. The other side of the vase shows a bearded satyr holding torches and a young woman with a tambourine (not on a stage).

FIGURE 7. 'Bell-krater' from Paestum, attributed to Asteas, 360–40 BC. Vatican Museums (inv. 17106 U19): photo copyright © Governorate of the Vatican City State—Directorate of the Vatican Museums. Two masked comic actors playing Zeus, with a ladder, and Hermes, with a candle in one hand and his *caduceus* in the other; the woman at the stage-set window is not masked.

exile who welcomed Herakles in Stesichorus' *Geryoneis*.[111] The temple was situated at the turning-point of the Circus Maximus, at the opposite end of Lucumo's *hippodromos* from where Demeter, Dionysus and Kore would be

111. Ovid *Fasti* 5.87-100, cf. nn. 58–9; for Evander as Hermes' son see Virgil *Aeneid* 8.138-9, Dionysius of Halicarnassus *Roman Antiquities* 1.31.1, Pausanias 8.43.2.

installed a few years later.[112] We can, I think, assume that the god's annual festival exploited that fairground space for whatever would best instruct and entertain his worshippers. As Plato pointed out, people learned about the gods 'by hearing the stories in prayers at sacrifices, and watching the shows accompanying them that the young most enjoy seeing and hearing'.[113] We needn't think of scripted plays, but we should certainly think of theatre in the broad sense, and of favourite scenarios presented every year.

An old story retold by Ovid could be one of them.[114] Mercury is accompanying his father Jupiter, who is hoping to seduce one of the nymphs of the Tiber. They are all summoned to hear Jupiter's instructions not to let Juturna evade his advances, but one of them, Lara, not only warns Juturna but even spills the beans to Juno as well. Furious, Jupiter tears out her tongue and tells Mercury as *psychopompus* to take her to the underworld; Mercury escorts Lara to the appropriate sacred grove, where he takes advantage of her inability to protest, and only then fulfils his mission.[115] In due course she gives birth to the Lares, Rome's guardian gods,[116] and is herself worshipped as 'The Silent Goddess'.[117]

One way of playing this story is suggested by the Paestan scene (fig. 7), but to keep it farcical throughout would defeat the object of the exercise, which was to teach people about the gods. The outcome of it all is shown in a quite different style on a near-contemporary bronze mirror (fig. 8), where the iconography clearly alludes to three Roman festivals that took place during the nine-day period in mid-February when contact with the world of the dead was believed to be possible.[118]

112. Ovid *Fasti* 5.669 (*templa . . . spectantia Circum*), Apuleius *Metamorphoses* 6.8.2 (*retro metas Murcias*); n. 78. Exact relative dating is impossible because our two authorities calculated the chronology differently, but Livy put the dedication of the Mercury temple in the twelfth year of the republic and Dionysius put that of the Ceres Liber Libera temple in the seventeenth.

113. Plato *Laws* 10.887d: καὶ μετὰ θυσιῶν ἐν εὐχαῖς αὐτοῦς ἀκούοντές τε, καὶ ὄψεις ὁρῶντες ἑπομένας αὐτοῖς ἃς ἥδιστα ὅγε νέος ὁρᾷ τε καὶ ἀκούει πραττομένας θυόντων.

114. Ovid *Fasti* 2.583-616 (introduced with *disce, per antiquos quae mihi nota senes*); Wiseman 2004, 80 and 116–17.

115. Modern readers naturally find this tale of mutilation and rape repugnant; one can only hope Ovid's casual retelling reflects an original comic staging that minimised the brutality.

116. For the *Lares praestites* see Ovid *Fasti* 5.129-6; Robinson 2011, 388–90.

117. Ovid *Fasti* 2.572 (*Tacitae*), 583 (*dea muta*), with Robinson 2011, 362–3; for Tacita cf. Plutarch *Numa* 8.6, who explained her as a reminder of the Pythagorean virtue of silence.

118. *Parentatio* (13–21 February): Ovid *Fasti* 2.533-70, Degrassi 1963, 408–13. Iconography: Wiseman 1995, 65–71.

FIGURE 8. 'Praenestine' bronze mirror, second half of the fourth century BC. Rome, Antiquario comunale (inv. MAI 49): *Monumenti inediti* 11 (1879) 3.1. She-wolf suckling twin boys. Surrounding figures, clockwise from top left: (1) Hermes/Mercury, identified by his *petasos* hat (Athenaeus 12.537f); (2) veiled female, no doubt Tacita, 'the Silent Goddess' (Ovid *Fasti* 2.583-616); (3) the god Quirinus, whose festival was on 17 February (*Quirinalia*), identified by his physiognomy (Crawford 1974, no. 427.2, plate LI) and by the spear he carries (Ovid *Fasti* 2.475-8, Plutarch *Quaestiones Romanae* 87); (4) a lion, perhaps referring to the *Feralia* ('wild-beast festival') on 21 February; (5) Pan Lykaios, whose Roman festival was on 15 February (*Lupercalia*), identified by the shepherd's staff he holds (*Homeric Hymn* 19.5, νόμιον θεόν) and the goat-skin knotted round his neck (Justin *Epitome* 43.1.7).

The twin boys in the main scene must be the Lares.[119] The figures above are their father Mercury and their mother, now a goddess of the underworld; she has evidently given birth on 15 February—the 'wolf-festival' (*Lupercalia*), nine months after Mercury's own festival on 15 May—and left her new-born children in the world of the living, to be nourished and protected by wild beasts. Their rescuers are the Arcadian god Pan Lykaios, son of Hermes (and like him, introduced to Roman cult by Evander),[120] and Quirinus, eponym of the Roman People, the *Quirites*.[121]

If this mirror was made about 330 BC (a reasonable guess), the buyer who commissioned it and the artist who engraved it had probably never heard of Romulus and Remus. Romulus' first appearance on the stage of history is an unimpressive one, quoted from the lost work of a little-known Sicilian historian writing some time in the fourth century BC:

> Alkimos says that Romulus was the son of Aeneas' wife Tyrrhenia, and from Romulus was born Aeneas' granddaughter Alba, whose son, called Rhodius [Rhomus?], founded the city of Rome.[122]

Just one in a sequence of patently aetiological 'speaking names',[123] this Trojan Romulus has no brother and no story. The tale of Romulus and Remus, twin founders of Rome, is first attested in 296 BC, as reported by Livy:

> Also in that year the curule aediles Cn. Ogulnius and Q. Ogulnius prosecuted several moneylenders, whose property was confiscated; from

119. For the Lares as twins see Ovid *Fasti* 2.615-16.

120. *Homeric Hymn* 19.1 (Ἑρμείαο φίλον γόνον); Ovid *Fasti* 2.271-80, 5.91-102, Dionysius of Halicarnassus *Roman Antiquities* 1.32.3 (Evander). For *Lupercalia* as a calque on Λύκαια see Ovid *Fasti* 2.423-4, Virgil *Aeneid* 8.343-4, Plutarch *Moralia* 280c = *Quaestiones Romanae* 68.

121. Varro *De lingua Latina* 5.73 (*Quirinus a Quiritibus*), Festus (Paulus) 43L (*a Quirino Quirites*), cf. Ovid *Fasti* 2.479. The temple of Quirinus on the Quirinal was vowed by L. Papirius Cursor (Livy 10.46.7, Pliny *Natural History* 7.213), probably in 326 BC as consul or 325 BC as dictator.

122. Alkimos *BNJ* 560 F4 (Festus 326-8L): *Alcimus ait Tyrrhenia Aeneae natum filium Romulum fuisse, atque eo ortam Albam Aeneae neptem, cuius filius nomine Rhodius condiderit urbem Romam.* Another fourth-century Sicilian historian (Kallias *BNJ* 564 F5a) named Romulus as one of the three sons of Latinos and Rhome, 'one of the Trojan women who came into Italy with the other Trojans' (Dionysius of Halicarnassus *Roman Antiquities* 1.72.5).

123. Tyrrhenia = the land over which Latinos ruled (Hesiod *Theogony* 1011-16); Romulus = Rome (but *not* named as its founder); Alba = *mons Albanus*, federal cult-site of the Latins (Varro *De lingua Latina* 6.25, Pliny *Natural History* 3.68-9). Francis Cairns (email to TPW, 23 May 2024) explains 'Rhodius' as a misreading of Ῥῶμος in Alkimos' text, 'a Syracusan splayed mu mistaken for delta iota'.

FIGURE 9. Reverse of a 'Romano-Campanian' silver didrachm, c. 290 BC (Crawford 1974, 137, no. 20.1; Coarelli 2013, 44–6): Bibliothèque nationale de France, REP-1364, Gallica Digital Library. The she-wolf stands with her head turned back and down to attend to the twins below. Legend in exergue: *Romano(rum)*.

> the share that came to the public treasury . . . they set up at the *ficus Ruminalis* images of the founders of the city as infants under the teats of a she-wolf.[124]

The *ficus Ruminalis* was at the Lupercal,[125] and the bronze statue-group there was immediately used as a symbol of Rome itself, on one of the very earliest Roman coin issues (fig. 9).[126] These two very different uses of the same mythological motif presuppose a fast-changing Roman world.

124. Livy 10.23.11-12: *eodem anno Cn. et Q. Ogulnii aediles curules aliquot faeneratoribus diem dixerunt; quorum bonis multatis ex eo quod in publicum redactum est . . . ad ficum Ruminalem simulacra infantium conditorum urbis sub uberibus lupae posuerunt.* For the twins as joint founders of the city see also Cassius Hemina *FRHist* 6 F14, Diodorus Siculus 37.11.1, Varro *Res rusticae* 2.pref.4 and 2.1.9, Conon *BNJ* 26 F1.48.7, Strabo 5.3.2 C229, Pliny *Natural History* 15.77, Servius on Virgil *Aeneid* 6.777, *CIL* 6.33856; the joint foundation is also implied (*pace* Briscoe 2013, 167) by Virgil *Aeneid* 1.292-3, Propertius 2.11.23 and 4.1.9-10.

125. Pliny *Natural History* 15.77; for the statue-group see Dionysius of Halicarnassus *Roman Antiquities* 1.79.8 (χαλκᾶ ποιήματα παλαιᾶς ἐργασίας).

126. The image is repeated on other coins of the third and second centuries BC: Crawford 1974, 150, 235, 267, 302 (nos 39.3, 183.1–6, 235.1, 287.1).

The mirror was a wealthy lady's private property, decorated with a piously educational religious scene; the coin-type was a statement of national identity, announcing the guaranteed currency 'of the Romans' (*Romanorum*). What had happened in the forty or so years between the engraving of the mirror and the engraving of the coin-type was the Romans' extraordinary achievement of military and political dominance throughout central Italy. As their surveyors marked out conquered land for settlement and their engineers altered the landscape with roads and bridges,[127] 'Roman Italy' was being made permanent.

This new reality changed the way the Romans presented themselves to the world. In the story on the coin-type, the twin boys suckled by the she-wolf at the Lupercal were not the sons of Mercury and a river-nymph; they were the sons of Mars and Aeneas' daughter Ilia, 'lady of Troy'.[128] Perhaps the 'Greek Rome' inherited from Lucumo's dynasty, reflected in Stesichorus' origin-legend of Arcadian Evander (section 1.3 above), seemed less appropriate now that the Greek cities of the south were potential adversaries.[129] Whatever the reason, a new diplomatic identity had been created. When the Greeks of Taras called in king Pyrrhos of Epirus to help them against Rome in 280 BC, as a descendant of Achilles he regarded it as a war against Trojan colonists.[130]

Ordinary Romans were probably not much concerned about such questions. What they needed to know about gods and men in the distant past, they learned from what they saw at the public festivals.[131] We can be sure that the story of the she-wolf suckling Remus and Romulus was dramatised for them, because we have evidence for it from only two generations later.[132]

127. Velleius Paterculus 1.34.3-4 lists ten colonial settlements founded by the Romans in Italy between 334 and 295 BC; Diodorus Siculus 20.36.2 describes the effect (and expense) of the Via Appia, built from Rome to Capua in 312 BC.

128. Cf. Servius *auctus* on Virgil *Aeneid* 1.273 (*Naeuius et Ennius Aeneae ex filia nepotem Romulum conditorem urbis tradunt*), with Ennius *Annales* 56 and 60 Sk and Servius on Virgil *Aeneid* 6.777 for the name Ilia. For the adaptation of the Mercury–Lara story see Schwegler 1853, 432–5, Wiseman 1995, 71.

129. The hostility of Taras, the most powerful of them, is first attested in 282 BC, when a Roman ambassador there was regarded as a *barbaros* (Dionysius of Halicarnassus *Roman Antiquities* 19.5.1).

130. Paus. 1.12.1: στρατεύειν γὰρ ἐπὶ Τρώων ἀποίκους Ἀχιλλέως ὢν ἀπόγονος. Cf. Timaeus *BNJ* 566 F36 and 59, assuming Rome's Trojan origin despite an alleged foundation date of 814 BC (F60, synchronised with Carthage).

131. Compare Plato *Laws* 10.887d (n. 113) with Varro *De lingua Latina* 6.18: *cur hoc,* [*fabula*] *togata data eis Apollinaribus ludis docuit populum.*

132. Donatus on Terence *Adelphoe* 537 (*dicitur interuenisse lupam Naeuianae fabulae alimonio Remi et Romuli dum in theatro ageretur*); see Manuwald 2001, 141–61 on Naevius' *Romulus*.

1.6. The phlyax *authors*

Pyrrhos failed to protect Taras, which was taken by the Romans in 272 BC. They were now masters of a long-established Greek city, one which already, like Athens, had a permanent stone-built theatre for its festival of Dionysus.[133] What effect the new situation had on Tarantine theatre culture we can only guess; what we do know, however, is that Rhinthon, one of their leading playwrights, had an effect on the theatre culture of Rome.

Born in Syracuse, working in Taras in the early third century BC, Rhinthon pioneered the dramatic form of 'cheerful tragedy' or 'foolery' (*phlyax* in Greek), 'transforming tragic themes into the laughable'; it was also called 'Italian comedy'.[134] A fellow-poet wrote a charming epitaph for him:

> Laugh aloud as you go by, and give me a friendly word. I am Rhinthon of Syracuse—only a minor songbird of the Muses, but from my tragic fooleries I gathered ivy that was all my own.[135]

When Roman scholars centuries later came to list the various types of comedy performed in Rome, one of the categories they identified was that of *fabulae Rhinthonicae*.[136]

Three other *phlyax*-writers are known by name (their fragments gathered in the first volume of *Poetae Comici Graeci*): Skiras, also from Taras; Sopatros, from Paphos in Cyprus; and Blaisos of Capri, whose neighbours included the Latin colonists of Paestum, Suessa and the Pontiae islands.[137] To judge by their titles, it was Euripides above all who gave them their plots.[138] That should remind us of the scene on the bronze *cista* (fig. 4),

133. Attested in 282 BC: Dionysius of Halicarnassus *Roman Antiquities* 19.5.2-3, Florus 1.13.3-4, Dio Cassius 9.39.5. The Theatre of Dionysus at Athens was built about half a century earlier.

134. *Suda* R 171 = 4.295 Adler (Ῥίνθων, Ταραντῖνος κωμικός, ἀρχηγὸς τῆς καλουμένης ἱλαροτραγῳδίας, ὅ ἐστι φλυακογραφία. υἱὸς δ' ἦν κεραμέως καὶ γέγονεν ἐπὶ τοῦ πρώτου Πτολεμαίου [306–282 BC]); Stephanus Byzantinus 603.1 (Ῥίνθων, Ταραντῖνος φλύαξ, τὰ τραγικὰ μεταρρυθμίζων ἐς τὸ γελοῖον); Athenaeus 9.402b (τῆς Ἰταλικῆς καλουμένης κωμῳδίας).

135. *Hellenistic Epigrams* 2827-30 Gow-Page (*Anthologia Palatina* 7.414): καὶ καπυρὸν γελάσας παραμείβεο, καὶ φίλον εἰπὼν | ῥῆμ' ἐπ' ἐμοί. Ῥίνθων εἴμ' ὁ Συρακόσιος, | Μουσάων ὀλίγη τις ἀηδονίς· ἀλλὰ φλυάκων | ἐκ τραγικῶν ἴδιον κισσὸν ἐδρεψάμεθα.

136. *De comoedia* 6.1 (Kaibel 1899, 68), Evanthius *De fabula* 4.1 (Kaibel 1899, 66), Lydus *De magistratibus* 40: probably from Suetonius (sections 3.3 and 3.4 below).

137. Settlements founded in 273 (Paestum) and 315 BC. Blaisos wrote a *Satournos* (Athenaeus 11.487c), a Greek spelling of the Latin name of the Greek god who gave Latium its name (Virgil *Aeneid* 8.322-3, Ovid *Fasti* 1.238).

138. E.g. *Herakles* (Rhinthon), *Hippolytus* (Sopatros), *Iphigeneia at Aulis* (Rhinthon), *Iphigeneia in Tauris* (Rhinthon), *Medea* (Rhinthon), *Meleagros* (Rhinthon, Skiras), *Orestes* (Rhinthon, Sopatros), *Telephus* (Rhinthon).

which could well count as Euripidean 'tragic foolery'. As we saw (section 1.4 above), those fourth-century Latin bronzes shared their iconography with contemporary Italian red-figure vases, and it is from the latter source that current scholarship confidently infers local familiarity with classic Athenian tragedy, and local willingness to mock its plots.[139]

That must still have been true in Rhinthon's time,[140] and despite the inconsistent dates it has always been tempting to identify the fourth-century tragic burlesque illustrated on the vases with the third-century tragic burlesque attributed to *phlyax* plays.[141] The simplest hypothesis, that Rhinthon was the first to produce such performances with written scripts, may well be right: the absence of earlier texts would give later readers the idea that Rhinthon had invented the entire genre.[142] Whatever the truth of that, it is certain that 'Rhinthon-style' plays were a familiar part of the subsequent Roman theatre repertoire.

One of the late authors who tell us about *fabulae Rhinthonicae* also puts them in a surprising wider context:

> We know that Rhinthon, Skiras, Blaisos and the other Pythagoreans were educators of no minor teachings in Magna Graecia, and especially Rhinthon, who was the first to write comedy in hexameters. Taking his start from him, the Roman Lucilius was the first to produce comedy in heroic verse. After him and his successors, whom the Romans call *satyrikoi*, the later authors imitated the style of Cratinus and Eupolis, and using the metres of Rhinthon and the mockeries of those just mentioned, strengthened satyric comedy.[143]

What this deeply puzzling passage means is something to be addressed in later chapters (sections 3.4 and 4.4 below), but three points are worth noting immediately: first, the *phlyax* authors' Pythagoreanism, otherwise unattested, implies an ongoing tradition from Epicharmus two centuries

139. See above all Taplin 1993 and 2007 (esp. 2007, 108–219 on Euripidean plots).

140. Rhinthon's father was a potter (*Suda* R 171 = 4.295 Adler, n. 134), though by then red-figure was no longer being made.

141. See especially Trendall 1959 on '*phlyax* vases', and Taplin 1993, 48–54; for the mismatch of the dates see already Webster 1948, 19.

142. Trendall 1959, 9, despite *Suda* R 171 = 4.295 Adler (ἀρχηγός).

143. Lydus *De magistratibus* 1.41: Ῥίνθωνα καὶ Σκίραν καὶ Βλαῖσον καὶ τοὺς ἄλλους τῶν τῶν Πυθαγορείων ἴσμεν οὐ μικρῶν διδαγμάτων ἐπὶ τῆς μεγάλης Ἑλλάδος γενέσθαι καθηγητάς, καὶ διαφερόντως τὸν Ῥίνθωνα, ὃς ἑξαμέτροις ἔγραψε πρῶτος κωμῳδίαν· ἐξ οὗ πρῶτος λάβων τὰς ἀφορμὰς Λουκίλιος ὁ Ῥωμαῖος ἡρωικοῖς ἔπεσιν ἐκωμῴδησεν. μεθ' ὃν καὶ τοὺς μετ' αὐτόν, οὓς καλοῦσι Ῥωμαῖοι σατυρικούς, οἱ νεώτεροι τὸν Κρατίνου καὶ Εὐπόλιδος χαρακτῆρα ζηλώσαντες τοῖς μὲν Ῥίνθωνος μέτροις, τοῖς δὲ τῶν μνημονευθέντων διασυρμοῖς χρησάμενοι, τὴν σατυρικὴν ἐκράτυναν κωμῳδίαν.

before;[144] second, the reference to Cratinus and Eupolis equally suggests a continuing Italian engagement with classical Athenian drama; and third, even the reference to 'satyric comedy', whatever Lydus' source may have meant by that, is reminiscent of the satyrs piping and dancing to the Iphigeneia story on the *cista* (fig. 4) and mocking the serious participants at the *ludi Romani*.[145]

A younger contemporary of Rhinthon was Andronikos of Taras, who may have been still a child when the city fell to the Romans in 272 BC. He was evidently enslaved and subsequently freed, taking as his Roman citizen name the name of his ex-master, Lucius Livius.[146] It was Lucius Livius Andronicus whose production of a play at the *ludi Romani* of 240 BC was recorded on the old documents Atticus and Cicero referred to, thus giving rise to the idea that he was the first-ever Latin dramatist (section 1.1 above). Livy named him as the first to write plays with plots, as if the Romans had never had any notion of drama before.[147]

1.7. Time for a rethink

Theatre historians have always taken what Cicero and Livy say as authoritative history, and that's understandable, because it fits in with the belief that 'the Greeks came before the Romans'. But thanks to the material evidence for the sixth and early fifth centuries BC, first assembled and analysed in an epoch-making exhibition in 1990,[148] it is now clear that Rome at that time was an integral part of the archaic Greek cultural world; similarly, the corpus of surviving bronze *cistae* from Rome and Latium, now systematically collected and discussed,[149] reveals a deep familiarity with Greek culture in the fourth century too.

It takes time, however, for new information to affect long-held beliefs, and even the best scholarship on Roman drama has been reluctant to take account of the shift in historical understanding. Gesine Manuwald, for instance, admits only a hint of uncertainty: 'Although

144. See n. 67.

145. Fabius Pictor *FRHist* 1 F15 = Dionysius of Halicarnassus *Roman Antiquities* 7.72.10-12 (ἐπὶ τὰ γελοιότερα μεταφέροντες . . . σατυρικὴ παιδιὰ καὶ ὄρχησις); section 1.4 above.

146. Cicero *Brutus* 72, with Kaster 1995, 48–9.

147. Livy 7.2.8 (*Liuius . . . ausus est primus argumento fabulam serere*); section 3.1 below.

148. Cristofani 1990 ('La grande Roma dei Tarquini'), fully exploited by major syntheses on terracotta decoration (Winter 2009) and architecture (Hopkins 2016).

149. Battaglia and Emiliozzi 1979 and 1990 (catalogue), Menichetti 1995, Emiliozzi and Maggiani 2002, Wiseman 2004, 89–118 and 2008, 86–124; surprisingly ignored in La Rocca 2020.

Livy does not give an objective report about the emergence of scenic performances in Rome, the core facts need not be doubted.'[150] Similarly, Mark Griffith in the *Cambridge Companion* takes it as read that 'the largely Hellenized cities of Lucania, Apulia and Sicily existed quite independently of Rome and its small range of local concerns'.[151] I hope the material presented in this chapter has demonstrated that that position is no longer tenable.

An unexamined premise has been tacitly assumed: that the innovation in the mid-third century BC of Latin *literature*—poetry preserved as text—was the point at which the Romans first understood what Greek drama was.[152] But why should that be so? Although it is very likely that Livius Andronicus was the first Latin poet to have his lines copied on to papyrus,[153] there is no reason at all to think that his production of a Latin tragedy in 240 BC was the start of something 'qualitatively different from what had happened before'.[154]

A better understanding is only possible if we take seriously the likelihood that Rome as a city-state was the creation of an exiled Corinthian aristocrat and entrepreneur, who in the late seventh century BC constructed a market-place (the Roman Forum) and a showground (the Circus Maximus) for lavish festivals (the 'great games').[155] His successor, known to the later tradition as 'Servius Tullius', built the first stone temple in Rome, archaeologically dateable to about 580 BC and with the same frontal decoration as the contemporary Artemis temple at the Corinthian colony of Corcyra;[156] it was dedicated to Matuta, the Latin name for Leukothea, whose main cult was at the Isthmus of Corinth.[157]

150. Manuwald 2011, 24, cf. 30 ('Elements in this narrative agree with information in other literary sources [*sic*] or with what is generally plausible for drama in the early stages of its development'); see now Fulkerson and Tatum 2024, 9–10 for a similar position.

151. Griffith 2007, 27. Contrast Bradley 2020, 256: 'Rome was a Hellenised society that regularly drew on the cultural experiences of neighbours, particularly the Greek cities of southern Italy.'

152. For Roman drama as a 'literary genre', to be identified as 'Greek-style drama', see Manuwald 2011, 1, 15 and *passim*. For 240 BC as the moment when 'a distinctive set of circumstances launched [the Romans] on their strange experiment of taking over into their own vernacular one of the most prestigious aspects of [Greek] culture', see Feeney 2016, 4, 205 and *passim*.

153. Cf. Wiseman 2015, 45–7 on Alexandria as the likely model.

154. Feeney 2016, 113 (cf. n. 11).

155. Section 1.2 above, esp. nn. 46–8.

156. Winter, 2009, 190–2, Potts, 2015, 44–5, Hopkins, 2016, 53–60; for Servius as the founder see Ovid *Fasti* 6.477-80.

157. Ovid *Fasti* 6.541-50; Pausanias 1.44.8, 2.2.1.

Matuta's story (she had been Ino, the nurse of Dionysus) was no doubt first told at the temple's dedication on 11 June (*Matralia*),[158] and told again on that date every year thereafter for the education of the citizens. It featured Herakles, in Rome with the cattle of Geryon;[159] his altar, founded on that occasion, was just the other side of the river harbour from the temple,[160] and when the Matuta temple was rebuilt in the early fifth century BC his deification was represented on the roof (fig. 2). We know the tale of Ino-Leukothea-Matuta only from Ovid, in whose treatment it looks very like a stage scenario,[161] implying that at some point its annual retelling had become an acted performance.

At what stage is that likely to have happened? Given the Dionysiac slant of the narrative,[162] I think the default position should be the early fifth century BC, when Rome's temples sported the same sort of satyr-antefixes as in Sicily, and when the confident new republic set up the cult of Ceres, Liber and Libera, combining the two Sicilian patron-goddesses with Dionysus.[163] It is a reasonable conjecture that what Rome learned from Sicily at this time included the pioneering Dionysiac drama of Epicharmus and his colleagues,[164] contemporary with the first dramatists in Athens.

Thus far the evidence is only circumstantial. The proof comes in the following century (say, 330 BC), with the stage-window and the satyrs piping and dancing in the Iphigeneia scene on the bronze *cista* (fig. 4). But that alone is enough to disprove the 'orthodox version' of the origin of Roman theatre.

Cicero was entitled to be pleased with the foray into the archives that enabled him to date the first recorded play at the *ludi Romani* (section 1.1 above), and if he made a wrong inference from it ('we Romans came late to poetry'), that's perfectly understandable. He did know that the son of Corinthian Demaratus had introduced Rome to Greek culture and

158. Ovid *Fasti* 6.481-550, esp. 495-500 for the Isthmus.

159. Ovid *Fasti* 6.519: *appulerat ripae uaccas Oetaeus Hiberas.*

160. See for instance the plan at Coarelli 1988, 104–5.

161. Ovid *Fasti* 6.523-6, with Wiseman 1998, 50–51: Ino tells her story to Hercules (and the audience).

162. Ovid *Fasti* 6.483-4 (*Bacche . . . derige uatis opus*), 503 (grove of Semele), 507 (*Bacchae* of Latium), 514 (*Thyiades*).

163. See nn. 71–2 (antefixes), 76–8 (new cult).

164. See nn. 68–70.

founded the *ludi Romani*,[165] but he also believed that the early Romans regarded the stage and all its works as disgraceful.[166]

He didn't have the archaeological evidence that has enabled recent scholarship to rethink its understanding of archaic Rome, and it's very unlikely that he had read the early western-Greek authors whom Dionysius of Halicarnassus took the trouble to consult (section 1.2 above). He shared the common Roman low opinion of Greeks in general,[167] and took for granted the undesirability of Dionysiac rites, as decreed by the Senate four generations earlier.[168] Naturally, he had no notion of Rome as a 'Greek city' that knew about drama from the start and honoured Dionysus and his satyrs.

Nevertheless, as I hope this chapter has demonstrated, from the sixth to the third century BC that is just what Rome was.

165. Cicero *De republica* 2.34 (*influxit enim non tenuis quidam e Graecia riuulus in hanc urbem*), 2.36 (*eundem primum ludos maximos, qui Romani dicti sunt, fecisse accepimus*).

166. Cicero *De republica* 4.10 = Augustine *City of God* 2.13.3: *cum artem ludicram scaenamque totam in probro ducerent.*

167. See for instance Cicero *Ad Q. fratrem* 1.2.4 on the vices of the *tota natio* ('irresponsible, obsequious, dishonest'), a private opinion matching the general prejudice he could exploit in lawcourt speeches (e.g. *Pro Flacco* 9-12).

168. Cicero *De legibus* 2.37 (*seueritatem maiorum senatus uetus auctoritas de Bacchanalibus . . . declarat*), referring to 186 BC.

CHAPTER TWO

Cicero at the Theatre

PARADOXICALLY, OUR best source for Roman theatre is an author who never wrote for the stage (though he did once defend a famous actor in a court case). What makes Cicero's evidence so valuable is the sheer extent of it. Not all his huge output has survived, but the extant texts of thirty-seven volumes of collected letters, forty-one forensic and political speeches and eighteen oratorical and philosophical treatises in about forty volumes make the years from 86 to 43 BC—from *De inuentione* to the last surviving letters—by far the most thoroughly documented period in the whole of Roman history.

Cicero seldom had cause to give a direct description of theatrical events.[1] They were something his contemporaries took for granted and didn't need to have explained to them. But if we read his work carefully enough, there is precious evidence to be found where Cicero unwittingly tells us something about Roman theatre while talking to his own audience about something quite different.

2.1. *Education*

Take for instance a brief sentence in a letter to Atticus in July 45 BC, referring to Atticus' six-year-old daughter, who had been unwell:

> Good decision about Attica. It's worth it just to have her spirits raised, by watching the show and by what it says about religion as well.[2]

1. *Ad Atticum* 2.19.3, 4.15.6, *Pro Sestio* 115-23 and *Ad familiares* 7.1.2-3 will be discussed in sections 2.2–4 below.

2. Cicero *Ad Atticum* 13.44.2: *de Attica probo. est quiddam etiam animum leuari cum spectatione tum etiam religionis opinione et fama.*

Atticus had taken his little girl to the games, and the date makes it certain that they were the *ludi Apollinares*. The shows were put on in the Circus Flaminius—a piazza, not a race track—in front of the old temple of Apollo *medicus*. Twenty years later the temple was rebuilt as a gleaming marble showpiece of Augustan Rome, but when Atticus and his daughter were there it was still the venerable building that had been vowed to the god when plague struck Rome nearly four centuries before.[3] He was Apollo the Healer, and though Cicero himself took little account of the gods, even he could see that the *religionis opinio et fama* would do her good.

Such *opiniones* are mentioned again in a more formal context, a passage in *De legibus* on the superiority of sense-perception over mere belief:

> In the case of our senses no parent or nurse or teacher or poet or *stage-show* distorts them, nor does popular opinion lead them astray. For our minds, however, all kinds of traps are laid, either by the people just mentioned, who on receiving young untrained minds stain them and twist them as they please, or else by that power which lurks within, entwined with every one of our senses, namely pleasure, which masquerades as goodness but is in fact the mother of all ills.[4]

The stage was an education, teaching people what to believe, and several other passages in Cicero's philosophical works enable us to see how it worked. In *De diuinatione*, for instance, he was discussing the Stoic belief in the gods' goodwill for mankind:

> Who's going to grant you that? Epicurus, who says the gods don't care about themselves or anything else? Or our own Ennius, who gets great applause from an approving populace when he says 'I've always said the race of heavenly gods exists, and I always will say it, but I don't think they care about what the human race does.'[5]

3. Livy 4.25.3, cf. 40.51.6 (*ad aedem Apollinis medici*).

4. *De legibus* 1.47: *nam sensus nostros non parens, non nutrix, non magister, non poeta, non* <u>*scaena*</u> *deprauat, non multitudinis consensus abducit; at uero animis omnes tenduntur insidiae, uel ab iis quos modo enumeraui, qui teneros et rudes cum acceperunt inficiunt et flectunt ut uolunt, uel ab ea quae penitus in omni sensu inplicata insidet, imitatrix boni, uoluptas, malorum autem mater omnium.*

5. *De diuinatione* 2.104: *quis hoc uobis dabit? Epicurusne? qui negat quicquam deos nec alieni curare nec sui. an noster Ennius? qui magno plausu loquitur assentiente populo: 'ego deum genus esse semper dixi et dicam caelitum, | sed eos non curare opinor quid agat humanum genus.'*

It wasn't Ennius himself saying it, but a character in his tragedy *Telamo*,[6] and the 'approving populace' was the audience in the theatre.

Cicero used a similar scene in *De finibus* to illustrate the emotion people feel at hearing or reading of a deed of magnanimity:

> I'm not talking about us, who were born, brought up and educated to praise and honour. But what acclamations are shouted by the unsophisticated crowd in the theatre when these lines are spoken! 'I am Orestes!'—but then the other—'No, no, I tell you *I* am Orestes!' Then too, when they each give the confused and blundering king a way out,[7] as they beg that they may be killed together, is this scene, whenever it's acted, ever received without the greatest enthusiasm?[8]

As a philosopher, Cicero was well aware of the theatre's power to teach false doctrine. Discussing the immortality of the soul in his *Tusculan Disputations*, he blamed 'the poets' for the fact that people cannot conceive of souls without bodily form:

> People thought the dead had a subsequent life underground, and many erroneous beliefs followed from that, which the poets have magnified. The crowded audience in the theatre, including women and children, is moved to hear so grand an aria: 'I come, I come from Acheron, barely by a deep and desperate way, through caverns built of huge harsh overhanging rocks, where the gloom of the underworld stands thick and solid!' . . . This [error] is the origin of the whole of Homer's *Underworld*, and of those necromantic rites[9] my friend Appius used to practise.[10]

6. Cf. *De natura deorum* 3.79, *De diuinatione* 1.132; Jocelyn 1969, 127–8.

7. Thoas, king of the Taurians; the play was probably Pacuvius' *Chryses* (Warmington 1936, 192–207).

8. *De finibus* 5.63: *quid loquar de nobis qui ad laudem et ad decus nati suscepti instituti sumus? qui clamores uulgi atque imperitorum excitantur* <u>*in theatro*</u>, *cum illa dicuntur: 'ego sum Orestes' contraque ab altero 'immo enimuero ego sum, inquam, Orestes'! cum autem etiam exitus ab utroque datur conturbato errantique regi, ambo ergo se una necari cum precantur, quotiens hoc agitur, ecquandone nisi admirationibus maximis?*

9. For necromancy in Rome see Ogden 2001, 149–59, esp. 150–51 on Appius Claudius (consul 54 BC).

10. *Tusculan Disputations* 1.36–7: *sub terra censebant reliquam uitam agi mortuorum; quam eorum opinionem magni errores consecuti sunt, quos auxerunt poetae. frequens enim* <u>*consessus theatri*</u>, *in quo sunt mulierculae et pueri, mouetur audiens tam grande carmen: Adsum atque aduenio Acherunte uix uia alta atque ardua | per speluncas saxis structas asperis pendentibus | maxumis, ubi rigida constat crassa caligo inferum. . . . inde Homeri tota* νέκυια, *inde ea quae meus amicus Appius* νεκυομαντεῖα *faciebat.*

Homer's *Underworld* (*Odyssey* book 11) was an afterthought; the poets Cicero meant in the first place were playwrights, misleading the theatre audience.

These examples from the philosophical dialogues were written for a well-educated minority ('I'm not talking about us') with a clear sense of superiority over the 'unsophisticated crowd'. In his lawcourt speeches, addressing not just the senatorial and equestrian jurors but also the people standing round in the Forum,[11] Cicero adopted a more inclusive tone. Here he is in the defence of Plancius in 54 BC, quoting Accius' famous tragedy *Atreus*:

> I always teach [my son] what that famous king descended from Jupiter taught his sons: 'You must always be alert, there are many traps for the good', and 'what many men envy'—you know the rest. Surely that serious and talented poet wrote what he wrote in order to incite us and our children to hard work and good reputation, not those royal children who no longer existed?[12]

And in the same year he defended Gaius Rabirius, who had had the misfortune to work for king Ptolemy:

> We all know how kings behave, even if we haven't experienced it. These are kings' orders: 'Pay attention and obey', 'If you go beyond what's asked'. These are their threats: 'If I find you here tomorrow, you will die.' We should read and watch those scenes not merely for enjoyment but to learn just how to take care and avoid them.[13]

We don't know which tragedy was being quoted, but the message was the same: we watch these plays to learn from them. He made the same point ten years later in a speech to the Senate:

> To be feared and hated is odious, detestable, fragile and short-lived. Even in the play we see that 'let them hate, so long as they fear' was disastrous to the very character who said it.[14]

11. For the importance of the crowd (*corona*) see Cicero *Brutus* 192, 290, *De finibus* 4.74, Catullus 53, Quintilian 12.10.74.

12. *Pro Plancio* 59: *haec illi soleo praecipere . . . quae rex ille a Ioue ortus suis praecepit filiis: 'uigilandum est semper, multae insidiae sunt bonis', 'id quod multi inuideant' nostis cetera. nonne quae scripsit grauis ille et ingeniosus poeta, scripsit non ut illos regios pueros, qui iam nusquam erant, sed ut nos et nostros liberos ad laborem et laudem excitaret?*

13. *Pro Rabirio Postumo* 29: *nemo nostrum ignorat, etiam si experti non sumus, consuetudinem regiam. regum autem sunt haec imperia: 'animaduerte ac dicto pare' et 'praeter rogitatum si plus' et illae minae: 'si te secundo lumine hic offendero | moriere'. quae non ut delectemur solum legere et spectare debemus sed ut cauere etiam et effugere discamus.*

14. *Philippics* 1.33-4: *metui uero et in odio esse inuidiosum detestabile imbecillum caducum. quod uidemus etiam in fabula illi ipsi qui 'oderint dum metuant' dixerit perniciosum fuisse.*

That was Accius' *Atreus* again, as seen in the theatre.

A particularly spectacular stage lesson was provided by the matricide tragedies of Orestes and Alcmaeon.[15] The young Cicero referred to it in his defence of Sextus Roscius, who was accused of killing his own father:

> Do you see that those whom the poets have handed down to us as avenging their fathers by inflicting capital punishment on their mothers, even though they are said to have done it on the orders and by the oracles of the immortal gods, are still hounded by the Furies and never allowed any rest, because they couldn't even do their duty without committing a crime? . . . Well, don't imagine that those who have committed some impious wickedness are hounded and terrified by the blazing torches of the Furies, in the manner you see all the time in plays. It's each man's own guilt and terror that most torments him, each man's own wrongdoing that hounds him and inflicts madness on him, each man's own bad thoughts and bad conscience that terrify him. For the wicked, *these* are the Furies, constant and personal.[16]

He used it again as an ex-consul decades later, attacking Clodius in the Senate:

> What greater punishment can the immortal gods inflict on a man than madness and insanity? Unless you think that the characters you see in tragedies, agonised and consumed by a wound and physical pain, are suffering more grievous angers of the immortal gods than those who come on stage in a state of madness. Those screams and groans of Philoctetes, dreadful though they are, are not as pitiful as the exultation of Athamas and the melancholy of the matricides.[17]

15. E.g. Ennius *Alcmeo* (Goldberg and Manuwald 2018, 14–21), Pacuvius *Dulorestes* (Warmington 1936, 208–35), Accius *Alcmeo* (Warmington 1936, 332–7).

16. *Pro Roscio Amerino* 66-7: *uidetisne quos nobis poetae tradiderunt patris ulciscendi causa supplicium de matre sumpsisse, cum praesertim deorum immortalium iussis atque oraculis id fecisse dicantur, tamen ut eos agitent Furiae neque consistere umquam patiantur, quod ne pii quidem sine scelere esse potuerunt? . . . nolite enim putare, quem ad modum in fabulis saepenumero uidetis, eos qui aliquid impie scelerateque commiserint agitari et perterreri Furiarum taedis ardentibus. sua quemque fraus et suus terror maxime uexat, suum quemque scelus agitat amentiaque adficit, suae malae cogitationes conscientiaeque animi terrent; hae sunt impiis adsiduae domesticaeque Furiae.*

17. *De haruspicum responso* 39: *a dis quidem immortalibus quae potest homini maior esse poena furore atque dementia? nisi forte in tragoediis quos uulnere ac dolore corporis cruciari et consumi uides grauiores deorum immortalium iras subire quam illos qui furentes inducuntur putas. non sunt illi eiulatus et gemitus Philoctetae tam miseri, quamquam sunt acerbi, quam illa exsultatio Athamantis et quam senium matricidarum.*

And again, attacking Piso:

> I had forgotten that these are the surest punishments inflicted by the immortal gods on the wicked and the sinful. Do not imagine, senators, that wicked men are terrified at the gods' command by the blazing torches of the Furies, as you see it on the stage. It is each man's own guilt, his own crime, his own over-boldness, that throws him out of his sound mind. These are the Furies, these are the flames, these are the burning brands. Must I not think you more insane than the famous Orestes or Athamas in the tragedies?[18]

By that time it was a cliché of optimate political rhetoric that the *populares* were *furiosi*,[19] madmen driven by the Furies (section 7.4 below).

Even in the sober context of the *De legibus* dialogue, Cicero still had the Furies' stage appearances in his mind's eye. There must be a penalty to pay for crimes against men and offences against the gods, and the courts cannot be relied on to deliver it:

> So it is not by judicial sentence that they pay the penalty. . . . The Furies hound them and pursue them, not with blazing torches *as in the plays* but with the anguish of conscience and the torture of guilt.[20]

It is a tribute to the power of the Roman stage that such images remained with Cicero throughout his adult life.

2.2. *Music and politics*

With his long dialogues 'On the republic' and 'On the laws', Cicero was following very deliberately in the footsteps of Plato. He was much influenced by Plato's political thinking,[21] particularly the doctrine in book 8 of the

18. *In Pisonem* 46-7: *me tamen fugerat deorum immortalium has esse in impios et conceleratos poenas certissimas. nolite enim ita putare, patres conscripti, ut in scaena uidetis, homines consceleratos impulsu deorum terreri furialibus taedis ardentibus. sua quemque fraus, suum facinus, sua audacia de sanitate ac mente deturbat; hae sunt impiorum Furiae, hae flammae, hae faces. ego te non tragico illo Oreste aut Athamante dementiorem putem?*

19. Cicero *Pro Sestio* 97 (*furiosi*), 99 (*animi furor*); cf. *Ad Atticum* 4.3.4 (Clodius' *contiones furiosissimae*), *Philippics* 2.1 (*audacior quam Catilina, furiosior quam Clodius*), [Sallust] *In Ciceronem* 7 (*qui tibi ante optimates uidebantur, eosdem dementes ac furiosos uocas*); cf. Virgil *Aeneid* 8.668-9 (*et te, Catilina, minaci | pendentem scopulo Furiarumque ora trementem*).

20. *De legibus* 1.40: *itaque poenas luunt non tam iudiciis . . . sed eos agitant insectanturque Furiae, non ardentibus taedis sicut in fabulis sed angore conscientiae fraudisque cruciatu.*

21. See for instance *Ad Q. fratrem* 1.1.29 (*princeps ingeni et doctrinae*), *Ad Atticum* 4.16.3 (*deus ille noster Plato*), *Ad familiares* 1.9.12 (*scripta diuinitus*) and 18 (*quo ego*

Republic that popular government leads to tyranny,[22] and in *De legibus* he introduced his model law-code with a specifically Platonic preface on the need to make the citizens believe in the reality of divine punishment for wrongdoing.[23] The Furies on stage would certainly help to that end, which may be why, despite his misgivings about some of the lessons they taught, Cicero was not tempted to follow Plato in banishing the poets and dramatists from his republic.

The ideal state whose law-code Cicero presented was supposedly that of the Roman republic itself, plus a few added items that he claimed were among 'the customs of our ancestors' in any case.[24] There was no mention of theatre as such, but his rule for the *ludi* was as follows:[25]

> Let them control popular merriment with public games, whether it happens with chariot-racing and physical competition, or with singing and strings and pipes, and let them associate it with honour of the gods.[26]

The two categories were *ludi circenses* and *ludi scaenici*, circus games and stage games, with the latter defined as musical performances. At first sight, that is surprising: what about drama?

To a contemporary it wouldn't be surprising at all: drama *was* musical. The modern reader, however, only has texts, and thus loses an entire dimension of performance. As so often, it's the throw-away remarks that show us what we miss, as when Cicero as oratorical theorist, discussing rhythmical language, comments on a passage in Ennius' *Thyestes*:

---

uehementer auctore moueor), *De legibus* 1.15 (*quem tu admiraris, quem omnibus anteponis, quem maxime diligis*), *Orator* 10 (*grauissimus auctor et magister*).

22. Plato *Republic* 8.562a-569c, whence Cicero *De republica* 3.45; cf. *Ad Atticum* 10.8.6 (*illa Platonis de tyrannis*).

23. *De legibus* 2.14-16: *ut uir doctissimus fecit Plato . . . habes legis prooemium; sic enim appellat Plato.* As Quintus is made to point out, however (*De legibus* 2.17), his treatment is very different from Plato's.

24. *De legibus* 2.22, 3.12, referring back to *De republica* 2.41-3. In fact the additions were changes the *optimates* would like to see: permanent censorship (*De legibus* 3.7), the Senate's decrees binding on all (*De legibus* 3.10, 28), voting not by secret ballot (*De legibus* 3.10, 33-9).

25. *De legibus* 2.22: *loedis publicis, quae siue curriculo et certatione corporum, siue cantu et fidibus et tibiis fiat, popularem laetitiam moderanto eamque cum diuum honore iungunto.*

26. For the *ludi* as honour to the gods see for instance *In Verrem* 2.5.36, *De haruspicum responso* 21-4 (Wiseman 2008, 168–70).

'without a pipe-player accompanying it, that's very much like prose'.[27] Or when Cicero as moral philosopher, discussing life after death, observes that in Pacuvius' *Iliona* a scene of the apparition of the heroine's murdered son Deipylus 'is sung in subdued and plaintive melodies, to move whole theatres to tears'.[28]

Waiting for the play to begin (Pacuvius or Ennius), the audience first heard music:

> How much in song escapes us! The experts in that discipline hear it, and at the first note from the pipe-player say it's *Antiopa* or *Andromacha*, when we don't have the least idea.[29]

In both tragedy and comedy, much of the text was not spoken but sung.[30] There was always a pipe-player, whose name would be recorded along with those of the playwright, the principal actor, the aediles who gave the games and the consuls in office that year.[31]

In that context, it was natural for Cicero to defend his law-code rule for the games by stressing the importance of music in education:

> I agree with Plato that nothing can so easily influence young and impressionable minds as the various sounds of song. One can hardly express what power they have in both ways, by stirring up the languid and calming down the excited, now letting the emotions go, now pulling them in.[32]

Hence Plato's prohibition of musical innovation in book 4 of the *Republic*, invoked by Cicero with a verbatim quotation: 'he says the rules for music

27. *Orator* 184: *uelut illa in Thyeste: 'quemnam te esse dicam? qui tarda in senecta' et quae sequuntur; quae, nisi cum tibicen accessit, orationis sunt solutae simillima.*

28. Cicero *Tusculan Disputations* 1.106 (Warmington 1936, 238–41): *haec cum pressis et flebilibus modis, qui totis theatris maestitiam inferant, concinuntur.* Iliona was a daughter of Priam and Hecuba; her son's opening words '*Mater, te appello*' became a familiar quotation (Cicero *Pro Sestio* 126, Horace *Satires* 2.3.61).

29. *Academica* 2.20: *quam multa quae nos fugiunt in cantu exaudiunt in eo genere exercitati, qui primo inflatu tibicinis Antiopam esse aiunt aut Andromacham, cum id nos ne suspicemur quidem!*

30. For details see Marshall 2006, 203–44 (comedy), Čulík-Baird 2022, 173–96 (tragedy).

31. See the 'didascalia' appended to Plautus *Stichus* (200 BC) and to Terence *Hecyra* (165), *Heauton timorumenos* (163), *Eunuchus* (161), *Phormio* (161) and *Adelphoe* (160).

32. *De legibus* 2.38: *adsentior enim Platoni nihil tam facile in animos teneros atque molles influere quam uarios canendi sonos, quorum dici uix potest quanta sit uis in utramque partem; namque et incitat languentes et languefacit excitatos et tum remittit animos, tum contrahit.*

cannot be changed without the public laws being changed too'.[33] At that point Cicero demurred:

> My own view is that it isn't as alarming as that, but it shouldn't be ignored either. I do notice that [in theatres] that used to be filled with enjoyable strictness by the tunes of Livius and Naevius, [people] now jump up and twist their necks and roll their eyes in time with the inflexions of the music. Ancient Greece used to punish that severely.[34]

So was he on Plato's side or not? Praise of Livius Andronicus comes oddly from Cicero, who declared that Livius' plays weren't worth reading twice.[35]

No doubt he wanted it both ways, valuing theatre for its educational effect while deploring innovations he thought might be dangerous. Consistent or not, his engagement with Plato implies a shared conviction that theatre was not mere entertainment, but vital to the social and political health of the republic. Certainly he was well aware of its political importance at the day-to-day level, not least as a barometer of public opinion.

As always, it's the passing comments that are valuable. In the summer of 61 BC, eighteen months after the dramatic and contentious end of his consulship, Cicero was out of favour with the Roman populace. However, he had struck up a good relationship with the popular hero Gnaeus Pompeius ('Pompey the Great'), so he was in good spirits when reporting to Atticus on his political situation:

> The crowd at public meetings—the miserable starving *plebs*, that leech of the treasury—thinks the Great Man is devoted to me alone! And yes indeed, we've been brought together by a lot of pleasant familiarity—so much so that those conspiratorial drunkards, the boys with the little beards, call him Gnaeus Cicero in their discussions. And so I get away with wonderful applause, both at the games and at the gladiators, without any shepherd-style whistling.[36]

33. *De legibus* 2.39 (*negat enim mutari posse musicas leges sine mutatione legum publicarum*), after Plato *Republic* 4.424c (οὐδαμοῦ γὰρ κινοῦνται μουσικῆς τρόποι ἄνευ πολιτικῶν νόμων τῶν μεγίστων).

34. *De republica* 2.39: *ego autem nec tam ualde id timendum nec plane contemnendum puto; illud quidem <uideo>, quae solebant quondam conpleri seueritate iucunda Liuianis et Naeuianis modis, nunc ut eadem exsultent <et> ceruices oculosque pariter cum modorum flexionibus torqueant. grauiter olim ista uindicabat uetus illa Graecia.* For the problematic text see Dyck 2004, 359.

35. Cicero *Brutus* 71 (*non satis dignae quae iterum legantur*); Cicero never quotes Livius, and Naevius only rarely (full list of quotations in Čulík-Baird 2022, 255–72).

36. *Ad Atticum* 1.16.11: *illa contionalis hirudo aerari, misera ac ieiuna plebecula, me ab hoc Magno unice diligi putat; et hercule multa et iucunda consuetudine coniuncti inter*

Senators had reserved seats at the theatre,[37] and their reception on arrival was an index of their popularity. Whistling was the way the crowd expressed its disapproval,[38] so it seems Cicero had been on the receiving end of it before Pompey's friendship shielded him.

He was happy to mock his enemies for avoiding the theatre games so as not to be whistled at,[39] but it's clear that he himself, and other prominent senators, regularly chose to be out of Rome when the games were on.[40] He may, however, have made an exception for the *ludi Apollinares* in July, which were under the control of the urban praetor, not the aediles.[41] On the few occasions when he refers to being present, those are the games concerned.

When the time for the *ludi Apollinares* came round in 59 BC, one of the great ideological power struggles of Roman history had just been played out. Caesar, the first *popularis* consul for nearly twenty years, had forced through two land-reform bills against stubbornly intransigent optimate opposition, and Cicero was in despair. 'Everything's lost', he wrote to Atticus: 'the republic is dead.'[42] However, Caesar's necessarily ruthless tactics had caused a backlash:

> Public opinion has become clear above all at the theatre and the shows. At the gladiators both the master of the troupe and his guests were torn to bits with the whistling, and at the *ludi Apollinares* the tragic actor Diphilus made a nasty attack on our friend Pompey: 'You are great by our misfortune' was encored again and again, and the whole theatre applauded when he said 'the time will come when you'll groan aloud at that very same prowess'—and the rest of the speech too.[43]

---

nos sumus, usque ut nostri isti comissatores coniurationis, barbatuli iuuenes, illum in sermonibus Cn. Ciceronem appellant. itaque et ludis et gladiatoribus mirandas ἐπισημασίας *sine ulla pastoricia fistula auferebamus.*

37. Cicero *Pro Cornelio* fr. 27 Crawford, *De haruspicum responso* 24, Asconius 69–70C; it was a contentious privilege (Livy 34.54.4-8).

38. E.g. Caelius in *Ad familiares* 8.2.1, on Q. Hortensius in 51 BC.

39. *Pro Sestio* 115-6 (*populares*), *In Pisonem* 65 (L. Piso), *Philippics* 1.37 (*populares*).

40. *In Clodium et Curionem* fr. 19 Crawford, *Ad Atticum* 4.8a.1, *Ad Q. fratrem* 3.1.1, 3.4.6, *De oratore* 1.24, *De finibus* 3.8; Wiseman 2015, 83–5, and section 6.1 below.

41. Livy 25.12.9-15, 27.23.5; no doubt the praetor's lictors could ensure proper respect for dignified senators.

42. *Ad Atticum* 2.19.5 (*certi sumus perisse omnia*), 2.20.3 (*ciuitas moritur*), 2.21.1 (*res publica . . . tota periit*).

43. *Ad Atticum* 2.19.3 (July 59 BC): *populi sensus maxime theatro et spectaculis perspectus est. nam gladiatoribus qua dominus qua aduocati sibilis conscissi, ludis Apollinaribus Diphilus tragoedus in nostrum Pompeium petulanter inuectus est: 'nostra miseria tu es magnus' miliens coactus est dicere, 'eandem uirtutem istam ueniet tempus cum grauiter gemes' totius theatri clamore dixit itemque cetera.*

Pompey was Caesar's son-in-law and close ally. The spectacular triumph for his Asiatic conquests had taken place two years earlier,[44] and now he was in Campania supervising the distribution of land to his veterans under Caesar's law. It is not known which tragedy Diphilus was playing, but we may assume that the praetor in charge of the games had chosen one with a suitable plot, of a hero who turned into a tyrant:

> In fact those lines could have been composed for the occasion by an enemy of Pompey. The speech beginning 'If neither laws nor customs can compel' was delivered to much noisy acclamation. When Caesar arrived there was feeble applause, and he was followed by young Curio. For him the applause was of the sort Pompey used to get when the republic was still alive. Caesar was annoyed, and it's said that a letter is speeding to Pompey in Capua. They're hostile to the *equites*, who gave Curio a standing ovation, and enemies of everyone.[45]

The republic, however, was not dead, and six months later the Roman People, on the proposal of one of their tribunes, voted Cicero into exile.[46]

Eventually he was recalled, with Pompey's help, but the price was the loss of his political independence. He hated that,[47] but at least it meant that once again Pompey's friendship got him a good reception at the games. Here he is at the *ludi Apollinares* of 54 BC:

> I came back to Rome for Fonteius' sake on 9 July.[48] I went to the show, and the first thing is that I got loud and steady applause—but never mind that, it's stupid of me to write it down. Then I looked out for Antipho. He was given his freedom before coming on stage. To get to the point, he won the prize. But I never saw anything so puny, so voiceless, so—but please keep that to yourself! At least in *Andromacha* he

44. Pliny *Natural History* 7.97-9, 37.13, Degrassi 1947, 566 (September 61 BC).

45. Cicero *Ad Atticum* 2.19.3: *nam et eius modi sunt ii uersus ut in tempus ab inimico Pompei scripti esse uideantur. 'si neque leges neque mores cogunt' et cetera magno cum fremitu et clamore sunt dicta. Caesar cum uenisset mortuo plausu, Curio filius est insecutus. huic ita plausum est ut salua re publica Pompeio plaudi solebat. tulit Caesar grauiter. litterae Capuam ad Pompeium uolare dicebantur. inimici erant equitibus, qui Curioni stantes plauserant, hostes omnibus.*

46. For putting Roman citizens (the Catilinarian conspirators) to death without trial when he was consul in 63; he had depended on the authority of the Senate, but the *populares* insisted that it was illegal to execute any citizen *iniussu populi* (Cicero *Pro Rabirio perduellionis reo* 12); see Lintott 1999, 89–93 for the issues involved.

47. See especially *Ad Q. fratrem* 3.5.4 (autumn 54 BC): *angor, mi suauissime frater, angor nullam esse rem publicam.*

48. Probably Fonteius was the *praetor urbanus*, responsible for the games.

> was bigger than Astyanax,[49] but there was no-one else his size in the cast. As for Arbuscula,[50] they really liked her. The games were splendid and successful. The beast-hunt was postponed to another time.[51]

It looks as if Cicero had been asked to report to Atticus (who was in Greece) on two young performers making their debut.

Arbuscula was a *mima*—actress, singer and dancer in the variety-show genre known as 'mime'—and the order of Cicero's comments implies that the programme scheduled a 'mime' to follow the tragedy.[52] Normally the 'mimes' were beneath his notice, of interest only if they made satirical comments on current affairs.[53] Shortly after the murder of Caesar, for instance, Cicero was at his villa at Tusculum. On 9 April 44 BC, the day before the *ludi Megalenses* began, he sent a note to Atticus in Rome:

> Write back if you have any hard news. If not, please give me a full account of popular demonstrations and what the mime-actors have to say.[54]

2.3. A special case

One conspicuous piece of Ciceronian evidence requires separate treatment. His long excursus on *optimates* and *populares* in the speech for Sestius includes a vivid picture of Roman theatre games,[55] but it is evidence of a different sort from the passages we have dealt with so far. There,

49. Andromache, widow of Hector (see Goldberg and Manuwald 2018, 28–41 for Ennius' play); Astyanax, infant son of Priam and Hecuba.

50. On whom see Horace *Satires* 1.10.76-7 (with scholiasts), Servius on Virgil *Eclogues* 10.6 (*nobilis meretrix*).

51. *Ad Atticum* 4.15.6: *redii Romam Fontei causa a.d. VII Id. Quint. ueni spectatum, primum magno et aequabili plausu—sed hoc ne curaris, ego ineptus qui scripserim. deinde Antiphonti operam. is erat ante manu missus quam productus. ne diutius pendeas, palmam tulit. sed nihil tam pusillum, nihil tam sine uoce, nihil tam—uerum haec tu tecum habeto. in Andromacha tamen maior fuit quam Astyanax, in ceteris parem habuit neminem. quaeris de Arbuscula. ualde placuit. ludi magnifici et grati, uenatio in aliud tempus dilata.*

52. So too *Ad familiares* 9.16.7: the previous custom (undated) had been to follow the tragedy with a *fabula Atellana*.

53. *Ad familiares* 7.11.2; Wiseman 2023, 43–6. For his usual dismissive attitude see for instance *Pro Caelio* 64, *Ad familiares* 7.1.2, *Pro Rabirio Postumo* 35, *Orator* 88.

54. *Ad Atticum* 14.3.2: *tu si quid* πραγματικὸν *habes rescribe; sin minus, populi* ἐπισημασίαν *et mimorum dicta perscribito*. Cf. 14.2.1 (*bona signa consentientis multitudinis*), referring to the mime-writer Publilius.

55. Cicero *Pro Sestio* 96-143, esp. 115-23 on *ludi scaenici*; for the political issues involved see Kaster 2006, 1–14, Wiseman 2009, 5–14.

our information consisted of what Cicero took for granted about theatrical experience when talking about something else; in the *pro Sestio* passage, by contrast, Cicero was quite deliberately giving information and insisting on how to interpret it. It is 'a tendentious and deceptive part of a tendentious and deceptive speech',[56] but it repays close attention all the same.

The trial of Sestius took place in February 56 BC, five months after Cicero's return from exile. Cicero claimed, no doubt rightly, that the prosecution was politically motivated, attacking Sestius for supporting the campaign to get Cicero recalled. The other defence speakers having dealt with the charges, he could use the final speech to deliver his own version of the events leading to his exile, and that meant countering the powerful *popularis* case that his banishment was well deserved.[57] Presenting the final section of the speech as a lesson to the young men present,[58] Cicero offered his account of *ludi scaenici* as a particular example for them:

> I undertook at this point to educate the young about which people counted as *optimates*, and to explain that question I need to show that not all those who are considered *populares* really are so. I'll achieve that most easily if I describe the true and uncorrupted judgement of the whole people, and the innermost feelings of the citizen body.[59]

The argument that follows takes it for granted that the theatre audience at *ludi scaenici* represented the entire Roman People, *populus Romanus uniuersus*.[60]

The particular occasion Cicero chose to describe was not one that he had seen himself. It took place in late May or early June 57 BC,[61] when he was still in exile and the consul Publius Lentulus was working hard to get him recalled. Part of Lentulus' strategy was to exploit the reputation of

56. Kaster 2006, 35 ('its primary audience . . . was the wealthy and conservative panel of judges, to whom it told a story they would have wanted to hear'). Cf. also Wiseman 2009, 7: 'the tendentious self-justification of a controversial politician at the crisis of his career'.

57. See n. 46.

58. Cicero *Pro Sestio* 96 (*rem quaeris praeclaram iuuentuti ad discendum nec mihi difficilem ad perdocendum*), 136 (*uosque adulescentes*).

59. *Pro Sestio* 119: *sed mihi sumpsi hoc loco doctrinam quandam iuuentuti, qui essent optimates. in ea explicanda demonstrandum est non esse populares omnes eos qui putentur. id facillime consequar, si uniuersi populi iudicium uerum et incorruptum et si intimos sensus ciuitatis expressero.*

60. *Pro Sestio* 122, 124 (also 125 on gladiatorial shows); cf. *Philippics* 1.36, Pliny *Natural History* 36.119-20.

61. For the chronology see Kaster 2006, 400 n. 25; *pace* Palombi 1996, 35, who arbitrarily dates it to 1 May when the *ludi Florales* were on.

the *popularis* hero Gaius Marius,[62] who like Cicero came from Arpinum. He therefore called a meeting of the Senate at the temple of Honos and Virtus, built by Marius from the spoil of his great victory over the Cimbri and Teutones in 101 BC,[63] and organised *ludi scaenici* in honour of Honos and Virtus on the same day.[64]

The Senate approved Lentulus' motion that all who wished for the good of the republic should come to Rome to vote for Cicero's recall.[65] That is where Cicero began his description of the events he hadn't seen, to illustrate his allegation that *populares* like Clodius kept away from the games for fear of being whistled at:

> Only once, I say, did that '*popularis*' individual ever venture to the games, and it was when honour was being paid to virtue in the temple of Virtue, when the monument of Gaius Marius, the man who saved this empire, provided a site for the recall to safety of his fellow-townsman [Cicero himself, of course], a man who also defended the republic.[66]

The Romans called the temple 'the monument(s) of Marius',[67] and the piazza in front of it will have displayed the trophies of his victory.[68] There had to be space there for sacrifices at the altar on festival days (at other

62. As Cicero himself had done as consul (*Pro Rabirio perduellionis reo* 27-30); for the ideological significance of Marius' memory see Velleius Paterculus 2.43.4 (*aduersante nobilitate*), Suetonius *Diuus Iulius* 11 (*aduersante optimatium factione*), Plutarch *Caesar* 6.1-4 (δυεῖν δὲ οὐσῶν ἐν τῇ πόλει στάσεων).

63. *CIL* 11.1831.17-19 (*de manubiis Cimbric. et Teuton. aedem Honori et Virtuti uictor fecit*); Palombi 1996. The temple was at the top of the Sacra Via, where the remains of Hadrian's great Venus and Rome temple are today (Festus 446-8L, with Coarelli 1983, 101–3); it may have been adjacent to Marius' house, which we know was close to the Forum (Plutarch *Marius* 32.1).

64. *Scholia Bobiensia* 136 Stangl: *ludos Honoris atque Virtutis, qui celebrabantur in memoriam et honorem C. Marii, a quo res bello Cimbrico feliciter gestae sunt.*

65. Cicero *Post reditum in senatu* 24-5; the vote itself took place on 4 August (Cicero *Ad Atticum* 4.1.4).

66. Cicero *Pro Sestio* 116: *semel, inquam, se ludis popularis homo commisit omnino, cum in templo Virtutis honos habitus est uirtuti Gaique Mari conseruatoris huius imperii monumentum municipi eius et rei publicae defensori sedem ad salutem praebuisset.*

67. So described also at Cicero *Pro Plancio* 78, *De diuinatione* 1.59, Valerius Maximus 1.7.5 (where *Iouis* is either a confusion or a textual error), 4.4.8.

68. Piazza: Valerius Maximus 2.5.6 (temple of Febris *in area Marianorum monumentorum*); for such *areae* in front of temples see for instance *CIL* 10.1781.5-6 (*area quae est ante aedem Serapi*, Puteoli), Livy 2.41.11 (*area ante Telluris aedem*), 40.19.2 (*area Volcani et Concordiae*), Solinus 1.18 (*area Apollinis*). Of the two sets of Marian trophies in Rome (Valerius Maximus 6.9.14 *bina tropaea*) the other was on the Capitol (Propertius 3.11.45-6, Plutarch *Caesar* 6.1); Reusser 1999.

times there may have been an open-air market),[69] and since games were regularly held in front of temples, where the divinity being honoured could see them,[70] the piazza is surely where we must imagine the temporary theatre set up for the *ludi scaenici* specially organised by Lentulus.

Cicero had to imagine it too, though he carefully concealed the fact. His account continues:

> What feelings the Roman People manifested at that time was demonstrated in two ways: there was unanimous applause, first for the fact itself and for the Senate in absence, when [news of] the Senate's decree had been heard, and then for the individual senators as they came back from the meeting to watch the show; and when the consul himself, the organiser of the games, took his seat, [the audience] standing with hands outstretched, giving thanks and weeping for joy, demonstrated their goodwill and compassion for me.[71]

That, Cicero claimed, was the one and only time Clodius showed himself at the games:

> When that madman arrived, driven by that insane mentality of his,[72] the Roman People could hardly restrain itself, they could barely keep their hatred from his foul and polluted body, and all poured forth shouts and loud curses, shaking their fists.
>
> But why do I record the spirit and courage of the Roman People, catching sight of freedom after long subjection, in the case of a man whom not even actors spared as he sat there in front of them, even though he was then already a candidate for the aedileship?[73] When a *togata* comedy was being played ('The Pretender', I think),[74] the whole

69. Cf. Varro *Res rusticae* 1.2.10 (fruit sellers *summa sacra uia*).

70. E.g. Cicero *De haruspicum responso* 24 (*ante templum in ipso Matris magnae conspectu*), Arnobius *Aduersus nationes* 7.33 (*si suis in ludis flagitiosas conspexerit res agi*), on the *ludi Megalenses* and *Florales* respectively; cf. n. 26.

71. Cicero *Pro Sestio* 117: *quo quidem tempore quid populus Romanus sentire se ostenderet, utroque in genere declaratum est, primum cum audito senatus consulto rei ipsi atque absenti senatui plausus est ab uniuersis datus, deinde cum senatoribus singulis spectatum e senatu redeuntibus; cum uero ipse qui ludos faciebat consul assedit, stantes ei manibus passis gratias agentes et lacrimantes gaudio suam erga me beneuolentiam ac misericordiam declararunt.*

72. More likely by defiance: Clodius had of course opposed the Senate's resolution, and must have known the audience at Lentulus' games would not be friendly.

73. Long delayed by the *optimates*, Clodius' election as aedile was a recent event when Cicero spoke in Sestius' trial.

74. *Simulans* was a play by L. Afranius, on whom see Cicero *Brutus* 167 (*homo perargutus, in fabulis . . . disertus*), *De finibus* 1.7 (his borrowings from Menander).

> company leant forward in the face of that foul man and harangued him loudly in unison: 'After your origins [?], Titus, the end of your vicious life'.[75] He sat there dumbstruck—he who used to fill his own harangues with abuse from singers was being shown the door by the voices of the singers themselves.[76]

What *togatae* comedies were, and when and why they were introduced, are questions for the next chapter (section 3.6 below). The interesting point here is the emphasis on singers (*cantores*); it's both a reminder of how much music there was in Roman drama (section 2.2 above) and also evidence for the use of derisive song as a weapon in the street politics of Rome.[77]

With an apology to the jurors for this unusual style of forensic oratory, Cicero switched from comedy to tragedy:

> Since I've mentioned the games, I shouldn't omit the fact that in a huge variety of stage speeches there was never a single passage where something said by the playwright that seemed to apply to my situation was missed by the entire Roman People or not brought out by the actor himself. . . .
>
> This is what I mean: when news of the decree of the Senate passed in the temple of Virtus had just been brought to the games and the theatre, in front of a huge audience a superlative artist—a man who I swear has always been among the best in our state as well as the best on the stage—weeping with fresh joy mingled with grief and longing for me, stated my case before the Roman People with much weightier words than I myself could have done.
>
> He expressed the genius of a great poet not only by his acting skill but also by his own distress.[78]

75. Text and significance uncertain: perhaps the only point was *exitus uitiosae uitae.*

76. *Pro Sestio* 117-18: *at cum ille furibundus incitata illa sua uaecordi mente uenisset, uix se populus Romanus tenuit, uix homines odium suum a corpore eius impuro atque infando represserunt; uoces quidem et palmarum intentus et maledictorum clamorem omnes profuderunt. sed quid ego populi Romani animum uirtutemque commemoro, libertatem iam ex diuturna seruitute dispicientis, in eo homine cui tum petenti iam aedilitatem ne histriones quidem sedenti pepercerunt? nam cum ageretur togata Simulans, ut opinor, caterua tota clarissima concentione in ore impuri hominis inminens contionata est: 'haec, Tite, tua post principia atque exitus | uitiosae uitae.' sedebat exanimatus, et is qui antea cantorum conuicio contiones celebrare suas solebat, cantorum ipsorum uocibus eiciebatur.*

77. Cf. Cicero *Ad Q. fratrem* 2.3.2: *cum omnia maledicta, uersus denique obscenissimi in Clodium et Clodiam dicerentur.*

78. Cicero *Pro Sestio* 118, 120-21: *et quoniam facta mentio est ludorum, ne illud quidem praetermittam, in magna uarietate sententiarum numquam ullum fuisse locum in quo aliquid a poeta dictum cadere in tempus nostrum uideretur, quod aut populum uniuersum*

As senators and *equites* who might well have been there at the time, the jury at Sestius' trial didn't need to be told that the actor concerned had been the veteran Aesopus, and the play Lucius Accius' *Eurysaces*.[79] Some of them may also have been aware that Aesopus had taught the young Cicero the same techniques of emotional delivery that Cicero was now using on them.[80] For instance:

> With what power [he spoke the lines]
>
> > 'He who with determined mind aided the commonwealth,
> > established it, stood by the Achaeans . . .'
>
> He was saying I stood by you, he pointed to your ranks![81] It was encored by the entire audience.
>
> > 'When things were in doubt he never doubted
> > to offer his life, never spared his head.'
>
> To what great applause did he act those lines! When 'our greatest friend in the greatest conflict' was being applauded for the poet's words, the actor's enthusiasm and the expectation of my return, there was no need for a gesture, because the actor himself generously added the phrase 'endowed with greatest talent', and perhaps people approved of it because they missed me somewhat.
>
> To what groans from the Roman People did the same actor perform the famous 'O my father . . .' scene a little later in the same play! He was thinking of me, me in my absence, as the father to be lamented, the man Quintus Catulus and many others in the Senate had often named 'the father of our country'.[82] To what weeping for the arson and destruction I suffered did he lament a father driven out, a country afflicted, a house burned and overthrown, to such effect that when he pointed out former prosperity and then turned to the audience with 'all

---

fugeret aut non exprimeret ipse actor. . . . quid fuit illud, quod recenti nuntio de illo senatus consulto quod factum est in templo Virtutis ad ludos scaenamque perlato, consessu maximo summus artifex et mehercule semper partium in re publica tam quam in scaena optimarum flens et recenti laetitia et mixto dolore ac desiderio mei egit apud populum Romanum multo grauioribus uerbis meam causam quam egomet de me agere potuissem. summi enim poetae ingenium non solum arte sua sed etiam dolore exprimebat.

79. *Scholia Bobiensia* 136 Stangl; already famous in the 80s BC (*Rhetorica ad Herennium* 3.34), Aesopus was embarrassingly past it in 55 (Cicero *Ad familiares* 7.1.2).

80. Plutarch *Cicero* 5.3, cf. Cicero *De diuinatione* 1.80.

81. Senators and equestrians had their own demarcated seating areas at the games.

82. No doubt in December 63; cf. Cicero *In Pisonem* 6, *Ad Atticum* 9.10.3.

> these things I have seen in flames',[83] he brought tears to the eyes even of my enemies and ill-wishers.[84]

We can see from this what liberties could be taken with a classic play-text if the producer—in this case the consul Lentulus—wanted to make a topical point. A half-line was added to make the contemporary reference clear, and then an appropriate whole passage was inserted from a different play.[85]

Cicero left to the end the scene that must have been the reason why Lentulus chose Accius' play in the first place. We don't know the plot of the *Eurysaces*, but it seems it was directly applicable to Cicero's situation:

> Great heavens! How he spoke that other scene, the one that seems to me to have been so acted and written that it could have been admirably spoken even by Quintus Catulus if he had come back to life, since it was his custom to be free in his censure and criticism of the People's occasional rashness or the Senate's mistakes:
>
> 'O ungrateful Argives, irresponsible Greeks, forgetful of benefits!'
>
> In fact that wasn't true: they weren't ungrateful, just wretched because they couldn't give safety to the man who had given it to them. No-one was ever more grateful to anyone than everyone was to me. But still, it was for me that a most eloquent poet wrote the scene and a most courageous actor (not just an excellent one) acted it, when he pointed to each of the orders and accused the Senate, the Roman knights and the general populace:
>
> 'You allow him to be in exile, you allowed him to be banished,
> you put up with his banishment!'

83. It was a passage from Ennius' *Andromacha* (Cicero *Tusculan Disputations* 3.44-5 and 53); Jocelyn 1969, 81–7.

84. Cicero *Pro Sestio* 120-21: *qua enim <ui> 'qui rem publicam certo animo adiuuerit | statuerit steterit cum Achiuis'—uobiscum me stetisse dicebat, uestros ordines demonstrabat! reuocabatur ab uniuersis. 're dubia | haut dubitarit uitam offerre nec capiti pepercit'. haec quantis ab illo clamoribus agebantur! cum iam omisso gestu uerbis poetae et studio actoris et exspectationi nostrae plauderetur 'summum amicum summo in bello'—nam illud ipse actor adiungebat amico animo et fortasse homines propter aliquod desiderium adprobabant: 'summo ingenio praeditum'. iam illa quanto cum gemitu populi Romani ab eodem paulo post in eadem fabula sunt acta! 'o pater'—me, me ille absentem ut patrem deplorandum putabat, quem Q. Catulus, quem multi alii saepe in senatu patrem patriae nominarant. quanto cum fletu de illis nostris incendiis ac ruinis, cum patrem pulsum, patriam adflictam deploraret, domum incensam euersamque, sic egit ut demonstrata pristina fortuna cum se conuortisset: 'haec omnia uidi inflammari' fletum etiam inimicis atque inuidis excitaret!*

85. By 'later in the same play' (*paulo post in eadem fabula*) Cicero evidently meant 'later in the same performance by Aesopus'.

> I was only told, and those who were there can more easily judge, what the expressed feeling of the whole audience was at that time, how the entire Roman People declared its goodwill in the cause of one who was not a *popularis*.
>
> And since my speech has brought me to this point, the actor, as he pleaded my cause with such emotion, wept so often for what happened to me that that splendid voice of his was choked with tears; the poets, whose genius I have always loved, did not fail me when I needed them; and the Roman People showed its approval not only by its applause but even by its audible distress.[86]

And that was what the whole rhetorical *tour de force* had been meant to prove, that Cicero's *popularis* enemies did not speak for the Roman People.

Spelling out his lesson for the younger generation now in more sober tones, Cicero still had one more example to give:

> So if the Roman people had been at liberty, was it proper that it should be Aesopus or Accius speaking so on my behalf, or that it should be the leaders of the state? In the *Brutus* I was mentioned by name—'Tullius, who had established freedom for the citizens'—and it was encored time after time. Wasn't that enough to show that in the Roman People's judgement the thing depraved citizens accused me of overthrowing was established by the Senate and myself?[87]

86. Cicero *Pro Sestio* 122-3: *pro di immortales! quid? illa quem ad modum dixit idem! quae mihi quidem ita et acta et scripta uidentur esse ut a Q. Catulo, si reuixisset, praeclare posse dici uiderentur; is enim libere reprehendere et accusare populi non numquam temeritatem solebat aut errorem senatus: 'o ingratifici Argiui, immunes Graii, immemores benefici!' non erat illud quidem uerum; non enim ingrati sed miseri, quibus reddere salutem a quo acceperant non liceret, nec unus in quemquam umquam gratior quam in me uniuersi; sed tamen illud scripsit disertissimus poeta pro me, egit fortissimus actor, non solum optumus, de me, cum omnes ordines demonstraret, senatum, equites Romanos, uniuersum populum Romanum accusaret: 'exsulare sinitis, sistis pelli, pulsum patimini!' quae tum significatio fuerit omnium, quae declaratio uoluntatis ab uniuerso populo Romano in causa hominis non popularis, equidem audiebam, existimare facilius possunt qui adfuerunt. et quoniam huc me prouexit oratio, histrio casum meum totiens conlacrumauit, cum ita dolenter ageret causam meam, ut uox eius illa praeclara lacrimis impediretur; neque poetae, quorum ego semper ingenia dilexi, tempori meo defuerunt; eaque populus Romanus non solum plausu sed etiam gemitu suo comprobauit.*

87. *Pro Sestio* 123: *utrum igitur haec Aesopus potius pro me aut Accium dicere oportuit, si populus Romanus liber esset, an principes ciuitatis? nominatim sum appellatus in Bruto: 'Tullius, qui libertatem ciuibus stabiliuerat.' milliens reuocatum est. parumne uidebatur populus Romanus iudicare id a me et a senatu esse constitutum, quod perditi ciues sublatum per nos criminabantur?*

Lentulus had chosen a variety of items for his special games: a *togata* comedy by Afranius, a tragedy by Accius, and a historical play (*fabula praetexta*) by Accius on the expulsion of Tarquin by Lucius Brutus.[88] That could have been dangerous for Cicero (the *populares* said he had acted like a tyrant),[89] but evidently the emphasis was placed on Tarquin's admirable predecessor Servius Tullius, whose name could be used as another prompt for applause.

We may well be sceptical of Cicero's repeated claim—the premise of his entire argument—that the audience at Lentulus' games in the piazza was the voice of the whole Roman People,[90] but it did the job on the day and Sestius was unanimously acquitted.[91] It has done a job for modern readers too, in providing a reason for Cicero actually to *describe* what went on at a Roman theatre.

2.4. Ludi Graeci

Another such reason came up the following year, with the games put on by Pompey as consul to inaugurate the grand new theatre he had built in the Campus Martius. The first-ever permanent theatre in Rome, it was a huge building with a stage evidently designed for large-scale spectacle. Cicero described the occasion in a letter to Marcus Marius, who lived at Stabiae on the bay of Naples. You did well not to go, he told his friend:

> If you're interested, the games were very elaborate, but not to your taste, if I may guess from my own. . . . They didn't even have the charm that ordinary games usually have, because looking at the stage business took away all the enjoyment. I don't doubt you're very content to have missed it, for what pleasure is there in six hundred mules in the *Clytemnestra*, or three thousand mixing-bowls in *The Trojan Horse*, or variously equipped infantry and cavalry in some battle or other? They got plenty of popular admiration, but wouldn't have given you any pleasure.[92]

88. Details in Manuwald 2001, 220–37, and see section 7.5 below.

89. E.g. Cicero *Ad Atticum* 1.16.10 (*'quousque hunc regem feremus?'*), *Pro Sulla* 21 (*regnum meum ferre non posse*), [Sallust] *In Ciceronem* 5 (*erepta libertate*).

90. Cf. Cicero *De domo* 89-90 for a similar argument a few months earlier.

91. Cicero *Ad Q. fratrem* 2.4.1: *quod uehementer interfuit rei publicae, . . . omnibus sententiis absolutus est.*

92. Cicero *Ad familiares* 7.1.2 (September 55 BC): *ne id quidem leporis habuerunt quod solent mediocres ludi. apparatus enim spectatio tollebat omnem hilaritatem; quo quidem apparatu non dubito quin animo aequissimo carueris. quid enim delectionis habent*

Meaninglessly extravagant productions became a regular thing, as we know from Horace a generation later.[93]

Cicero's next comment takes us in a historically much more interesting direction.

> I don't suppose you'd have wanted to see the Greek or Oscan games, especially since you can see Oscan ones even on your local council, and you're so anti-Greek that you don't even use the Greek road to go to your villa![94]

The jokes are lost on us, but the casual reference to Greek and Oscan *ludi* at Pompey's games is a valuable addition to knowledge, precisely because of its casualness. There is no suggestion that such games were in any way unusual, just that Marius wouldn't enjoy them any more than the ones in Latin.

There happens to be corroborative evidence for Oscan *ludi*. The geographer Strabo mentions the Osci as one of the peoples who once occupied the coastal area between Latium and Campania, and he notes a strange thing about them:

> The Osci have died out, but their language is maintained among the Romans to the extent of putting their verses on stage in a traditional festival and performing them as mimes.[95]

For Rome as a multilingual city we may note also Suetonius' report that at the games put on by Caesar and Augustus there were separate stages for performances 'in all languages'.[96] In particular, there would be nothing strange about performances in Greek, which was always the international language of poetry and drama. For them too the evidence is worth digging out.

---

sescenti muli in Clytemnestra aut in Equo Troiano creterrarum tria milia aut armatura uaria peditatus et equitatus in aliqua pugna? quae popularem admirationem habuerunt, delectationem tibi nullam attulissent.

93. Horace *Epistles* 2.1.187-93, on triumphal processions occupying the stage for hours on end.

94. Cicero *Ad familiares* 7.1.3: *non enim te puto Graecos aut Oscos ludos desiderasse, praesertim cum Oscos uel in senatu uestro spectare possis, Graecos ita non ames ut ne ad uillam quidem tuam uia Graeca ire soleas.*

95. Strabo 5.3.6 C233: τῶν μὲν γὰρ Ὄσκων ἐκλελοιπότων ἡ διάλεκτος μένει παρὰ τοῖς Ῥωμαίοις, ὥστε καὶ ποιήματα σκηνοβατεῖσθαι κατά τινα ἀγῶνα πάτριον καὶ μιμολογεῖσθαι. Not to be confused with *fabulae Atellanae*, which of course were in Latin (Varro *De lingua Latina* 7.29).

96. Suetonius *Diuus Iulius* 39.1 (*ludos etiam regionatim urbe tota et quidem per omnium linguarum histriones*), *Diuus Augustus* 43.1 (*etiam uicatim ac pluribus scaenis per omnium linguarum histriones*). No doubt including Etruscan: cf. Varro *De lingua Latina* 5.55 on Volnius, who wrote *tragoediae Tuscae.*

At some point in the first century BC a promising young performer called Licinia Eucharis died at the age of fourteen. She was given a fine tombstone, and on it she addressed the passers-by in the iambic *senarii* she would have used on stage:

> Skilled and taught almost by the Muses' hand,
> I who recently graced with my dancing the games of the nobles
> and played the lead before the People on the Greek stage—
> see how the cruel Fates with their song
> have laid down my body's ashes in the tomb.[97]

There is no indication of anything unusual: 'the Greek stage' was evidently something familiar, one of the places a gifted young dancer might perform.

We know there were *ludi Graeci* at the stage games for Gaius Marius' triumph in 101 BC, but only because it was noticed that he didn't stay to watch them.[98] *Ludi Graeci* at the annual games of Apollo are attested only by another throw-away comment in Cicero's correspondence.[99] The two theatres at Caesar's victory games in 46, for shows respectively in Greek and Latin, only happen to be mentioned because young Gaius Octavius (the future Augustus) was put in charge of the Greek one.[100] That Augustus' own *ludi saeculares* in 17 BC featured two different types of Greek performance, in the theatres of Pompey and Marcellus respectively, is known only from the chance survival of parts of the inscription required by the Senate to record the details of the event.[101]

What sort of plays were performed at the 'Greek games'? There may be a hint in Virgil's description of his poetic beginnings:

> At first my Thalea saw fit to play in Syracusan verse, and didn't blush to inhabit the woodland.[102]

97. *CIL* 1^2.1214.11-15 = *ILLRP* 803.11-15: *docta erodita paene Musarum manu,| quae modo nobilium ludos decoraui choro | et* <u>*Graeca in scaena*</u> *prima populo apparui, | en hoc in tumulo cinerem nostri corporis | infestae Parcae deposierunt carmine.* Note that *prima apparui* does not mean 'I was the first to appear' (as assumed in Wiseman 1985, 31).

98. Plutarch *Marius* 2.2, used as evidence for Marius' lack of Greek learning; the occasion was his dedication of the temple of Honos and Virtus (n. 63).

99. Cicero *Ad Atticum* 16.5.1 (July 44 BC): *scis enim quid ego de ludis Graecis existimem.*

100. Nicolaus of Damascus *Vita Caesaris* 19; the occasion was the dedication of the temple of Venus Genetrix in Caesar's new forum (Dio 43.22.2-4).

101. *CIL* 6.32323.156-8, with Wiseman 2015, 154–5.

102. Virgil *Eclogues* 6.1-2: *prima Syracosio dignata est ludere uersu | nostra neque erubuit siluas habitare Thalea.*

The Syracusan poet–playwrights were Epicharmus and Sophron in the fifth century BC and Theocritus in the third, who honoured Epicharmus and imitated Sophron.[103] Virgil was of course referring to Theocritean 'pastoral', but Thalea, Muse of comedy,[104] reminds us that it too was meant to be performed.

At this point we can return to Cicero, who quotes Epicharmus twice in Greek (in private correspondence) and again in Latin translation (in a philosophical dialogue). The first time is in a long letter to Atticus in March 60 BC, reporting among other things Cicero's good relations with Pompey:

> But I'm involved in these new friendships only so far as Epicharmus, that cunning Sicilian, keeps whispering his old song in my ear: 'Keep sober, remember, don't be trusting; that's what holds good sense together.'[105]

He urged similar caution in a later letter to his brother Quintus: 'I'm surprised you've forgotten Epicharmus' advice "Find out how he deals with others."'[106] And in one of his dialogues Cicero quoted Epicharmus as saying 'I don't want to die, but I don't care about being dead'.[107]

Given all that, and the fact that Varro quoted Sophron verbatim in his treatise on the Latin language,[108] it's a reasonable inference that the Syracusan tradition of Doric Greek poetry for performance was familiar to educated Romans of the late republic. The question is, did they know it from reading texts, or from seeing and hearing the works performed at the

103. *Anthologia Palatina* 9.600 (Theocritus' Doric inscription for a bronze statue of Epicharmus in Syracuse); *Scholia in Theocritum uetera* 269-70 Wendel (τὴν δὲ Θεστυλίδα ὁ Θεόκριτος ἀπειροκάλως ἐκ τῶν Σώφρονος μετήνεγκε Μίμων), 305 Wendel (παρέπλασε δὲ τὸ ποιημάτιον ἐκ τῶν παρὰ Σώφρονι Ἴσθμια θεωμένων καὶ κεχωρισμένον ἐστὶ τοῦ ποιητικοῦ προσώπον). For Sophron as a dramatist, see Demetrius *On Style* 156 (δράματα), Solinus 5.13 (*in scaena*).

104. See for instance *Anthologia Palatina* 9.504.10; Wiseman 2015, 112.

105. Cicero *Ad Atticum* 1.19.8: *atque ita tamen his nouis amicitiis implicati sumus ut crebro uafer ille Siculus insusurret Epicharmus cantilenam illam suam,* νᾶφε καὶ μέμνασ' ἀπιστεῖν· ἄρθρα ταῦτα τᾶν φρενῶν. Quintus Cicero had quoted the same aphorism translated into Latin (*Commentariolum petitionis* 39): Ἐπιχάρμειον *illud teneto 'neruos atque artus esse sapientiae non temere credere'*.

106. Cicero *Ad Q. fratrem* 3.1.23: *soleo admirari . . . nihil te recordari . . . de praeceptis Epicharmi,* γνῶθι πῶς ἄλλῳ κέχρηται.

107. Cicero *Tusculan Disputations* 1.15: *'emori nolo, sed me esse mortuum nihili aestimo'*.

108. Varro *De lingua Latina* 5.179: *mutuum, quod Siculi* μοῖτον*; itaque scribit Sophron* μοῖτον ἀντὶ μοίτου.

ludi Graeci? I think a likely answer can be found, but it requires a careful look at all the Greek quotations in Cicero's letters.

2.5. Greek in the head

In Shackleton Bailey's edition of Cicero's correspondence, the four extant collections contain a total of 914 letters: 426 to Atticus, 435 to other friends and acquaintances (*ad familiares*), 27 to his brother Quintus and 26 to Marcus Brutus.[109] Cicero used Greek very freely in the letters to Atticus and to Quintus, and quoted from Greek authors without translating. A good deal of scholarly work has been done on Cicero's use of Greek,[110] but there is more to be learned from the Greek quotations in particular.[111] Again, the importance of the material is its casualness: here if anywhere, informally to his brother or Atticus, he will have written or dictated what came immediately to mind.

According to my count, there are 97 Greek quotations in the *ad Atticum* collection and 11 in *ad Q. fratrem*, a total of 108 in 453 letters.[112] By contrast, there are a mere 15 in the whole *ad familiares* collection, and seven of those occur in a single letter, to Caesar in 46 BC, where Cicero draws attention to this 'novel style' of correspondence.[113] Of a total of 123 quotations in Greek, 56 are from Homer, 39 from drama, 20 from other poets, and 8 from prose authors.

The preponderance of Homer is easy to explain. Homer was where literary schooling began, and many educated Romans must have had their heads full of the *Iliad* and *Odyssey*.[114] Their political world being highly

109. Other editors reach different totals: for a convenient summary see White 2010, 172–3.

110. E.g. Steele 1900, Rose 1921, Jocelyn 1973, Horsfall 1979, Baldwin 1992, Dubuisson 1992, Adams 2003, 308–47. See now Čulík-Baird 2022, 58–66 ('Cicero and the Greek Poets'), 66–76 ('Latin Translations of Greek Poets'), 273–8 (list of Cicero's references to Greek poetry); however, the Epicharmus references (nn. 105–7) are inexplicably omitted.

111. Steele 1900, 392–400 is an excellent catalogue, but offers no serious discussion.

112. See the Appendix to this volume; Čulík-Baird's list does not include the prose quotations at *Ad Atticum* 5.20.3, 7.1.6, 9.13.4, 10.8.7, 13.42.3, 16.11.1, *Ad familiares* 7.26.1, 15.19.2.

113. Cicero *Ad familiares* 13.15.2: *genere nouo sum litterarum ad te usus.*

114. Horace *Epistles* 2.2.41-2, Petronius *Satyrica* 5.11-12, Quintilian 1.8.5, Pliny *Letters* 2.14.2. Cf. Steele 1900, 394 on the places where just a brief phrase is quoted, 'merely as a key to the thought which Cicero wished to bring before the mind of the reader. Two or three words might bring up an entire Homeric picture.'

competitive,[115] it came naturally to them to think of prominent politicians as Homeric heroes.[116] Cicero himself certainly lived by that ethos;[117] again and again in the correspondence we see Iliadic examples guiding him at the key moments in his public life.[118]

The other great influence was Plato, whose authority Cicero regarded as divine.[119] He too was a point of reference when big decisions had to be made,[120] but prose is much less memorable than verse. There are only eight Greek prose quotations in the whole correspondence,[121] and the one from Plato was no doubt quoted in the original only because Cicero had recently re-read it.[122] It was the Greek poets above all whose words he could recall unprompted—and among the poets, after Homer it was the dramatists, especially Athenian tragedy.[123]

115. Lucretius 2.11 (*certare ingenio, contendere nobilitate*), 5.1123-4 (*ad summum succedere honorem | certantes*); for *certare* and *contendere* as applied to politics, see for instance Lucilius 1232-4 Marx, Varro *Menippean Satires* 450 Astbury, Cicero *Pro Sulla* 49, 90, Horace *Odes* 3.1.12-13. Roman aristocrats had always sought to be *optimus* ('the best') or *primarius* ('number one'): *CIL* 1^2.8-9 (L. Scipio *cos.* 259 BC), Pliny *Natural History* 7.139-40 (L. Metellus *cos.* 251 and 247 BC), Cicero *De senectute* 61 (A. Calatinus *cos.* 258 and 254 BC). For political life as a Homeric duel (*dimicatio*), see for instance Cicero *Pro Sestio* 1, *Pro Caelio* 47, *Orator* 42.

116. See for instance Cicero *Ad Atticum* 1.18.3 (Memmius as Paris, M. Lucullus as Menelaus), *Ad familiares* 3.7.6 (Cicero and Appius as Agamemnon and Achilles), Plutarch *Pompey* 67.3 (Domitius on Pompey as Agamemnon); Champlin 2003a.

117. See for instance *Ad Atticum* 2.3.4 on *Iliad* 12.243 (*non opinor esse dubitandum quin semper nobis uideatur* εἷς οἰωνὸς ἄριστος ἀμύνεσθαι περὶ πάτρης); *Ad Q. fratrem* 3.5.4 on *Iliad* 4.182 = 8.150 (*illud uero quod a puero adamaram,* πολλὸν ἀριστεύειν καὶ ὑπείροχον ἔμμεναι ἄλλων); *Ad Atticum* 9.5.3 on *Iliad* 18.96-9 (*sicut apud Homerum . . . ego uero haec officia mercanda uita puto*).

118. E.g. when aiming for the consulship in 65 (*Ad Atticum* 1.1.4, *Iliad* 22.159-61), opposing Caesar and Pompey in 59 (*Ad Atticum* 2.3.4, *Iliad* 12.243), staying with the *optimates* in 59 and 50 (*Ad Atticum* 2.5.1 and 7.1.4, *Iliad* 22.100-5), following Pompey in 49 (*Ad Atticum* 9.5.3, *Iliad* 18.96-9).

119. *Ad Atticum* 4.16.3 (*deus ille noster Plato*), *Ad familiares* 1.9.12 (*scripta diuinitus*); nn. 21–2.

120. As in May 49, whether to join Pompey: *Ad Atticum* 10.8.6 (*sed tamen, mi Attice, auguria quoque me incitant . . . illa Platonis de tyrannis*).

121. *Ad Atticum* 5.20.3 (*Corpus Paroem. Gr.* 1.300), 7.1.6 (Thucydides 1.97.2), 9.13.4 (Plato *Epistles* 7.329d), 10.8.71 (Thucydides 1.138.3), 13.42.3 (*Corpus Paroem. Gr.* 1.421), 16.11.1 (Heraclitus fr. 49 Diels), *Ad familiares* 7.26.1 (Epicurus ap. Diog. Laert. 10.22), 15.19.2 (Epicurus ap. Diog. Laert. 10.132).

122. *Ad Atticum* 9.13.4 (March 49 BC): Plato *Epistles* 7.329d. Similarly *Ad Atticum* 7.1.6 (October 50) and 10.8.7 (May 49): quotations from Thucydides book 1, appropriate re-reading for a time of conflict leading to war.

123. Čulík-Baird 2022, 276–8 (Aeschylus 2, Sophocles 4, Euripides 15); add *Ad Q. fratrem* 3.4.2 (Aeschylus). The only quotation from Aristophanes (*Ad Atticum* 5.10.3, *Wasps* 1431) was essentially a proverb (*Tusculan Disputations* 1.41); cf. *De republica* 4.11 (Scipio) for Cicero's disapproval of the political licence of Old Comedy.

Did he know those words from drama just from reading book-texts, or was it from hearing them delivered in the theatre? Having spent two years in Greece (79–77 BC), Cicero had had plenty of opportunity to hear the classic plays performed. He was studying oratorical technique as well as philosophy,[124] and the way tragic actors used voice and gesture was a vital part of that.[125] If classic Greek tragedy was ever staged in Rome, we can be sure Cicero was a knowledgeable spectator. One way or another, it's clear that he had a good stock of Greek tragic speeches readily available in his memory.

How he used them, along with Homer, is wonderfully illustrated by the letter to Caesar mentioned above. It was written in 46 BC, after the civil war; Cicero had been on the wrong side, and now made his peace with the victor by playing on their shared knowledge of classic Greek literature. In what started as a routine letter of recommendation, he mentioned that young Precilius' father had wanted Cicero to accept Caesar's offers of political alliance:

> 'But he did not ever persuade the heart in my breast',[126] because I was listening to our men of distinction, as they kept shouting 'Be brave, so that posterity may praise you'.[127] 'At these words a black cloud of grief covered him.'[128] But he does console me too. Though I've been burned once, even now they want to fire me with glory, and this is what they say: 'Let me not die without a fight, unrenowned, but having done some mighty deed to be heard of by men to come.'[129] But nowadays, as you see, they have less influence on me. I turn from Homer's grand style to the true advice of Euripides: 'I hate a sage who's not sage to himself.'[130] It's a verse the elder Precilius does well to praise, and he tells me one can look 'to the future as well as the past',[131] and nevertheless 'be ever the best and out in front of the others'.[132]

124. Cicero *Brutus* 314-6, cf. Plutarch *Cicero* 4.

125. Cicero *De oratore* 1.128, 1.251, 2.193 (exemplified at 3.213-27); cf. Seneca *Controuersiae* 3.pref.3, Quintilian 12.5.5.

126. Odysseus, resistant to Calypso and Circe (*Odyssey* 7.258, 9.33): Cicero, resistant to the elder Precilius.

127. Athene to Telemachus (*Odyssey* 1.302): the *optimates* working on Cicero.

128. Laertes, before Odysseus reveals himself (*Odyssey* 24.315): Cicero, exiled by Clodius' tribunician law.

129. Hector's self-encouragement before the fight with Achilles (*Iliad* 22.304-5).

130. From an unknown play (*TrGF* fr. 905); the *optimates* were urging Cicero, not themselves.

131. Achilles to Agamemnon's messengers, or the wise old Ithacan Halitherses (*Iliad* 1.343, *Odyssey* 24.452).

132. Hippolochus to Glaucus, Peleus to Achilles (*Iliad* 6.208, 11.784). *Ad familiares* 13.15.1-2 (evidently 45 BC): ἀλλ' ἐμὸν οὔ ποτε θυμὸν ἐνὶ στήθεσσιν ἔπειθεν. *audiebam enim nostros proceres clamitantis* ἄλκιμος ἔσσ', ἵνα τίς σε καὶ ὀψιγόνων ἐὺ εἴπῃ. ὣς φάτο, τὸν δ'ἄχεος νεφέλη ἐκάλυψε μέλαινα. *sed tamen idem me consolatur etiam. hominem <enim> perustum*

Addressed to the man who had defeated the *optimates*, this delicately phrased sequence of allusions enabled Cicero to save his dignity while renouncing his old allegiance.[133]

So far, so good: the quotations attest a mind well stocked with classic Greek texts immediately ready for use. The concentration on the well-known classics was noted a century ago by H. J. Rose, who could find only three quotations from 'post-Attic writers' and one of them wasn't even Cicero's own.[134] Two of those three, and a third not noticed by Rose,[135] are of particular historical interest, precisely because there is no obvious reason why Cicero should have had them in his head.

2.6. *Rhinthon and Sopatros*

The 'Greek games' in Rome (section 2.4 above) may provide such a reason, an explanation why three of the Greek quotations in the letters are not from the classic texts that any well-educated Roman might be expected to know.

The first comes in a letter to Atticus in May 60 BC, reflecting on Cicero's sense of political isolation:

> What I want you to consider is this. Since the death of Catulus I've been keeping to this optimate line without any support or company. As Rhinthon (I think) says, 'Some count for nothing, others don't care at all.' The jealousy towards me of our friends with the fishponds is something I'll write to you about another time, or keep for when we meet.[136]

---

etiamnum gloria uolunt incendere atque ita loquuntur: μὴ μὰν ἀσπουδί γε καὶ ἀκλειῶς ἀπολοίμην, ἀλλὰ μέγα ῥέξας τι καί ἐσσομένοισι πυθέσθαι. *sed me minus iam mouent, ut uides. itaque ab Homeri magniloquentia confero me ad uera praecepta* Εὐριπίδου*:* μισῶ σοφιστήν ὅστις οὐχ αὑτῷ σοφός. *quem uersum senex Precilius laudat egregie et ait posse eundem et* ἅμα πρόσσω καὶ ὀπίσσω *uidere et tamen nihilo minus* αἰὲν ἀριστεύειν καὶ ὑπερείροχον ἔμμεναι ἄλλων.

133. Cf. Hutchinson 1998, 15: 'The Greek in the letter to Caesar also enables Cicero to write with the distance, and the community, of cultured discourse about his difficult political relationship with his addressee (whatever exactly he may be saying here).' I don't know why Čulík-Baird (2022, 59) should describe the letter as 'infamous'.

134. Rose 1921, 114 ('post-Attic' left Epicharmus out of account): *Ad Atticum* 1.20.3 (Rhinthon), 8.5.1 ('Alexandrian'); Rose's third example was a line of Leonidas (*Hellenistic Epigrams* 2490 Gow-Page = *Anthologia Palatina* 10.1.1), used by Atticus in March 49 BC and picked up by Cicero as a shorthand phrase for 'time to join Pompey' (*Ad Atticum* 9.7.5, 9.18.3, 10.2.1).

135. *Ad Atticum* 1.19.2 (March 60 BC), n. 138.

136. Cicero *Ad Atticum* 1.20.3: *illud tamen uelim existimes, me hanc uiam optimatem post Catuli mortem nec praesidio ullo nec comitatu tenere. nam ut ait Rhinthon, ut*

We have met Rhinthon already (section 1.6 above) as the author of 'tragic fooleries' in third-century BC Taras (Tarentum). But even his contemporaries thought of Rhinthon as only a 'minor songbird of the Muses';[137] whatever could have brought him, of all people, into Cicero's mind at such a moment?

Among the other *phlyax*-writers of the time was Sopatros, whom Cicero may have quoted to Atticus just two months earlier:

> The Senate has resolved . . . that ambassadors with full powers be sent to approach the peoples of Gaul and try to prevent them joining the Helvetii. They are Q. Metellus Creticus, L. Flaccus, and ('myrrh on the lentils!') Lentulus son of Clodianus.[138]

The quotation was a proverb, but the source that identifies it as such provides some other information as well:

> Sopatros in his *Underworld* refers [to lentils] as follows: 'Ithacan Odysseus is here, the myrrh on the lentils. Take courage, my soul!' Clearchus the Peripatetic in his *On Proverbs* records 'myrrh on the lentils' as a proverb, and Varro who is called the Menippean refers to it too.[139]

Varro used the phrase as a title,[140] and since Menippean satire was evidently a stage genre in the same serio-comic (*spoudogeloion*) category as the *phlyax*,[141] it is quite possible that he took it from Sopatros. The quotation comes from a play called *Nekuia*, the name also given to book 11 of

---

opinor, οἱ μὲν παρ'οὐδέν εἰσι, τοῖς δ'οὐδὲν μέλει. *mihi uero ut inuideant piscinarii nostri aut scribam ad te alias aut in congressum nostrum reseruabo.* Q. Catulus (consul 78 BC) was a hardline optimate regarded by the *populares* as 'more brutal than Sulla' (Sallust *Histories* 3.15.9 Ramsey); the *piscinarii* were L. Lucullus (consul 74 BC) and Q. Hortensius (consul 69 BC), whose seaside villas featured notoriously elaborate artificial fishponds (Varro *Res rusticae* 3.17.5-9).

137. *Anthologia Palatina* 7.414.3: Μουσάων ὀλίγη τις ἀηδονίς.

138. *Ad Atticum* 1.19.2 (March 60 BC): *senatus decreuit ut . . . legati cum auctoritate mitterentur qui adirent Galliae ciuitates darentque operam ne eae cum Heluetiis coniungerent. legati sunt Q. Metellus Creticus et L. Flaccus et,* τὸ ἐπὶ τῇ φακῇ μύρον, *Lentulus Clodiani filius.*

139. Athenaeus 4.160b-c (Sopatros fr. 13 *PCG*): ὁ Σώπατρος . . . ἐν Νεκυίᾳ μνημονεύει οὕτως· Ἴθακος Ὀδυσσεύς, τοὐπὶ τῇ φακῇ μύρον, | πάρεστι· θάρσει, θυμέ. Κλέαρχος δὲ ὁ ἐπὶ τοῦ περιπάτου ἐν τοῖς Περὶ παροιμιῶν ὡς παροιμίαν ἀναγράφει τὸ ἐπὶ τῇ φακῇ μύρον, ἧς μέμνηται καὶ Οὐάρρων ὁ Μενίππειος καλούμενος.

140. Varro *Menippean Satires* 549-51 Astbury (Nonius 100L, 230L, 319L); the piece was subtitled περὶ εὐκαιρίας.

141. Strabo 16.2.29 C759 (Menippus σπουδογέλοιος); Stephanus Byzantinus 357 (Blaisos σπουδογελοίων ποιητής). Stage genre: see Wiseman 2009, 132–43 (Varro) and 2015, 172–5 (Lucian).

the *Odyssey*, where Odysseus visits the underworld.[142] Menippus too was fond of underworld scenes.[143]

In March 49 BC, Caesar wanted Cicero to return to Rome and lend dignity to a now depleted Senate.[144] Atticus' advice on the subject contained a striking phrase:

> If Manius Lepidus and Lucius Vulcatius stay here, then I think you should stay, provided that if Pompey is safe and has made a base somewhere, you abandon this *Underworld* and prefer to be defeated with him than to rule with Caesar in the cesspit that is clearly to be expected.[145]

Cicero picked it up when reporting on Caesar's personal visit and his own refusal to comply:

> So I don't think he's pleased with me—but I was pleased with myself, something I haven't been used to for a long time. As for the rest, good heavens! What a retinue, what an *Underworld*, as you like to call it! Celer was among the heroes[?] there.[146]

Atticus wasn't necessarily referring to *Odyssey* book 11. In Cicero's Rome the underworld scene was something people saw on the stage.

We noticed earlier (section 2.1 above) that Cicero blamed 'the poets' for the fact that people cannot conceive of souls without bodily form: 'This [error] is the origin of the whole of Homer's *Underworld*.'[147] But *Odyssey* book 11 was Cicero's afterthought in that passage; the poets he meant in the first place were playwrights. Of course he had tragedy in mind,[148] but the underworld scenario could equally well be staged in comic, satiric

142. E.g. Diodorus Siculus 4.39.3, Plutarch *Moralia* 740e.

143. See Lucian's Μένιππος ἢ Νεκυομαντεία, and Menippus' role as protagonist in Lucian's *Dialogues of the Dead* (Loeb ed. vol. 4, 72–109 and vol. 7, 1–175). Cf. also *Suda* Φ 180, where Menippus presents himself as coming from Hades as an inspector of sins, to report back to the powers below.

144. *Ad Atticum* 9.6a (Caesar to Cicero), *ut tuo consilio gratia dignitate ope omnium rerum uti possim*; reported by Cicero to Atticus at 9.9.3.

145. Quoted in *Ad Atticum* 9.10.7: *si M'. Lepidus et L. Vulcatius remanent, manendum puto, ita ut, si saluus sit Pompeius et constiterit alicubi, hanc* νέκυιαν *relinquas et te in certamine uinci cum illo facilius patiaris quam cum hoc in ea quae perspicitur futura colluuie regnare.*

146. *Ad Atticum* 9.18.1-2 (28 March): *credo igitur hunc me non amare. at ego me amaui, quod mihi iam pridem usus non uenit. reliqua, di boni! qui comitatus, quae, ut tu soles dicere,* νέκυια! *in qua erat* ἥρως *Celer.* The final sentence depends on a modern emendation.

147. *Tusculan Disputations* 1.37: *inde Homeri tota* νέκυια.

148. He quoted an underworld scene from an unknown Roman tragedy (*TrRF* 1.50).

or erotic mode.[149] One of those who did so was Sopatros, and the pattern of quotation and allusion makes it likely that Cicero and Atticus were familiar with his work.

After Rhinthon and (probably) Sopatros, the third of the anomalous post-classical Greek quotations in Cicero's letters is a hexameter that H. J. Rose thought had 'an Alexandrian flavour';[150] it comes in a letter to Atticus written at Formiae in February 49 BC. Cicero had had a visit from Atticus' freedman Dionysius, whom he found insufferably rude and arrogant:

> He's never been more demented than in this business. What I didn't put in my letter to you is that I heard afterwards that on that occasion he went from the third milestone 'constantly raging in vain with his horns in the air'—that is, after a great deal of bad language.[151]

The line, evidently a familiar one, appears also in Catullus, translated into Latin.[152] But who wrote it?

After Rose's time the line was confidently attributed to Callimachus' *Hecale*, and understood as referring to the Marathonian bull.[153] But why should we suppose that here, and only here in the whole correspondence, Cicero had Callimachus in mind? Given his ironical attitude to contemporary enthusiasts for Hellenistic poetry,[154] that would be surprising. If it described the bull of Marathon, why should Catullus use it of the Minotaur? The spondaic ending may suggest an 'Alexandrian' context, but exactly the same feature is found in one of the hexameter fragments of Epicharmos more than two centuries earlier.[155]

Catullus' use of the line suggests a different explanation. Rhinthon and his fellow *phlyax*-writers liked Euripidean plots,[156] and Euripides

149. Laberius *Necyomanteia* (Aulus Gellius 16.7.12, 20.6.6 = frr. 42-3 Panayotakis). For Laberius and other mimographers as satirical commentators on current events, see Cicero *Ad familiares* 7.2.3 (53 BC), *Ad Atticum* 14.3.2 (44 BC). Erotic: Ovid *Fasti* 5.197-8, with Wiseman 2008, 226–7; cf. Laberius fr. 59 Panayotakis (Aulus Gellius 16.7.4), *tollet bona fide uos Orcus nudas in catomum.*

150. Rose 1921, 114.

151. *Ad Atticum* 8.5.1: *numquam autem cerritior fuit quam in hoc negotio. nam quod ad te non scripseram, postea audiui a tertio miliario tum eum isse* πολλὰ μάτην κεράεσσιν ἐς ἠέρα θυμήναντα, *multa, inquam, mala cum dixisset.*

152. Catullus 64.111: *nequiquam uanis iactantem cornua uentis.*

153. Pfeiffer 1949, 467, Hollis 1990, 323–4: now listed as Callimachus fr. 732 Pf.

154. Cicero *Tusculan Disputations* 3.45 (on *cantores Euphorionis*), *Ad Atticum* 7.2.1 (on οἱ νεωτέροι).

155. Epicharmus fr. 121 *PCG* (λαοὶ τοξοχίτωνες, ἀκούετε Σειρηνάων).

156. *Herakles* (Rhinthon), *Hippolytus* (Sopatros), *Iphigeneia at Aulis* (Rhinthon), *Iphigeneia in Tauris* (Rhinthon), *Medea* (Rhinthon), *Meleagros* (Rhinthon, Skiras), *Orestes* (Rhinthon, Sopatros), *Telephus* (Rhinthon).

brought the Minotaur into at least one of his plays.[157] Rhinthon is said to have written 'hexameter comedy',[158] so a *phlyax* scenario with a speaking Minotaur could have occurred to Cicero à propos of Dionysius' furious language—more probably, I suggest, than the bull of Marathon in Callimachus' *Hecale*.

The conclusion is that some of the phrases that spontaneously occurred to Cicero as he wrote or dictated his letters may have been in his mind because he had heard them delivered, in Greek, on the stage in Rome: Rhinthon and Sopatros in 60 BC, Rhinthon again perhaps in 49. They too provide precious contemporary evidence for the lost world of Roman public entertainment, in this case for the place within it of the non-Attic, western-Greek dramatic tradition from Epicharmus through to the third century BC.

157. Plutarch *Theseus* 15.2 (Euripides *TrGF* frr. 996-7); Tzetzes *Chiliades* 11.555 (the Minotaur in Euripides' *Theseus*). For an interpretation of Catullus 64 as itself a script for performance, see Wiseman 2023, 103–40.

158. Lydus *De magistratibus* 1.41 (τὸν Ῥίνθονα, ὃς ἑξαμέτροις ἔγραψε πρῶτος κωμῳδίαν), evidently from Suetonius (section 4.4 below).

CHAPTER THREE

Historical Evidence

MUCH OF the Cicero evidence is information he didn't know he was giving us, glimpses of what people in his time didn't need to be told. The situation is quite different with authors who *intended* to provide information for their readers: in their case we must try to imagine not only their own times but also the times, centuries earlier, that they claimed to be explaining. How much could they know? Where did they find their information?

This chapter looks at four authors who offered factual accounts of the origins and nature of Roman theatre, and close attention to what they said will lead us in some unexpected directions. Since their evidence involves more than a thousand years of history, reference to the time-chart in the Preface (fig. 1) may be needed to keep track of the chronology.

3.1. Narrative history: the evidence of Livy

Our first authority is Titus Livius, known to English speakers as 'Livy'. His huge history of Rome, from the origins down to his own time, was planned at a time when the Roman state was in crisis: as he put it in his preface, 'we can endure neither our vices nor the remedies needed to cure them'.[1] Not surprisingly, civil strife was a recurring theme, prominent even in the Romulus and Remus foundation story.[2]

It was a theme emphasised in Livy's narrative of 367 BC, where he reported 'enormous struggles' over the right of plebeians to hold political

1. Livy pref. 9 (trans. T. J. Luce), written probably in the mid-30s BC.

2. Livy 1.6.4 (*interuenit . . . auitum malum, regni cupido, atque inde foedum certamen coortum*), where the phraseology refers back to a programme passage in the preface on how history provides examples of behaviour to avoid (pref. 10, *foedum inceptum foedum exitu quod uites*); cf. 1.17.1 (*certamen regni ac cupido*).

power, leading to the threat of civil war.[3] A compromise was found (each year two consuls would be elected, one of whom might be a plebeian), and 'great games' were decreed to celebrate it.[4] But who was to pay for them? The plebeian aediles declined the responsibility, so a new 'curule' aedileship was introduced to administer this 'gift to the immortal gods'.[5]

Meanwhile, Rome was afflicted by plague.[6] The newly reformed government took action in 364 BC:

> Since neither human policies nor divine aid alleviated the violence of the plague, people's minds were overcome by superstitious terror. Among other attempts to placate the wrath of heaven, it is said that stage games were also instituted—something new to a warlike people, since hitherto there had been only the spectacle of the *circus*.[7] But it was a small matter, as beginnings usually are.
>
> The thing itself was foreign. There was no singing, no acting in imitation of song: the players summoned from Etruria danced to the accompaniment of a pipe-player's measures and made quite graceful movements in the Etruscan manner. Then the young men began to imitate them, at the same time exchanging repartee in improvised verses, with movements appropriate to the words. So it was taken up and established by frequent repetition.
>
> The name given to these native performers was *histriones*, since *ister* was the Etruscan word for a player. They didn't throw out rough improvised exchanges like Fescennine verse,[8] as had been done previously, but began to perform *saturae* filled with musical measures in what was now a written song accompanied by a pipe-player and with appropriate movement.

3. Livy 6.42.9-10 (*per ingentia certamina . . . prope secessionem plebis res terribilesque alias minas ciuilium certaminum uenit*), with Kraus 1994, 330 and Wiseman 1995, 107–8 on Livy's narrative strategy at this point.

4. Livy 6.42.12. The *ludi magni* (later *ludi Romani*) had been instituted by 'Tarquinius Priscus' (section 1.2 above): Cicero *De republica* 2.36, Eutropius 1.6.1, *De uiris illustribus* 6.8; cf. ps.Asconius 217 Stangl (*sub regibus*).

5. Livy 6.42.13-14, 7.1.1 and 5-6; cf. 10.47.3-4 (293 BC), 27.6.19 (210).

6. Livy 5.13.4-5 (399 BC), 5.31.5 (392), 6.20.15 (384), 6.21.1 (383), 7.1.8 (365) 7.2.1 (364), 7.3.1-4 (363).

7. The ruler who first introduced the Roman games (section 1.2 above) also created the Circus Maximus in which they were held: Livy 1.35.8-9, Dionysius of Halicarnassus *Roman Antiquities* 3.68.1, Eutropius 1.6.1, *De uiris illustribus* 6.8.

8. *Versus Fescenninus* was abusive ribaldry, often sung at weddings: see Catullus 61.120, Horace *Epistles* 2.1.145-6, Festus (Paulus) 76L, Macrobius *Saturnalia* 2.4.21.

> It is said that Livius, some years later, who from *saturae* was the first to compose a play with a plot—he was of course the actor of his own songs, as they all were at that time—had made his voice hoarse from frequent encores and obtained permission to station a boy in front of the pipe-player to sing the song, and acted it with rather more energetic movement because he wasn't impeded by using his own voice.[9]

I have left *saturae* untranslated, because its meaning is controversial;[10] for the moment, it is enough to register that Livy understood it as a performance that was not a play with a plot.

'Livius' (no relation to the historian) was Lucius Livius Andronicus, the playwright whose production at the *ludi Romani* of 240 BC, recorded in 'ancient documents', was taken by Cicero and his friend Atticus as the beginning of all Roman literature (section 1.1 above).[11] That vague 'some years later' was therefore well over a century beyond the chronological context of Livy's narrative. And now he went on to describe equally undated subsequent developments, including the introduction of the Oscan farces known as *fabulae Atellanae*,[12] before ending with a moralising contrast

9. Livy 7.2.3-9: *cum uis morbi nec humanis consiliis nec ope diuina leuaretur, uictis superstitione animis ludi quoque scaenici—noua res bellicoso populo, nam circi modo spectaculum fuerat—inter alia caelestis irae placamina instituti dicuntur; ceterum parua quoque, ut ferme principia omnia, et ea ipsa peregrina res fuit. sine carmine ullo, sine imitandorum carminum actu ludiones ex Etruria acciti, ad tibicinis modos saltantes, haud indecoros motus more Tusco dabant. imitari deinde eos iuuentus, simul inconditis inter se iocularia fundentes uersibus, coepere; nec absoni a uoce motus erant. accepta itaque res saepiusque usurpando excitata. uernaculis artificibus, quia ister Tusco uerbo ludio uocabatur, nomen histrionibus inditum; qui non, sicut ante, Fescennino uersu similem incompositum temere ac rudem alternis iaciebant sed impletas modis saturas descripto iam ad tibicinum cantu motuque congruenti peragebant. Liuius post aliquot annis, qui ab saturis ausus est primus argumento fabulam serere, idem scilicet—id quod omnes tum erant—suorum carminum actor, dicitur, cum saepius reuocatus uocem obtudisset, uenia petita puerum ad canendum ante tibicinem cum statuisset, canticum egisse aliquanto magis uigente motu quia nihil uocis usus impediebat.*

10. See Oakley 1998, 55–8, and cf. Valerius Maximus 2.4.4 (*paulatim deinde ludicra ars ad saturarum modos perrepsit*), with Oakley 1998, 776–7. The question is discussed in the next chapter.

11. Cicero *Brutus* 71-2 (*in antiquis commentariis*), *Tusculan Disputations* 1.3, Aulus Gellius 17.21.42-3 (citing Varro *De poetis*). The *praenomen* is given by Gellius 17.21.42, the *cognomen* by Gellius 18.9.5, *Historia Augusta* 30.13.5 and *Grammatici Latini* 2.321 Keil (Priscian).

12. Livy 7.2.10-12 (*inde . . . postquam . . . postea*); on *fabulae Atellanae* see also Diomedes *De poematibus* 10.5 and 9 = *Grammatici Latini* 1.490 Keil (nn. 52 and 55).

between the innocent origins of Roman theatre and the insanely extravagant productions of his own time.[13]

How did Livy know what had happened in 364 BC? His earliest authority was Fabius Pictor, writing at the end of the third century,[14] and where Fabius got his information from can only be a matter of conjecture. The plague outbreak itself was the sort of portentous event that would be recorded by the *pontifex maximus* (and archived in the so-called *annales maximi*),[15] and the summoning of the performers from Etruria could have been part of that documentation. But Livy's digression on the consequences of the innovation was evidently inserted into his narrative from a quite different type of source.

The most striking aspect of it is the emphasis on music and dance.[16] Livius' production of plays with plots, epoch-making in the other sources,[17] is mentioned only in passing; what matters in this account is his alleged introduction of 'acting in imitation of song',[18] the silent actor miming what someone else was singing. That looks like a pseudo-historical origin-story for the great theatrical innovation of Livy's own time, the 'all-mime' dance drama (*pantomimus*) pioneered by Bathyllus and Pylades in the 20s BC.[19]

If that is what it was, we must rule out the common but unnecessary assumption that Livy's digression was taken from Varro.[20] However, Varro's treatment of Roman drama is important in its own right, and well worth trying to reconstruct. So he is the second of our four witnesses.

13. Livy 7.2.13 (*hanc uix opulentis regnis tolerabilem insaniam*); cf. Valerius Maximus 2.4.6 on the lavish decoration of theatres in the first century BC.

14. Livy 2.40.10 (*apud Fabium, longe antiquissimum auctorem*), 22.7.4 (Fabius cited on 217 BC); cf. Appian *Hannibalic War* 27.116 ('Fabius, the historian of these events', sent to Delphi in 216).

15. Cato *FRHist* 5 F80 ('the notice in the house of the *pontifex maximus*' recording food shortages and eclipses), cf. Cicero *De republica* 1.25 (an eclipse in the *annales maximi*); on the origin and nature of the *annales maximi* see the contrasting arguments of Rich 2018, 19–28 and Wiseman 2018, v–xiii.

16. Rightly emphasised by Oakley 1998, 42.

17. Cicero *Brutus* 72, *Tusculan Disputations* 1.3, *De senectute* 50; Aulus Gellius 17.21.42, Cassiodorus *Chronica* 2.128M.

18. Livy 7.2.4 (*sine imitandorum carminum actu*), 7.2.9 (*dicitur . . . canticum egisse*).

19. Athenaeus 1.20.d-e, Jerome *Chronica* Ol. 189.3 (22–21 BC), Seneca *Controuersiae* 3.pref.10; see Hall and Wyles 2008, and chapter 11 below.

20. See Oakley 1998, 42–51 for full discussion. An equally possible (and equally unprovable) source was Sinnius Capito, whose *libri spectaculorum* discussed the theatre and circus festivals (Lactantius *Diuinae institutiones* 6.20.35, cf. Festus 500L); he evidently wrote later than Varro, who doesn't mention him, but earlier than Verrius Flaccus, who disagreed with him about the *ludi Apollinares* (Festus 436-8L).

3.2. Historical research: the evidence of Varro

Cicero described Marcus Varro as 'the most scrupulous investigator of the past'.[21] In Latin, *inuestigator* was a live metaphor: *uestigia* meant literally 'tracks' or 'footprints',[22] and historical enquiry was like hunting for something by the traces it had left. Varro himself was very conscious of the analogy:

> There are few things that time does not corrupt, and many that it takes away completely. . . . What oblivion already robbed from our ancestors, not even the diligence of Mucius and Brutus, chasing what got away, can ever bring back. . . . For there is more than a little darkness in the wood where these things have to be caught.[23]

That was written to introduce book 5 of *De lingua Latina*, warning how difficult it was to identify the origins of particular words, and the men he referred to were senior senators whose work was remembered as the foundation of Roman civil law.[24] The *uestigia* they sought were serious business, historical evidence for the language and institutions of Rome.[25]

The same applied to Varro's work on the origins of Roman drama. His masterpiece, the 41-volume *Antiquitates*, which came out when Livy was about fourteen years old,[26] included as the tenth book of the 'divine antiquities' sequence a volume devoted to theatre festivals (*ludi scaenici*),[27] and that was only a part of Varro's extensive output on the subject. Practically nothing is left of that output, but thanks to St Jerome at least some titles are known.

21. Cicero *Brutus* 60: *diligentissimus inuestigator antiquitatis.*

22. For the extended sense as 'evidence' see *Oxford Latin Dictionary* s.v. *uestigium* 7b.

23. Varro *De lingua Latina* 5.5: *uetustas pauca non deprauat, multa tollit . . . illa quae iam maioribus nostris ademit obliuio, fugitiua secuta sedulitas Muci et Bruti retrahere nequit. . . . non mediocris enim tenebrae in silua ubi haec captanda.*

24. Pomponius in *Digest* 1.2.2.39 (*Publius Mucius et Brutus et Manilius, qui fundauerunt ius ciuile*): P. Mucius Scaevola, consul in 133 BC and *pontifex maximus* from 130 to 115, and Marcus Brutus, praetor about 140 BC; for Manius Manilius, consul in 149 BC, cf. Varro *De lingua Latina* 7.105 (cited on Plautus).

25. For Varro's regular use of *uestigia* in this sense, see *De lingua Latina* 5.42, 5.43, 5.154, 5.183, 6.18, *Res rusticae* 2.4.9.

26. Jerome *Chronica* Ol. 180.2 (Livy born 59 BC), Cicero *Academica* 1.9 (impact of publication), Augustine *City of God* 6.3 (contents list).

27. Augustine *City of God* 4.1.3, 6.3.4.

Jerome set himself to list Varro's entire *oeuvre*, but gave up after 39 items consisting of 480 volumes: 'I've copied out barely half the list, and it's wearisome for readers.'[28] The ones he did register are as follows:

title	**number of books**
1. *Antiquitates*	45[29]
2. *De uita populi Romani*	4
3. *Imagines*	15
4. λογιστορικοί	76
5. *De lingua Latina*	25
6. *Disciplinae*	9
7. *De sermone Latino*	5
8. *Quaestiones Plautinae*	5
9. *Annales*	3
10 *De origine linguae Latinae*	3
11. *De poemati<bu>s*	3
12. *De originibus scaenicis*	3
13. *De scaenicis actionibus*	3
14. *De actis scaenicis*	3
15. *De descriptionibus*	3
16. *De proprietate scriptorum*	3
17. *De bibliothecis*	3
18. *De lectionibus*	3
19. *De similitudine uerborum*	3
20. *Legationes*	3
21. *Suasiones*	3
22. *De Pompeio*	3
23. *Singulares*	10
24. *De personis*	3
25. *De iure ciuili*	15
26. ἐπιτομή *antiquitatum ex libris XLII*	9
27. ἐπιτομή *ex libris imaginum XV*	4

28. Jerome in Ritschl 1857, 150–51: *uix medium descripsi indicem et legentibus fastidium est.*

29. This numeral is either Jerome's mistake or a scribal error: see Augustine *City of God* 6.3.1 for the 41 books of *Antiquitates*, 25 for *res humanae* and 16 for *res diuinae.*

28. ἐπιτομή *de lingua Latina ex libris XV*	9
29. *De principiis numerorum*	9
30. *Res rusticae*	3
31. *De ualetudine tuenda*	1
32. *De sua uita*	3
33. *De forma philosophiae*	3
34. *Res urbanae*	3
35. *Saturae Menippeae*[30]	150
36. *Poemata*	10
37. *Orationes*	22
38. *Pseudotragoediae*	6
39. *Saturae*	4

The most obviously relevant titles are the nine volumes on 'theatrical origins', 'theatrical performances' and 'theatrical acts' (items 12–14) and the five volumes of 'problems in Plautus' (item 8), which may or may not be the three or more volumes 'on the comedies of Plautus' cited by Aulus Gellius.[31] All those works are lost, but an outline of Varro's treatment of Roman drama can be recovered from another late text, contemporary with Jerome.

At some point in the late fourth or early fifth century AD, a Greek grammarian called Diomedes composed in Latin a three-volume *Ars grammatica*, of which the third book was devoted to poetry and metre.[32] Having described the various combinations of short and long syllables that made metrical 'feet', he went on to discuss kinds of poems, *poematum genera*.[33] Following a centuries-old Greek scholarly tradition, he divided poems into three categories: first, dramatic or mimetic, in which characters speak without any intervention in the poet's voice; second, narrative or expository, in which the poet speaks without any intervention in other

30. As often happens, here and at item 39 the MSS use the spelling *satira* (or *satyra*); but the alleged derivation from the adjective *satur* (section 4.3 below) is enough to show that in Varro's time the proper spelling was *satura*.

31. Aulus Gellius 3.3.9: *M. Varro in libro de comoediis Plautinis primo.*

32. Kaster 1988, 270–72, Zetzel 2018, 294–5; the text is in Keil 1857, 297–529.

33. *Grammatici Latini* 1.299, 473, 482-92 Keil. The chapter *De poematibus* was edited by Friedrich Leo for inclusion in the first volume of Kaibel's edition of Greek comic fragments (Kaibel 1899, 53–61): I shall cite it by Leo's section numbers followed by the relevant page number in Keil's compendium.

characters' voices; and third, a mixture of the two, in which the poet both speaks in his own voice and brings on characters speaking in theirs.[34]

So far, so good: that scheme could be applied to Livy's narrative (section 3.1 above), with Livius Andronicus' innovation of 'plays with plots' belonging in the first category and the *saturae* that preceded them in the second. But Livy's narrative was all about Rome and Etruria, whereas Diomedes treated Roman drama as a form of Greek:

> Dramatic or mimetic poetry [the first category] consists of four types: among the Greeks, tragic, comic, satyric, mimic; among the Romans, 'purple-bordered', 'tavern-style', 'Atellan', 'flat-foot'.[35]

Such sub-divisions were of no interest to Livy.[36] For Diomedes, on the other hand, they were fundamental, and later in his chapter he discussed them in detail, citing Lucilius, Varro, Horace, Virgil and Suetonius.[37]

His main source was probably Varro. Suetonius wrote two volumes 'on Roman shows and competitions', no doubt updating Varro's classic works to take account of the new theatrical conditions of the principate,[38] but Varro's own works were still available in Diomedes' time, and it is Varro himself, with his constant urge to divide subjects of knowledge into *genera* and *species*,[39] who is likely to be the source for Diomedes' categories of drama.

Diomedes took for granted a basic distinction between tragedy and comedy.[40] Tragedy, in Greek or Latin, was *sui generis*, uniquely distinc-

34. Diomedes *De poematibus* 1.2-3 = *Grammatici Latini* 1.482 Keil; for the tradition see Janko 1984, 128–33, Nünlist 2009, 94–102.

35. Diomedes *De poematibus* 1.4 = *Grammatici Latini* 1.482 Keil: *poematos dramatici uel actiui genera sunt quattuor: apud Gaecos tragica comica satyrica mimica, apud Romanos praetextata tabernaria Atellana planipes*. (Note that these are not 'the four kinds of Roman drama' attributed to 'Roman literary history' at Fulkerson and Tatum 2024, 45, an unfortunately over-simplified account.)

36. He mentions 'Atellan' plays only as a later development (Livy 7.2.10-12, n. 12 above).

37. *De poematibus* 8–14 (= *Grammatici Latini* 1.487-90 Keil), esp. 8.2 (Varro fr. 304 Funaioli, Horace *Ars poetica* 220-21, Virgil *Georgics* 2.380-1, Horace *Ars poetica* 275-7, Lucilius book 12), 9.2 (Varro fr. 305 Funaioli), 10.2 (Varro fr. 306 Funaioli, Horace *Ars poetica* 288), 11.1-2 (Horace *Ars poetica* 179, 192), 12 (Horace *Ars poetica* 220-24), 14.5 (Suetonius in Roth 1858, 280).

38. *Suda* T 895 = 4.581 Adler: περὶ τῶν παρὰ Ῥωμαίοις θεωριῶν καὶ ἀγώνων βιβλία β′. See section 11.1 below.

39. E.g. Varro *De lingua Latina* 5.10-13, *De re rustica* 1.9.1-6, 2.1.11-12, *De philosophia* ap. Augustine *City of God* 19.1; see Rawson 1991, 327–9.

40. Tragedy: *De poematibus* 8 = *Grammatici Latini* 1.487-8 Keil. Comedy: *De poematibus* 9-10 = *Grammatici Latini* 1.88-90 Keil.

tive with its restricted range of mythological plots and the high platform-soled boots (*cothurni*) that its masked actors always wore. Everything else consisted of a huge range of different performance styles and different types of plot. How could it be categorised?

Diomedes, naming Varro among his sources, began his discussion of Roman comedy by distinguishing 'plays in the toga' (*fabulae togatae*) from 'plays in the Greek cloak' (*fabulae palliatae*):

> Comedies were originally called *togatae* because everything in public value was perceived to be in confusion;[41] these *togatae* were later divided into 'purple-bordered' [*praetextatae*] and 'tavern-style' [*tabernariae*]. The plays called *togatae* are those written according to the customs and conventions of people in togas, i.e. the Romans (for the toga is a Roman garment), just as Greek plays, according to Varro, were called *palliatae* from the [Greek] style of dress. Although *togatae* is a general name, its particular use instead of 'tavern-style' is due not only to the common error that calls Afranius' plays *togatae*,[42] but even to the poets, such as Horace,[43] who says 'whether they produced *praetextae* or *togatae*'.[44]

Diomedes' idea of a 'common error' may simply be his failure to realise that the phrase *fabula togata* was ambiguous in the late republic. We know that Varro regarded *praetexta* as a sub-division of *togata*,[45] whereas Horace's casual reference clearly implies that for him *praetexta* and *togata* were mutually exclusive.

41. This baffling sentence no doubt represents something in his source that Diomedes failed to understand. For a possible explanation of the origin of *togatae* see section 3.6 below.

42. In fact the comedies of Afranius (late second century BC) were always so described: Horace *Epistles* 2.1.1.57, Velleius Paterculus 2.9.3, Quintilian 10.1.100, Macrobius *Saturnalia* 6.1.4, Ausonius *Epigrams* 75.4.

43. Horace *Ars poetica* 288.

44. Diomedes *De poematibus* 10.1-2 = *Grammatici Latini* 1.489 Keil: *initio togatae comoediae dicebantur quod omnia in publico honore confusa cernebantur. quae togatae postea in praetextatas et tabernarias diuidebantur. togatae fabulae dicuntur quae scripta sunt secundum ritus et habitum hominum togatorum, id est Romanorum (toga namque Romana est), sicut Graecas fabulas ab habitu aeque palliatas Varro ait nominari. togatas autem, cum sit generale nomen, specialiter tamen pro tabernariis non modo communis error usurpat, qui Afrani togatas appellat, sed et poetae, ut Horatius, qui ait 'uel qui praetextas uel qui docuere togatas'.*

45. Varro *De lingua Latina* 6.18 (*togata praetexta data Apollinaribus ludis*); Wiseman 2008, 194–9.

Pursuing the Varronian line, and picking up his earlier summary,[46] Diomedes continued:

> There are as many types of *togata* plays as there are of *palliata*. The first type is *togatae* that are called 'purple-bordered', in which the concerns of commanders and public affairs used to be enacted, and Roman kings or leaders are brought on stage; they are like tragedies in the dignity and high status of their characters. They are called 'purple-bordered' because in this type of play the deeds of kings and magistrates are included, who use the purple-bordered [toga].[47]
>
> The second type is *togatae* that are called 'tavern-style'; they are like comedies in the low status of their characters and the similarity of their plots. In these plays not magistrates or kings but humble persons are brought on stage, and private houses, which once used commonly to be called *tabernae* because they were roofed with planks [*tabulae*].[48]
>
> The third type is Latin plays that are called 'Atellan' from the Oscan town Atella, in which they originated; in their plots and jokes they are like Greek satyr-plays.
>
> The fourth type is 'flat-foot', which in Greek is called *mimus* [μῖμος]. It is called 'flat-foot' in Latin because the actors come on stage 'flat-footed', i.e. barefoot, not in high boots [*cothurni*] like tragic actors or soft shoes [*socci*] like comic ones. Or else it's because once upon a time they used to act not on a raised stage but on the flat level of the *orchestra*, having laid aside their mimic equipment.[49] This 'flat-foot' type is mentioned by Atta, the writer of *togatae*,[50] in his 'Aedile's play': 'You're going to give money? The flat-foot jumps for joy!'

46. Diomedes *De poematibus* 1.4 = *Grammatici Latini* 1.482 Keil (n. 35): it was followed by his treatment of all the different types of poetry in turn (epic, elegy, iambus, epodes, *satyra*, bucolic, tragedy and comedy), the last of which contains the present passage. For '*satyra*' see chapter 4 below.

47. For the *toga praetexta* of Roman magistrates see for instance Cicero *Pro Cluentio* 154, *Ad familiares* 2.16.7.

48. An implausible derivation: 'the vast majority of Varronian etymologies are based on some loose outward similarity between two words, and this loose similarity is then justified by deriving one from the other, often via flimsy semantic routes' (De Melo 2019, 42).

49. Here too (cf. n. 41) the obscurity may result from Diomedes' failure to understand his source.

50. Cf. Jerome *Chronica* Ol. 175.4 (from Suetonius), reporting the death in 77–76 BC of *Titus Quintius Atta scriptor togatarum*.

However, any plays they had made from soft shoes [i.e. 'comedy'] they declaimed dressed in Greek[51] cloaks.[52]

At this point Diomedes had completed his programme of showing the Greek equivalents of the supposed four types of *fabulae togatae*. He now embarked on a similar demonstration of the differences:

The 'purple-bordered' *togata* differs from tragedy in that in tragedy heroes are brought on stage (for instance, Pacuvius wrote tragedies with heroic titles—*Orestes*, *Chryses* etc—as did Accius), whereas in 'purple-bordered' it is Roman leaders, as in the one entitled *Brutus*, or *Decius* and similarly *Marcellus*.[53]

The 'tavern-style' *togata* differs from comedy in that in comedy Greek customs and Greek characters—Laches, Sostrata etc—are brought on stage, whereas in 'tavern-style' it is Latin ones. 'Tavern-style' *togatae* were regularly brought to the stage by two men in particular, Lucius Afranius and Gaius Quintius, since Terence and Caecilius wrote comedies.[54]

Latin 'Atellan' differs from Greek satyr-plays in that in satyr-plays the characters brought on stage are generally satyrs, or else absurd

51. Presumably meaning that *comoedia* proper, symbolised by the *soccus*, had Greek scenes and Greek characters, as in Plautus and Terence; cf. Horace *Epistles* 2.1.168-76 on Plautus (who however admitted 'Atellan' elements too).

52. Diomedes *De poematibus* 10.3-6 = *Grammatici Latini* 1.489-90 Keil: *togatarum fabularum species tot fere sunt quot et palliatarum. nam prima species est togatarum quae praetextatae dicuntur, in quibus imperatorum negotia agebantur et publica et reges Romani uel duces inducuntur, personarum dignitate et sublimitate tragoediis similes. praetextatae autem dicuntur quia fere regum uel magistratuum, qui praetexta utuntur, in eius modi fabulis acta comprehenduntur. secunda species <est> togatarum quae tabernariae dicuntur et humilitate personarum et argumentorum similitudine comoediis pares, in quibus non magistratus regesue sed humiles homines et priuatae domus inducuntur, quae quidem olim quod tabulis tegerentur communiter tabernae uocabantur. tertia species est fabularum Latinarum quae a ciuitate Oscorum Atella, in qua primum coeptae, appellatae sunt Atellanae, argumentis dictisque iocularibus similes satyricis fabulis Graecis. quarta species est planipedis, qui Graece dicitur mimus. ideo autem Latine planipes dictus, quod actores pedibus planis, id est nudis, proscenium introirent, non ut tragici actores cum cothurnis neque ut comici cum soccis; siue quod olim non in suggestu scaenae sed in plano orchestrae positis instrumentis mimicis actitabant. cuius planipedis Atta togatarum scriptor ita in Aedilicia fabula meminit, 'daturin estis aurum? exultat planipes'. siquas tamen ex soccis fabulas fecerant, palliati pronuntiabant.*

53. For these plays on Roman historial themes see Manuwald 2001, 134–41 (Naevius' *Clastidium*—i.e. *Marcellus*?), 196–220 (Accius' *Decius*), 220–37 (Accius' *Brutus*).

54. See n. 51. 'Gaius Quintius' was presumably 'Titus Quintius Atta' (n. 50); it is not known which *praenomen* is correct, and the proper spelling of the *gentilicium* was 'Quinctius'.

and satyr-like—e.g. Autolycus, Busiris—whereas in 'Atellan' it is Oscan characters like Maccus.[55]

There is no comment on 'flat-foot' drama and *mimus*/μῖμος, no doubt because in that case there was no distinction to be made between Greek and Latin performances.

Although incorporated into Diomedes' 'comedy' chapter, this characteristically systematic Varronian taxonomy was concerned with all dramatic forms, including serious ones.[56] Not only that, but it treated them as a single phenomenon exemplified equally in Greek and Latin. *Tragoedia* and *comoedia* were Greek concepts and Greek inventions, but produced also in Latin by Pacuvius and Accius in one case, Terence and Caecilius in the other. So Varro's view was quite different from Livy's narrative (section 3.1 above), which took place in a totally Greek-free zone: there, the only influences were Etruscan and Oscan.[57]

3.3. Updating the record: the evidence of Suetonius

Our third authority is Suetonius Tranquillus, a scholar and imperial functionary writing in the first quarter of the second century AD. Like Varro, he wrote on a wide variety of subjects, and for him too we have an incomplete list of titles:[58]

1. 'On Greek games';
2. 'On Roman shows and competitions' (two volumes);[59]

55. Diomedes *De poematibus* 10.7-9 = *Grammatici Latini* 1.490 Keil: *togata praetextata a tragoedia differt, quod in tragoedia heroes inducuntur, ut Pacuuius tragoedias nominibus heroicis scripsit, Orestem Chrysen et his similia, item Accius, in praetextata autem <duces Romani, ut in ea> quae inscribitur Brutus uel Decius, item Marcellus. togata tabernaria a comoedia differt, quod in comoedia Graeci ritus inducuntur personaeque Graecae, Laches Sostrata, in illa uero Latinae. togatas tabernarias in scaenam datauerunt praecipue duo, L. Afranius et C. Quintius, nam Terentius et Caecilius comoedias scripserunt. Latina Atellana a Graeca satyrica differt, quod in satyrica fere satyrorum personae inducuntur aut siquae sunt ridiculae similes satyris, Autolycus Busiris, in Atellana Oscae personae, ut Maccus.*

56. On Roman *fabula praetexta* (or *praetextata*, as Diomedes preferred) see Kragelund 2016.

57. Livy 7.2.4 and 12: *ex Etruria . . . ab Oscis.*

58. *Suda* T 895 = 4.581 Adler lists items 1–10; see also Lydus *De magistratibus* 3.64 (Περὶ ἐπισήμων πορνῶν), Servius on Virgil *Eclogues* 3.8 and *Aeneid* 7.627 (*De uitiis corporalibus*), Priscian 6.8.41 (*De institutione officiorum*), Ausonius *Epistulae* 17.15 Green (*De regibus*), Iulius Romanus *ap.* Charisius 307 Barwick (*De rebus uariis*), Priscian 8.4.20 (*in VIII Pratorum*).

59. I.e. *De ludis scaenicis et circensibus*? See section 11.1 below for its likely content.

3. 'On the Roman year';
4. 'On bibliographical annotation';
5. 'On the *Republic* of Cicero, against Didymus';
6. 'On names and types of clothes, shoes etc';
7. 'On insults and bad language, and their origins';
8. 'On Rome, its customs and manners' (two volumes);
9. 'Family history of the Caesars, consisting of their lives and successions from Julius to Domitian' (seven volumes);
10. 'A garland of famous Romans' (several volumes);[60]
11. 'On famous prostitutes';[61]
12. 'On physical defects';
13. 'On the institution of offices';
14. 'On kings' (three volumes);
15. 'On various subjects', or 'Fields' (at least eight volumes).

We know him best from his lives of the Caesars (item 9), but the originality of that work may not be typical of his *oeuvre* as a whole. The title of item 5 implies close engagement with previous scholarship (polemical in this case), and for many of the subjects he covered his purpose may well have been to collect the findings of earlier scholars, criticise them where necessary, and bring their treatments up to date.

When Tertullian in about AD 200 was warning his fellow-Christians about the Roman games (cf. item 2), he referred them to 'Suetonius Tranquillus or the authors Tranquillus used';[62] when Censorinus in 238 was explaining the Roman calendar (cf. item 3), he cited 'Iunius Gracchanus, Fulvius, Varro and Suetonius';[63] when St Jerome in 392 dedicated to his friend Dexter a compilation of Christian literary lives (cf. item 10), he claimed a place in the tradition of 'Varro, Santra, Nepos, Hyginus and the

60. I.e. *De uiris illustribus*, on which see Wallace-Hadrill 1983, 50–61. Of its constituent parts *De grammaticis et rhetoribus* survives, and *De oratoribus ac poetis* was evidently lost in the mid-fifteenth century (Giovanni Pontano in Roth 1858, 288, cf. Wiseman 1985, 189–90).

61. No doubt used by Servius on Virgil *Eclogues* 10.6: *fuerunt autem uno tempore nobiles meretrices tres: Cytheris, Origo, Arbuscula.* All three were *mimae*: Cytheris, mistress of Antony, Cornelius Gallus and M. Brutus (*De uiris illustribus* 82.2), was the subject of the Virgil passage; for the other two see Horace *Satires* 1.2.55-6, 1.10.76-7, with the scholiasts on both passages.

62. Tertullian *De spectaculis* 5.8: *positum est apud Suetonium Tranquillum uel a quibus Tranquillus accepit.*

63. Censorinus *De die natali* 20.2: *magis Iunio Gracchano et Fuluio et Varroni et Suetonio aliisque credendum est.*

man you urge me to imitate, Tranquillus'.[64] It all points to Suetonius as the latest in a long succession of scholarship, providing the names of his predecessors that later readers repeated along with his own.

Jerome also exploited Suetonius' *De uiris illustribus* for his translation of Eusebius' chronicle of world history, into which he inserted 'numerous items carefully excerpted from Tranquillus and other well-known historians'.[65] The most easily identifiable are those from the *De poetis* section of Suetonius' work, occurring between Olympiads 135 (240–236 BC) and 210 (AD 61–64). The poets mentioned by Jerome are as follows:[66]

Quintus Ennius poeta: born c. 240–36 BC, died c. 168–4 BC;
Naeuius comicus: born 201/200 BC;
Plautus ex Vmbria Sarsinas: died 200/199 BC;
Titus [*sic*] *Liuius tragoediarum scriptor*: active c. 188–6 BC;[67]
Statius Caecilius comoediarum scriptor: active c. 179–6 BC;
Publius Terentius Carthaginiensis comoediarum scriptor: died 158/7 BC;
Pacuuius Brundisinus tragoediarum scriptor: active c. 154–2 BC;
Lucilius poeta, satyrarum scriptor; born 148/7 BC, died 103/2 BC aged 46;
L. Accius tragoediarum scriptor; born 170 BC,[68] active 139/8 BC;
M. Terentius Varro philosophus et poeta: born 116/15 BC;
Turpilius comicus: died 104/3 BC.
M. Furius cognomento Bibaculus: born 103/2 BC;
Titus Lucretius poeta: born c. 94–2 BC, died by suicide aged 44;
L. Pomponius Bononiensis Atellanarum scriptor: active 89/8 BC;
Gaius Valerius Catullus scriptor lyricus: born 87/6 BC, died 58–7 BC aged 30;[69]

64. Jerome *De uiris illustribus* pref.: *fecerunt quidem hoc . . . apud Latinos autem Varro, Santra, Nepos, Hyginus, et ad cuius nos exemplum prouocas, Tranquillus.*

65. Jerome *Chronica* pref. 4: *nunc addita nunc admixta sunt plurima quae de Tranquillo et ceteris inlustribus historicis curiosissime excerpsi.*

66. The text is most easily accessed in Brugnoli 1995, 25–55; Olympiad years ran from summer to summer, hence the double BC and AD dates (e.g. 201/200 BC, AD 63/4).

67. The poet's *praenomen* was Lucius (Aulus Gellius 6.7.11, 17.21.42); the evident confusion with Titus Livius the historian is more likely Jerome's fault than Suetonius'. The dates are also wrong, but that error went right back to Accius in the second century BC (Cicero *Brutus* 72-3); was Suetonius deceived by it, or did he mention it as an alternative tradition which Jerome carelessly took as true?

68. Jerome specifies *Mancino et Serrano consulibus.*

69. Since all the dateable poems of Catullus belong to 56–54 BC (Wiseman 2023, 4–5), the death-date Jerome gives must be wrong, and if Catullus' age at death is reliably reported, the birth-date must be wrong too. The two entries are mutually consistent, so it must have been Suetonius' error, not Jerome's.

Titus Quinctius Atta scriptor togatarum: died 77/6 BC;
Vergilius Maro: born 70 BC, died 19 BC;[70]
Horatius Flaccus satyricus et lyricus poeta: born 65/4 BC, died 9/8 BC;
Laberius mimorum scriptor: died 43 BC;[71]
Publilius mimografus: active 43/2 BC;
Ouidius Naso: born 43/2 BC, died AD 17/18;
Cornificius poeta: died 41/40 BC;
M. Bauius poeta: died 35/4 BC;
Cornelius Gallus Foroiuliensis poeta: died by suicide 27/6 BC;
Aemilius Macer Veronensis poeta: died 16/15 BC;
Persius Flaccus satyricus poeta: born AD 34/5, died AD 62/3;
M. Annaeus Lucanus Cordubensis poeta: died AD 63/4.

Varro too had written a *De poetis*, providing precise dates.[72] But since he probably didn't include authors alive in his own time,[73] the great succession of classic Roman poets from Lucretius onwards still remained to be documented.[74]

Of the twenty-seven poets named by Jerome, eleven are identified as working in a particular stage genre:[75]

comoedia	*tragoedia*	*Atellana*	*togata*	*mimus*
Naevius	Livius	Pomponius	Quinctius Atta	Laberius
Caecilius	Pacuvius			Publilius
Terentius	Accius			
Turpilius				

Suetonius refers to just the same categories in his surviving biographies.[76] That combined evidence is enough to show that he did not reproduce

70. Jerome specifies *Pompeio et Crasso consulibus* and *Sentio Saturnino et Lucretio conss.*

71. Jerome specifies *decimo mense post C. Caesaris interitum.*

72. Aulus Gellius 17.21.42-5 (Varro *De poetis* frr. 55-6 Funaioli) on L. Livius' first production in 240 BC, the birth of Ennius the following year, and Naevius' first production in 235.

73. For the convention of not naming contemporaries, cf. Quintilian 10.1.94 (satirists), 96 (lyric poets), 104 (historians), 122 (orators).

74. It is not clear how much help Suetonius got from Santra, Nepos and Hyginus (n. 64).

75. Plautus as a comic poet was perhaps too obvious to be specified; Jerome also ignores Ennius and Naevius as writers of tragedies.

76. *Comoedia*: Suetonius *Diuus Augustus* 89.1, *Gaius* 3.2, *Diuus Claudius* 11.2. *Tragoedia*: *Gaius* 54.1, *Diuus Vespasianus* 19.1. *Atellana*: *Tiberius* 45, *Gaius* 27.4, *Nero* 39.3, *Galba* 13.1. *Togata*: *Diuus Augustus* 45.4, *Nero* 11.2, *De grammaticis* 21.4. *Mimus*: *Diuus Iulius* 39.2, *Diuus Augustus* 53.1, *Gaius* 57.4, *De grammaticis* 18.2.

Varro's schematic paradigm, in which *togata* was the general category of all drama in Roman dress, whether comic or serious, but followed the view Diomedes regarded as a 'common error', that *togata* was a particular type of comedy, described by Varro as 'tavern-style'.[77]

If we are right to think of Suetonius as the later Roman empire's main source of scholarship, summarising and updating the previous tradition,[78] his own ideas of the nature of Roman drama may perhaps be detectable in what subsequent grammarians said about it. Since Terence was a favourite school-text,[79] teachers needed to explain the history of comedy to their pupils, and extracts on the subject from two fourth-century commentators happen to survive.[80]

Aelius Donatus provides just a brief summary. Having divided drama (*fabula*) into the two categories of tragedy and comedy, he goes on:

> Tragedy is called 'purple-bordered' (*praetexta*) if it has a Latin plot. Comedy has many categories: it is either 'in Greek dress' or 'in Roman dress' or 'tavern-style' or 'Atellan' or 'mime' or 'Rhinthonic' or 'flat-foot'.[81]

Fortunately Evanthius gives a bit more detail:

> It is important to remember that after the Greek 'New Comedy' the Latins introduced many types of plays: for instance 'in Roman dress', [so called] from their Latin performers and plots; 'purple-bordered', from the dignity of their tragic characters from Latin history; 'Atellan', from the Campanian town where they were first produced; 'Rhinthonic', from the name of their originator; 'tavern-style', from their low-class plots and manner; 'mime', from their long-standing imitation of vulgar plots and trivial characters.[82]

77. Diomedes *De poematibus* 10.2 = *Grammatici Latini* 1.489 Keil (n. 44 above): *togatas autem, cum sit generale nomen, specialiter tamen pro tabernariis . . . communis error usurpat.*

78. See above, nn. 62–4.

79. See for instance Ausonius *Protrepticus* 56-65 (along with Horace, Virgil and Sallust).

80. Edited by Friedrich Leo in Kaibel 1899, 62–71. For Aelius Donatus and Evanthius see Kaster 1988, 275–8 and 278–9, Zetzel 2018, 254 and 255–6.

81. *De comoedia* 6.1 (Kaibel 1899, 68): *<tragoedia,> si Latina argumentatio sit, praetexta dicitur. comoedia autem multas species habet: aut enim palliata est aut togata aut tabernaria aut Atellana aut mimus aut Rhinthonica aut planipedaria.* Compare Diomedes at nn. 35, 44, 52 above.

82. Evanthius *De fabula* 4.1 (Kaibel 1899, 66): *illud uero tenendum est, post* νέαν κωμῳδίαν *Latinos multa fabularum genera protulisse, ut togatas ab scaenicis atque argumentis Latinis, praetextatas a dignitate personarum tragicarum ex Latina historia,*

Evanthius' list of *fabulae* includes 'purple-bordered' (*praetextata* = Donatus' *praetexta*) without distinguishing it from the comic genres, and contains the usual confusion about *togatae* and *tabernariae*.[83] What is most striking, however, is the appearance in both authors of a category called *Rhinthonicae* (section 1.6 above).

Such plays were not mentioned by Diomedes, and so probably not by Varro either. However, as we noted in the previous chapter, the third-century Tarantine dramatist Rhinthon was in Cicero's head along with Homer and the great Athenian tragedians, and that surprising fact is best explained by an ongoing performance tradition of Rhinthon's plays at Rome.[84] It's understandable that it didn't feature in Varro's account: a type of Latin play named after a Greek playwright would be hard to fit into his symmetrical scheme of Greek and Latin correspondences (section 3.2 above). But how could Donatus and Evanthius know such a recondite fact from four centuries earlier if it wasn't in Varro?

Two centuries before their time, Suetonius had been in charge of the imperial libraries.[85] That gave him an unparalleled opportunity to seek out obscure texts from the late republic and the Augustan age, periods in which he clearly had a keen interest.[86] And it was not restricted to the texts themselves: he also wanted to understand the circumstances of their performance at the *ludi scaenici*.[87] Three examples from his extant biographies may give an idea of how his mind worked.

First, the literary scholar L. Crassicius Pansa (*né* Pasicles), who was best known for his commentary on Cinna's erudite poem *Zmyrna*; Suetonius also found out that he had been 'involved with the stage, helping the writers of mimes'.[88] Next, the learned Gaius Melissus, a freed slave appointed by Augustus to set up libraries in the Portico of Octavia; what Suetonius noted was his invention of a new type of *fabula togata*, played not in the toga but in the *trabea*, as worn by Romulus and the ancient

---

Atellanas a ciuitate Campaniae ubi actitatae sunt primae, Rhinthonicas ab auctoris nomine, tabernarias ab humilitate argumenti ac stili, mimos ab diuturna imitatione uilium rerum ac leuium personarum.

83. Both authors list them as separate categories, but Donatus a few lines later refers to *togatae . . . quas nonnulli tabernarias uocant* (Donatus *De comoedia* 6.5, Kaibel 1899, 6).

84. Cicero *Ad Atticum* 1.20.3; see section 2.6 above.

85. *Année Épigraphique* 1953, 73: [*a*] *studiis, a byblio*[*thecis, ab e*]*pistulis.*

86. As was demonstrated by Wallace-Hadrill 1983, 52–9.

87. As discussed in chapter 11 below.

88. Suetonius *De grammaticis* 18.2 (*circa scaenam uersatus est dum mimographos adiuuat*); Wiseman 1994a, 90–97.

Roman kings.[89] Finally, Germanicus Caesar, whose mini-biography (incorporated into that of his son Gaius 'Caligula') found space for the fact that his literary studies included the writing of comedies in Greek; Suetonius made a point of mentioning the later production of one of them by Germanicus' brother Claudius at a dramatic festival in Naples.[90]

Such particular curiosity about what was involved in writing for the stage makes it, I think, more likely than not that Suetonius could have found evidence for the production of 'Rhinthonic plays' in republican Rome, and that Donatus and Evanthius then used his work for the summaries of types of Roman drama that they compiled for their pupils.

3.4. Byzantine scholarship: the evidence of John Lydus

The fourth ancient author who tries to tell us what Roman drama consisted of is John Lydus ('the Lydian'), Iohannes Laurentius (or son of Laurentius), born in AD 490 at the town of Philadelphia in Lydia.[91] In 511 he entered the imperial civil service, just as Suetonius had done four centuries before; but the capital Suetonius knew had now been ruled by the Goths for a generation. Lydus lived and worked in Constantinople, and was already in his forties when Justinian embarked on the great campaign to reconquer the western empire, a project still in progress at the time of Lydus' death about 560.

The three works of Lydus that survive (none of them complete) were probably written after he retired from the praetorian prefect's office in 551. They are the four books 'On the months' (Περὶ μηνῶν, *De mensibus*), which also deal with the days of the week and the festival dates of the Roman year; the one-volume 'On sky-signs' (Περὶ διοσημειῶν, *De ostentis*), which also includes earthquakes as portentous events; and the three-volume work variously entitled 'On political offices', 'On powers' or 'On the magistracies of the Roman state' (περὶ πολιτικῶν ἀρχῶν, περὶ ἐξουσιῶν or περὶ ἀρχῆς τῆς Ῥωμαίων πολιτείας, *De magistratibus*), which develops into an account of Lydus' *bête noire* 'John the Cappadocian', who was appointed praetorian

89. Suetonius *De grammaticis* 21.4 (*fecit et nouum genus togatarum inscripsitque trabeatas*); cf. Ovid *Fasti* 1.37, 2.503 (Romulus), Livy 1.41.6 (Servius Tullius). Suetonius' works included *On Names and Types of Clothing* (*Suda* T 895 = 4.581 Adler) and *On Kings* (Ausonius *Epistulae* 17.15 Green).

90. Suetonius *Gaius* 3.2 (*inter cetera studiorum monimenta reliquit et comoedias Graecas*), *Diuus Claudius* 11.2 (*comoediam quoque Graecam Neapolitano certamine docuit ac de sententia iudicum coronauit*); cf. Tacitus *Annals* 15.33.2 for Naples as a *Graeca urbs*.

91. Kaster 1988, 306–9; his full name is attested only in the genitive, Ἰωάννου Λαυρεντίου Φιλαδελφέως τοῦ Λυδοῦ (Photius *Bibliotheca* 180).

prefect in 531. Surprisingly, it is the *De magistratibus* that contains a catalogue of types of Roman drama.

Much of the first book of *De magistratibus* consists of a numbered sequence of 'introductions' (προαγωγαί) of the various offices, presented in the supposed order of their institution:[92]

1. *Magister equitum*	1.14-15
2. *Patricii*	1.16-23
3. *Quaestores*	1.24-9
-. *Consules*	1.30-33
4. *Decemuiri* and *praefectus urbi*	1.34-5
5. *Dictator*	1.36-8
6. *Censores*	1.39-43
7. *Tribuni plebis*	1.44-8
8. *Praetores*	1.48-9
9. *Praefectus uigilum*	1.50

In the summary 'contents list' at the beginning of the text, the item on the censorship is announced as containing a digression:

> Sixth introduction, the so-called *censura*, containing also material on comedy and tragedy, and when they became known to the Romans.[93]

In the main text the digression is marked only at the end,[94] not at the beginning, so the reason for it can only be guessed.

Lydus begins this item by explaining that early Rome had a citizen army in which everyone had to provide his own equipment and food. Hence the need for *censores* to register each citizen's property and assess his contribution in time of war: 'for this reason the Greeks translated *censores* as "valuers"'.[95] He then goes on with a complete *non sequitur*:

> At that time the Roman comic poet Titinius produced a play in Rome. Drama is divided into two [types]: tragedy and comedy.
>
> Tragedy is itself divided into two [types]: *crepidata* and *praetextata*, of which *crepidata* has Greek plots, *praetextata* Roman ones.[96]

92. Lydus *De magistratibus* pref., 1.14-50; by an apparent oversight, the introduction of the consulship is not numbered. Item 7 on the tribunate is mainly devoted to a long list of military titles.

93. Lydus *De magistratibus* pref.: ἕκτη προαγωγὴ ἡ καλουμένη κηνσοῦρα· ἐν ᾧ καὶ περὶ κωμῳδίας καὶ τραγῳδίας, καὶ πότε Ῥωμαίοις ἐγνώσθησαν.

94. Lydus *De magistratibus* 1.42: καὶ ταῦτα μὲν περὶ τῆς ἀρχαίας κωμῳδίας τε καὶ τραγῳδίας.

95. Lydus *De magistratibus* 1.39: ὅθεν τοὺς κήνσωρας Ἕλληνες τιμητὰς καθ' ἑρμηνείαν ἐκάλεσαν.

96. *Crepidata* should mean 'wearing the Greek shoes or boots called κρηπῖδες (*crepidae*)', but there seems to be no parallel in either Greek or Latin for that type of footwear

> Comedy is divided into seven [types]: *palliata*, *togata*, *Atellana*, *tabernaria*, *Rhinthonica*, *planipedaria* and *mimica*. *Palliata* is comedy that has a Greek plot, *togata* an ancient Roman one; *Atellana* is [comedy] of the so-called *exodiarii*;[97] *tabernaria* is the 'stage' or 'theatre' comedy,[98] *Rhinthonica* the 'exotic',[99] *planipedaria* the 'finale'.[100] *Mimica* is of course the only one surviving nowadays; having nothing artistic about it, it attracts the crowd solely by meaningless laughter.[101]

This unexplained digression uses the same categories listed by Aelius Donatus and Evanthius,[102] including *Rhinthonica*. If our earlier inference was correct, that should mean that Lydus too was using Suetonius.

We know that Lydus had access, directly or indirectly, to more than one of Suetonius' works,[103] and the Suetonian treatise 'on the institution of public offices' would be an obvious resource when seeking material for his own *De magistratibus*. Not only that, but in this passage on the types of Roman drama Lydus' unique explanation of *Atellana* as 'comedy of the *exodiarii*' is precisely consistent with Suetonius' own usage.[104]

---

rather than κοθόρνοι (*cothurni*) being specific to tragedy.

97. For *exodius* (ἐξόδιος) as the closing performance after a tragedy see Plutarch *Alexander* 75.3, *Pelopidas* 34.1, *Crassus* 33.4; at Rome it was usually an *Atellana* or a mime (Cicero *Ad familiares* 9.16.7).

98. Perhaps because the stage was made of planks (*tabulae*), from which *taberna* was supposedly derived (Festus 490L, n. 48 above).

99. It is not clear why Rhinthon should be any more 'exotic' than the Greek 'New Comedy' playwrights on whose work the *palliatae* comedies of Plautus, Terence and Caecilius were based.

100. If the hybrid term καταστολαρία derives from καταστολή in the sense of 'finale of a play' (schol. Aristophanes *Peace* 1203), this definition duplicates that of *Atellana* (n. 97).

101. Lydus *De magistratibus* 1.40: τότε Τιτίνιος ὁ Ῥωμαῖος κωμικὸς μῦθον ἐπεδείξατο ἐν τῇ Ῥώμῃ. ὁ δὲ μῦθος τέμνεται εἰς δύο, <εἰς τραγῳδίαν καὶ κωμῳδίαν· ὧν ἡ τραγῳδία καὶ αὐτὴ τέμνεται εἰς δύο>, εἰς κρηπιδᾶταν καὶ πραιτεξτᾶταν· ὧν ἡ μὲν κρηπιδᾶτα Ἑλληνικὰς ἔχει ὑποθέσεις, ἡ δὲ πραιτεξτᾶτα Ῥωμαϊκάς. ἡ μέντοι κωμῳδία τέμνεται εἰς ἑπτά· εἰς παλλιᾶταν, τογᾶταν, Ἀτελλάνην, ταβερναρίαν, Ῥινθωνικήν, πλανιπεδαρίαν καὶ μιμικήν· καὶ παλλιᾶτα μέν ἐστιν ἡ Ἑλληνικὴν ὑπόθεσιν ἔχουσα κωμῳδία, τογᾶτα δὲ ἡ Ῥωμαϊκήν ἀρχαίαν· Ἀτελλάνη δέ ἐστιν ἡ τῶν λεγομένων ἐξωδιαρίων· ταβερναρία δὲ ἡ σκηνωτὴ ἢ θεατρικὴ κωμῳδία· Ῥινθωνικὴ ἡ ἐξωτική· πλανιπεδαρία ἡ καταστολαρία· μιμικὴ ἡ νῦν δῆθεν μόνη σῳζομένη, τεχνικὸν μὲν ἔχουσα οὐδέν, ἀλόγῳ μόνον τὸ πλῆθος ἐπάγουσα γέλωτι.

102. See nn. 81–2. The explanations differ from those offered by Evanthius; perhaps the two authors made different choices from multiple options in their common source.

103. Quotes from 'Tranquillus': Lydus *De magistratibus* 1.12 (Suetonius *Diuus Augustus* 40.5), 1.34 (from *De institutione officiorum*?), 2.6 (from the lost preface to the *Caesares*), 3.64 (from Περὶ ἐπισήμων πορνῶν).

104. Suetonius *Tiberius* 45 (*in Atellanico exhodio*); cf. Livy 7.2.11, Juvenal 6.71-2.

The conjecture seems to be confirmed by the way Lydus develops his digression:

> Because I think it's necessary to pursue the subject, I shall add this too. We know that Rhinthon, Skiras, Blaisos and the other Pythagoreans were educators of no minor teachings in Magna Graecia, and especially Rhinthon, who was the first to write comedy in hexameters. Taking his start from him, the Roman Lucilius was the first to produce comedy in heroic verse. After him and his successors, whom the Romans call *satyrikoi*,[105] the later authors imitated the style of Cratinus and Eupolis, and using the metres of Rhinthon and the mockeries of those just mentioned, strengthened satyric comedy. Horace did not go beyond the art, but Persius, wanting to imitate the poet Sophron, exceeded the obscurity of Lycophron. Turnus,[106] Juvenal and Petronius, going right to the limit with their abusive language, damaged the satyric rule.[107]

This passage was flagged as a problem in the opening chapter (section 1.6 above), and its factual content is a complex of problems that will engage us in the next chapter as well (section 4.4 below); what matters for the present argument is that the naming of Roman satirists up to and including the time of Suetonius makes it more likely than not that Suetonius was Lydus' source.[108]

So too does the phraseology. Suetonius was in the habit of referring to literary genres as if they were objects to be found and used, as for instance at the start of the surviving Greek epitome of his treatise 'On insults and bad language, and their origins':

105. It is not known how Lydus would have spelt the word in Latin, nor how (or whether) he distinguished 'Roman satire' from 'satyric' drama; see section 4.4 below.

106. For Turnus, a satirical poet of the late first and early second century AD, see Martial 7.97.7, 11.10, Rutilius Namatianus 1.603-4, Sidonius Apollinaris 9.266; Courtney 1993, 362–3 (the two surviving fragments).

107. Lydus *De magistratibus* 1.41: ὅτι δὲ ἀναγκαῖον οἶμαι ἐμβραδῦναι τῷ λόγῳ, προσθήσω καὶ τοῦτο. Ῥίνθωνα καὶ Σκίραν καὶ Βλαῖσον καὶ τοὺς ἄλλους τῶν τῶν Πυθαγορείων ἴσμεν οὐ μικρῶν διδαγμάτων ἐπὶ τῆς μεγάλης Ἑλλάδος γενέσθαι καθηγητάς, καὶ διαφερόντως τὸν Ῥίνθωνα, ὃς ἑξαμέτροις ἔγραψε πρῶτος κωμῳδίαν· ἐξ οὗ πρῶτος λάβων τὰς ἀφορμὰς Λουκίλιος ὁ Ῥωμαῖος ἡρωικοῖς ἔπεσιν ἐκωμῴδησεν. μεθ' ὃν καὶ τοὺς μετ' αὐτόν, οὓς καλοῦσι Ῥωμαῖοι σατυρικούς, οἱ νεώτεροι τὸν Κρατίνου καὶ Εὐπόλιδος χαρακτῆρα ζηλώσαντες τοῖς μὲν Ῥίνθωνος μέτροις, τοῖς δὲ τῶν μνημονευθέντων διασυρμοῖς χρησάμενοι, τὴν σατυρικὴν ἐκράτυναν κωμῳδίαν. Ὁράτιος μὲν οὐκ ἔξω τῆς τέχνης χωρῶν, Πέρσιος δὲ τὸν ποιητὴν Σώφρονα μιμήσασθαι θέλων τὸ Λυκόφρονος παρῆλθεν ἀμαυρόν. Τοῦρνος δὲ καῖ Ἰουβενάλιος καῖ Πετρώνιος, αὐτόθεν ταῖς λοιδορίαις ἐπεξελθόντες, τὸν σατυρικὸν νόμον παρέτρωσαν.

108. Presumably a late work written after Juvenal's death, which post-dates AD 127 (Juvenal 15.27) but probably not by much, since the following (and final) poem is incomplete. How long Suetonius lived is not known.

> The literary style [τρόπος] of insults was originally discovered by Homer and the poets close to him in time, and later augmented by writers of comedy and orators.[109]

Similarly in his *De grammaticis*, he identified the first person to 'bring the study of grammar into the city', and went on to name those who 'put it in order and augmented it in every aspect'.[110] So when Lydus tells us that Lucilius' successors 'strengthened' (ἐκράτυναν) the comic genre in which they wrote, and that Horace did not go beyond its proper art (τέχνη) but Turnus, Juvenal and Petronius 'damaged its rule' (τὸν νόμον παρέτρωσαν), the similar usage suggests that his source text was written by Suetonius.

Much still remains unexplained, however. For a systematic treatise on public magistracies Lydus may well have used Suetonius' 'On the institution of offices' (*De institutione officiorum*), and for information on the types of Roman drama he may well have turned to Suetonius' 'On Roman shows and competitions' (*De ludis scaenicis et circensibus*?);[111] the problem is the lack of a connection between the two. What caused him to insert this digression on drama into his account of the Roman censorship? Before trying to find an answer, we need to understand how Lydus used the texts that were available to him.

3.5. Lydus and his sources

The preface to Lydus' *De magistratibus* begins with the assertion that the first public authorities in Rome were priests. 'When Tyrrhenos migrated from Lydia to the west he taught the Lydians' mystic rites to the people who were then called Etruscans',[112] and from them the knowledge came to the Romans 'because king Numa took the insignia of the magistrates from the Etruscans and introduced them to the state'.[113] Lydus named his

109. Taillardat 1967, 48: τὸν τῶν βλασφημιῶν τρόπον κατέδειξε μὲν ἀρχῆθεν Ὅμηρος καὶ οἱ συνεγγὺς τῷ χρόνῳ ποιηταί, ἐπηὔξησαν δὲ ὕστερον κωμικοί τε καὶ ῥήτορες.

110. Suetonius *De grammaticis* 2.1 (*studium grammaticae in urbem intulit Crates Mallotes*), 3.1 (*instruxerunt auxeruntque ab omni parte grammaticam L. Aelius Lanuuinus generque Aeli Ser. Clodius*); pointed out as a Suetonian mannerism by Power 2014, 9–10.

111. See nn. 58–9.

112. Lydus *De magistratibus* pref.: Τυρρηνοῦ ἐπὶ τὴν ἑσπέραν ἐκ τῆς Λυδίας μεταναστάντος τοὺς τότε καλουμένους Ἐτρούσκους (ἔθνος δὲ ἦν Σικανόν) τὰς Λυδῶν τελετὰς διδάξαντος. For Tyrrhenos' migration see Herodotus 1.94, Strabo 5.2.2 C219.

113. Ibid.: τὰ γὰρ ἐπίσημα τῶν ἀρχόντων ἀπὸ Θούσκων λαβὼν ὁ βασιλεὺς Νουμᾶς τῇ πολιτείᾳ εἰσήγαγεν.

sources as 'Capito and Fonteius, and from them also the most informative Varro, all of them Romans'.[114]

Lydus took a particular interest in this ancient Etruscan lore that had come from his native land. He treated it at length in *De ostentis*, where more detail is provided about his sources:

> Since for us (I mean those from Italy) the originator of the subject is Tages, it is consistent to use his own words—or rather the sense of them, since they are composed in rather archaic vocabulary and are hard to follow and not very clear.[115]

Tages was a supernatural being who miraculously appeared from a ploughed furrow and revealed to the Etruscans the science of haruspicy (prophecy from the entrails of sacrificial beasts); before he vanished again his words were recorded verbatim in a question-and-answer interview by Tarchon, pupil and companion of the Tyrrhenos who led the Lydian emigration.[116] Lydus evidently thought Tarchon's text survived:

> We shall make use also of the other [sources], Tarchon the *haruspex* and Tarquitius the hierophant [?] and Capito the priest, to interweave a precise structure of the matter from what all these men have said.[117]

Tarquitius was an expert on Etruscan divination writing in the late republic;[118] Capito is named again a few lines later along with Fonteius, who wrote on Etruscan matters.[119] Perhaps these authorities claimed that their material went back to Tarchon's transcription of Tages.

Capito and Fonteius appear together also in the *De magistratibus* preface, as the authors from whom 'the most informative Varro' took his

114. Ibid.: καὶ μάρτυρες μὲν τούτων ὅ τε Καπίτων καὶ Φοντήιος, ἐξ ὧν καὶ ὁ διδασκαλικώτατος Οὐάρρων, Ῥωμαῖοι πάντες.

115. Lydus *De ostentis* 2: ἐπειδὴ δὲ ἡμῖν, τοὺς ἐξ Ἰταλίας φημί, Τάγης ἀρχηγὸς τοῦ πράγματος γέγονεν, ἀκόλουθον τοῖς αὐτοῦ ῥήμασι χρήσασθα[ι, μ]ᾶλλον δὲ τῇ τούτων ἐννοίᾳ· τοῖς γὰρ ἀρχαιοτέροις ὀνόμασιν ἐκεῖνα συγκείμενα δυσπαρακολούθητα πώς ἐστιωκαὶ οὐ σφόδρα σαφῆ.

116. Cicero *De diuinatione* 2.50-51, Lydus *De ostentis* 3. For Tarchon see Strabo 5.2.2 C219 (Tyrrhenos' companion), Cato *FRHist* 5 F70 (Tyrrhenos' son).

117. Lydus *De ostentis* 2: [χρησόμεθα δὲ καὶ τοῖς] λοιποῖς, Ταρχοντί τε τῷ θυοσκόπῳ καὶ Ταρκυτίῳ τῷ [τελεστῇ καὶ Κα]πίτωνι ἱερεῖ, ὥστε ἐκ τῶν πᾶσι τούτοις εἰρημέ[νων γλαφυράν] τινα διαπλέξαι τοῦ πράγματος ἁρμονίαν.

118. Macrobius *Saturnalia* 3.7.2, *CIL* 11.3370 = *ILS* 2924 (with Heurgon 1953); cf. Festus 340L, [Virgil] *Catalepton* 5.3, and the lists of *auctores* for Pliny *Natural History* 1 and 11.

119. Lydus *De ostentis* 3: ἔκ τε τῶν Θούσκων ἔκ τε τῶν ἄλλων ὅσοι τούτους ἡρμήνευσαν, Καπίτωνός τέ φημι καὶ Φοντηίου. Fonteius' Etruscan thunder-lore is referred to at *De ostentis* 39 (title), though what follows clearly comes from an east-Greek source.

information.[120] What Lydus did not realise was that they were the same person, the priest (probably *pontifex*) C. Fonteius Capito, a friend of Mark Antony who became one of the suffect consuls of 33 BC.[121] Presumably Lydus' mistake arose from his source-text citing Capito variously by *cognomen* or *gentilicium* (but not both).[122]

Reading between the lines, we can begin to see what John Lydus' scholarship involved. He was clearly proud of his command of Latin, and twice refers to an oracle supposedly given to Romulus, that when the Romans ceased to use their language, fortune would desert them.[123] The imperial libraries, to which as a civil servant he had easy access, must have had a good stock of Latin texts, including no doubt the wide-ranging and educationally useful works of Varro and Suetonius; on the other hand, there is no reason to think that Constantine's Christian capital would take care to preserve or copy specialist texts on the intricacies of pagan ritual. Most of the works Lydus cites by name were probably known to him only at second or third hand: when he named 'Capito and Fonteius, and from them the most informative Varro' as his sources for the priesthoods of regal Rome, he must have meant 'Varro, who himself cited Capito and Fonteius'.[124]

Lydus was trying to reach back into the thought-world of pre-Christian Rome, an aim not everyone approved of. Proceeding with the preface to *De magistratibus*, he felt he had to justify himself:

> It remains to give an account of the public authorities, and [to show] that they evolved from a priestly arrangement to the public form. Let no-one consider me alien to what has been handed down from the distant past—unless perhaps [the critic] happens to be out of tune with rational sense and from mere hostility subverts approval [of the past]. I am aware that the legal authors report that a certain Gracchianus wrote on this subject long ago,[125] but those writings are perhaps not

120. See n. 114.

121. *IG* 12.4.1.266 = Crawford 1996, 499 line 3: [Γάιος] Φωντήιος Γαίου υἱὸς Καπίτων ἱερεύς. See *PIR*² F 465, with Weinstock 1950 (properly cautious but surely correct).

122. As happened with the scholar Aurelius Opillus (Suetonius *De grammaticis* 6, Funaioli 1907, 86–95), as cited by Varro *De lingua Latina* 7.50 (*Opillus*), 7.65 (*Aurelius*), 7.67 (*Opillus*), 7.70 (*Aurelius*), 7.79 (*Opillus*), 7.106 (*Aurelius*).

123. Lydus *De magistratibus* 2.12 = 3.42, from 'Fonteius the Roman'.

124. Lydus *De magistratibus* pref. (n. 114); i.e., Varro who cited Fonteius Capito.

125. I.e. Iunius Gracchanus, so called from his friendship with Gaius Gracchus (Pliny *Natural History* 33.36). He wrote *De potestatibus* and a commentary on the calendar *fasti* (fragments translated in Hooker 2007, 190–94).

> extant anywhere, Time having simultaneously brought them into being and utterly concealed them.[126]

One senses Lydus' frustration. Justinian's huge project to codify Roman law, one of the great intellectual achievements of the time, had identified the ancient authority Lydus needed for his work, but had not transmitted the texts. Somehow, he had to get back to 'Gracchianus', as he called him, and find what had been 'handed down from the distant past'.

How he did it may be seen from a case where his source-text survives. His treatment of the quaestorship, the third of the 'introductions' to the various offices in book I of *De magistratibus*, begins as follows:

> Credibility for writers is provided by the testimony of the men of old. For instance, Iunius Gracchianus in 'On powers' [writes] about the magistrate called *quaestor* by the Romans, in these very words:[127]

Before we read Lydus' supposedly verbatim quotation (from an author whose texts he has said were lost), we must first read his source. It is the chapter *De officio quaestoris* in the *Digest* of Roman law published by Justinian's commissioners in 533:

> Ulpian, in his one-volume work *De officio quaestoris*:
>
> The origin of appointing quaestors is very ancient, almost before all [other] magistrates. In fact Iunius Gracchanus reports in book VII of *De potestatibus* that even Romulus himself and Numa Pompilius had quaestors, whom they appointed not by their own decree but by the vote of the people. But just as it is doubtful whether the quaestor existed in the reigns of Romulus and Numa, so on the other hand it is certain that there were quaestors when Tullus Hostilius was king; and indeed the more usual opinion among the old [authors] is that Tullus Hostilius was the first to introduce quaestors into the state.
>
> Iunius, Trebatius and Fenestella write that at the start they were called 'quaestors' from the type of enquiry [they undertook].

126. Lydus *De magistratibus* pref.: ὥστε ὑπόλοιπον περὶ τῶν πολιτικῶν ἀφηγήσασθαι ἐξουσιῶν καὶ ὅτι ἀπὸ ἱερατικῆς τάξεως ἐπὶ τὸ πολιτικὸν μετεφύησαν σχῆμα. μὴ οὖν ἡμᾶς ἀλλοίους πρὸς τὰ πάλαι δοθέντα κρίνοι τις, πλῆν εἰ μὴ τυχὸν ἀπηχὲς λογικῆς ἀσφαλείας ὑφιστάμενος φθόνῳ τὸν ἔπαινον μεταβάλοι. ὅτι δὲ καὶ Γρακχιανός τις πάλαι περὶ τούτων ἔγραφεν, ἴσμεν τοὺς νομογράφους ἀναφέροντας· οὐδαμοῦ δὲ τὰ γραφεντα φέρεται ἴσως αὐτά, πάντως δὲ καὶ αὐτὰ τοῦ χρόνου τεκόντος ἅμα καὶ κρύψαντος.

127. Lydus *De magistratibus* 1.24: τὸ πιστὸν τοῖς γράφουσιν ἡ τῶν ἀρχαίων ἐπιτίθησι μαρτυρία. Ἰούνιος τοίνυν Γρακχιανὸς ἐν τῷ Περὶ ἐξουσιῶν αὐτοῖς ῥήμασι τοῦ καλουμένου παρὰ Ῥωμαίοις κυαίστωρος.

Some of the quaestors used to be allocated by lot to the provinces, by a decree of the Senate made in the consulship of Decimus Drusus and Porcina.[128] Certainly not all quaestors were allocated provinces, and indeed the quaestors of the *princeps* were exempted; for they are kept free for the sole task of reading the *princeps*' messages in the Senate.

From these, as we are saying, there are some who used to be called 'candidates of the *princeps*', and they read his messages in the Senate.[129]

No doubt abbreviated by the compilers of the *Digest*, Ulpian's text was written some time about AD 215, when good information about the work of the republican scholars was evidently still available.

Lydus now presented it as the testimony of Iunius Gracchanus more than three centuries earlier, 'in these very words':

'They were appointed by a vote of the people. After them Tullus the *rex* decided that the office of the *quaestores* was necessary, with the result that the majority of historians attributed that rank to him and him alone. Iunius, Trebatius and Fenestella said that they were so named from enquiry.'

And after other things [he says]:

'Except that later candidates of the emperor were picked out as *quaestores*, who were kept free solely for the reading of the emperor's messages, and the same men also read out public resolutions of the Senate on behalf of those who were being promoted in honour.'[130]

128. There was no such consulship, but Decimus Brutus was consul in 138 BC and M. Lepidus Porcina in 137; the confusion could be either Ulpian's or his excerptor's.

129. *Digest* 1.13.1: *Ulpianus libro singulari de officio quaestoris. origo quaestoribus creandis antiquissima est et paene ante omnes magistratus. Gracchanus denique Iunius libro septimo de potestatibus etiam ipsum Romulum et Numam Pompilium binos quaestores habuisse, quos ipsi non sua uoce sed populi suffragio crearent, refert. sed sicuti dubium est an Romulo et Numa regnantibus quaestor fuerit, ita Tullo Hostilio rege quaestores fuisse certum est: et sane crebrior apud ueteres opinio est Tullum Hostilium primum in rem publicam induxisse quaestores.* [1] *et a genere quaerendi quaestores initio dictos et Iunius et Trebatius et Fenestella scribunt.* [2] *ex quaestoribus quidam solebant prouincias sortiri ex senatus consulto, quod factum est Decimo Druso et Porcina consulibus. sane non omnes quaestores prouincias sortiebantur, uerum excepti erant candidati principis: hi enim solis libris principalibus in senatu legendis uacant.* [3] *hodieque optinuit indifferenter quaestores creari tam patricios quam plebeios: ingressus est enim et quasi primordium gerendorum honorum sententiaeque in senatu dicendae.* [4] *ex his, sicut dicimus, quidam sunt qui candidati principis dicebantur quique epistulas eius in senatu legunt.*

130. Lydus himself received such a ψῆφος in 551 (*De magistratibus* 3.30), which no doubt accounts for this gratuitous addition to what the *Digest* extract says.

> That is what Iunius [writes]; but the jurist Ulpian adequately discusses the quaestor in his *De officio quaestoris*, 'On the office of quaestor'.[131]

Lydus seems not to have noticed that he has made Iunius cite himself, along with Trebatius and Fenestella who wrote a century after his time.[132]

Of course Lydus knew where his 'verbatim' quotations really came from: a page or two later he repeated the information about the *candidati principis* who read out imperial communications in the Senate, and properly attributed it to 'Ulpian the jurist in his one-volume work on the office of quaestor'.[133] But Ulpian had cited the seventh book of Iunius Gracchanus' *De potestatibus*, and that was enough to let Lydus claim that the whole passage was precious 'testimony from the men of old'.[134]

Even so, he didn't use all of it. Perhaps, like Ulpian, he was doubtful about Gracchanus' statement that Romulus and Numa appointed quaestors by popular vote.[135] For whatever reason, he omitted that, and the effect of the omission is to make the next sentence meaningless. 'After them', he says (μετὰ τούτους), and attentive readers will ask 'After whom?' It is a *non sequitur* very like the one in Lydus' account of the censorship and its digression on Roman drama; the digression began 'At that time' (τότε), and attentive readers will ask 'What time?' We can now return to that passage, in the hope that this lengthy examination of Lydus' citation technique will have helped us to make sense of it.

131. Lydus *De magistratibus* 1.24 (following from n. 127 above): προεχωρήσαντο ψήφῳ τοῦ δήμου. Τοῦλλος δὲ ὁ ῥὴξ μετὰ τούτους ἀναγκαίαν εἶναι τὴν τῶν κυαιστώρων ἀρχὴν ἔκρινεν, ὡς τοὺς πλείους τῶν ἱστορικῶν αὐτῷ τὴν τοιαύτην ἀναγράψαι καὶ μόνῳ. ἀπὸ δὲ τῆς ζητήσεως οὕτως ὀνομασθῆναι αὐτοὺς Ἰούνιος καὶ Τρεβάτιος καὶ Φενεστέλλας εἶπον. καὶ μεθ' ἕτερα· πλὴν ὕστερον ἐξῃρέθησαν οἱ κανδιδᾶτοι τοῦ βασιλέως κυαίστωρες οἳ πρὸς ἀνάγνωσιν τῶν βασιλικῶν γραμμάτων καὶ μόνην ἐσχόλαζον· οἱ δὲ αὐτοὶ καὶ ψήφους ἀπὸ τοῦ κοινοῦ τῆς βουλῆς ἀπεγίνωσκον ὑπὲρ τῶν εἰς ἀξιώματα προαγομένων. ταῦτα μὲν ὁ Ἰούνιος, ὁ νομικὸς δὲ Οὐλπιανὸς ἐν τῷ *De officio quaestoris*, ἀντὶ τοῦ <Περὶ τοῦ κυαίστωρος τάξεως> περὶ κυαίστωρος ἀποχρώντως διαλεγεται.

132. For an even more horrendous mix-up compare Lydus' *De magistratibus* 3.63 with his source-text, Pliny *Natural History* 9.60-62 (Panayotakis 2010, 400–403): 'Cornelius Nepos and the poet Laberius, both Romans', are cited as referring to a freedman of the emperor Claudius a century after their time.

133. Lydus *De magistratibus* 1.28: Οὐλπιανοῦ τοῦ νομικοῦ . . . ἐν μονοβίβλῳ Περὶ τῆς τοῦ κυαίστωρος τάξεως.

134. See n. 127.

135. Compare the texts at nn. 129 and 131.

3.6. A significant censorship

Explaining the censorship (which in his day had been obsolete for nearly five hundred years), Lydus described the censors' role as financial assessors, and then, without warning, cut to 'At that time the Roman comic poet Titinius produced a play in Rome'.[136] He had presumably changed his source, and we have seen above (section 3.4) that the source he now turned to was almost certainly Suetonius. The question is, what was there in Suetonius' account of the office to link the censors' role to the production of a particular play?

All we know about Titinius is that he was active probably in the first quarter of the second century BC,[137] and that he wrote *fabulae togatae*.[138] Lydus' Suetonian list of styles defined *togata* as 'comedy that has an ancient Roman plot',[139] which no doubt explains his oddly emphatic statement here that 'a Roman poet produced a play in Rome'. The natural assumption is that his source was reporting an innovation, the first time a comedy had been performed in Roman dress. But when was it, and what did it have to do with the censorship?

The most likely context is the climate of hostility to Greek culture that followed the wars with Philip V (200–197 BC) and Antiochus III (191–88). In 186 BC the Senate decided that Dionysiac worship ('Bacchanalia') was an alien import, and instructed the consuls to stamp it out.[140] As censor in 184 Marcus Cato aimed to restore traditionally austere values against the Romans' growing taste for luxury, which he evidently blamed on Greek influence. 'Consider this as spoken by a prophet', he wrote: 'when that race gives us its literature it will corrupt everything.'[141] In 181 the tomb

136. Lydus *De magistratibus* 1.40 (n. 101). *Pace* Wünsch 1903, xxxv, τότε can hardly refer to 219 BC, the last date mentioned in Lydus' text (*De magistratibus* 1.38): that was in a quite different context, in the chapter on the dictatorship.

137. Guardí 1984, 18–19. The main evidence is the order of names *Titinio Terentio Attae* at Charisius 315B (citing Varro *De lingua Latina*).

138. Serenus Sammonicus *Liber medicinalis* 1037–8 (*praecepit Titini sententia . . . qui ueteri claras expressit more togatas*), confirmed by his Latin titles (Guardí 1984, 30–78 for the fragments).

139. Lydus *De magistratibus* 1.40 (n. 101): καὶ παλλιᾶτα μέν ἐστιν ἡ Ἑλληνικὴν ὑπόθεσιν ἔχουσα κωμῳδία, τογᾶτα δὲ ἡ Ῥωμαϊκὴν ἀρχαίαν.

140. Livy 39.8-19, esp. 15.3 (*prauis et externis religionibus*), 16.8 (*magistratibus negotium est datum uti sacra externa fieri uetarent*). As Liber Pater, Dionysus had had his cult and festival at Rome ever since 493 BC (Dionysius of Halicarnassus *Roman Antiquities* 6.17.2-4, Ovid *Fasti* 3.713-90).

141. Pliny *Natural History* 29.14 (Cato addressing his son): *hoc puta uatem dixisse: quandoque ista gens suas litteras dabit, omnia corrumpet.* At the *ludi scaenici* audiences

of Numa Pompilius was discovered, containing carefully preserved texts of Pythagorean lore; the urban praetor consulted the Senate and had the books burnt in public 'because it was not appropriate that they should be read and preserved'.[142]

The next censors (179 BC) were two famously hostile aristocratic rivals who began their year of office with a formal act of reconciliation.[143] They then requested substantial public funding,[144] which they each used in innovative ways. Fulvius Nobilior, who was patron of the 'half-Greek' poet Ennius and ten years earlier had stripped the Greek city of Ambracia of its statues and other works of art,[145] now made a grand philhellenic gesture:

> He used his censorial funding to create a temple to 'Hercules of the Muses' in the Circus Flaminius. What led him to it was not just his own literary culture and the friendship of a great poet, but the fact that when in command in Greece he had learned that Herakles was a Μουσαγέτης, which means comrade and leader of the Muses. Fulvius was the first to consecrate the nine Muses' statues,[146] taken from Ambracia, under the protection of the strongest of divinities.[147]

His colleague Marcus Lepidus had fiercely denounced the plunder of the Ambracia statues.[148] Now, reconciliation notwithstanding, Lepidus successfully petitioned the Senate for extra funds to pay for theatre games

---

had been enjoying tragedies on Greek mythological subjects by Livius Andronicus, Naevius and Ennius ever since 240 BC.

142. Cassius Hemina *FRHist* 5 F35 = Pliny *Natural History* 13.86 (*in his libris scripta erant philosophiae Pythagoricae*), Livy 40.29.12 (*legi seruarique non oportere*). A statue of Pythagoras as 'the wisest of the Greeks', erected on the instruction of Pythian Apollo, had been standing in the Comitium ever since the fourth century BC (Pliny *Natural History* 34.26, Plutarch *Numa* 8.10).

143. Livy 40.45.6-46.15 (M. Aemilius Lepidus and M. Fulvius Nobilior).

144. Livy 40.46.16: *censoribus deinde postulantibus ut pecuniae summa sibi qua in opera publica uterentur adtribueretur, uectigal annuum decretum est.*

145. Ennius: Cicero *Pro Archia* 27, Suetonius *De grammaticis* 11.2 (*semigraecus*), cf. Festus 374L (*utpote Graecus Graeco more usus*). Ambracia: Livy 38.43.1-44.6, 39.4-5.

146. For the statue group see Wiseman 2004, 181–2, fig. 71 (coins of 66 BC), Ovid *Fasti* 6.811-12.

147. Eumenius *Pro instaurandis scholis* (= *Panegyrici Latini* 9) 7.3: *aedem Herculis Musarum in circo Flaminio Fuluius ille Nobilior ex pecunia censoria fecit, non id modo secutus, quod ipse litteris et summi poetae amicitia duceretur, sed quod in Graecia cum esset imperator acceperat Heraclem Musagetem esse, id est comitem ducemque Musarum, idemque primus nouem signa Camenarum ex Ambraciensi oppido translata sub tutela fortissimi numinis consecrauit.*

148. Livy 38.43.6, 38.44.3-5.

at the dedication of two temples he himself had vowed earlier in a war against the Ligurians.[149] It was a conspicuous counter-demonstration:

> Having dedicated the temples, both in the Circus Flaminius, he gave *ludi scaenici* for three days after the dedication of the temple of Juno and for two days after the dedication of the temple of Diana, with one day of *ludi circenses* for each.[150]

The exact site of the Diana temple is not known, but that of Juno was next door to Fulvius' temple of 'Hercules of the Muses', and surely meant to compete with it.[151]

Since there seems to be no parallel for a censor putting on public games, it's reasonable to suppose that 179 BC provided the missing link between the censorship and dramatic performance that Lydus' account requires. If so, then Titinius' play was a deliberate innovation, a skirmish in Rome's culture wars: the first-ever comedy in Roman dress would enable Lepidus pointedly to upstage Fulvius' Greek Muses in the neighbouring temple. Suetonius may well have mentioned such a conspicuous event, either in his *De institutione officiorum*, as anomalous censorial expenditure, or in his *De ludis scaenicis et circensibus*, as anomalous censorial presidency of public games.[152] We must assume that Lydus deliberately omitted it, just as he omitted Romulus and Numa appointing quaestors,[153] thus leaving (in each case) a *non sequitur* in his text.

Lydus did the best he could with the material he had, and sometimes even succeeded in recovering 'the testimony of the men of old'. Despite his limitations and the difficulties involved, his chapter on the censorship has enabled us to infer that Suetonius probably dated the introduction of *fabulae togatae* to 179 BC. That fits the chronological progression implied by Evanthius two hundred years before: 'It is important to remember that after the Greek "New Comedy" the Latins introduced many types

149. Livy 40.52.1: *ut sibi dedicationis causa templorum reginae Iunonis et Dianae . . . pecunia ad ludos decerneretur.*

150. Livy 40.52.2-3: *dedicauit eas aedes, utramque in circo Flaminio, ludosque scaenicos triduum post dedicationem templi Iunonis, biduum post Dianae, et singulos dies fecit in circo.*

151. See *Forma urbis Romae* frr. 30-31 for the post-Augustan situation: the temple of Juno enclosed by the portico of Octavia, that of Hercules Musarum by the adjacent portico of Philippus.

152. See respectively Priscian 6.8.41 and *Suda* T 895 = 4.581 Adler (Περὶ τῶν παρὰ Ῥωμαίοις θεωριῶν καὶ ἀγώνων).

153. *Digest* 1.13.1 (n. 129), Lydus *De magistratibus* 1.24 (n. 131).

of plays.'[154] No doubt Suetonius counted Plautus and Terence as New Comedy,[155] and went on to report, with dates where possible,[156] the subsequent introduction of each of the other types.

Varro had defined *fabulae togatae* as all plays, comic and otherwise, that were performed in Roman dress; for him, *togata* was a generic title that included *praetexta* (serious plays on Roman history) as a subspecies.[157] For Horace, on the other hand, those two categories were alternatives, plays in Roman dress either comic or serious:

> Our poets have left no genre unattempted, and earned not the least honour when daring to leave Greek tracks and celebrate our own deeds, whether they produced *praetextae* or *togatae*.[158]

It is clear that there were two incompatible opinions on the subject, each held by serious, well-informed people.[159] But we know (section 3.3 above) that Suetonius took the same view as Horace, treating *togatae* not as the primary category of all plays with a Roman scene, but as a specific (and datable) sub-category of comedy.[160] Now we can add the likelihood that he reported the introduction of the genre in 179 BC.

3.7. *Whom to believe?*

It has taken a lot of difficult argument to get back to Varro through Diomedes, and to get back to Suetonius through Jerome, Evanthius and John Lydus; but at least a reasonably clear picture has emerged of their respective treatments of Roman drama. Varro evidently thought of it as a unitary

154. Evanthius *De fabula* 4.1 = Kaibel 1899, 66 (n. 82).

155. As they did themselves: Plautus *Asinaria* 10-11, *Casina* 31-4, *Mercator* 9-10, *Trinummus* 18-19; Terence *Adelphoe* 6-7, *Andria* 9-14, *Eunuchus* 19-34, *Heauton timoroumenos* 4-9, *Phormio* 24-6.

156. As suggested by his specific dating of Pylades' introduction of 'all-mime' dance to 22/21 BC (Jerome *Chronica* Ol. 189.3).

157. Diomedes *De poematibus* 10.1-6 = *Grammatici Latini* 1.489-90 Keil (nn. 44 and 52); *praetextae* were already being staged in the third century BC (see Manuwald 2001, 134–61 on Naevius' *Clastidium* and *Romulus*).

158. Horace *Ars poetica* 285–8: *nil intemptatum nostri reliquere poetae, | nec minimum meruere decus uestigia Graeca | ausi deserere et celebrare domestica facta, | uel qui praetextas uel qui docuere togatas.*

159. The fact that Diomedes four hundred years later called Horace's view an error (n. 44) means only that as a teacher he had to choose which doctrine to give his pupils; he was in no position to make an informed judgement.

160. See nn. 76–7: he listed Quinctius Atta as a *scriptor togatarum* (Jerome *Chronica* Ol. 175.4), and referred to *togatae* as a comic genre at *Diuus Augustus* 45.4, *Nero* 11.2 and *De grammaticis* 21.4.

concept to be analysed in its logical structure, while Suetonius, looking back over a longer perspective, treated it diachronically as an organism of which the stages of development could be traced and dated.

Both took it for granted that drama was a seamlessly Greco-Roman phenomenon. Varro's whole structure was simultaneously Greek and Latin:

> Dramatic poetry consists of four types: among the Greeks, tragic, comic, satyric, mimic; among the Romans, 'purple-bordered', 'tavern-style', 'Atellan', 'flat-foot'.[161]

Suetonius' account was similarly symmetrical, and added the Greek genre of *Rhinthonica* to the list of Latin comedy-types.[162] (He even went on to derive the whole tradition of Roman satire from the plays of Rhinthon and his contemporaries,[163] a puzzle to be addressed in the next chapter.)

Given the popularity of Athenian tragedy and comedy in south Italy and Sicily from the fifth century onwards (section 1.4 above),[164] it would not be at all surprising if the development of Roman drama was along Greek lines, as Varro and Suetonius implied. What *is* surprising is Livy's account of its supposed origin (section 3.1 above), which ignored Greek drama altogether. According to Livy the Romans in 364 BC knew nothing of *ludi scaenici*; Etruscan dancers and musicians were introduced, but no acting was involved; subsequent improvised dialogue by amateur performers was a purely local development.[165]

Livy's digression on the later progress of the genre took the same line, giving no dates but beginning with an event of 240 BC:

> It is said that Livius some years later . . . was the first to compose a play with a plot; he was of course the actor of his own songs, as they all were at that time. He had made his voice hoarse from frequent encores and obtained permission to station a boy in front of the pipe-player to sing the song, and acted it with rather more energetic movement because he wasn't impeded by using his own voice.[166]

161. Diomedes *De poematibus* 1.4 = *Grammatici Latini* 1.482 Keil (n. 35).

162. Donatus *De comoedia* 6.1 (Kaibel 1899, 68), Evanthius *De fabula* 4.1 (Kaibel 1899, 66), Lydus *De magistratibus* 1.40 (nn. 81–2 and 101).

163. Lydus *De magistratibus* 1.41 (n. 107).

164. Contemporary evidence from vase-painting has been thoroughly documented and discussed: see for instance Taplin 1993, Todisco 2002, Taplin 2007, Taplin 2020, Todisco 2020.

165. Livy 7.2.3-7 (n. 9): *noua res bellicoso populo . . . sine carmine ullo, sine imitandorum carminum actu . . . imitari deinde . . . uernaculis artificibus.*

166. Livy 7.2.8-9: *Liuius post aliquot annis, qui . . . ausus est primus argumento fabulam serere, idem scilicet—id quod omnes tum erant—suorum carminum actor, dicitur,*

But 'Livius' was Livius Andronicus, a Greek from Taras, and his plays were Greek tragedies in Latin.[167] The digression continues:

> Then it began to be sung to the gestures of the actors [?],[168] with only the dialogue left to the actors' voices. By the use of this rule for plays it became detached from laughter and loose joking, and after performance gradually developed into an art the young men left the acting of plays to [professional] actors. They themselves began to throw jokes stitched into verses at each other in the old style, from which there arose what were later called 'after-pieces', attached in particular to 'Atellan' plays.[169] Performances of that kind, taken over from the Oscans, the young men retained, and would not let them be degraded by [professional] actors. That is why the custom remains that those who act 'Atellan' [plays] are not demoted from their civic status [by the censors],[170] and why they [are allowed to] serve in the army, as being uninvolved with the professional stage.
>
> Among other things that have had small beginnings,[171] it seemed worth while also to set out the origin of [theatre] games, to make it clear from what a healthy start the thing has come to its present insanity, hardly tolerable even in wealthy kingdoms.[172]

---

cum saepius reuocatus uocem obtudisset, uenia petita puerum ad canendum ante tibicinem cum statuisset, canticum egisse aliquanto magis uigente motu quia nihil uocis usus impediebat. For the date (section 1.1 above) see Cicero *Brutus* 71–2, *Tusculan Disputations* 1.3, Varro *De poetis* in Aulus Gellius 17.21.42–3.

167. Suetonius rightly called him *tragoediarum scriptor* (n. 67); the known titles are *Achilles, Aegisthus, Aiax magistophoros, Andromeda, Danae, Equus Troianus, Hermiona* and *Tereus* (Warmington 1936, 2–15). Cf. Cicero *Brutus* 72 (from Accius, misdated) for his Tarantine origin.

168. The text is probably corrupt: see Oakley 1998, 65–6 for possible meanings.

169. For the text and meaning here see Oakley 1998, 67–8, with nn. 97 and 104 on *exodia*.

170. As professional actors could be (Augustine *City of God* 2.13.3 = Cicero *De republica* 4.10), i.e. *omnes propter praemium in scaenam prodeuntes* (Ulpian in *Digest* 3.2.2.5).

171. A reference back to the beginning of his account (7.2.4, n. 9): *parua quoque, ut ferme principia omnia.*

172. Livy 7.2.10–12: *inde †ad manum cantari histrionibus† coeptum deuerbiaque tantum ipsorum uoci relicta. postquam lege hac fabularum ab risu ac soluto ioco res auocabatur et ludus in artem paulatim uerterat, iuuentus histrionibus fabellarum actu relicto ipsa inter se more antiquo ridicula intexta uersibus iactitare coepit; unde exorta quae exodia postea appellata consertaque fabellis potissimum Atellanis sunt; quod genus ludorum ab Oscis acceptum tenuit iuuentus nec ab histrionibus pollui passa est; eo institutum manet, ut actores Atellanarum nec tribu moueantur et stipendia, tamquam expertes artis ludicrae, faciant. inter aliarum parua principia rerum ludorum quoque prima origo ponenda uisa est, ut appararet quam ab sano initio res in hanc uix opulentis regnis tolerabilem insaniam uenerit.*

The oddity of Livy's procedure here was noted in Stephen Oakley's magisterial commentary: 'whether due to ignorance (which is hard to credit), oversight, slavish adherence to his source, or Italian chauvinism, he manages to avoid mentioning Greek drama throughout the digression'.[173]

Ignorance can be ruled out. At the time the young Livy was getting what must have been a first-rate education, the best authorities treated Roman drama as a continuation of Greek:

> In the consulship of C. Claudius Centho, son of Appius Caecus, and M. Sempronius Tuditanus [240 BC] the poet Lucius Livius was the first of all to produce plays at Rome, more than 160 years after the deaths of Sophocles and Euripides and about 52 years after the death of Menander.[174]

Livy deliberately took a different line, and his closing comment suggests a reason why.

The idea of drama developing from a small but 'healthy' beginning (*quam ab sano initio*) into something intolerably extravagant matches quite precisely the overall vision of Roman history that inspired Livy to write his history:

> The task is immense, since Rome's history stretches back over seven hundred years and since the state has now grown so large from small beginnings that it struggles under the incubus of its own great size. . . . My wish is that each reader will . . . follow in his mind how, as discipline broke down bit by bit, morality at first foundered; how it next subsided in even greater collapse and then began to topple headlong in ruin—until the advent of our own age, in which we can endure neither our vices nor the remedies needed to cure them.[175]

For an event before 'discipline broke down',[176] Greek involvement was not something Livy could admit. Regarding Greeks in general as morally

173. Oakley 1998, 54.

174. Aulus Gellius 17.21.42, from Varro's *De poetis* and/or Cornelius Nepos' *Chronica*; see the citations at 17.21.3, 8, 24, 43 and 45.

175. Livy pref. 4 and 9 (trans. T. J. Luce): *res est praeterea et immensi operis, ut quae supra septingentesimum annum repetatur et quae ab exiguis profecta initiis eo creuerit ut iam magnitudine laboret sua. . . . ad illa mihi pro se quisque . . . labante deinde paulatim disciplina uelut dissidentes primo mores sequatur animo, deinde ut magis magisque lapsi sint, tum ire coeperint praecipites, donec ad haec tempora quibus nec uitia nostra nec remedia pati possumus peruentum est.*

176. In 364 BC the Romans were still 'a warlike people' (Livy 7.2.3, n. 9), hence the emphasis on the role of the young men.

inferior to Romans,[177] he believed that early Rome was totally innocent of any contact with the Greek world.[178] It was evidently easy for him to think, as Horace did, that Roman knowledge of Greek drama was a comparatively recent phenomenon,[179] and could thus be associated with the 'collapse' of Roman morality.

It is now known that this schematic idea was entirely unhistorical. As we saw in the first chapter, from the sixth century BC onwards Rome was an integral part of the Greek cultural world. That is quite consistent with the Greco-Roman view of drama that Varro and Suetonius evidently presented, but utterly at variance with Livy's version of events.

This chapter has tested the evidence of four authors who aimed to inform their readers about the history of Roman theatre. The first is the most easily accessible, Livy's great history with its confident narrative about events that happened long before the time of his earliest sources (section 3.1). The relevant works of our second and third authors are lost, and have to be reconstructed from their use by later scholars: we were able to get back to Varro via Diomedes (section 3.2), and to Suetonius via Jerome and Evanthius (section 3.3) and our fourth author, John Lydus (sections 3.4–6). A necessarily complex argument revealed that Varro, a historical researcher interested in the details of the past for their own sake,[180] and Suetonius, following the same line with additions of his own,[181] understood Roman drama as continuous with Greek, a position clearly in conflict with Livy's morally improving narrative of innocent small beginnings.

Although modern literary scholarship has been content to accept Livy's picture,[182] the material record of early Roman culture has made that position untenable. It makes much better historical sense to trust what Varro and Suetonius were able to discover.

177. E.g. Livy 8.22.8, 9.18.4-7, 42.47.5-7; contrast pref. 11 on the Romans (*nulla umquam res publica nec maior nec sanctior nec bonis exemplis ditior fuit*).

178. E.g. Livy 1.18.3 (Numa as a pupil of Pythagoras impossible *a priori*), 1.56.6 (Tarquin's sons go to Delphi 'through unknown lands and even more unknown seas').

179. 'In the peace after the Punic wars' (Horace *Epistles* 2.1.161-3).

180. Cicero *Brutus* 60 (*diligentissimus inuestigator antiquitatis*).

181. E.g. *fabulae Rhinthonicae* (section 3.3) and the date of the introduction of *fabulae togatae* (section 3.6).

182. See most recently Fulkerson and Tatum 2024, 9–10 and 113.

CHAPTER FOUR

Roman Satire and Roman Theatre

THE ENGLISH word 'satire' is derived from the Latin noun *satura*, but what *satura* meant is surprisingly uncertain. The earliest surviving uses of the word come from two contemporaries, the poet Horace and the historian Livy, writing in the period 35–25 BC. We have seen already (section 3.1 above) that in his account of the origins of Roman theatre Livy used *satura* to describe a performance genre, 'a written song accompanied by a pipe-player and with appropriate movement'.[1] Only a decade or so earlier, however, Horace had described as *satura* his own informal hexameter poetry in the collection he called *sermones* ('conversations');[2] and Horace prided himself on *not* writing for public stage performance.[3]

Most modern scholarship avoids the issue by treating 'Roman satire' as a genre of hexameter poetry invented by Lucilius in the second century BC, with a canon of four authors only.[4] That is indeed how Horace and his successors constructed it, and the artificiality of the construction is well understood:

1. Livy 7.2.7: *impletas modis saturas descripto iam ad tibicinum cantu motuque congruenti peragebant.*

2. Horace *Satires* 2.1.1, 2.6.17 (*satura*); *Epistles* 1.4.1, 2.1.250 (*sermones*).

3. Horace *Satires* 1.10.37-9 (*haec ego ludo | quae neque in aede sonent certantia iudice Tarpa, | nec redeant iterum atque iterum spectanda theatris*), *Epistles* 1.19.41-2 (*spissis indigna theatris | scripta pudet recitare et nugis addere pondus*).

4. See for instance Ferriss-Hill 2022 (summarised as 'Keywords: Roman satire—Lucilius—Horace—Persius—Juvenal'), with full bibliography. For Lucilius as the originator see Horace *Satires* 1.4.56-7 (*ego quae nunc, | olim quae scripsit Lucilius*), 1.10.48 (*inuentor*), Persius 1.114-8, Juvenal 1.19-20 and 165-7.

> The rather-too-neat generic genealogies of Horace, Persius and Juvenal implement a collective, almost collusive, literary *damnatio memoriae* against a number of writers of the genre known from other sources.[5]

Nevertheless, Latinists have often been content to go along with it and allow those other authors to stay forgotten.[6] I think it's time to give them their due.

4.1. What was satura*?*

We can start with an older contemporary of Livy and Horace, the prodigiously erudite *inuestigator antiquitatis* Marcus Varro, whose taxonomy of Greek and Roman theatre was explored in the previous chapter (section 3.2 above). Varro was a man of action in public life, a senator and a military and naval commander,[7] and the last five items on Jerome's list of his written works (well over a third of the total in volume numbers) reveal yet another of his many talents: he didn't just investigate the history of Roman performance culture, he also contributed to it as a creative artist.

The astonishing 150 volumes of 'Menippean *saturae*' (93 titles are known) were evidently scripts for performance to a theatre audience,[8] including dialogue between characters on stage.[9] The wide variety of metres attested (as well as prose) is consistent with Livy's description of *saturae* as 'filled with musical measures';[10] the fragments suggest that these performances consisted of conversations interspersed with music and dance in various styles.[11] The basic format may have been a cross-talk act between 'Marcus', the author, and Menippus of Gadara, a Cynic philosopher of the third century BC, of whom it was said that 'he polished up his *saturae* with poetry of every kind'.[12]

5. Ferriss-Hill 2022, 2.

6. E.g. Ferriss-Hill 2022, 9 ('if we exclude Ennius, Pacuvius, and Varro at the Roman verse satirists' behest'), 76 (Varro's Menippean satires 'outside the scope of this study'). But see now Fedeli 2024, 65–74, Fulkerson and Tatum 2024, 111–26.

7. For a sketch of his public career see Wiseman 2009, 107–29.

8. Varro *Menippean Satires* frr. 218 = Nonius 510L (*uosque in theatro*), 355 = Nonius 593L (*ualete et me palmulis producite*); Wiseman 2009, 137–43. All references to the *Menippean Satires* are numbered as in Astbury's Teubner edition.

9. E.g. Varro *Menippean Satires* fr. 277 = Nonius 499L; Wiseman 2015, 77.

10. Livy 7.2.7 (n. 1): *impletas modis saturas*.

11. For *saturae* as conversations (*sermones*) see Lucilius fr. 1039M = Nonius 502L, Horace *Epistles* 1.4.1, 2.1.250. Music and dance: Wiseman 2015, 77–8.

12. Ps.Probus on Virgil *Eclogues* 6.31, p. 336 Hagen (*is quoque omnigeno carmine satiras suas expoliuerat*); cf. Cicero *Academica* 1.9 for Varro's use of Menippus ('imitations, not translations'), and *Suda* s.v. *Phaios* (Φ180 Adler) for Menippus' own performance style.

It seems likely that Varro's other four volumes of *saturae* (item 39 on Jerome's list) were the same sort of thing but without Menippus, just 'Marcus' addressing the audience in prose or verse, or else in conversation with other persons.[13] Varro was interested in the question of how *saturae* should be composed, as we happen to know from Nonius' dictionary of early Latin usage, where the Greek loan-word *pareutactoi* ('cadets') is illustrated by a quotation from an otherwise unattested Varronian work, *De compositione saturarum*. The text is totally baffling,[14] but seems to be in dialogue:

> 'The girl cadets are here.'
> 'A woman . . .'
> 'What woman?'
> 'Venus!'

Perhaps Varro's treatment of the theory of *satura* was itself composed in *satura* form.

Varro's channelling of a Greek predecessor, with Greek titles and subtitles and Greek words and phrases scattered liberally in the text,[15] was certainly not an innovation of his own. A century or more earlier Ennius too had written *saturae*, collected into at least four volumes.[16] They are much less well attested than Varro's, but the surviving fragments reveal the same features: metrical variety,[17] dialogue,[18] conversation with the author,[19] and presentation of classic Greek predecessors (Aesop and the scurrilous Sotades).[20]

'Marcus': *Menippean Satires* frr. 45-70, 175, 269-92, 505, cf. 562 ('Varro'). Menippus: frr. 516-39, 542.

13. It is possible, though far from certain, that one of these *saturae* was Τρικάρανος ('Three Heads') on the triple alliance of Pompey, Crassus and Caesar in 60 BC (Appian *Civil Wars* 2.9.33).

14. Nonius 93L: *Varro De compositione saturarum: pareutactae adsunt mulier quae mulier Venus.*

15. Well over half of the known titles are wholly or partly Greek; of the 591 surviving fragments, 44 contain Greek words or phrases.

16. Porphyrio on Horace *Satires* 1.10.46 (*Ennius, qui quattuor libros saturarum reliquit*); cf. Donatus on Terence *Phormio* 339, where the reading *e sexto saturarum Ennii* is textually uncertain.

17. Iambic, trochaic, hexameter and sotadean lines are securely attested (Ennius frr. 7-19 Blänsdorf).

18. See Quintilian 9.2.36 on personification (προσωποποιία): *ut Mortem ac Vitam, quas contendentes in satura tradit Ennius.*

19. Nonius 48L: *Ennius satyrarum lib. III: 'Enni poeta, salue.'*

20. Aulus Gellius 2.29.3 (*hunc Aesopi apologum Q. Ennius in saturis . . . composuit*), 18.2.7 (Sotadean verses *qui sunt in saturis Quinti Enni*); it seems likely that 'the *Sota* of

Born at Greek Rhodiae (Rudiae) in the heel of Italy,[21] Ennius was trilingual in Greek, Oscan and Latin.[22] At Rome, his engagement with classic Greek literature took many forms, most notably his production of tragedies based on fifth-century Athenian plays by Euripides and Aristarchus,[23] and his spectacular self-presentation at the start of the *Annales* as a Pythagorean reincarnation of Homer himself.[24] Even though he created their great national epic,[25] the Romans still thought of Ennius as a Greek.[26]

His ways of entertaining them included impersonation of the myth-historian Euhemerus of Messene (in prose),[27] the mock-epic gourmet poet Archestratus of Gela (in hexameters),[28] and the early Syracusan comic dramatist Epicharmus (in trochaic *septenarii*).[29] It is not certain that these 'minor works' were part of the *saturae* collection, but they may well have been; one of the few things we are told about the early tradition of *satura* is that it used prose as well as a variety of poetic metres.[30]

Particularly interesting is Ennius' choice of Epicharmus, a contemporary of Pythagoras who was well known for popularising the philosopher's ethical teachings:

> Those who wish to propound maxims about the conduct of life cite as authority the wise sayings of Epicharmus; nearly all philosophers know these by heart. . . . [Epicharmus] put the thoughts of the Pythagoreans

---

Ennius' (Varro *De lingua Latina* 5.62, Festus 448L, Sotadean lines at frr. 1-6 Blänsdorf) was one of the *saturae*.

21. Cicero *De oratore* 3.168, Pomponius Mela 2.66; Strabo 6.3.5 C281 (ἐπὶ Ῥοδιῶν πόλεως Ἑλληνίδος, ἐξ ἧς ἦν ὁ ποιητὴς Ἔννιος).

22. Aulus Gellius 17.17.1: *Quintus Ennius tria corda habere sese dicebat, quod loqui Graece et Osce et Latine sciret.*

23. *Glossaria Latina* 1.568 (*tragoedias autem fere omnes ex Graecis transtulit, plurimas Euripidis, nonnullas Aristarchi*), with Jocelyn 1969, 44–5.

24. Horace *Epistles* 2.1.10-12 (with Porphyrio), Persius 6.10-11 (with scholiast); Skutsch 1985, 147–53.

25. Diomedes *De poematibus* 3.2 = *Grammatici Latini* 1.484 Keil: *epos Latinum primus digne scripsit Ennius, qui res Romanorum decem et octo complexus est libris.*

26. Festus 374L (*utpote Graecus Graeco more usus*), cf. Suetonius *De grammaticis* 1.2 (*semigraecus*).

27. Varro *De re rustica* 1.48.2 (*apud Ennium . . . in Euhemeri libris uersis*), Lactantius *Diuinae institutiones* 1.11.33 (*hanc historiam et interpretatus est Ennius et secutus*); *BNJ* 63 F12-26.

28. Apuleius *Apologia* 39 = Ennius fr. 28 Blänsdorf; for Archestratus see Wilkins and Hill 1994.

29. Cicero *Academica* 2.51 (*Ennium . . . in Epicharmo*), Varro *De lingua Latina* 5.668 (*Epicharmus Enni*); Ennius frr. 35-41 Blänsdorf.

30. Quintilian 10.1.95: *non sola carminum uarietate mixtum.*

in metre, and under the guise of foolery published the secret teachings of Pythagoras.[31]

The Romans were familiar with Pythagoras: they had made him an honorary citizen after the expulsion of Tarquin,[32] and put up a statue to him in the Comitium at the time of the Samnite wars, having been told by Delphi to honour 'the wisest of the Greeks'.[33] Perhaps, like Varro with Menippus, Ennius used Epicharmus to give the authority of Greek wisdom to his comments on contemporary life.[34]

Chronologically midway between Ennius and Varro, and similarly known only from fragmentary quotations, the *saturae* of Gaius Lucilius were produced during the last three decades of the second century BC.[35] Because of his lack of metrical variety (he soon settled on the hexameter as his constant metre), Lucilius is often thought of as the founder of a wholly new literary genre, familiar to us from the later satires of Horace, Persius and Juvenal.[36] In all other respects, however, the fragments reveal just the same characteristics as those of Varro and Ennius.

Firstly, the author was the chief character.[37] Sometimes he was in narrative mode, as in the tale of his trip to Sicily;[38] more often he was in conversation, outspoken and often combative.[39] Secondly, dialogue was evidently normal: even though practically all of the surviving fragments are very short, several of them clearly represent cross-talk between two people.[40] Thirdly, the text was full of Greek, transliterated

31. Iamblichus *De uita Pythagorica* 29.166, 35.266 (trans. John Dillon and Jackson Hershbell): οἵ τε γνωμολογῆσαί τι τῶν κατὰ τὸν βίον βουλόμενοι τὰς Ἐπιχάρμου διανοίας προφέρονται, καὶ σχεδὸν πάντες αὐτὰς οἱ φιλόσοφοι κατέχουσι. . . . εἰς μέτρον δ'ἐντεῖναι τὰς διανοίας τῶν ἀνδρῶν, μετὰ παιδιᾶς κρύφα ἐκφέροντα τὰ Πυθαγόρου δόγματα.

32. Epicharmus *ap.* Plutarch *Numa* 8.9; for the historical context see Wiseman 2024, 10–12.

33. Pliny *Natural History* 34.26, Plutarch *Numa* 8.10; Coarelli 1985, 119–23. For 'Roman Pythagoras' in general see Volk 2016.

34. See Cicero *Academica* 1.8 for Varro's account of his method (*multa admixta ex intima philosophia, multa dicta dialectice*).

35. For excellent summary accounts see Gratwick 1982, 162–71; Fulkerson and Tatum 2024, 116–25.

36. See nn. 4–6.

37. As Horace put it (*Satires* 2.1.32-4), Lucilius' whole life was on view there; for his self-presentation, see Lucilius 791-2 = Nonius 54L, 481L. Lines of Lucilius are numbered according to Warmington's Loeb edition.

38. Porphyrio on Horace *Satires* 1.5.1.

39. E.g. Lucilius 186-93, 763-5, 1075 = Aulus Gellius 18.8.2, Nonius 125L, 181L.

40. E.g. Lucilius 588-9, 817-8, 940, 946 = Nonius 568L, 519L, Charisius in *Grammatici Latini* 1.96 Keil, Nonius 53L.

or otherwise;[41] at one point Lucilius even called himself 'half a Greek' (*semigraecus*).[42]

Like Ennius and Varro, Lucilius was interested in Greek philosophy. Clitomachus, the head of the Academy, wrote a treatise on scepticism for him,[43] and references to Academics, Socratics and Stoics turn up regularly in the fragments.[44] He also engaged with Greek tragedy,[45] and according to Horace, who knew his work very well, his whole approach was taken from Athenian 'Old Comedy':

> The poets Eupolis, Cratinus and Aristophanes, and the others to whom Old Comedy belongs, used to brand with great frankness anyone who deserved to be called out for being a villain or a thief, for being an adulterer or a murderer or notorious for some other reason. Lucilius depends on them completely; they were the ones he followed, just changing the metres and rhythms.[46]

Like them, as Horace knew, he delivered his social criticism from the stage.[47]

But the Old Comedy authors were playwrights composing for actors and a dancing chorus. It's true that the *saturae* in Livy's narrative (section 3.1 above) were performances that included music and movement (though Lucilius seems to have done without the musical element), but Livy carefully distinguishes *saturae* from 'plays with a plot'.[48] What influenced Lucilius must have been the *parabasis* of Athenian Old Comedy, where the actors left the scene and the chorus, taking off their robes, 'stepped forward' to address the audience in anapaests about subjects and personalities of current concern, either impersonating the author or speaking directly on his behalf.[49]

41. Examples are countless; for a characteristic bilingual *tour de force* see Lucilius 567-73 = Nonius 37-8L.

42. Lucilius 391 = Velius Longus in *Grammatici Latini* 7.47 Keil.

43. Cicero *Academica* 2.102 (and another for L. Marcius Censorinus the consul of 149 BC).

44. Lucilius 35, 789, 822, 835, 1189-90 = Lactantius *Diuinae institutiones* 5.15.3, Nonius 288L, 668L, 353L, Porphyrio on Horace *Satires* 1.3.124.

45. See Aulus Gellius 6.3.28 for his criticism of Euripides.

46. Horace *Satires* 1.4.1-7: *Eupolis atque Cratinus Aristophanesque poetae | atque alii quorum comoedia prisca uirorum est, | si quis erat dignus describi quod malus ac fur, | quod moechus foret aut sicarius aut alioqui | famosus, multa cum libertate notabant. | hinc omnis pendet Lucilius, hosce secutus | mutatis tantum pedibus numerisque.*

47. Horace *Satires* 2.1.71 (*scaena*), often dismissed as metaphorical, but for no good reason.

48. Livy 7.2.8: *Liuius . . . qui ab saturis ausus est primus argumento fabulam serere.*

49. E.g. Aristophanes *Acharnians* 624-66, *Knights* 498-610, *Clouds* 510-626, *Wasps* 1009-120, *Peace* 729-817, *Frogs* 674-737.

This investigation of what is left of the *saturae* of Ennius, Lucilius and Varro has had two results: it confirms Livy's statement that a *satura* was a stage performance but not a play, and it attests a constant involvement with Greek that is alien to Livy's picture but consistent with Varro's taxonomy of Greek and Roman drama as a unitary phenomenon (section 3.2 above).

4.2. *Restricting the genre*

By its nature, satire can quickly go out of date. Varro's *saturae* belonged to the 70s and 60s BC,[50] before Horace was born or when he was still a child in Venusia; a generation later they were no longer topical entertainment but texts to be read.[51] Even so, one would expect Horace to have read them, which makes his account of the current state of the genre a very surprising one:

> It was this, tried without success by Varro Atacinus and certain others, that I was able to write better—though not up to the inventor's standard; I wouldn't dare to deprive *him* [Lucilius] of the crown that sticks to his head with so much praise.[52]

Why should Horace refer to a *different* Varro, a poet not even known for satire, while ignoring one of the most famous authors of the age, who was still alive and writing at the time?[53] There must have been some non-literary explanation; it's possible, for instance, that Marcus Varro was *persona non grata* in the circle of Maecenas.[54]

Whatever the reason, this evasive passage encouraged the false belief that there had been no satire before Lucilius, and no significant satire between Lucilius and Horace himself. Nearly a century later Persius

50. See Wiseman 2009, 147 for the likely dates.

51. Cf. Cicero *Academica* 1.8 (45 BC), where Varro, as a character in the dialogue, assumes readers (*minus docti . . . ad legendum inuitati*) rather than an audience.

52. Horace *Satires* 1.10.46-9 (trans. P. Michael Brown): *hoc erat, experto frustra Varrone Atacino | atque quibusdam aliis, melius quod scribere possem, | inuentore minor; neque ego illi detrahere ausim | haerentem capiti cum multa laude coronam.* The 'certain others' may have included the learned freedmen Sevius Nicanor and Pompeius Lenaeus (Suetonius *De grammaticis* 5.1, 15.2).

53. See Courtney 1993, 235–53 for P. Terentius Varro 'Atacinus', author of *Bellum Sequanicum, Argonautae* and *Chorographia.* Still writing: Varro *De re rustica* 1.1.1 (*annus octogesimus*, 37 BC).

54. 'The more famous M. Terentius Varro . . . had recently been proscribed by Antony, and equally proscribed from H[orace]'s satirical genealogy' (Gowers 2012, 327).

defined the tradition in the same way, staking his own claim to be the third in line.[55] Quintilian, Persius' longer-lived contemporary, gave a slightly more nuanced version of the same view:

> As for satire, it is completely our own. Lucilius was the first to win outstanding praise for it, and he still has admirers so devoted that they do not hesitate to class him above all other poets, not merely all other satirists. I am as far from their view as from that of Horace, who thinks that Lucilius 'flows along muddily' and that there are things in him that you could well be rid of.[56] He has astonishing learning and outspokenness—and, as a result of that, acerbity: and a great deal of wit. Horace is much more concise and pure: unless I am biased by my love for him, he is the best. Persius won a good deal of genuine fame, despite writing only one book. There are brilliant satirists today,[57] whose names will be celebrated in the future.
>
> The other type of satire, an earlier invention, was exploited by Terentius Varro, in his case with prose as well as a variety of metres. This most learned among Romans composed very many books of vast erudition. He was highly skilled in the Latin language and every aspect of antiquity, together with both Greek and Roman history; but he has more to offer to learning than to eloquence.[58]

It would have been helpful if Quintilian had given more detail on the 'earlier invention', but his purpose, the education of the budding orator, didn't require that.

55. Persius 1.114-8; cf. also 1.123-4, from Horace *Satires* 1.4.1-7.

56. Horace *Satires* 1.4.11, 1.10.50-1.

57. E.g. Turnus (n. 88 below), and perhaps already Juvenal (cf. Martial 7.24, 7.91, 12.18.1-6); see Courtney 1993, 362–3 for what little is known of Turnus, evidently a major figure in his time.

58. Quintilian 10.1.93-5 (trans. Russell and Winterbottom 1972, 394): *satura quidem tota nostra est, in qua primus insignem laudem adeptus Lucilius quosdam ita deditos sibi adhuc habet amatores, ut eum non eiusdem modo operis auctoribus sed omnibus poetis praeferre non dubitent. ego quantum ab illis tantum ab Horatio dissentio, qui Lucilium fluere lutulentum et esse aliquid quod tollere possis putat. nam eruditio in eo mira et libertas atque ita acerbitas et abunde salis. multum est tersior ac purus magis Horatius et, nisi labor eius amore, praecipuus. multum et uerae gloriae quamuis uno libro Persius meruit. sunt clari hodieque et qui olim nominabuntur. alterum illud etiam prius saturae genus, sed non sola carminum uarietate mixtum condidit Terentius Varro, uir Romanorum eruditissimus. plurimos hic libros et doctissimos composuit, peritissimus linguae Latinae et omnis antiquitatis et rerum Graecarum nostrarumque, plus tamen scientiae collaturus quam eloquentiae.*

Two casual phrases are particularly revealing. First, satire is 'completely our own', in contrast with genres that were originally Greek, like epic and elegy.[59] But both Horace and Persius took it for granted that what Lucilius did was what Athenian Old Comedy had done, with just the metre changed.[60] Quintilian's comment only makes sense if he thought of Roman satire as a necessarily hexameter genre. Secondly, he mentions 'the other type' (*alterum illud genus*) only as an afterthought, defining it by its use of various metres, and even prose, as if that made it generically different. It seems clear that Horace's artificial restriction of the genre to what he himself did was followed by Quintilian as an axiom of literary history; and the mainstream of modern scholarship has followed his example.[61]

Quintilian's dismissive implication that the Varronian style was now obsolete is disproved by the existence of Seneca's *Apocolocyntosis*, a brilliant skit in mixed prose and verse that advertises its generic credentials with a quotation from Varro himself.[62] However, as a publicly funded professor Quintilian could hardly draw attention to mockery of a deified emperor.[63]

Another contemporary masterpiece he omitted to mention—not surprisingly, given its low-life subject matter—was Petronius' *Satyrica*, a multi-volume picaresque narrative which is sometimes assumed to be an example of 'Menippean satire'.[64] In fact it is generically unclassifiable,[65] and since the story has nothing to do with satyrs or satyr-play, the meaning of the title is a mystery.[66] But its inclusion of poetic passages, long and short, was indeed a feature in common with the Varronian style of *satura*.

59. Cf. Quintilian 10.1.85-6 (Virgil second only to Homer), 93 (*elegia quoque Graecos prouocamus*).

60. Horace *Satires* 1.4.1-7 (n. 46, *mutatis tantum pedibus numerisque*), Persius 1.123-4.

61. See n. 4; Fedeli 2024 now presents a much more nuanced account.

62. Seneca *Apocolocyntosis* 8.1 = Varro *Menippean Satires* fr. 583; for the work as a 'Menippean satire' see Coffey 1976, 165–77, Eden 1984, 13–16.

63. Jerome *Chronica* Ol. 216.4 (AD 88) on Quintilian: *primus Romae publicam scholam et salarium e fisco accepit.* Cf. Wiseman 2023, 33 on his caution in dealing with Catullus' attacks on Caesar.

64. E.g. Coffey 1976, 178–203, cf. Schmeling and Setaioli 2011, xxxiv; that generic category is used very loosely in modern scholarship (Weinbrot 2005, Wiseman 2009, 137–8).

65. Described by Macrobius (*In somnium Scipionis* 1.2.8) simply as a *fabula* like Apuleius' *Metamorphoses*; see Schmeling and Setaioli 2011, xxx–xxxviii for the possibilities.

66. Priapus, whose hostility to the narrator Encolpius drives the plot, is sometimes found in the company of satyrs in narratives of a different kind (e.g. Ovid *Fasti* 1.392-400, 6.319-24, *Metamorphoses* 14.637-41), and at one point his priestess Quartilla administers an aphrodisiac called *satyrion* (Petronius *Satyrica* 20.7, 21.1).

4.3. Diomedes on satyra

Now we go forward three hundred years, to Diomedes' *De poematibus*. The literary treatise that gave us access at second hand to Varro's taxonomy of Greek and Roman drama (section 3.2 above) is important also for the question of *satura*.

Diomedes divided *poemata* into three categories:[67] (1) dramatic or mimetic, for which his examples were Virgil's *Eclogues* 1 and 9; (2) narrative or expository, exemplified by Virgil's *Georgics* 1–3, the first part of *Georgics* 4, and Lucretius; and (3) a mixture of the two, for instance Homer's *Iliad* and *Odyssey* and Virgil's *Aeneid*.[68] He was evidently not thinking at all of drama, which would have been the obvious example to use for the first category. Similarly, the stage was not at the front of his mind when he went on to discuss the particular poetic genres in turn:[69] epic, elegy, iambus, epodes, *satyra*,[70] bucolic, and only then tragedy and comedy (at length), added at the end as something different.

It's clear that Diomedes didn't think of *satyra* as a performance genre. But he did know that dramatists had once written it:

> *Satyra* is a Roman verse form which nowadays is insulting and composed to censure people's vices in the style of Old Comedy, as written by Lucilius and Horace and Persius; but formerly *satura* was the name given to a verse form that consisted of various smaller pieces of poetry, as written by Pacuvius[71] and Ennius.[72]

This presented the same distinction Quintilian had made, between satire in the modern sense (as defined by Horace) and what had been called

67. Diomedes *De poematibus* 1.2-3 = *Grammatici Latini* 1.482 Keil.

68. Diomedes extends his treatment at *De poematibus* 1.4-6 = *Grammatici Latini* 1.482-3 Keil, giving further examples of the three kinds (including drama proper for the first), clearly from a different source.

69. *De poematibus* 3-14 = *Grammatici Latini* 1.483-92 Keil.

70. As Leo points out in his critical apparatus (Kaibel 1899, 55), that is how Diomedes consistently spelt it; the editors systematically 'correct' it to *satira* (Keil) or *satura* (Leo), but my translation keeps the author's spelling except where he was referring to Latin sources.

71. The *saturae* of Pacuvius are mentioned also by Porphyrio on Horace *Satires* 1.10.46, but no fragments survive and nothing is known of them.

72. *De poematibus* 6.1 = *Grammatici Latini* 1.485 Keil (Leo's text): *satura dicitur carmen apud Romanos, nunc quidem maledicum et ad carpenda hominum uitia archaeae comoediae charactere compositum, quale scripserunt Lucilius et Horatius et Persius; set olim carmen quod ex uariis poematibus constabat satura uocabatur, quale scripserunt Pacuuius et Ennius.*

satura in earlier times; but unlike Quintilian, Diomedes exemplified the latter by naming two of Rome's great tragic dramatists as authors of *uaria poemata*.

Diomedes now went on to give four possible reasons for the name of the genre:

> *Satyra* is named either (1) from 'satyrs', because in this verse form ridiculous and shameful things are said in the same way that they are uttered and done by satyrs, or (2) from the 'full' dish that the men of old used to offer to the gods that was stuffed with many varied first-fruits and called *satura* from the 'fullness' of it.[73] That type of dish is also mentioned by Virgil in the *Georgics*, when he says 'and on concave dishes we present steaming offal' and 'we shall bring dishes and cakes'.[74]
>
> Or else (3) [*satyra* is named] from a type of stuffing filled with many ingredients, which Varro says was called *satura*. This is how he defines it in the second book of his *Plautine Questions*: '*satura* is raisins, polenta and pine kernels soaked in honey-wine, to which some people add pomegranate seeds'.
>
> Others think (4) [*satyra* is named] from *lex satura*, a 'stuffed law' that contains many items in a single bill,[75] clearly because many poems are included together in the *satyra* verse form. Lucilius mentions this *lex satura* in his first book: 'an aedile elected by means of a stuffed [law] to provide legal immunity'. So does Sallust in his *Jugurtha*:[76] 'then, after opinions had been sought by means of a stuffed [proposal], he was received in surrender'.[77]

73. The derivation is from the Latin adjective *satur*, 'full, replete'. Leo brackets *copia* as a gloss on *saturitate*; Keil (following MS *A*) reads *copia et saturitate*, 'from the abundance and fullness of it'.

74. Virgil *Georgics* 2.194, 2.394.

75. Cf. Festus 416L: *satura et cibi genus ex uariis rebus conditum est et lex multis aliis legibus conferta*.

76. Sallust *Jugurthine War* 29.5; the context was Jugurtha's presence at the *consilium* of the consul L. Calpurnius Bestia in 111 BC: 'the council members' opinions seem to have been sought on all aspects of the surrender simultaneously rather than item by item' (Woodman 2007, 177).

77. *De poematibus* 6.2 = *Grammatici Latini* 1.485-6 Keil: *satura autem dicta siue a satyris, quod similiter in hoc carmine ridiculae res pudendaeque dicuntur uelut quae a satyris proferuntur et fiunt; siue satura a lance, quae referta uariis multisque primitiis in sacro apud priscos dis inferebatur et a [copia] saturitate rei satura uocabatur (cuius generis lancium et Vergilius in Georgicis meminit, cum hoc modo dicit: 'lancibus et pandis fumantia reddimus exta' et 'lancesque et liba feremus'); siue a quodam genere farciminis, quod multis rebus refertum saturam dicit Varro uocitatum. est autem hoc positum in II*

The second, third and fourth explanations are different ways of applying a derivation from the Latin adjective *satur*, 'full', the significance of which is made clear by the Varro quotation: *satura* was a variety performance, as full of different items as stuffing was full of different ingredients. That fits well with Diomedes' description of the earlier type of *satura* as 'a verse form consisting of various smaller pieces of poetry', and it might even be applicable to Livy's idea of *satura* as 'a written song accompanied by a pipe-player and with appropriate movement'.[78]

Much more surprising is the explanation Diomedes put first, 'the ridiculous and shameful things that are said and done by satyrs'. That certainly didn't come from Varro, Diomedes' source on types of drama, who listed satyr-play only as a Greek form (section 3.2 above).[79] It is true that satyr-play was familiar in Rome, and Horace even offered advice on how it should be composed,[80] but there is no very obvious analogy between satyr-play and Roman satire in any of its surviving forms.

Nevertheless, Diomedes got the idea from somewhere. He knew about '*satyra*' from a source who post-dated Persius, and in a later passage, on comedy, he named his source as 'Tranquillus'.[81] So it seems very likely that the derivation from satyrs was taken from Suetonius.

4.4. John Lydus again

Another reader of Suetonius was John Lydus in the mid-sixth century AD, whose anomalous digression on Roman drama we have discussed twice already (sections 1.6 and 3.4 above). In the previous chapter the question

---

libro Plautinarum quaestionum: 'satura est uua passa et polenta et nuclei pinei [*ex*] *mulso consparsi; ad haec alii addunt et de malo punico grana'. alii autem dictam putant a lege satura, quae uno rogatu multa simul comprehendat, quod scilicet et satura carmine multa simul poemata comprehenduntur; cuius saturae legis Lucilius meminit in primo: 'per saturam aedilem factum qui legibus soluat' et Sallustius in Iugurtha: ' deinde quasi per saturam sententiis exquisitis in deditionem accipitur'.*

78. *De poematibus* 6.1 = *Grammatici Latini* 1.485 Keil (n. 72 above), Livy 7.2.7 (n. 1); *poemata* could of course be sung and danced (e.g. Ovid *Tristia* 2.519).

79. *De poematibus* 10.5 and 9 = *Grammatici Latini* 1.490 Keil (similarities to and differences from the Latin *fabula Atellana*); Varro is cited at 10.2. Cf. *De poematibus* 12 = *Grammatici Latini* 1.491 Keil: *satyrica est apud Graecos fabula in qua item tragici poetae ... satyros induxerunt.*

80. Horace *Ars poetica* 220–50; cf. Porphyrion on *Ars poetica* 221 (satyr-plays by Pomponius), Nicolaus of Damascus *FGrH* 90 F75 = Athenaeus 6.261c (Sulla's σατυρικαὶ κωμῳδίαι), Vitruvius 5.6.9 and 7.5.2 (stage-painting for satyr-play); Wiseman 1988 = 1994a, 68–85.

81. *De poematibus* 6.1 = *Grammatici Latini* 1.485 Keil (n. 72 above); *De poematibus* 14.5 = *Grammatici Latini* 1.490 Keil (discussed in detail in section 11.2 below).

was what relevance it had to Lydus' argument in the 'censorship' chapter of *De magistratibus*.[82] Now we must look more carefully at the content of it.

Having noted that 'at that time [unspecified] the Roman comic poet Titinius produced a play in Rome',[83] Lydus went on as follows:

> Drama is divided into two [types]:[84] tragedy and comedy.
>
> Tragedy is itself divided into two [types]: *crepidata* and *praetextata*, of which *crepidata* has Greek plots, *praetextata* Roman ones.
>
> Comedy is divided into seven [types]: *palliata*, *togata*, *Atellana*, *tabernaria*, *Rhinthonica*, *planipedaria* and *mimica*. *Palliata* is comedy that has a Greek plot, *togata* an ancient Roman one; *Atellana* is [comedy] of the so-called *exodiarii*; *tabernaria* is the 'stage' or 'theatre' comedy, *Rhinthonica* the 'exotic', *planipedaria* the 'finale'. *Mimica* is of course the only one surviving nowadays; having nothing artistic about it, it attracts the crowd solely by meaningless laughter.
>
> Because I think it's necessary to pursue the subject, I shall add this too. We know that Rhinthon, Skiras, Blaisos and the other Pythagoreans were educators of no minor teachings in Magna Graecia, and especially Rhinthon, who was the first to write comedy in hexameters. Taking his start from him, the Roman Lucilius was the first to produce comedy in heroic verse. After him and his successors, whom the Romans call *satyrikoi*, the later authors imitated the style of Cratinus and Eupolis,[85] and using the metres of Rhinthon and the mockeries of those just mentioned, strengthened satyric comedy. Horace did not go beyond the art, but Persius, wanting to imitate the poet Sophron,[86] exceeded the obscurity of Lycophron.[87] Turnus,[88] Juvenal and Petro-

82. See section 3.6 above on the censors of 179 BC.

83. Lydus *De magistratibus* 1.40: τότε Τιτίνιος ὁ Ῥωμαῖος κωμικὸς μῦθον ἐπεδείξατο ἐν τῇ Ῥώμῃ. His Latin source probably wrote *fabulam exhibuit*, with an explanation of the term *fabula togata* as 'a play set in Rome'.

84. 'Drama' translates the subject noun μῦθος, which must have been *fabula* in the Latin source; it could equally well be translated 'plot' or 'story'.

85. As stated by Horace (*Satires* 1.4.1-7, cf. 1.10.16-17), and repeated by Persius (1.123-5).

86. Sophron's 'mimes' were in prose (Aristotle *Poetics* 1.1447b10), but he is often called a ποιητής, and of course he wrote for stage performance: Demetrius *On Style* 156 (δράματα), Solinus 5.13 (*in scaena*).

87. Lycophron's *Alexandra* is in the form of a hyper-tragic messenger-speech in which Cassandra's jailer reports her riddling prophecy to king Priam.

88. On whom see Martial 7.97.7, 11.10, Rutilius Namatianus 1.603-4, Sidonius Apollinaris 9.266; Courtney 1993, 362–3 (the two surviving fragments).

nius, going right to the limit with their abusive language, damaged the satyric rule.

So much for ancient comedy and tragedy.[89]

Modern scholarship has often doubted Horace's assumption that Roman satire took its style and subject-matter from Athenian Old Comedy.[90] Here, however, is a history of the genre that not only assumes Old Comedy as its model but adds a whole range of other formative influences from different types of Greek stage performance. The mention of authors from the first and second centuries AD—Persius, Turnus, Juvenal, Petronius—makes it highly likely that Lydus' source here was Suetonius (section 3.4 above).

Among the many surprising features of this testimony is the way the author took for granted the now traditional Lucilius–Horace–Persius sequence that defined the genre as necessarily hexameter (section 4.2 above), but unlike Quintilian gave it a Greek pedigree.[91] He derived it not from Menippus, as in Varro's polymetric *saturae*, but from Rhinthon of Taras, that 'minor song-bird of the Muses' whose third-century 'fooleries' Cicero so surprisingly had in his head two hundred years later (section 2.6 above).[92] No hexameter fragments of Rhinthon happen to survive, but

89. Lydus *De magistratibus* 1.40-2: ὁ δὲ μῦθος τέμνεται εἰς δύο, <εἰς τραγῳδίαν καὶ κωμῳδίαν· ὧν ἡ τραγῳδία καὶ αὐτὴ τέμνεται εἰς δύο>, εἰς κρηπιδᾶταν καὶ πραιτεξτᾶταν· ὧν ἡ μὲν κρηπιδᾶτα Ἑλληνικὰς ἔχει ὑποθέσεις, ἡ δὲ πραιτεξτᾶτα Ῥωμαϊκάς. ἡ μέντοι κωμῳδία τέμνεται εἰς ἑπτά· εἰς παλλιᾶταν, τογᾶταν, Ἀτελλάνην, ταβερναρίαν, Ῥινθωνικήν, πλανιπεδαρίαν καὶ μιμικήν· καὶ παλλιᾶτα μέν ἐστιν ἡ Ἑλληνικὴν ὑπόθεσιν ἔχουσα κωμῳδία, τογᾶτα δὲ ἡ Ῥωμαϊκήν ἀρχαίαν· Ἀτελλάνη δέ ἐστιν ἡ τῶν λεγομένων ἐξωδιαρίων· ταβερναρία δὲ ἡ σκηνωτὴ ἢ θεατρικὴ κωμῳδία· Ῥινθωνικὴ ἡ ἐξωτική· πλανιπεδαρία ἡ καταστολαρία· μιμικὴ ἡ νῦν δῆθεν μόνη σῳζομένη, τεχνικὸν μὲν ἔχουσα οὐδέν, ἀλόγῳ μόνον τὸ πλῆθος ἐπάγουσα γέλωτι. ὅτι δὲ ἀναγκαῖον οἶμαι ἐμβραδῦναι τῷ λόγῳ, προσθήσω καὶ τοῦτο. Ῥίνθωνα καὶ Σκίραν καὶ Βλαῖσον καὶ τοὺς ἄλλους τῶν τῶν Πυθαγορείων ἴσμεν οὐ μικρῶν διδαγμάτων ἐπὶ τῆς μεγάλης Ἑλλάδος γενέσθαι καθηγητάς, καὶ διαφερόντως τὸν Ῥίνθωνα, ὃς ἑξαμέτροις ἔγραψε πρῶτος κωμῳδίαν· ἐξ οὗ πρῶτος λάβων τὰς ἀφορμὰς Λουκίλιος ὁ Ῥωμαῖος ἡρωικοῖς ἔπεσιν ἐκωμῴδησεν. μεθ' ὃν καὶ τοὺς μετ' αὐτόν, οὓς καλοῦσι Ῥωμαῖοι σατυρικούς, οἱ νεώτεροι τὸν Κρατίνου καὶ Εὐπόλιδος χαρακτῆρα ζηλώσαντες τοῖς μὲν Ῥίνθωνος μέτροις, τοῖς δὲ τῶν μνημονευθέντων διασυρμοῖς χρησάμενοι, τῆν σατυρικὴν ἐκράτυναν κωμῳδίαν. Ὁράτιος μὲν οὐκ ἔξω τῆς τέχνης χωρῶν, Πέρσιος δὲ τὸν ποιητὴν Σώφρονα μιμήσασθαι θέλων τὸ Λυκόφρονος παρῆλθεν ἀμαυρόν. Τοῦρνος δὲ καῖ Ἰουβενάλιος καῖ Πετρώνιος, αὐτόθεν ταῖς λοιδορίαις ἐπεξελθόντες, τὸν σατυρικὸν νόμον παρέτρωσαν. καὶ ταῦτα μὲν περὶ τῆς ἀρχαίας κωμῳδίας τε καὶ τραγῳδίας.

90. See for instance Brink 1963, 157 ('We may feel that there is little point in that doctrine'), Rudd 1966, 89 ('The only satisfactory answer is to regard the lines as a piece of special pleading'), Gowers 2012, 149 ('[It] looks like a retrospective fiction that constructs a genealogy and moral authority for Lucilian satire').

91. Not, therefore, *tota nostra* (as at Quintilian 10.1.93, n. 58).

92. Nossis *Anthologia Palatina* 7.414, cf. *Suda* R 171 = 4.295 Adler; Cicero *Ad Atticum* 1.20.3.

since his Syracusan predecessor Epicharmus occasionally used them,[93] it may well be that he did too.

Similarly, it is perfectly possible that Lucilius cited him as a predecessor.[94] Lucilius came from Suessa Aurunca in northern Campania,[95] and the ubiquity of Greek phrases in the surviving fragments shows how familiar he was with the multilingual cultural ambience of his neighbours to the south. The evidence is terribly scrappy, but there is enough to suggest that at this time hellenised southern Italy may have had a taste for serio-comic popular philosophy,[96] and Rhinthon himself is described in our sources both as a comic poet and as a philosopher.[97] So the reference to 'Rhinthon, Skiras, Blaisos and the other Pythagoreans' as 'educators of no minor teachings in Magna Graecia' is not as strange as it first appears.[98]

Of course it is impossible to estimate how far Lucilius was influenced by their work, and we know enough about Lydus' handling of his sources (section 3.5 above) to be aware that he may have unhelpfully rephrased whatever Suetonius said on the subject. For all his faults, however, Lydus did not invent such reports out of nothing. As an imperial librarian Suetonius surely had access to the full text of Lucilius' works,[99] where he must have found something to justify his evident belief that both Rhinthon and Lucilius wrote 'hexameter comedy'.[100] We can't be confident that 'satyric comedy' was Suetonius' own phrase, but he does seem to have taken it as self-evident that Roman satire was a performance genre.

On Persius, for instance, he assumed a similarly direct influence from the theatre world of 'Magna Graecia', in this case the fifth-century

93. Epicharmus *PCG* F113.415 (= Homer *Iliad* 9.63), F121, F224.

94. *Pace* Kaibel 1899, 184 ('*Rhinthonicas fabulas nemo legit praeter grammaticos et lexicographos Alexandrinos*'); if Cicero knew his work, of course Lucilius could have known it too.

95. Juvenal 1.20, Ausonius *Epistulae* 11.9-10; it had been a Latin colony since 313 BC (Livy 9.28.7).

96. E.g. Blaisos of Capri, σπουδογελοίων ποιητής (Stephanus Byzantinus 357), and the Samnite Nysius, Stoic and σπουδαιοπάρῳδος (*Index Stoicorum Herculanensis* 75 Traversa).

97. Rhinthon *PCG* T1, F14: *Suda* R 171 = 4.295 Adler (Ῥίνθων, Ταραντῖνος κωμικός), Hesychius s.v. ἄσεκτος (παρὰ Ῥίνθονι Ταραντίνῳ φιλοσόφῳ).

98. Lydus *De magistratibus* 1.41: Ῥίνθωνα καὶ Σκίραν καὶ Βλαῖσον καὶ τοὺς ἄλλους τῶν τῶν Πυθαγορείων ἴσμεν οὐ μικρῶν διδαγμάτων ἐπὶ τῆς μεγάλης Ἑλλάδος γενέσθαι καθηγητάς. Cf. n. 31 for Epicharmus as a Pythagorean dramatist.

99. *Année Épigraphique* 1953, 73 (he was *a bybliothecis*).

100. Lydus *De magistratibus* 1.41: τὸν Ῥίνθωνα, ὃς ἐξαμέτροις ἔγραψε πρῶτος κωμῳδίαν· ἐξ οὗ πρῶτος λάβων τὰς ἀφορμὰς Λουκίλιος ὁ Ῥωμαῖος ἡρωικοῖς ἔπεσιν ἐκωμῴδησεν. Perhaps one of Lucilius' satires was a dialogue between the author and Rhinthon?

Syracusan dramatist Sophron, whose philosophical style had made him Plato's favourite reading-matter.[101] Even the comparison of Persius with Lycophron may come from the same ambience, if Simon Hornblower is right in suggesting that Lycophron's notoriously obscure *Alexandra* was a product of Greek south Italy in the early second century BC, and probably intended for performance.[102]

The modern orthodoxy that Roman satire was written solely to be read in books, not delivered to an audience, fails to account for the fact that ten of the forty poems in the Horace, Persius and Juvenal collections were composed in dramatic form.[103] Both Persius and Juvenal repeatedly mentioned the theatre games and popular audiences as a normal and regular part of their experience.[104] Horace did not, but as a favoured protégé of Maecenas he was the exception that proved the rule: his disdain for poets performing at the regular *ludi* is evidence for his own privileged position.[105] He did perform in public, but only at the grandest of occasions,[106] and his pride in that status should not be mistaken for the attitude of all Roman satirists. On the contrary, later poets prayed in vain for a Maecenas in their own time.[107]

Thanks to John Lydus, therefore, we can see how Suetonius understood Roman *satura* as a performance genre for a public audience as well as a literary genre for readers of books, and how he re-connected it with the Greek traditions—dramatic and philosophical—that Ennius, Lucilius and Varro had taken for granted. That is an important step forward, in two contrasting ways. On the one hand, it confirms Livy's usage of the word for a type of performance (section 3.1 above); on the other, it contradicts Livy's supposedly Greek-free historical context in the fourth century BC.[108]

101. See n. 86: for Plato see Duris *FGrH* 76 F72, Quintilian 1.10.17, Diogenes Laertius 3.18.

102. See n. 87, with Hornblower 2015, 39–49.

103. Horace *Satires* 2.1, 2.3, 2.4, 2.5, 2.7, 2.8; Persius 1, 3, 5; Juvenal 9. Of the remaining monologues, only nine were addressed to named individuals, presumably for specific private occasions: Horace *Satires* 1.1, 1.6; Persius 6; Juvenal 8 and 12-16.

104. Specific *ludi*: Persius 5.178; Juvenal 6.67-9, 6.250, 11.193-7, 14.262. Popular audience: Persius 1.15-17, 1.42; Juvenal 8.188-9, 11.196-7. Theatre: Persius 1.81-2; Juvenal 3.154, 3.172-3, 7.93, 10.213-14, 14.256-7, 14.324. Circus: Juvenal 3.223, 10.37, 10.80, 11.53, 11.197. Praetor in charge: Juvenal 6.380, 10.36, 11.195, 11.257.

105. See n. 3, with Wiseman 2015, 142–6.

106. The obvious example is the *ludi saeculares* of 17 BC (*CIL* 6.32323.149, Horace *Odes* 4.6 and *Carmen saeculare*); but see also *Odes* 3.6 and 3.14, with Wiseman 2022.

107. Martial 1.107, 8.55, 11.3; Juvenal 7.94-5.

108. And also Quintilian's formulation 'satire is completely our own' (10.1.93, n. 58).

Greek or not-Greek? That question involves another puzzle. Diomedes, who used Suetonius, called the genre '*satyra*', and derived it in the first instance from satyrs;[109] the same notion is presupposed by Suetonius' naming of Petronius, author of the *Satyrica*, among those who offended against the 'law' of the genre.[110] So the question must be properly addressed: what relevance could satyrs or satyr-play have to Roman *satura*?

4.5. *Satyrs*

To get anywhere near a possible answer we need to go back as far as the seventh century BC.

The famous kitharode Arion of Lesbos, who originated the choral dithyramb in honour of Dionysus, was the first to 'bring in satyrs speaking verse'.[111] He worked in Corinth under Periander (c. 627–587 BC), but also undertook a very profitable tour of Italy and Sicily.[112] The ruler of Rome at about that time was Lucumo ('Lucius Tarquinius'), son of the exiled Corinthian Demaratus and heir to the wealth that Demaratus had taken abroad at the time of Cypselus' coup in about 657 BC (section 1.2 above).[113] Lucumo had used that wealth to institute lavish games at a specially created festival site with a *hippodromos* (the Circus Maximus).[114]

109. See nn. 70–77. Diomedes' Latin spelling seems more significant than the use of σατυρικός in Lydus' Greek.

110. Lydus *De magistratibus* 1.41 (n. 89): Τοῦρνος δὲ καῖ Ἰουβενάλιος καῖ Πετρώνιος, αὐτόθεν ταῖς λοιδορίαις ἐπεξελθόντες, τὸν σατυρικὸν νόμον παρέτρωσαν. For the idea of a *lex operis* (Horace *Ars poetica* 135) applied to *satura*, see Horace *Satires* 2.1.1-2, Juvenal 6.635.

111. *Suda* A 3886 = 1.351 Adler: λέγεται . . . πρῶτος χορὸν στῆσαι καὶ διθύραμβον ᾆσαι καὶ ὀνομάσαι τὸ ᾀδόμενον ὑπὸ τοῦ χοροῦ, καὶ σατύρους εἰσενεγκεῖν ἔμμετρα λέγοντας.

112. Herodotus 1.24.1 (he earned χρήματα μεγάλα).

113. Demaratus: Cicero *De republica* 2.34 (*fortunis facile ciuitatis suae principem . . . fugisse cum magna pecunia dicitur*), *Tusculan Disputations* 5.109 (*fugit Tarquinios Corintho et ibi suas fortunas constituit*), Dionysius of Halicarnassus *Roman Antiquities* 3.46.3-5 (μεγάλα κέρδη περιβαλόμενος). Lucumo: Livy 1.34.1 (*uir impiger ac diuitiis potens*), 1.34.11 (*Romanis conspicuum eum nouitas diuitiaeque faciebant*); Zonaras 7.8 (πολλὰ πατρόθεν διαδεξάμενος). For the context see Wiseman 2024, 1–6.

114. Cicero *De republica* 2.36 (*primum ludos maximos, qui Romani dicti sunt, fecisse accepimus*), Livy 1.35.8-9 (*tum primum circo qui nunc maximus dicitur designatus locus est . . . spectauere furcis duodenos ab terra spectacula alta sustinentibus pedes*), Dionysius of Halicarnassus *Roman Antiquities* 3.68.1 (κατεσκευάσε δὲ καὶ τὸν μέγιστον τῶν ἱπποδρόμων . . . ποιήσας περὶ αὐτὸν καθέδρας . . . ἐπ' ἰκρίοις, δοκῶν ξυλίναις σκηναῖς ὑποκειμένων), Eutropius 1.6.1 (*circum Romae aedificauit, ludos magnos instituit qui ad nostram memoriam permanent*), *De uiris illustribus* 6.8 (*circum maximum aedificauit, ludos magnos instituit*). Cf. ps.Asconius 217 Stangl: *Romani ludi sub regibus instituti sunt magnique appellati, quod magnis impensibus dati.*

We don't know where in Italy Arion earned his prize-money, but Lucumo's newly-formed *polis* is an obvious possibility.[115]

Satyrs are first seen in a narrative context on Athenian black-figure pottery showing the return of Hephaestus to Olympus. The story featured on a painting in the temple of Dionysus Eleuthereus in Athens:

> The Greeks say that when Hephaestus was born [his mother] Hera threw him out; bearing a grudge against her, he sent as a gift a throne with invisible fetters, and when she sat down she was held fast. Hephaestus could not be persuaded by any of the other gods, but Dionysus, who was particularly trusted by Hephaestus, got him drunk and brought him back to heaven.[116]

The procession, with Hephaestus riding an ithyphallic mule and escorted by satyrs and nymphs, features among the scenes on the famous 'François Vase' (c. 570 BC) found in the Fonte Rotella necropolis at Clusium in Etruria.[117] Less well known but equally significant is the surviving fragment of another large black-figure *krater*, of similar date and painted with the same scene, from the archaic cult site of Volcanus in the *comitium* at Rome.[118] The choice of subject is unlikely to be accidental, particularly as the ruler of Rome about that time—'Servius Tullius', protégé of the Tarquins—was said to be a son of the fire-god.[119]

Sixty years or so later the Tarquins were expelled, and their ancestral wealth expropriated.[120] A combination of archaeological and textual

115. See Ammerman 1990 and Hopkins 2016, 27–34 for the creation of the site of the Roman Forum in the second half of the seventh century BC; an *agora* may be taken as defining a *polis*. Note that the earliest attested name from the site of Rome is a Greek one ('Kleiklos' or 'Ktektos'), scratched on a seventh-century Corinthian pot from the Esquiline cemetery: Musei Capitolini, inv. AC 12648; Solin 1983, Damiani and Parisi Presicce 2019, 329 (g125.48).

116. Pausanias 1.20.3: λέγεται δὲ καὶ τάδε ὑπὸ Ἑλλήνων, ὡς Ἥρα ῥίψαι γενόμενον Ἥφαιστον, ὁ δὲ οἱ μνησικακῶν πέμψαι δῶρον χρυσοῦν θρόνον ἀφανεῖς δεσμοὺς ἔχοντα, καὶ τὴν μὲν ἐπεί τε ἐκαθέζετο δεδέσθαι, θεῶν δὲ τῶν μὲν ἄλλων οὐδενὶ τὸν Ἥφαιστον ἐθέλειν πείσασθαι, Διόνυσος δὲ (μάλιστα γὰρ ἐς τοῦτον πιστὰ ἦν Ἡφαίστῳ) μεθύσας αὐτὸν ἐς οὐρανὸν ἤγαγε.

117. Florence, Museo archeologico nazionale, inv. 4209 (signed by Kleitias as painter and Ergotimos as potter); Bundrick 2019, 216–17. The same scene, with padded komast dancers instead of satyrs, had already featured on Corinthian pottery (Carpenter 2007, 44–6, Shaw 2014, 33–9); the story was soon dramatised in Epicharmus' Κωμασταί ἢ Ἥφαιστος (*Suda* H 481 = 2.585 Adler).

118. Antiquario del Foro, inv. 901; Coarelli 1983, 176–7 (cf. 161–9 for the identification of the *lapis niger* site as the *Volcanal*), Cristofani 1990, 56 (3.1.22) and tav. II.

119. Dionysius of Halicarnassus *Roman Antiquities* 4.2.3 (Hephaestus), Ovid *Fasti* 6.627 (Volcanus).

120. For the date (508–7 BC) see Polybius 3.22.2. The Tarquins tried in vain to recover their property: Livy 2.3.5-6 (*bona repetentes*), 2.4.3 (*reddenda bona*), 2.19.10 (*ob erepta bona*), 2.34.4 (*pro bonis Tarquiniorum*); Zevi 2014, 65–8.

evidence suggests that in the next twenty or thirty years it was spent on new temples, beautifully decorated with painted terracotta mouldings, and on ambitious annual festivals in honour of the new cults.[121] Various new buildings at this time, not only at Rome itself but in Latium and south Etruria too, featured antefixes decorated with satyr-faces (or masks) and satyrs dancing with nymphs, a fashion that appears elsewhere only in eastern Sicily (section 1.3 above).[122]

As we saw in the first chapter, this was when 'satyr-play' was first organised at the festival of Dionysus Elethereus at Athens,[123] and when an already existing tradition of Sicilian drama featured Epicharmus of Syracuse, 'the champion of Bacchus and the satyrs'.[124] At Rome, the cult of Liber (Dionysus) was joined with that of Ceres and Libera (Demeter and Kore) at an elaborate temple built in 493 BC at the starting-point of the *hippodromos*;[125] the expensive games founded at the same time took place each year at the *Liberalia* (17 March) and *Cerialia* (19 April).[126]

The next contemporary evidence comes in the fourth century BC, on the engraved bronze mirrors and caskets (*cistae*) produced at that time in Rome and Latium (section 1.4 above). Much of the iconography is Dionysiac, just as it is on fourth-century Italian red-figure pottery; in both media satyrs appear in very varied contexts, including mythological stories not obviously involving Dionysus,[127] and they are often represented as dancers or musicians,

121. See Hopkins 2016, 137–71 (the architectural 'continuity of splendor' after the Tarquins), Wiseman 2024, 11–14. Temples: e.g. Saturnus (501/498/497 BC), Mercurius (495), Ceres, Liber and Libera (493), Castor and Pollux (484). Festivals: see Dionysius of Halicarnassus *Roman Antiquities* 6.1.4 for Saturnus (φασὶ . . . δημοτελεῖς ἀναδειχθῆναι τῷ θεῷ καθ' ἕκαστον ἐνιαυτὸν ἑορτάς τε καὶ θυσίας); 6.10.1 and 6.17.2 for Ceres, Liber and Libera (θυσίας τε μεγάλας ἀπὸ πολλῶν ἐπιτελέσειν χρημάτων καὶ ἀγῶνας καταστήσεσθαι πολυτελεῖς, οὓς ἄξει ὁ Ῥωμαίων δῆμος ἀνὰ πᾶν ἔτος . . . ἀπὸ δὲ τῶν λαφύρων ἐξελόμενος τὰς δεκάτας ἀγῶνάς τε καὶ θυσίας τοῖς θεοῖς ἀπὸ τετταράκοντα ταλάντων ἐποίει).

122. Marconi 2006, 81–7, Shaw 2014, 71–3.

123. *Suda* Π 2230 = *TrGF* 4 T1 (supposedly introduced by Pratinas of Phlius in the 70th Olympiad, 499–6 BC); for the probable origins of satyr-drama, and the nature of Pratinas' innovation, see O'Sullivan and Collard 2013, 22–8 and 242–7, Shaw 2014, 28–55, Wright 2016, 14–17.

124. Shaw 2014, 56–77, cf. Csapo and Wilson 2020, 308–33; *Anthologia Palatina* 7.82 (Δωρίδος ἐκ Μούσης κεκορυθμένον ἀνέρα Βάκχῳ | καὶ σατύροις Σικελὸν τῇδ' Ἐπίχαρμον ἔχω), Aristotle *Poetics* 3, 5 (1448a32-4, 1449b5-7).

125. Dionysius of Halicarnassus *Roman Antiquities* 6.94.3 (date and site); Cicero *In Verrem* 2.4.108 (*pulcherrimum et magnificentissimum*), Vitruvius 3.3.5 (Etruscan style, terracotta decoration), Pliny *Natural History* 35.154 (archaic inscription naming terracotta artists Damophilos and Gorgasos), Cicero *Pro Balbo* 55 (*sacra . . . adsumpta de Graecia*, with Greek priestesses).

126. Dionysius of Halicarnassus *Roman Antiquities* 6.10.1, 6.17.2 (n. 121); Degrassi 1963, 425–6, 442–3.

127. For details see Wiseman 2008.86-124, esp. 92–6, figs 21–5.

as on figure 4. The magnificent 'Ficoroni *cista*', made by Novius Plautius in Rome, shows an Argonautic episode in the presence of Dionysus, Silenus and the satyrs. As we saw, that was a story taken from drama: Sophocles' satyr-play *Amykos*, and before that Epicharmus' play of the same name.[128]

Another signed piece, a mirror engraved by *Vibis Pilipus* (Vibius Philippus, a Latin speaker with a Greek name), showed the satyr Marsyas in a dance competition with 'little Pan' for an amphora wreathed in Bacchic ivy.[129] At the *comitium* in Rome there was a statue of Marsyas as the symbol of freedom, under the protection of Dionysus ('Liber *pater*');[130] no doubt he also featured at the god's games, the *Liberalia*, where freedom of speech was specifically celebrated.[131]

This material evidence from fifth- and fourth-century Rome makes it very hard to believe Livy's assertion that in 364 BC dramatic festivals were an unprecedented novelty.[132] Familiarity with satyrs ought to imply familiarity with the sort of performances in which satyrs appeared,[133] and the various festival games already provided frequent opportunities to stage them.[134] No doubt Livy had his own reasons for presenting the early Roman republic as innocent of any influence from Greece (section 3.7 above); fortunately, however, even from that ill-documented period there is enough contemporary evidence to prove him wrong.

4.6. Philosophers

One very unexpected feature of the iconography of the bronze *cistae* is the 'satyr philosopher', mature, serious, clothed in a mantle leaving one shoulder bare.[135] One such was Marsyas, symbol of Roman *libertas*, who was

128. Athenaeus 3.94e, 9.400b (Sophocles), scholiast on Apollonius Rhodius 2.98 (Epicharmus): section 1.4 above.

129. *ILLRP* 1201 (Rome, Villa Giulia), Wiseman 2008, 59, fig. 10; for *Paniskoi* in the context of nymphs and satyrs see Cicero *De natura deorum* 3.43.

130. Scholiasts on Horace *Satires* 1.6.116, Crawford 1974, 377–8, no. 363; cf. Servius on *Aeneid* 3.20 (*in tutela Liberi patris*) and 4.58 (*libertatis indicium*). Full discussion in Torelli 1982, 99–106, Coarelli 1985, 91–119: the statue probably dated from the late fourth century BC.

131. Naevius *ap.* Festus (Paulus) 103L: *libera lingua loquimur ludis Liberalibus.*

132. Livy 7.2.3 (section 3.1 above): *ludi quoque scaenici—noua res bellicoso populo, nam circi modo spectaculum fuerat.*

133. Not of course confined to the specific conventions of Athenian satyr-play: see Shaw 2014 for the many varieties of 'satyr drama'.

134. See n. 114 (Lucumo's *ludi Romani*) and n. 121 (games for Ceres and Liber); also ps. Asconius 217 Stangl on the *ludi plebeii*, introduced soon after the expulsion of the Tarquins.

135. Battaglia and Emiliozzi 1990, 240, 308: nos 72 and 96 (Rome, Villa Giulia inv. 51199 and 51197); in the former case he is playing pipes (Wiseman 2008, 91, fig. 20).

famous for his wisdom and self-control.[136] The Pythagoreans believed that self-control was a kind of harmony,[137] and the effect of Marsyas' musicianship (he was a virtuoso pipe-player) was described by Alcibiades in Plato's *Symposion*:

> I'm saying that Socrates is like Marsyas the satyr. . . . Marsyas used his instruments to charm people by the power of what came from his lips, and his melodies alone can cause anyone who plays them even today . . . whether it's a skilled musician or a mere flute-girl, to bring about enchantment and to mark out, thanks to their divine nature, those who long for the gods and their mysteries.[138]

As it happened, statues of Alcibiades and Pythagoras—'the bravest and the wisest of the Greeks'—shared the honorific space of the Comitium in Rome with that of Marsyas himself.[139]

These tantalising scraps of contemporary evidence suggest a cultural continuity from the time of Epicharmus of Syracuse two centuries earlier, a long-standing western-Greek tradition of comic and satyric performance and Pythagorean philosophy.[140] Livy was either unaware of that tradition or preferred to ignore it, but the *saturae* he reported as an innovation in 364 BC could easily have been a part of it. He described them as metrical texts written for performance accompanied by a pipe-player, and distinguished them from plays with a fictional plot (*argumentum*).[141] It's not hard to imagine them as monologues or cross-talk acts on topical subjects with appropriately varied musical accompaniment, and one obvious format would be discussion of contemporary *mores* with a philosopher—or even a philosophical satyr.

In Greek such a performance would be called σπουδογέλοιον, 'seriocomic'. It was a popular style in the Hellenistic world of the third century

136. Diodorus Siculus 3.58.3: Μαρσύαν τὸν Φρύγα, θαυμαζόμενον ἐπὶ συνέσει καὶ σωφροσύνῃ.

137. Plato *Republic* 4.430d-e and 431e-432a, with Guthrie 1962, 31.

138. Plato *Symposion* 215b-c: καὶ φημὶ αὖ ἐοικέναι αὐτὸν τῷ σατύρῳ τῷ Μαρσύᾳ . . . ὁ μέν γε δι' ὀργάνων ἐκήλει τοὺς ἀνθρώπους τῇ ἀπὸ τοῦ στόματος δυνάμει, καὶ ἔτι νυνὶ ὃς ἂν τὰ ἐκείνου αὐλῇ . . . τὰ οὖν ἐκείνου ἐάντε ἀγαθὸς αὐλητὴς ἐάντε φαύλη αὐλητρίς, μόνα κατέχεσθαι ποιεῖ καὶ δηλοῖ τοὺς τῶν θεῶν τε καὶ τελετῶν δεομένους διὰ τὸ θεῖα εἶναι.

139. Pliny *Natural History* 34.26, Plutarch *Numa* 8.10 (n. 33).

140. See nn. 31 (Epicharmus as Pythagorean), 32 (Epicharmus' knowledge of Rome) and 124 (Epicharmus as 'champion of Bacchus and the satyrs').

141. Livy 7.2.7-8 (section 3.1 above): *impletas modis saturas descripto iam ad tibicinum cantu motuque congruenti peragebant. Liuius . . . ab saturis ausus est primus argumento fabulam serere.*

BC, used for instance by the Cynic philosopher Menippus (later exploited for Varro's *saturae*) and by Blaisos of Capri, one of a school of Pythagorean playwrights in south Italy.[142] At Rome it was associated with satyrs, as we know from the eye-witness evidence of Fabius Pictor:[143] in the late third century BC the procession at the *ludi Romani* featured *choroi* of satyr-performers doing the Greek dance called *sikinnis*, who 'mocked and mimicked the serious movements, turning them into something laughable'.[144]

At this point we must return to Diomedes (section 4.3 above) and John Lydus (section 4.4 above), who each preserved something of what Suetonius had said about Roman satire. First, '*satura* was once the name given to a verse form that consisted of various smaller pieces of poetry, as written by Pacuvius and Ennius';[145] though not the same as a play with a plot, *saturae* were nevertheless composed by well-known playwrights. Second,

> we know that Rhinthon, Skiras, Blaisos and the other Pythagoreans were educators of no minor teachings in Magna Graecia, and especially Rhinthon, who was the first to write comedy in hexameters. Taking his start from him, the Roman Lucilius was the first to produce comedy in heroic verse.[146]

Rhinthon was active in the third century BC.[147] He and his colleagues were evidently following in the tradition of Epicharmus, who 'put the thoughts of the Pythagoreans in metre, and under the guise of foolery published the secret teachings of Pythagoras'.[148] At Rome a century later the tradition continued, with Ennius' impersonation of Epicharmus (no doubt in his *saturae*) and his self-presentation as Homer reborn via Pythagorean *metempsychosis*.[149]

142. Strabo 16.2.29 C759 (Menippus σπουδογέλοιος), section 4.1 above; Stephanus Byzantinus 357.1 (Βλαῖσος σπουδογελοίων ποιητὴς Καπριάτης), Lydus *De magistratibus* 1.41 (Pythagoreans), section 4.4 above.

143. Dionysius of Halicarnassus *Roman Antiquities* 7.71.1: πίστιν . . . ἐξ ὧν αὐτὸς ἔγνω παρεχόμενος.

144. Dionysius of Halicarnassus *Roman Antiquities* 7.72.10 = Fabius Pictor *FRHist* 1 F15: οἱ τῶν σατυριστῶν ἐπόμπευον χοροὶ τὴν Ἑλληνικὴν εἰδοφοροῦντες σίκιννιν . . . οὗτοι κατέσκωπτόν τε καὶ κατεμιμοῦντο τὰς σπουδαίας κινήσεις ἐπὶ τὰ γελοιότερα μεταφέροντες.

145. Diomedes *De poematibus* 6.1 = *Grammatici Latini* 1.485 Keil (Leo's text): *olim carmen ex uariis poematibus constabat satura uocabatur, quale scripserunt Pacuuius et Ennius*. See section 4.1 above for Ennius' *saturae*; those of Pacuvius are mentioned by Porphyrio on Horace *Satires* 1.10.46.

146. Lydus *De magistratibus* 1.41 (n. 89).

147. *Suda* R 171 = 4.295 Adler: γέγονεν ἐπὶ τοῦ πρώτου Πτολεμαίου.

148. Iamblichus *De uita Pythagorica* 35, 266 (n. 31).

149. Ennius frr. 35-41 Blänsdorf, Skutsch 1985, 147–53 (nn. 24 and 29).

Even allowing for Lydus' ability to misrepresent his sources (section 3.5 above), it seems clear that Suetonius had surprisingly good information about the Greek antecedents of Roman *satura*. He evidently took it for granted that *satura* was a performance genre composed by playwrights, involving music and metre as well as prose, with a varied content exploiting the ethical teaching of philosophers.

What, if anything, he said about satyrs is unfortunately beyond conjecture. The spellings *satyra* and *satyrici* used by the intermediary sources may not go back to Suetonius himself, and his inclusion of Petronius' *Satyrica* in the genre of 'satire' could be a mere coincidence. That satyrs were involved in early *satura* is certainly a possibility, but the only evidence for it is circumstantial. In any case, such involvement would have ended in 186 BC, when '*Bacchanalia*' were declared to be an alien import and officially banned.[150]

Fortunately there is no doubt about the assertion that Lucilius' type of *satura* was inspired by Rhinthon and his colleagues, who wrote for stage performance with a philosophical agenda. Indeed, Suetonius evidently went on to say that Greek dramatic poets influenced the whole subsequent history of Roman satire, right down to Persius.[151]

4.7. The bigger picture

We have been able to recover enough of Suetonius' lost treatment of Roman satire to see that it contradicted both Livy and Quintilian. Despite what Livy said, the Romans of the early republic were not unfamiliar with stage performances (*ludi scaenici*), and despite what Quintilian said, satire was not 'completely our own', but imitated Greek precedents.[152] We are also in a position to judge that his view is more likely than theirs to be accurate, since the archaeological evidence we have used along the way (material available to us but not to them) implies Roman familiarity with Greek culture, particularly with Dionysus, god of drama, and his followers, the satyrs.

By taking Suetonius' view seriously we can dispense with the modern dogma that Roman satire was a non-Greek and non-dramatic genre created by Lucilius and consisting of four authors only.[153] What it should

150. Livy 39.8-19, esp. 15.3 (*prauis et externis religionibus*), 16.8 (*magistratibus negotium est datum uti sacra externa fieri uetarent*); Pailler 1988.

151. Lydus *De magistratibus* 1.41: Eupolis, Cratinus, Sophron, Lycophron (nn. 85–7).

152. *Contra* Livy 7.2.3 (n. 141), Quintilian 10.1.93 (n. 58).

153. See nn. 4–6.

lead us to infer instead is a continuous serio-comic performance tradition in both Greek and Latin, one that might well date back to the archaic world of the Roman festivals founded under the Tarquins and after their expulsion (section 1.2 above).

The ongoing influence of Pythagorean philosophy can be traced from Epicharmus in the early fifth century BC, through Rhinthon in the mid-third, to Ennius at the beginning of the second; and though Pythagoras then fell under official disapproval, as shown by the burning of Numa's books in 181 BC,[154] fifty years later the greatest of the Roman satirists evidently still found him of interest.[155] Fifty years later again, the philosopher of choice was the Cynic Menippus, a constant presence in Varro's voluminous satiric output.[156] But why should a stage-performance genre be so concerned with philosophical teachings?

Part of the answer is that philosophers were always good targets for mockery, as in Aristophanes' treatment of Socrates.[157] We know that Lucilius made fun of the Stoics,[158] and in one of Varro's satires the sayings of philosophers were likened to a sick man's fevered dreams.[159] No less important, perhaps, was the histrionic style of the philosophers themselves, particularly the Cynics. Here is a description of how one Cynic philosopher went about his business:

> He went about in the guise of a Fury, saying that he had come from Hades to look out for sins being committed, and was going to return and report them to the powers down below. This was his costume: a grey tunic reaching to his feet, a crimson girdle round it, an Arcadian hat on his head embroidered with the twelve signs of the Zodiac, tragic boots, a very long beard and an ash staff in his hand.[160]

154. Cassius Hemina *FRHist* 5 F35 = Pliny *Natural History* 13.86 (*in his libris scripta erant philosophiae Pythagoricae*), Livy 40.29.12 (*legi seruarique non oportere*); Volk 2015, 41–2. See section 3.6 above for the climate of hostility to Greek culture.

155. As implied by Lucilius 'taking his start' from Rhinthon (Lydus *De magistratibus* 1.41), whatever Suetonius/Lydus may have meant by that.

156. See n. 12; Wiseman 2009, 137–43.

157. Very sensibly discussed by Dover 1968, lii–lvi.

158. Porphyrio on Horace *Satires* 1.3.124: *Lucilius . . . per derisum Stoicorum dicit.*

159. Varro *Menippean Satires* 122 = Nonius 79L: *postremo nemo aegrotus quicquam somniat | tam infandum quod non aliquis dicat philosophus.*

160. Hippobotus *ap.* Diogenes Laertius 6.9.102 (of Menedemus) = *Suda* Φ 180 (of Menippus): Ἐρινύος ἀναλαβὼν σχῆμα περιῄει, λέγων ἐπίσκοπος ἀφῖχθαι ἐξ ᾅδου τῶν ἁμαρτονομένων, ὅπως πάλιν κατιὼν ταῦτα ἀπαγγέλλοι τοῖς ἐκεῖ δαίμοσιν. ἦν δὲ αὐτῷ ἡ ἐσθὴς αὕτη· χιτὼν φαιὸς ποδήρης, περὶ αὐτῷ ζώνη φοινικῆ, πῖλος Ἀρκαδικὸς ἐπὶ τῆς κεφαλῆς ἔχων ἐνυφασμένα τὰ δώδεκα στοιχεῖα, ἐμβάται τραγικοί, πώγων ὑπερμεγέθης, ῥάβδος ἐν τῇ χειρὶ μειλίνη.

Such characters would provide ready-made entertainment for a theatre audience, and one of them evidently appeared in Varro's Menippean satire *Ulysses and a Half*: 'here in his tragic boots, explaining the ways and the sound of the star-bearing heaven with hollow bronze.'[161]

No such outlandish figure ever took part in the 'conversations' Horace wrote for private performance to Maecenas and his guests.[162] In his evident determination to make *satura* respectable, Horace rejected the polymetric style of Ennius and Varro (section 4.1 above), 'full of varied items' as the etymology of the name suggests,[163] and took as his model just one aspect (the hexameter) of just one of his predecessors (Lucilius), with far-reaching consequences for literary history.

Horace also made a point of avoiding outspoken political comment, unlike Lucilius and in deliberate contrast with the norms of the recent past:

> On the same page Lucilius is praised because he scoured the city with plenty of salty wit. Granted—but I wouldn't give him the rest of it, because in that case I'd have to admire the mimes of Laberius as fine poems too. So it's not enough just to get the audience open-mouthed with laughter; and yet there's a virtue in that too. . . . Humour is often better and more effective than ferocity in cutting through great affairs. It's in this way that those great men whose writings were Old Comedy succeeded, it's for this that they should be imitated. But handsome Hermogenes has never read them, nor has that ape who's trained to sing nothing but Calvus and Catullus.[164]

The subtly elusive sequence of ideas enables Horace to have it both ways: yes, satire was descended, via Lucilius, from Aristophanic comedy, but that didn't mean it should imitate the slanderous treatment of contemporaries for which Aristophanic comedy was famous.[165]

161. Varro *Menippean Satires* 465 = Nonius 465L: *uias stelligeras aetheris explicans aere cauo sonitum hic in cothurnis.*

162. *Sermones*: Horace *Satires* 1.4.41-2, *Epistles* 1.4.1, 2.1.250. Private performance: Horace *Satires* 1.4.73 (*non recito cuiquam nisi amicis*), 1.6.23, 1.10.37-9.

163. Diomedes *De poematibus* 6.2 = *Grammatici Latini* 1.485-6 Keil (nn. 72–8).

164. Horace *Satires* 1.10.3-8, 14–19: *at idem, quod sale multo | urbem defricuit, charta laudatur eadem. | nec tamen hoc tribuens dederim quoque cetera; nam sic | et Laberi mimos ut pulchra poemata mirer. | ergo non satis est risu diducere rictum | auditoris; et est quaedam tamen hic quoque uirtus | . . . ridiculum acri | fortius et melius magnas plerumque secat res. | illi scripta quibus comoedia prisca uiris est | hoc stabant, hoc sunt imitandi: quos neque pulcher | Hermogenes umquam legit neque simius iste | nil praeter Caluum et doctus cantare Catullum.*

165. Cf. Cicero *De republica* 4.11 = Augustine *City of God* 2.9.3, approving of attacks on Cleon, Cleophon and Hyperbolus (*populares improbos*) but not on Pericles.

Who *was* imitating it? Leaving aside Hermogenes and the ape, topical allusions we can no longer catch,[166] the authors mentioned are Laberius, Calvus and Catullus. The last two were well known for political invective in epigrammatic form,[167] but they didn't write *satura*. Their contemporary Decimus Laberius did write for the stage, but his genre was the *mimus*.[168] What all three had in common was the social standing necessary for uninhibited comment on prominent contemporaries: Calvus was of senatorial rank, Laberius and Catullus equestrian.[169]

Cicero knew how satirical Laberius could be. Early in 53 BC he wrote to the young lawyer Trebatius, who was on Caesar's staff in Gaul:

> If you come back soon there won't be any talk, but if you're away too long with no result I'm terrified not just of Laberius but of our friend Valerius too. A legal expert from Britain would be a wonderful character to bring on stage![170]

'Our friend Valerius' was very probably Catullus, who seems to have turned to writing *mimus*-drama in the last few years of his short life.[171] He wrote a play called *Phormio*, the one line of which that happens to survive—'What are you doing here with your tragic verses and trailing robe?'—attests his use of stage conversations with those picturesquely comic intellectuals.[172]

For his redefinition of *satura* Horace took from Lucilius what he could use—hexameter format, autobiographical content—while avoiding the high-profile personal criticism Lucilius was most famous for. As examples

166. M. Tigellius Hermogenes was a famous singer, now dead (Horace *Satires* 1.2.1-3, with Porphyrio *ad loc.*), but the Tigellius of this satire (1.10.90-1) was evidently a teacher of literature.

167. Calvus: Suetonius *Diuus Iulius* 49.1 and 73, Seneca *Controuersiae* 7.4.7. Catullus: Quintilian 10.11.96, Tacitus *Annals* 4.34.5, Suetonius *Diuus Iulius* 73, Pliny *Natural History* 36.48, Porphyrio on Horace *Odes* 1.16.24; Wiseman 2023, 30–35.

168. Jerome *Chronica* Ol. 184.2 (*mimorum scriptor*), cf. Suetonius *Diuus Iulius* 39.2, Macrobius *Saturnalia* 2.6.6, 2.7.2; full details in Panayotakis 2010.

169. For Laberius see Macrobius *Saturnalia* 2.7.2 (*asperae libertatis equitem Romanum*), with examples of his *libertas* at 2.6.6 and Seneca *Controuersiae* 7.3.10 (put-downs of Clodius and Cicero respectively).

170. Cicero *Ad familiares* 7.11.2: *denique si cito te rettuleris, sermo nullus erit; si diutius frustra afueris, non modo Laberium sed etiam sodalem nostrum Valerium pertimesco. mira enim persona induci potest Britannici iureconsulti.*

171. Catullus as 'Valerius': Varro *De lingua Latina* 7.50, Pollio *ap.* Charisius 124B (Panayotakis 2010, 331). Catullus as *mimographus*: Martial 5.30.3-4, 12.83.3-4, Juvenal 8.185-8, 13.110-11, Tertullian *Aduersus Valentinianos* 14; for the full argument see Wiseman 2023, 39–46.

172. Priscian 6.7 = *Grammatici Latini* 2.200 Keil (Bonaria 1965, 79): *Valerius in Phormione: quid hic cum tragicis uersis et syrma facis?* Cf. n. 161 (Varro).

of those who did not avoid it he named three authors who did not write *satura* anyway; two of them, however, wrote for the stage. Paradoxical at first sight, his procedure only makes sense if he and his readers took it for granted that *satura* too was a public-performance genre.

Livy defined *satura* as 'a written song accompanied by a pipe-player and with appropriate movement'; dancing to a pipe-player's tune was also what mime-actors did.[173] Livy distinguished *satura* from 'a play with a plot'; Cicero applied exactly the same distinction to mime-performances.[174] Diomedes, probably using Suetonius, defined *satura* as 'consisting of various smaller pieces of poetry', and therefore named from 'a type of stuffing filled with many ingredients';[175] a similar variety of content, ranging from vulgar buffoonery to ethical exhortation,[176] accounts for the notorious impossibility of defining the nature of 'mime' as a single concept.[177] Another common element was reference to philosophers, including Pythagoreans and Cynics,[178] a shared interest that went back to Plato's favourite reading, the mimes of Sophron from fifth-century BC Syracuse.[179] For mime too we need to bear in mind the ongoing, multifarious tradition of performance at stage festivals all over the Greek world (including Rome) from the archaic period onwards.

Of course there were specific differences between the two genres: in mime, the physical clowning and the glamorous showgirls;[180] in *satura*,

173. Livy 7.2.7 (*impletas modis saturas descripto iam ad tibicinum cantu motuque congruenti*); Aulus Gellius 1.11.12 (*ut planipedi saltanti . . . tibicen incineret*), cf. Ovid *Ars amatoria* 1.501-2, Porphyrio on Horace *Satires* 2.6.72.

174. Livy 7.2.8 (*Liuius . . . qui ab saturis ausus est primus argumento fabulam serere*); Cicero *Pro Caelio* 64–5 (*quam est sine argumento . . . mimi ergo iam exitus, non fabulae*).

175. Diomedes *De poematibus* 6.1, 6.2 = *Grammatici Latini* 1.485-6 Keil (*carmen quod ex uariis poematibus constabat satura uocabatur . . . a quodam genere farciminis, quod multis rebus refertum saturam dicit Varro uocitatum*). The plays of Laberius and Publilius are described as *poemata* by both Cicero (*Ad familiares* 12.18.2) and Horace (*Satires* 1.10.6).

176. See respectively Cicero *De oratore* 2.242, 251; Seneca *Epistles* 8.8-9, *De tranquillitate animi* 11.8.

177. For detailed treatment see Panayotakis 2010, 1–32 (esp. 10–11 nn. 19–20 on the wide range of attested subjects).

178. Aulus Gellius 10.17.4 (*uersus Laberiani sunt: Democritus Abderites physicus philosophus*), Tertullian *Apologeticus* 48.1 (*ut ait Laberius de sententia Pythagorae*), Nonius 312L (*Laberius Compitalibus: sequere <me> in latrinum, ut aliquid gustes ex Cynica haeresi*), Priscian 6.7 = *Grammatici Latini* 2.199 Keil (*Laberius in Cancro: nec Pythagoream dogmam doctus*). Cf. nn. 160–65.

179. Duris *FGrH* 76 F72 (Athenaeus 11.504b), Diogenes Laertius 3.18. For Roman interest in Sophron cf. Statius *Siluae* 5.3.156-8, Lydus *De magistratibus* 1.41 (n. 86).

180. For the latter, see Wiseman 2008, 175–86 and 2023, 103–41 (discussing their roles in historical and mythological scenarios).

the author as the protagonist conducting the conversations,[181] and perhaps acting as master of ceremonies for the variety show. But there was enough common ground of subject-matter to make it natural for Horace to use mime as the counter-example to his tidied-up version of satire. He wasn't going to write like Laberius and Catullus, just as he wasn't going to write like Varro and Ennius (section 4.1 above).

Horace presented himself as unwilling to compose for the public stage,[182] but that was because his audience was the company at Maecenas' house. The inference that Roman satire was not meant for performance at all is a modern preconception. On the contrary, thanks to Diomedes and John Lydus, who had read Suetonius' well-informed treatment of the subject, we can be certain that *satura* was always for performance, a conspicuous part of the lost history of Roman theatre.

181. Easily detectable in the fragments: e.g. Ennius *ap.* Nonius 48L (*Enni poeta, salue*), Lucilius *ap.* Nonius 181L (*Nunc, Gai, quoniam incilans nos laedis uicissim*), Varro *ap.* Nonius 770L (*Erras, Marce, accusare nos*).

182. Horace *Satires* 1.10.37-9, *Epistles* 1.19.41-2 (n. 3).

CHAPTER FIVE

Religion, Ideology and Theatre

THE FESTIVAL OF ANNA PERENNA

ANNA PERENNA was a minor divinity, and the 'mimographer' Decimus Laberius wrote a play about her; her annual festival was on the Ides of March, a date made infamous by the murder of Caesar in 44 BC; some of her various stories were told in Ovid's *Fasti*, and one of them was re-told in Silius Italicus' *Punica*; her cult-site and its sacred spring, with inscriptions honouring victors in performance competitions, was discovered in 1999. This chapter was first composed, at the editors' invitation, for a multi-author volume that aimed 'to highlight the importance of Anna Perenna, the fluidity of her identity, and the intricacies of her various manifestations in text and material culture'.[1]

Intended as a historical overview, it began with a warning about the sheer volume of scholarship accumulated by the separate intellectual traditions—literary, historical, archaeological—that claim to offer an understanding of the ancient world. Literary scholars concentrate on the great classic texts, archaeologists on the material remains revealed by excavation; when they try to access each other's insights, neither group can possibly master all the scholarly literature in the other's field, or even always judge what counts as a good or bad argument in an unfamiliar intellectual environment.

That makes it all the more necessary to concentrate attention on the primary evidence—the texts and artefacts that happen to have survived to our own time—on which all the traditions, in their different ways, ultimately depend. 'Above all', said Erasmus, 'we must hasten to

1. McIntyre and McCallum 2019, x.

the sources'—and his phrase *ad fontes* is particularly appropriate in the case of Anna Perenna, at whose sacred spring altars were dedicated *gratis fontibus.*[2]

5.1. Anna and Peranna

Our best source for the annual festivals of the Roman republic is the fragmentary calendar, discovered in 1915, that was painted on the walls of a room in a Roman villa at Antium (modern Anzio) at some time between 84 and 46 BC.[3] Known nowadays as the *fasti Antiates maiores*, the calendar includes annotations for fifty-one of the days of the year, almost all of them naming the deity or deities to whom cult was due on that day. For the Ides of March the annotation reads *ANN(ae)* | *PERENNAE*, on two separate lines. Since the calendar lists multiple cult recipients in asyndeton (see for instance the annotation for 8 December, *TIBERINO* | *GAIAE*),[4] it is not clear whether the day was the festival of a single deity, Anna Perenna, or of two, Anna and Perenna.

The question matters because a contemporary source names Anna and Peranna (*sic*) as separate entities:

> I call on you, Anna and Peranna, and you, Panda, Pales, Nerienes and Minerva, Fortuna and Ceres.[5]

The quotation is from *Fighting Shadows: On Nonsense*, one of the 150 'Menippean satires' composed by Varro probably in the 70s and 60s BC (section 4.1 above). Why the speaker should invoke such a strange

2. *Année Épigraphique* 2003, 251, 7–8; cf. Erasmus *De ratione studii ac legendi interpretandique auctores* (Paris 1511), in Waszink 1971, 120: *in primis ad fontes ipsos properandum.*

3. *ILLRP* 9 = Degrassi 1963, 1–28. The *terminus post quem* is the last date on the consular list that accompanied the calendar; the *terminus ante quem* is Caesar's calendar reform.

4. Gaia was evidently Gaia Taracia or Fufetia, reported in *annales antiqui* as a Vestal Virgin who was honoured by the Roman People for bequeathing the Campus Martius to them in her will: see Pliny *Natural History* 34.25, Aulus Gellius 7.7.1 (at Plutarch *Publicola* 8.4 she is named Tarquinia). Not to be confused with Gaia Caecilia, who was identified with queen Tanaquil (Pliny *Natural History* 8.194, Festus 85L, cf. Plutarch *Roman Questions* 30).

5. Varro *Menippean Satires* fr. 506 Astbury: *te Anna ac Peranna, Panda, te calo, Pales,* | *Nerienes <et> Minerua, Fortuna ac Ceres,* cited from Σκιαμαχία περὶ τύφου by Aulus Gellius 13.23.4, who was interested in the vocative *Nerienes* (instead of *Nerio*). Cicero makes Varro describe his Menippean satires as an early work (Cicero *Academica* 1.8: *in illis ueteribus nostris*).

collection of major and minor deities is, alas, unknown, but we do at least know something about the first two names:

> In the same month [March] people go to Anna Perenna to sacrifice both publicly and privately, that they may prosperously *annare* and *perannare*.[6]

The first of the two verbs is unparalleled, but must mean something like 'pass the year'; the second is glossed by the *Oxford Latin Dictionary* as 'to continue for a long time, endure'. They were evidently not synonyms, and therefore Anna and Peranna could have been two separate deities in charge of two separate functions. For Macrobius, of course, writing long after Ovid and Silius Italicus created their narratives about her, Anna Perenna was a single entity. But that was not necessarily the case in the late republic.

The naming of specialist divinities with very particular functions was the responsibility of the Roman *pontifices*. Servius' commentary on Virgil explains:

> As for [Virgil] saying 'those [gods] whose work it is to protect the fields', these names of divine powers are found in the *indigitamenta*—that is, in the books of the *pontifices* that contain the names of the gods and the reasons for their names. Varro also states them. For as we said earlier, it is well known that divine powers are named after their functions, as for example the god Occator from *occatio* (harrowing), Sarritor from *sarritio* (hoeing), Sterculinius from *stercoratio* (manuring), Sator from *satio* (sowing).[7]

The reference to Varro is evidently to his *Divine Antiquities*, which were written precisely to help his fellow-citizens understand which deities to worship, and why:

> Not merely can a man not live well, [Varro] says, but he cannot live at all if he is unaware of who is a craftsman, or a baker, or a plasterer,

6. Macrobius *Saturnalia* 1.12.6 (on March as the original first month of the Roman year): *eodem quoque mense et publice et priuatim ad Annam Perennam sacrificatum itur, ut annare perannareque commode liceat.* Some MSS read *perennareque*, but I think *perannareque* is preferable as the *lectio difficilior*.

7. Servius on Virgil *Georgics* 1.21: *quod autem dicit 'studium quibus arua tueri', nomina haec numinum in indigitamentis inueniuntur, id est in libris pontificalibus, qui et nomina deorum et rationes ipsorum nominum continent, quae etiam Varro dicit. nam, ut supra diximus, nomina numinibus ex officiis constat inposita, uerbi causa ut ab occatione deus Occator dicatur, a sarritione Sarritor, a stercoratione Sterculinius, a satione Sator.*

> or whom to go to to obtain something he needs, or whom to call on to assist or guide or teach you. He maintains that similarly no-one doubts that knowledge of the gods is useful only if you know the power, skill, and competence which individual gods possess in their particular spheres.[8]

In book 14 of the *Divine Antiquities* Varro discussed a long sequence of such specialist deities under the heading *di certi*—presumably gods who were 'certain' because their names and functions were guaranteed by inclusion in the pontifical books.[9] We don't know whether Anna and Peranna were on his list, but Mena (from *mensis*) certainly was, as the month-goddess who looked after menstruation.[10]

These one-purpose deities were seized on by Christian polemicists eager to ridicule pagan beliefs, above all by Augustine in the *City of God*, who had a great admiration for Varro and a detailed knowledge of his works.[11] It was probably from Varro that he took his metaphor of 'plebeian gods' to distinguish the countless specialist deities from the great Olympians; the latter were dealt with in book 16 of the *Divine Antiquities* under the heading of *di praecipui atque selecti*.[12] Certainly the divine hierarchy reflected the social structure of Varro's own time:

> We can see that the *di selecti* themselves are equally involved in these minute functions that are minutely allotted to the multiple gods, just like the Senate with the *plebs*.[13]

8. Varro *Antiquitates diuinae* fr. 3 Cardauns (Augustine *City of God* 4.22.1, trans. P. G. Walsh): *dicens non modo bene uiuere sed uiuere omnino neminem posse, si ignoret quisnam sit faber, quis pistor, quis tector, a quo quid utensile petere possit, quem adiutorem adsumere, quem ducem, quem doctorem; eo modo nulli dubium esse asserens ita esse utilem cognitionem deorum, si sciatur quam quisque deus uim et facultatem ac potestatem cuiusque rei habeat.*

9. Augustine *City of God* 6.3.4 = Varro *Antiquitates diuinae* fr. 4 Cardauns (cf. frr. 87-203 Cardauns for the surviving items of his list).

10. Augustine *City of God* 7.2.3, 7.3.1 = Varro *Antiquitates diuinae* fr. 95 Cardauns.

11. See for instance Augustine *City of God* 3.4.1 (*uir doctissimus*), 3.17.22 (*magna peritia Varronis*), 4.1.3 (*uir doctissimus et grauissimae auctoritatis*), 4.31.3 (*auctor acutissimus et doctissimus*); 6.2-9 *passim* for use of the *Divine Antiquities*, 7.9.5 and 7.34.2 for use of *De cultu deorum*, 18.2-23 *passim* for use of *De gente populi Romani*.

12. Augustine *City of God* 4.11.3 (*in illa turba quasi plebeiorum deorum*), 6.1.7 (*ex illa turba uel quasi plebeiorum uel quasi procerum deorum*), 7.2.1 (*illam quasi plebeiam numinum multitudinem minutis opusculis deputatam*); cf. 7.3.1 on Vitumnus and Sentinus, each described as *obscurus et ignobilis*. For the *di praecipui atque selecti* see Varro *Antiquitates diuinae* frr. 4 and 229 Cardauns (Augustine *City of God* 6.3.4, 7.2.1).

13. Augustine *City of God* 7.3.7: *in his minutis operibus, quae minutatim diis pluribus distributa sunt, etiam ipsos selectos uideamus tamquam senatum cum plebe pariter operari.*

Since Varro used the term *ignobilis* to describe the humbler deities,[14] we may reasonably infer that he thought of the Olympian gods as the divine *nobilitas*.

Varro's *Divine Antiquities* were dedicated to Julius Caesar as *pontifex maximus*.[15] So too was Granius Flaccus' *De indigitamentis*, which also dealt with the deities named in the books of the *pontifices*.[16] At about the same time, a work in at least three volumes *On the Names of the Gods* was written by a Cornificius who may have served under Caesar as quaestor in 48 BC.[17] It is worth asking why the subject should have been so popular at just this time.

5.2. *The People's* pontifex

At the beginning of the republic, oppressed by the domination of the rich and powerful,[18] the plebeians left Rome *en masse* and occupied the Mons Sacer; this 'secession' was only ended with the creation of plebeian tribunes to protect the ordinary citizen against exploitation and the abuse of power. For centuries thereafter the republic managed its political differences without violence, but in 133 BC the tribune Tiberius Gracchus was murdered at a public assembly by a group of senators and their attendants, and no-one was ever prosecuted for the crime. From that moment on the republic was again 'split into two parts', as Cicero put it,[19] and the use of violence became commonplace.[20] When the inevitable civil war came, the 'cause of the *nobilitas*' prevailed;[21] Sulla drastically reduced the tribunes' powers, effectively reversing the outcome of the secession.

14. Varro *Antiquities diuinae* fr. 2b Cardauns (Augustine *City of God* 7.3.8).

15. Lactantius *Institutiones* 1.6.7, Augustine *City of God* 7.35.2.

16. Censorinus *De die natali* 3.2 (on Genius and Lar), Arnobius 3.8 (on the *di nouensiles*); cf. Macrobius *Saturnalia* 1.18.4 (on Apollo and Liber).

17. Priscian *Institutiones* 6.73 (*Grammatici Latini* 2.257 Keil), Macrobius *Saturnalia* 1.9.11, 1.17.62; cf. [Caesar] *De bello Alexandrino* 42–3 (Q. Cornificius, Caesar's *quaestor pro praetore* in Illyricum), Cicero *Ad familiares* 12.17.3 (Q. Cornificius' *summum ingenium* and *studia optima*).

18. Cicero *Pro Cornelio I* fr. 48 Crawford = Asconius 76C (*propter nimiam dominationem potentium*), Sallust *Histories* 1.10.2 Ramsey (*iniuriae ualidiorum*); cf. Livy 2.23.1-8 for an example.

19. Cicero *De republica* 1.31: *mors Tiberii Gracchi et iam ante tota illius ratio tribunatus diuisit populum in duas partes*.

20. Velleius Paterculus 2.3.2-3 (*hoc initium in urbe Roma ciuilis sanguinis gladiorumque impunitatis fuit*); Appian *Civil Wars* 1.1.1, 1.2.4-5; cf. Dionysius of Halicarnassus *Roman Antiquities* 2.11.2-3, who dates the turning point a decade later.

21. Cicero *Pro Roscio Amerino* 135, 138 (*causa nobilitatis*), cf. 142 (*uictoria nobilium*).

The rich and powerful now called themselves 'aristocrats' (*optimates*, translating the Greek *aristoi*), and their opponents on behalf of the Roman People (*populares*) were patronisingly described as 'those who wanted their words and deeds to be welcome to the multitude'.[22] The historian Sallust, in his powerful contemporary analysis of the corruption of the republic, used different terms to describe the two sides: the conflict was between an oligarchy ('the powerful few'), sometimes called the *nobilitas*, and the *plebs* or *populus* itself.[23] Our best evidence for the views of the *populares*, a necessary counterweight to Cicero's optimate sympathies, comes from the speeches Sallust gives to their spokesmen: the tribune C. Memmius in 111 BC, the consul M. Lepidus in 78, the tribune Licinius Macer in 73, and the centurion C. Manlius in 63. All four of them refer back to the ancient secession of the *plebs* as an admirable precedent.[24]

As a young man, Caesar had taken part in the agitation for the restoration of the tribunes' powers,[25] which eventually happened in 70 BC. Seven years later, at the time of his election as *pontifex maximus*, the consul at a Senate meeting described him as 'one who has taken what is called the *popularis* line in public life', and the election itself was a demonstration of the People's will.[26] Why it mattered to them becomes clear in our sources for Numa's original creation of the pontificate:

> The *pontifex maximus* had the duty of expounding and interpreting the divine will, or rather of directing sacred rites . . . as well as teaching whatever was requisite for the worship or propitiation of the gods.[27]

22. Cicero *Pro Sestio* 96: *qui ea quae faciebant quaeque dicebant multitudini iucunda uolebant esse.*

23. Those opposing terms appear in various combinations at Sallust *Catiline* 39.1, *Jugurtha* 5.1, 27.1, 30.3, 31.2, 31.20, 40.3-5, 41.5-7, 42.1, *Histories* 3.15.27 Ramsey. For the oligarchy (*pauci potentes, paucorum potentia*), see *Catiline* 20.7, 58.11, *Jugurtha* 3.4, 31.19, *Histories* 1.12, 3.15.6 Ramsey; also Caesar *De bello ciuili* 1.22.5 (*populum Romanum factione paucorum oppressum*), Hirtius *De bello Gallico* 8.50.2 (*contra factionem et potentiam paucorum*).

24. Sallust *Jugurtha* 31.6 and 17 (Memmius), *Histories* 1.49.23 Ramsey (Lepidus), 3.15.1 and 15 Ramsey (Macer), *Catiline* 33.3 (Manlius).

25. Suetonius *Diuus Iulius* 5, cf. 11 on Caesar in the mid-60s (*conciliato populi fauore . . . aduersante optimatium factione*).

26. Cicero *In Catilinam* 4.9 (*is in re publica uiam quae popularis habetur secutus est*); Dio Cassius 37.37.2 on the election (ἐν τῷ πλήθει τὴν ἐλπίδα αὐτῆς . . . λάβων).

27. Plutarch *Numa* 9.4 (trans. Bernadotte Perrin): ὁ δὲ μέγιστος τῶν ποντιφίκων οἷον ἐξηγητοῦ καὶ προφήτου, μᾶλλον δὲ ἱεροφάντου τάξιν εἴληχεν . . . καὶ διδάσκων ὅτου τις δέοιτο πρὸς θεῶν τιμὴν ἢ παραίτησιν.

> [Numa] entrusted to his keeping all sacral lore which, written out and authenticated, specified with what victims, on what days, and at what temples sacrifices were to be made, and with what moneys expenses were to be paid. He then subjected all other public and private religious matters to the decrees of the pontiff; it was to him that the *plebs* should come for advice.[28]

In the politically polarised late republic, the selection of *pontifices* became a *popularis* issue.[29] A tribune's law in 104 BC replaced the old co-optation system with popular election, but that was repealed by Sulla.[30]

The *pontifex maximus* appointed in Sulla's time was his close ally Q. Metellus Pius, the loyal son of a notoriously arrogant optimate.[31] We may doubt whether many craftsmen, bakers or plasterers would consult *him* about the forms of worship appropriate to their needs. Caesar, on the other hand, lived among them in the noisy, crowded Subura.[32] When Metellus Pius died, it was time to change the system back:

> The popular assembly, on the proposal of [the tribune] Labienus with Caesar's support, returned the election of priests to the People, renewing Domitius' law [of 104 BC] against that of Sulla.[33]

Once Caesar was elected, no doubt the manner of the pontiff's exercise of his duties changed too. It can only be guesswork, but the new 'people-friendly' circumstances of Caesar's pontificate may explain why so many Roman authors at just this time were offering their own learned interpretations of the names and personalities of the 'plebeian' deities.

28. Livy 1.20.5-6 (trans. T. J. Luce): *eique sacra omnia exscripta exsignataque attribuit, quibus hostiis, quibus diebus, ad quae templa sacra fierent, atque unde in eos sumptus pecunia erogaretur. cetera quoque omnia publica priuataque sacra pontificis scitis subiecit, ut esset quo consultum plebes ueniret.*

29. Cicero *De lege agraria* 2.18, *De amicitia* 96.

30. Velleius Paterculus 2.12.3, Suetonius *Nero* 2.1 (*lex Domitia*); Dio Cassius 37.37.1 (Sulla).

31. Asconius 79C, Plutarch *Caesar* 7.1. Close ally: Plutarch *Sulla* 6.5 (Pius and Sulla consuls together, 80 BC). Loyal son of Q. Metellus Numidicus: Diodorus Siculus 36.16, Valerius Maximus 5.2.7. Arrogant optimate: Sallust *Jugurtha* 64.1 (*inerat contemptor animus et superbia, commune nobilitatis malum*); Cicero *Pro Sestio* 37, Valerius Maximus 4.1.13 (opposition of *populares*).

32. Suetonius *Diuus Iulius* 46; cf. Martial 12.18.2 (*clamosa Subura*), Juvenal 11.51 (*feruenti Subura*).

33. Dio Cassius 37.37.1: τὰς αἱρέσεις τῶν ἱερέων, γράψαντος μὲν τοῦ Λαβιήνου σπουδάσαντος δὲ τοῦ Καίσαρος, ἐς τὸν δῆμον αὖθις ὁ ὅμιλος παρὰ τὸν τοῦ Σύλλου νόμον ἐπανήγαγεν, ἀνανεωσάμενος τὸν τοῦ Δομιτίου. Cf. 37.38.1 on the goodwill of οἱ πολλοί towards Caesar.

5.3. Anna's stories

One (or two) of those deities was Anna Perenna, who had a story of her own at least by the 50s or 40s BC, when the playwright Decimus Laberius was active.[34] It would be good to know what the plot of Laberius' *Anna Peranna* was,[35] and whether he invented it himself or found it in Varro or Cornificius or some other learned author.[36] Four of the six versions listed by Ovid look like conjectures from that sort of literature:

> There are those for whom this goddess is Luna, because she fills up the year with months. Some think she is Themis, some the Inachian cow [Io]. You will find people, Anna, who say you're a nymph, daughter of Azan, and that you gave Jupiter his first food.[37]

Why Themis or Io, nobody knows;[38] but Azan was an Arcadian hero, and Jupiter—to whom the Ides of every month were sacred—was born in Arcadia in one version of the myth.[39]

Ovid's other two stories are of Anna the Phoenician princess and Anna the old baker-woman of Bovillae. Phoenician Anna was mentioned in Naevius' epic on the Punic War: commenting on Virgil's first reference to *Anna soror*, Servius observes laconically, 'Whose daughters Anna and Dido were, Naevius tells us', but does not give a name.[40] By Varro's time, at least, she had a story:

34. Cicero *Ad familiares* 7.11.2 (53 BC), Macrobius *Saturnalia* 2.6.6 (Clodius' aedileship in 56); Laberius died in 43 (Jerome *Chronica* Ol. 184.2).

35. So spelt in the sources: Aulus Gellius 16.7.10, Nonius 129L (Laberius frr. 2-3 Panayotakis).

36. E.g. his contemporary Gavius Bassus (cf. Aulus Gellius 3.9.4 and 8), whose book *De dis* is cited by Macrobius *Saturnalia* 1.9.13 and Lydus *De mensibus* 4.2. The *De dis* of P. Nigidius Figulus, praetor in 58 BC, was at least 19 books long (Marcobius *Saturnalia* 3.44.6, cf. Nonius 215L, 312L, Servius *auctus* on Virgil *Eclogues* 4.10) but probably too esoteric to provide such stories: see Volk 2024 for the nature of Nigidius' work.

37. Ovid *Fasti* 3.657-60: *sunt quibus haec Luna est, quia mensibus impleat annum,* | *pars Themin, Inachiam pars putat esse bouem.* | *inuenies, qui te nymphen Azanida dicant* | *teque Ioui primos, Anna, dedisse cibos.* The *fasti Verulani* (Degrassi 1963, 166–7) mark the Ides of March as *feriae Ioui*.

38. Themis was the mother of Evander in the Greek tradition (Dionysius of Halicarnassus *Roman Antiquities* 1.31.1-3, 1.32.3); section 1.3 above.

39. Ovid *Fasti* 1.56, Macrobius *Saturnalia* 1.15.15 (sacred to Jupiter); Pausanias 8.4.2-3 (Azan), 8.38.2 (infancy of Zeus).

40. Servius on Virgil *Aeneid* 4.9 (*cuius filiae fuerint Anna et Dido, Naeuius dicit*); cf. *Aeneid* 1.621 for Belus (Phoenician Baal) as Dido's father, but elsewhere (on *Aeneid* 1.343) Servius names him as Mettes.

> Varro says that Anna, not Dido, was driven by love for Aeneas to kill herself on the funeral pyre. . . . It is certainly worth knowing that Varro says Aeneas was loved by Anna.[41]

Varro was interested in the Trojans' voyage to Italy, and had visited some of their landfalls already in 67 BC, when he commanded a fleet in the Adriatic in the war against the pirates.[42] But would he have invented this story himself? How Naevius' view of Carthage and Rome evolved into Virgil's,[43] and what other lost versions may once have existed, are matters beyond our knowledge. In particular, it is impossible to say what authors, if any, identified Dido's sister as Anna Perenna before Ovid did so.

With Anna of Bovillae, we are much better placed. She gave out hot cakes to the plebeians at the time of their secession—and the secession, as we have noticed already, was a story with topical relevance in the ideological struggles of the late republic.[44] Not only that, but Bovillae, supposedly a colony of Alba Longa,[45] was the family cult centre of the *gens Iulia*.[46] Help coming from there to needy plebeians is an idea that might have appealed to Laberius, who liked to use current affairs for his comic plots.[47]

The second half of Ovid's story about Anna of Bovillae,[48] the farcical tale of Anna, Minerva and Mars, is a perfect example of what Varro deplored about the dramatic literature of the time:

> There are three kinds of theology or ways of explaining the gods, the first of them being termed the mythical, the second the physical, and the third the civic. . . . The first theology is associated chiefly with the theatre, the second with the universe, and the third with the city. . . . The first type which I mentioned contains much fiction prejudicial to the dignity and the nature of the immortals.[49]

41. Servius *auctus* on Virgil *Aeneid* 4.682 (Varro *Antiquitates humanae* fr. 2.11 Mirsch): *Varro ait non Didonem sed Annam amore Aeneae impulsam se super rogum interemisse.* Servius on Virgil *Aeneid* 5.4: *sane sciendum est Varronem dicere Aenean ab Anna amatam.*

42. Varro *Antiquitates diuinae* frr. 2.6-18 Mirsch, esp. fr. 12 (Servius *auctus* on Virgil *Aeneid* 3.349); cf. Varro *Res rusticae* 2.pref.6 for his command ('from Delos to Sicily').

43. For Virgil's use of Naevius, see Macrobius *Saturnalia* 6.2.31, Servius *auctus* on Virgil *Aeneid* 1.198.

44. Ovid *Fasti* 3.661-744; cf. n. 24.

45. *Origo gentis Romanae* 17.6; cf. 9.6, 10.4, 11.3, 15.4-5, 16.4, 17.3, 18.5, 20.3 for L. Caesar's *Pontificalia* as one of the anonymous author's sources, and Livy 1.30.2 for the Iulii as one of the *gentes* that came to Rome from Alba.

46. Tacitus *Annals* 2.41.1, 15.23.2; *CIL* 14.2387 = 1^2.1439 = *ILLRP* 270.

47. Cf. Cicero *Ad familiares* 7.11.2 for the sort of scenario Laberius would use.

48. Linked to the first by *nuper erat dea facta* at *Fasti* 3.677.

49. Varro *Antiquitates diuinae* frr. 7 and 10 Cardauns (Augustine *City of God* 4.5.1, 4.5.7, 4.5.2, trans. P. G. Walsh): *tria genera theologiae dicit esse, id est rationis quae de*

It is clear from Augustine's use of the *Divine Antiquities* that what Varro objected to were plays with burlesque mythological plots put on at the *ludi scaenici*;[50] in particular, he disliked stories in which gods were portrayed as thieves (like Mercury) or adulterers (like Jupiter) or slaves to a mortal (like Hercules).[51] The deception of amorous Mars would certainly count as such a plot.

It is important not to overlook this authoritative body of evidence for a late-republican dramatic genre that is otherwise practically unattested. The nearest thing we have to confirmation of it is another fragment from one of Varro's own Menippean satires, where the speaker is commenting on the ruinous expense of keeping slaves and hunting dogs:

> Believe me, more masters have been eaten up by their slaves than by their dogs. If Actaeon had got in first and eaten his dogs before they ate him, he wouldn't be rubbish for dancers in the theatre.[52]

Actaeon was a subject for tragedy, with even a special mask equipped with antlers for the protagonist,[53] but the comic exploitation of tragic plots had been familiar in Italy since the third century BC, when Rhinthon pioneered the dramatic form called 'cheerful tragedy' (section 1.6 above).[54] Since *fabulae Rhinthonicae* are listed by the grammarians as a recognised type of Roman comedy,[55] it would be an economical hypothesis to identify them with the performances Varro complained about.

Note too that the role of Actaeon was *danced*. Cicero mentions in one of his speeches a dancer called Dionysia who charged 200,000 sesterces

---

diis explicatur, eorumque unum mythicon appellari, alterum physicon, tertium ciuile . . . prima, inquit, theologia maxime accommodata est ad theatrum, secunda ad mundum, tertia ad urbem . . . primum, inquit, quod dixi, in eo sunt multa contra dignitatem et naturam immortalium facta.

50. Augustine *City of God* 4.31.1; 6.5.5-6.7.5 *passim*, esp. 6.6.3 (*di poetici theatrici ludicri scaenici*), 6.7.1 (*theologia fabulosa theatrica scaenica*).

51. Varro *Antiquitates diuinae* fr. 7 Cardauns = Augustine *City of God* 6.5.2 (*ut di furati sint, ut adulterarint, ut seruierint homini*).

52. Varro *Menippean Satires* 513 Astbury: *crede mihi, plures dominos serui comederunt quam canes. quod si Actaeon occupasset et ipse prius suos canes comedisset, non nugas saltatoribus in theatro fieret.* Cf. Lucretius 4.978-83 for music and dancers on stage at the *ludi scaenici.*

53. Pollux 4.141 (τὰ δ' ἔκσκευα πρόσωπα Ἀκταίων ἐστὶ κερασφόρος).

54. Rhinthon *PCG* T 1-2 = *Suda* R 171, 4.295 Adler (Ταραντῖνος κωμικός, ἀρχηγὸς τῆς καλουμένης ἱλαροτραγῳδίας, ὅ ἐστι φλυακογραφία), Stephanus Byzantinus 603.1 (Ταραντῖνος φλύαξ, τὰ τραγικὰ μεταρρυθμίζων ἐς τὸ γελοῖον). It was also called 'Italian comedy' (Athenaeus 9.402b).

55. Rhinthon *PCG* T 5 = Caesius Bassus in *Grammatici Latini* 6.312 Keil, Euanthius *De fabula* 4.1, Donatus *De comoedia* 6.1, Donatus on Terence *Adelphoe* 7, Lydus *De magistratibus* 1.40; probably derived from Suetonius (see sections 3.3 and 3.4 above).

for a single performance.[56] She too must be part of this ill-attested dramatic culture, a style of performance preceding—and perhaps developing into—the hugely popular *pantomimus* dance-drama associated with Bathyllus and Pylades in the 20s BC.[57]

Pylades specialized in tragic roles, but Bathyllus' style was 'more cheerful' (the word used of Rhinthon's burlesques), exemplified by 'the nymph Echo or some Pan or satyr revelling with Eros'.[58]

Paying proper attention to this scattered and neglected evidence, and bearing in mind Varro's strictures on material 'unworthy of the divine majesty',[59] we should remember Propertius 4.9, where thirsty Hercules utters 'words unworthy of a god', or Ovid's account of the 'silent goddess' in *Fasti* 2, where Jupiter, lusting after Juturna, 'put up with many things so great a god shouldn't have to endure'.[60] If we ask, as we should, where the poets found such stories, the answer may be that they were 'attested by the stage'.[61]

Erotic plots like Jupiter's amorous pursuits were evidently typical of this theatrical tradition (fig. 7),[62] and in Varro's time erotic entertainment was particularly associated with the *ludi Florales*. It was a popular spectacle in both senses of the word: when Marcus Cato, the most outspoken of the *optimates* and Caesar's life-long enemy, was present at the *ludi Florales* in 55 BC (he was standing for election as praetor at the time), the audience would not allow the show to begin until he got up and left.[63] The three authors who refer to this event use the term *iocus* to describe

56. Cicero *Pro Roscio comoedo* 23; cf. Aulus Gellius 1.3.3 for Dionysia as a *notissima saltatricula*.

57. Seneca *Controuersiae* 3.pref.10 and 16, Macrobius *Saturnalia* 2.7.12-19; Jerome *Chronica* Ol. 189.3 (22–21 BC), Lucian *Saltatio* 34 (Augustus' time), Dio Cassius 54.17.4-5 (18 BC).

58. Athenaeus 1.20e (ἡ δὲ Βαθύλλειος ἱλαρωτέρα), Plutarch *Moralia* 711f; cf. Persius 5.123 (*ad numeros satyrum moueare Bathylli*).

59. Augustine *City of God* 6.6.5 (*maiestati indigna diuinae*); cf. 4.27.1 (*multa de diis fingantur indigna*), 6.1.1 (*falsa atque indigna*), 6.7.1 (*indignitatis et turpitudinis plena*), 6.8.4 (*de diis indigna*).

60. Propertius 4.9.32 (*et iacit ante fores uerba minora deo*), Ovid *Fasti* 2.586 (*multa tulit tanto non patienda deo*).

61. Ovid *Fasti* 4.326 (*mira, sed et scaena testificata loquar*), on the arrival of Magna Mater.

62. Augustine, *City of God* 4.26.1-3, 4.27.5; presumably from Varro, who is cited at 4.31.1.

63. Valerius Maximus 2.10.8, Seneca *Epistulae* 97.8. Cato and Caesar: Caesar *De bello ciuili* 1.3.4 (*ueteres inimicitiae*); for details cf. Plutarch *Cato the Younger* 23.1-2, 24.1-2, 31.3, 32.1-2, 33.1-3, 43.5, 49.1, 51.1-52.4, 58.6, 64.5, 72.2.

Flora's games; so too does Ovid in the *Fasti*, and he calls Flora's naked showgirls a 'plebeian chorus'.[64]

Ovid also uses the word *iocus* of the stories of Priapus' attempt on the nymph Lotis, of Faunus' pursuit of Omphale, of Priapus' attempt on Vesta, and negatively (no *ioci* here) of a non-erotic tale involving satyrs.[65] Since Faunus was identified as Pan, and the two Priapus stories are set at divine festivals attended by satyrs, Pans and nymphs,[66] this is all reminiscent of Bathyllus' dance world of nymphs, Pans and satyrs revelling. The notion of *iocus* occurs twice more in the *Fasti*: to describe the old songs sung by the pipers on the Ides of June (the first of all pipers was a satyr, Marsyas),[67] and the indecent songs sung by the girls at the festival of Anna Perenna (who was a nymph in two of the stories Ovid knew).[68]

The girls on the Ides of March sang 'specific obscenities' (*certa probra*), a puzzling adjective that seems to suggest a fixed form of words. If Varro's *di certi* were so called because they featured in the books of the *pontifices*, perhaps set formulae for the cult of Anna Perenna were listed there too. We cannot know; but if we are right to infer a change of pontifical style after Caesar's election in 63 BC, it is conceivable that new liturgies as well as new stories were being created for the 'plebeian' deities.

What we do know is that Ovid was very familiar with the idea of a divine *plebs*. In book 5 of the *Fasti*, Polyhymnia—the Muse who looked after the *pantomimus* dance genre—reports an early divine world in which all rank was equal and a 'plebeian god' might sit on the throne of Saturn.[69] The *locus classicus* for the idea of plebeian divinities comes in Ovid's curse-poem from exile:

64. Valerius Maximus 2.10.8 (*priscum morem iocorum*), Seneca *Epistulae* 97.8 (*Florales iocos*), Martial 1.pref. (*iocosae . . . sacrum Florae*); Ovid *Fasti* 4.946 (*scaena ioci morem liberioris habet*), 5.183 (*mater ades florum, ludis celebranda iocosis*), 5.331-2 (*quare lasciuia maior | his foret in ludis liberiorque iocus*). Showgirls: *Fasti* 5.349 (*turba meretricia*), 352 (*plebeio choro*). For the full argument see Wiseman 2023, 105–21.

65. Ovid *Fasti* 1.396 (*di quicumque iocis non alienus erat*), 2.304 (*traditur antiqui fabula plena ioci*), 6.320 (*est multi fabula parua ioci*); 3.735 on Silenus' discovery of honey (*non habet ingratos fabula nostra iocos*).

66. Ovid *Fasti* 1.393-90 (a Greek festival of Bacchus), 2.269-82 (Faunus as Pan), 6.321-4 (Cybele's festival on Mount Ida).

67. Ovid *Fasti* 6.692 (*et canere ad ueteres uerba iocosa modos*), cf. 704-8 on Marsyas. Pipers played at the *ludi scaenici*: *Fasti* 6.659 (*cantabat tibia ludis*), 667 (*quaeritur in scaena caua tibia*).

68. Ovid *Fasti* 3.675-6 (*puellae*), 695 (*inde ioci ueteres obscaenaque dicta canuntur*), cf. 653 and 659 on Anna as a *nympha*.

69. Ovid *Fasti* 5.18-20 (*par erat omnis honor | . . . ausus de media plebe sedere deus*); cf. *Metamorphoses* 1.595 (Apollo to Daphne, '*nec de plebe deo*'). Polyhymnia and *pantomimus*: *Anthologia Palatina* 9.505.17-18 (cf. 504.7), Nonnus *Dionysiaca* 5.104-7.

> You too, the *plebs* of the heavenly ones, Fauns and satyrs and *Lares* and rivers and nymphs and the race of half-gods.[70]

Already, in the great opening sequence of his epic, Ovid had presented Jupiter convening the Olympian Senate to the 'heavenly Palatine', where the *atria* of the *nobiles* are crowded like those of their mortal counterparts.[71] 'The dwellings of the *plebs* are elsewhere', and in his speech Jupiter tells us where:

> 'I have [to think about] the half-gods, the countryside divinities, nymphs and Fauns and satyrs and mountain-dwelling Silvani; since we do not yet deem them worthy of heaven, let us at least allow them to inhabit the earth that we have granted them.'[72]

'Not *yet* worthy of heaven', but there was always the chance of promotion, for instance from nymph to goddess, like Flora or Juturna.[73]

Promotion came also to the mortal Anna of Bovillae, and it was the Roman plebeians who brought it about by setting up a cult statue.[74] We might express it in a different idiom, and suggest that under the *popularis* pontificate of Julius Caesar the merely functional concept of Anna Perenna (or Anna and Peranna) evolved into an anthropomorphic divinity, accumulating a collection of stories to explain her name and her plebeian status.

5.4. *The Ides of March*

The plebeians who honoured Anna of Bovillae were 'still unprotected by any tribunes':[75] the secession itself enforced the creation of the tribunate of the *plebs*, to protect the Roman People from the abuse of power.

70. Ovid *Ibis* 81-2: *uos quoque, plebs superum, Fauni satyrique Laresque | fluminaque et nymphae semideumque genus.* Cf. also Martial 8.49.3-4 (*qua bonus accubuit genitor cum plebe deorum | et licuit Faunis poscere uina Iouem*).

71. Ovid *Metamorphoses* 1.172 (*atria nobilium*), 176 (*magni Palatia caeli*); cf. 1.200-5 for the explicit parallel with the Augustan Senate.

72. Ovid *Metamorphoses* 1.173: *plebs habitat diuersa locis.* 1.192-5: *'sunt mihi semidei, sunt rustica numina nymphae | Faunique satyrique et monticolae Siluani; | quos, quoniam caeli nondum dignamur honore, | quas dedimus certe terras habitare sinamus.'*

73. Ovid *Fasti* 5.197-212 (Flora), Virgil *Aeneid* 12.139-42 (Juturna); cf. also Ovid *Metamorphoses* 14.623-41 (Pomona as a nymph pursued by satyrs, Pans, Silenus and Priapus), Varro *De lingua Latina* 7.45 = Ennius *Annales* 118 Skutsch (*flamen Pomonalis*, implying divine status).

74. Ovid *Fasti* 3.673 (*signum posuere Perennae*), cf. 677 (*nuper erat dea facta*).

75. Ovid *Fasti* 3.663 (*nullis etiam nunc tuta tribunis*).

Four and a half centuries later, in January 49 BC, the *optimates* drove two tribunes out of Rome, to prevent them from exercising their legal right of veto.[76] The tribunes fled to Caesar, now proconsul of Gaul. Caesar marched his army into Italy, making it clear in a public statement what was at stake:

> [He said] he had left his province not for any criminal purpose, but to defend himself against the slanders of his enemies, to restore to their proper place the tribunes of the *plebs* who had been expelled from the city for that reason, and to bring about the freedom of himself and the Roman People from oppression by a faction of a few men.[77]

Caesar had enthusiastic popular support,[78] expressed after the war was over by the honorific title 'Father of the nation' (*parens patriae*).[79]

The Roman People were outraged by the murder of Caesar, and demanded vengeance.[80] It was provided by Caesar's heir and adopted son, whom they elected as consul at the age of nineteen, and as '*triumuir* for the establishment of the republic' (*rei publicae constituendae*) at the age of twenty.[81] One of the first acts of the triumvirs was the establishment of a cult for *Diuus Iulius*, the deified Caesar, with a temple to be built in the Forum at the place where the Roman People had insisted on burning his body.[82] Celebrations would be held on Caesar's birthday,[83] in the month now called 'July' (material for Ovid's seventh book, if the *Fasti* had ever been finished).

76. Caesar *De bello ciuili* 1.2.7-8, 1.5.1-5, 1.7.2-8.1; Dio Cassius 41.1-3. Cf. Cicero *Ad Atticum* 11.7.1: Caesar regarded as invalid all senatorial resolutions made after the expulsion of the tribunes.

77. Caesar *De bello ciuili* 1.22.5: *se non malefici causa ex prouincia egressum sed uti se a contumeliis inimicorum defenderet, ut tribunos plebis in ea re ex ciuitate expulsos in suam dignitatem restitueret, ut se et populum Romanum factione paucorum oppressum in libertatem uindicaret.*

78. As admitted even by the optimate Cicero: *Ad Atticum* 7.3.5, 7.7.6, 8.3.4, 10.4.8 (December 50–April 49 BC); cf. Appian *Civil Wars* 1.4.16 on Caesar as δημοτικώτατος.

79. Crawford 1974, 491 (no. 480.19); Degrassi 1947, 182–3 (*fasti Ostienses* on 44 BC: *Caesar pare[ns patriae occisus]*). Or *pater patriae*: *ILLRP* 407–8, Appian *Civil Wars* 2.106.442, 2.144.602, Dio Cassius 44.4.4.

80. Appian *Civil Wars* 1.4.17, 2.147.613-4, 3.60.247.

81. Augustus *Res gestae* 1.4, 2; cf. Appian *Civil Wars* 3.95.392 (assassins condemned by due legal process), 4.7.27 (triumvirate set up by a tribunician law), 4.8.31 (triumvirs elected ἁρμόσαι καὶ διορθῶσαι τὰ κοινά).

82. Dio Cassius 47.18.3-4, cf. 51.22.2 for its dedication in 29 BC.

83. Dio Cassius 47.18.5-6; Degrassi 1963, 188–9, 208 (*fasti Amiternini* and *fasti Antiates ministrorum*, 12 July).

For the Ides of March a quite different sort of annual remembrance was proposed:

> It was voted that the hall in which he was slain be walled up, that the Ides of March be called the Day of Parricide, and that a meeting of the Senate should never be called on that day.[84]

But though 'parricide' long remained the accepted phrase for the assassination,[85] *Parricidium* never appears on the surviving Augustan calendars; the Ides are marked only as Anna Perenna's cult day.[86]

Perhaps it was thought that giving the day *any* special name would be an inappropriate glorification. That may be the reason for Ovid's intention to say nothing about the murder, and certainly his change of mind, encouraged by Vesta, deals with the event in a way his audience would approve, emphasising the elder Caesar's divinity and the younger Caesar's dutiful exaction of vengeance.[87] The audience would not need reminding that the younger Caesar, now Caesar Augustus, had been granted the powers of that very tribunate of the *plebs* that the secession of the plebeians had first won and the elder Caesar had gone to war to defend.[88]

5.5. *A movable feast*

The festival of Anna Perenna took place close to the Tiber on the north side of Rome, at the first milestone on the Via Flaminia.[89] That information allows us to place Ovid's scene quite precisely. In modern terms, it is the neighbourhood of Via di Ripetta from Piazza del Popolo south to the Mausoleum of Augustus, bounded by the river to the west and the Corso (Via Flaminia) to the east.

The sacred-spring site found in 1999 at Piazza Euclide, identified epigraphically as a cult centre for Anna Perenna and the 'consecrated nymphs',[90]

84. Suetonius *Diuus Iulius* 88 (trans. J. C. Rolfe): *curiam in qua occisus est obstrui placuit Idusque Martias Parricidium nominari, ac ne umquam eo die senatus ageretur.* See also Dio Cassius 47.19.1.

85. Cicero *Ad Atticum* 12.3.1, *Philippics* 2.31; Valerius Maximus 1.5.7, 1.8.8, 3.1.3, 6.4.5, 6.8.4; Tacitus *Annals* 4.34.3, Florus 2.17.1.

86. Degrassi 1963, 172–3, 255 (*fasti Vaticani* and *fasti Farnesiani*).

87. Ovid *Fasti* 6.697 (*praeteriturus eram gladios in principe fixos*), 698-702 (Vesta), 703-4 (divinity), 705-10 (piety and vengeance).

88. Augustus *Res gestae* 10.1 (granted 'by law'), Tacitus *Annals* 1.2.1 (*ad tuendam plebem*).

89. Ovid *Fasti* 3.524 (*non procul a ripis, aduena Thybri, tuis*); Degrassi 1963, 172–3 (*fasti Vaticani*). It makes no significant difference whether the road was measured from the 'golden milestone' in the Forum (Plutarch *Galba* 24.4) or from the nearby Porta Fontinalis below the north-eastern slope of the Capitol (cf. Festus 97L for a gate as the start of a road).

90. *Année Épigraphique* 2003, 251–3, Blennow 2019, 96–9, figs 6.1–3.

is two kilometers north of Piazza del Popolo as the crow flies; it is not on the Via Flaminia, and it is nowhere near the Tiber bank. It is therefore not the scene of Anna Perenna's festival as described by Ovid. The earliest of the many coins found in the basin are of Augustan date, but we cannot know how long they had been in circulation when the site first came into use.

A change in the circumstances of Anna's cult is also suggested by Martial's poem about the villa of Julius Martialis. He describes the villa as 'on the long ridge of the Janiculum', but in fact the view it commanded is the view from Monte Mario:

> On one side you may see the seven imperial mounts and appraise all Rome; likewise the hills of Alba and Tusculum and whatever cool spot lies near the city, ancient Fidenae and little Rubrae and the fruitful grove of Anna Perenna that rejoices in the blood of virgins. On the other side the traveller on the Flaminian and Salarian way is on view; but his carriage makes no sound, lest the wheel disturb soothing slumbers that neither boatswain's call nor bargee's shout can interrupt, even though Mulvius [the Milvian bridge] be so near and keels glide rapidly down sacred Tiber.[91]

There was no grove in Ovid's account of Anna Perenna, and the girls who sang and danced on that easy-going occasion were clearly not virgins.

What Anna's grove 'rejoiced in' at line 16 must be either human sacrifice, obviously impossible in Martial's time, or the sort of pre-marriage 'initiation' of brides that was associated with Mutunus Tutunus, another 'functional' deity with a double name:

> Let him [the 'one god' of the pagans] be Mutunus or Tutunus, whom the Greeks call Priapus . . . Priapus who is all too masculine, on whose most enormous and foul member the new bride used to be ordered to sit, in the most honourable and pious custom of married women.[92]

91. Martial 4.64.11-24 (trans. D. R. Shackleton Bailey): *hinc septem dominos uidere montis | et totam licet aestimare Romam, | Albanos quoque Tusculosque colles | et quodcumque iacet sub urbe frigus, | Fidenas ueteres breuesque Rubras, | et quod uirgineo cruore gaudet | Annae pomiferum nemus Perennae. | illinc Flaminiae Salariaeque | gestator patet essedo tacente, | ne blando rota sit molesta somno, | quem nec rumpere nauticum celeuma | nec clamor ualet helciariorum, | cum sit tam prope Muluius sacrumque | lapsae per Tiberim uolent carinae.* Cf. 4.64.3: *longo Ianiculi iugo.*

92. Varro *Antiquitates diuinae* fr. 151 Cardauns (Augustine *City of God* 4.11.4, 6.9.7): *ipse sit Mutunus uel Tutunus, qui est apud Graecos Priapus . . . Priapus nimis masculus, super cuius immanissimum et turpissimum fascinum sedere noua nupta iubebatur, more honestissimo religiosissimo matronarum.* See also *City of God* 7.24.7, Lactantius *Institutiones* 1.20.36. For *uirgineus cruor* in a bridal context, cf. Claudian *Fescennini* 4.27, Ausonius *Cento nuptialis* 118.

We happen to know that Mutunus Tutunus had a shrine on the Velia, which was converted into baths for the house of Cn. Domitius Calvinus (consul in 53 and 40 BC);[93] but what happened to his cult after that?

Another Martial passage may be relevant, warning his female readers of obscene poems in the rest of his volume:

> Henceforth tipsy Terpsichore, laying modesty aside after the wine and roses, knows not what she is saying, naming openly and with no ambiguous turn of phrase that object which Venus proudly welcomes in the sixth month, which the bailiff sets for guard in the middle of the garden, which a good girl eyes behind her hand.[94]

The object is of course Priapus' erect member, and the sixth month, after the Ides of June, was the well-omened time for weddings.[95] At some point Anna's festival (*Annae sacrum*) was moved from 15 March to 18 June.[96] The *terminus ante quem* for the change is AD 354, but Martial's allusion seems already to presuppose it.

Priapus and the nymphs were fellow-revellers,[97] and a hymn to the phallic god set up some time in the first century AD suggests what his relationship may have been with the *nymphae sacratae* of Anna Perenna's grove and spring:

> Come together all of you, you girls who dwell in the sacred grove, you girls who dwell in the sacred waters, come together all of you and sing with seductive voice to handsome Priapus: 'Greetings, holy Priapus, father of all things.' Then plant countless kisses on his groin, put sweet-smelling garlands round his member, and sing again: 'Greetings, holy Priapus, father of all things.'[98]

93. Festus 142L (*sacellum . . . de quo aris sublatis balnearia sunt facta domus*).

94. Martial 3.68.5-10 (trans. D. R. Shackleton Bailey): *hinc iam deposito post uina rosasque pudore, | quid dicat nescit saucia Terpsichore, | schemate nec dubio, sed aperte nominat illam | quam recipit sexto mense superba Venus, | custodem medio statuit cum uilicus horto, | opposita spectat quam proba uirgo manu.* The word he elaborately avoids using is *mentula*.

95. Ovid *Fasti* 6.223-4: *post sacras monstratur Iunius Idus | utilis et nuptis, utilis esse uiris.*

96. Degrassi 1963, 248–9 (*fasti Furii Filocali*).

97. Petronius *Satyricon* 133.3 (*nympharum Bacchique comes . . . Dryadumque uoluptas*), *Priapeia* 33 (*Naiadas antiqui Dryadasque habuere Priapi*).

98. *CIL* 14.3565.13-22 = *Musa Lapidaria* 155.13-22 Courtney: *conuenite simul quot es[tis om]nes, | quae sacrum colitis [ne]mus [pu]ellae, | quae sacras colitis a[q]uas puellae, | conuenite quot estis atque [be]llo | uoce dicite blandula Priapo | 'salue, sancte pater Priape rerum'. | [i]nguini oscula figite inde mille, | [fasci]num bene olentibus [cor]onis | [cing]ite illi iterumque dicite omnis | ['salue, san]cte pater Priape rerum'.* It is inscribed

The 'girls' are of course nymphs, addressed a few lines further on as *deae puellae*.

The evidence therefore suggests that during the first century the cult of Anna Perenna acquired a new site, a new date and a new purpose. That needn't surprise us: we have already seen the eighty years from Varro's Menippean satires to Ovid's *Fasti* transform her from two verbal personifications (*Anna ac Peranna*) into a nymph or goddess with many different meanings, and there is no reason to think that the nature of her cult was any more static during the next eighty years, from Ovid's *Fasti* to Martial. For us, the challenge is to pay proper attention to the sources in their chronological order.

The ex-consul Silius Italicus was composing his huge epic poem *Punica* in the 80s and 90s AD. The excursus in the eighth book, on Anna Perenna as Punic princess and Roman goddess, obviously draws on the first of Ovid's Anna stories, though one or two of the details—the glassy caves, the sisterhood of nymphs—may perhaps reflect conditions new since Ovid wrote.[99] But Carthaginian Anna was part of an epic tradition going back to Virgil and Naevius; Ovid's plebeian Anna would have been less easy for Silius to assimilate.

The *popularis* ideology of Julius Caesar and Caesar Augustus was still a living force in AD 25, when praise of the assassins was a crime of high treason, and in AD 41, when the Senate hoped to re-establish an optimate republic and the Roman People wanted a Caesar to prevent them from doing so.[100] But that soon changed, in part thanks to the brilliant success of Lucan's *Pharsalia* in mythologizing the *optimates*: his Caesar was the tyrannical enemy of freedom, his Cato and Brutus the heroes of a doomed but noble cause. By the time Tacitus wrote his *Annals* in the early second century, the assassination was simply a historical event about which opposite opinions were equally legitimate: 'to some the worst of acts, to others

---

on a phallic herm dedicated to the *Genius numinis Priapi* by an imperial freedman whose name, *Iulius* Agathemerus, gives the approximate date.

99. Excursus: Silius Italicus 8.44-199. Details: 8.190-1 (*Numicius illam | suscepit gremio uitreisque abscondidit antris*), 8.198 (*inter caeruleas uisa est residere sorores*). This was written on the assumption that lines 8.144-223 are genuine, as argued by Heitland 1896 and Goold 1956, 9–12, and tacitly accepted by Reeve 1983, 390; however, they are rejected by the Teubner editor (Delz 1987, lxiv–lxviii), and Heyworth 2019, 194 states without argument that they are merely 'a sixteenth-century attempt to fill the lacuna'. Caution is appropriate where the experts are in such disagreement, but it seems to me that the differences from Ovid's scenario, compatible (as argued in Wiseman 2006, 58–9) with new evidence that no forger could have known about, are an argument in favour of authenticity.

100. AD 25: Tacitus *Annals* 4.34-5 (trial of Cremutius Cordus). AD 41: Josephus *Jewish Antiquities* 19.166-87 (Senate), 19.227-8 (opposition of Senate and People).

the finest'.[101] Moreover, it is likely that by then Anna's cult no longer had anything to do with the Ides of March.

About two generations after Silius and Tacitus, the cult site of Anna Perenna received two new altars, each inscribed with a short poem in iambic *senarii*. The first is headed 'to the consecrated nymphs' and dated at the end to 5 April AD 156:

> Suetonius Germanus with his wife Licinia, the vow which they had undertaken to Anna Perenna, that if they established themselves as victors they would place a marble altar, once again made victors, we deservedly repay the vow.[102]

The other has no heading or date, but is signed at the end 'Eutychides the freedman':

> The vow [which] once I had made to the consecrated nymphs, who deserved it because of the victory of my good patron Gaius Acilius Eutyches, we pay; and we attest in verses that [the nymphs] are sacred, and we dedicate an altar to the welcome springs.[103]

What sort of competition was this? The name of the victorious Acilius Eutyches may suggest an answer, if we compare an honorific inscription set up in AD 169 for the 'noble *archimimus*' Lucius Acilius Eutyches (perhaps his brother), who was 'honoured by the tragic, comic, and all other corporations concerned with the stage'.[104] The competitiveness of such performers is well attested in the epigraphic record, as for example in a second-century statue-base from Rome:

> Marcus Ulpius Apolaustus, freedman of the emperor [Trajan], crowned twelve times as the top *pantomimus* against the actors and all the professionals of the stage.[105]

101. Tacitus *Annals* 1.8.6, trans. A. J. Woodman (*aliis pessimum aliis pulcherrimum facinus*).

102. *Année Épigraphique* 2003, 252, Blennow 2019, 98, fig. 6.2: *Suetonius Germanus cum Licinia coniuge, | Annae Perennae uotum quod susceperant | si se uictores statuerent | aram marmoream se posituros, denuo | uictores facti uotum meriti soluimus.* The third line is four syllables short.

103. *Année Épigraphique* 2003, 251, Blennow 2019, 96, fig. 6.1: *uotum sacratis quondam nymphis feceram | boni patroni meritis ob uictoriam | C. Acili Eutychetis reddimus | et esse sanctas confitemur uersibus | aramque gratis dedicamus fontibus.*

104. *CIL* 14.2408 = *ILS* 5196: *L. Acilio L.f. Pompt. Eutyche*[*ti*] *nobili archimimo, commun. mimor. adlecto, diurno parasito Apoll., tragico comico et omnibus corporib. ad scaenam honor., decurioni Bouillis.*

105. *CIL* 6.10114 = *ILS* 5184: *M. Ulpius Aug. lib. Apolaustus | maximus pantomimus | coronatus aduersus histriones | et omnes scaenicos | artifices XII.* Cf. *ILS* 5185-94 for

The dedicators of the two altars at the Piazza Euclide site used iambic *senarii*, the regular metre of dramatic dialogue. If they owed their victories to Anna Perenna and the nymphs, it may be because those divinities had a long history of association with the stage, and in particular with 'mime' in its various forms.[106]

The Piazza Euclide site was evidently in use from the first century AD to the late fourth. The lead curse-tablets and 'voodoo dolls' found in the pool may belong to the latter part of that long period, but the magical practices they attest were commonplace throughout antiquity. One of the lead cylinders containing one of the dolls bears finger-prints evidently of a woman.[107] There's not much one can do with this evidence, but it may be helpful to remember the witches Canidia and Sagana in Horace's satire, or the nameless old woman and her group of girls 'binding hostile tongues' in Ovid's account of the Feralia.[108] It seems that in that respect too, Anna Perenna was a deity for the Roman *plebs*. They knew her stories not from reading them in books but from seeing them performed.

---

further examples: each inscription honours a *hieronica* or *hieronica coronatus*, '(crowned) victor in the sacred contest'.

106. Varro *Antiquitates diuinae* fr. 3 Cardauns (Augustine *City of God* 4.22) for nymphs in mime; and Laberius' play *Anna Peranna* was of course a *mimus*. Priapus too appeared in mime (Augustine *City of God* 6.7.2).

107. Museo Nazionale Romano, sezione epigrafica, inv. no. 475549.

108. Horace *Satires* 1.8.23-45, cf. 1.8.10 for the setting (*hoc miserae plebi stabat commune sepulcrum*); Ovid *Fasti* 2.571-82.

CHAPTER SIX

Politics and the People

THIS CHAPTER was written for an occasion in honour of Sir Fergus Millar, to vindicate his account of 'the crowd in Rome in the Roman republic' against critics who have argued that the republic was always an oligarchy, and that the general population of the city had neither the time nor the inclination to interest itself in politics.[1] The contemporary evidence that refutes that view also offers significant information about the *ludi scaenici* as occasions for popular politics, and how stage performances could influence later historians' political narratives.

6.1. Roman holidays

We begin with the contrasting testimony of two poets who knew the Roman scene incomparably better than any modern historian can hope to do, Gaius Lucilius and Quintus Horatius Flaccus:

> Now indeed from dawn to dusk, on holidays and workdays, all the People and all the senators alike busy themselves in the Forum, never leaving it. All have given themselves over to one and the same study and art—to be able to swindle without getting caught, to fight by cunning, to compete by smooth talking, pretend to be a fine fellow, to lay traps as if all are enemies of all.[2]

1. See for instance Mouritsen 2001, 36 ('Political activity in republican Rome was extremely time-consuming, and the urban *plebs* clearly had other more pressing concerns'), 89 ('the *plebs* naturally remained outside the sphere of politics'). *Contra* Millar 1998, Wiseman 2009, 5–32.

2. Lucilius 1145–51W (Lactantius *Institutiones* 5.9.20), trans. Frances Muecke: *nunc uero a mani ad noctem festo atque profesto | totus item pariterque die populusque patresque | iactare indu foro se omnes, decedere nusquam; | uni se atque eidem studio omnes dedere*

> We, both on working days and at festivals amid the gifts of playful Liber, with our wives and children will first pray duly to the gods, and then, in song mingled with Lydian pipes, sing of the leaders who lived virtuously in the ancestral way, and of Troy and Anchises and the offspring of kindly Venus.[3]

I quote these two very different scenes together, because in each case the poet happens to have made explicit something that Romans didn't need to be reminded of but we moderns are in constant danger of forgetting. Every day of the Roman year had its own character, defined not only by the legal categories of *dies fasti, nefasti, comitiales* and *intercisi*, or the religious categories of *feriae* and *dies atri*, but more generally as holidays or working days, *dies festi* and *profesti*.[4]

Chief among the *dies festi* were the annual series of public games:[5] the *ludi Megalenses* and *Ceriales* in April, the *ludi Florales* from late April into May, the *ludi Apollinares* in July, the *ludi Romani* in September and the *ludi plebeii* in November. Since our sources consistently refer to the theatre audience at the *ludi scaenici* as *populus Romanus*, or even *populus Romanus uniuersus*,[6] I think we are entitled to use evidence about the games as a reliable index of what the Roman People did or did not care about.[7]

A few passing comments from Cicero's correspondence may start us off in the right direction. First, some advice to C. Trebatius in Gaul in 53 BC:

> Besides, there won't be any talk if you come back soon, but if you stay away longer to no effect I'm afraid not only of Laberius but of our friend Valerius as well. A lawyer from Britain would be a marvellous character to put on stage.[8]

---

et arti, | uerba dare ut caute possint, pugnare dolose, | blanditia certare, bonum simulare uirum se, | insidias facere ut si hostes sint omnibus omnes.

3. Horace *Odes* 4.15.25-32: *nosque et profestis lucibus et sacris | inter iocosi munera Liberi | cum prole matronisque nostris | rite deos prius apprecati | uirtute functos more patrum duces | Lydis remixto carmine tibias | Troiamque et Anchisen et almae | progeniem Veneris canemus.*

4. On which see Michels 1967, 81–3.

5. Cicero *Pro Caelio* 1 (*diebus festis ludisque publicis, omnibus forensibus negotiis intermissis*), cf. 21 (*iam quae sit multitudo in foro, quae genera, quae studia, quae uarietas hominum uidetis*); it was evidently the time of the *ludi Megalenses*.

6. E.g. Cicero *Pro Sestio* 106, 116-27 (section 2.3 above), *De haruspicum responso* 22-5, *In Pisonem* 65. For *p. R. uniuersus* see Cicero *Pro Sestio* 119, 122, 124-5, *Philippics* 1.36; Pliny *Natural History* 36.119-20.

7. Cicero *Ad Atticum* 2.16.3: *populi sensus maxime theatro et spectaculis perspectus est.*

8. Cicero *Ad familiares* 7.11.2: *denique, si cito te rettuleris, sermo nullus erit; si diutius frustra afueris, non modo Laberium sed etiam sodalem nostrum Valerium pertimesco. mira enim persona induci potest Britannici iuris consulti.*

Satirical comment on current events was evidently a feature of the theatre games, as we see also in the letters to Atticus after the Ides of March:

> I got two letters from you yesterday. From the first I heard about the theatre and Publilius, good signs that the crowd are on our side. But it seemed to me that the applause given to Lucius Cassius was a joke. . . . Write back with any hard news you have. Failing that, give me a full account of popular applause and what the mime-actors say.[9]

The first thing to notice is that Decimus Laberius, Valerius Catullus and Publilius Syrus were dramatists who specialised in 'mime'.[10] That was a term that embraced a very wide range of performance styles,[11] but it is obvious from Cicero's references to the three authors and to the *mimorum dicta* that their repertoire included topical satire. That must include politics, if it was through them that he hoped to find out where the sympathies of the Roman People lay in the aftermath of Caesar's murder.

Cicero was also interested in the applause, or lack of it, given to individual senators as they entered to take their seats in the *orchestra*. The Greek word he used for such manifestations first appears in a letter written seventeen years earlier:

> The crowd at public meetings—the miserable starving *plebs*, that leech of the treasury—thinks the Great Man is devoted to me alone! And yes indeed, we've been brought together by a lot of pleasant familiarity—so much so that those conspiratorial drunkards, the boys with the little beards, call him Gnaeus Cicero in their discussions. And so I get away with wonderful applause, both at the games and at the gladiators, without any shepherd-style whistling.[12]

9. Cicero *Ad Atticum* 14.2.1 (8 April 44 BC) and 14.3.2 (9 April): *duas a te accipi epistulas heri. ex priore theatrum Publiliumque cognoui, bona signa consentientis multitudinis. plausus uero L. Cassio datus etiam facetus mihi quidem uisus est. . . . tu si quid* πραγματικὸν *habes rescribe; sin minus, populi* ἐπισημασίαν *et mimorum dicta perscribito.*

10. For the first two, see the *testimonia* and fragments collected by (respectively) Panayotakis 2010 and Wiseman 1985, 258–9, cf. 183–210 for his identity.

11. E.g. physical clowning (Cicero *De oratore* 2.251), obscene language (*De oratore* 2.242, *Orator* 88), Alexandrian plots (*Pro Rabirio Postumo* 35), improvisation (*Pro Caelio* 64, Macrobius *Saturnalia* 2.7.7), personal abuse (*Rhetorica ad Herennium* 1.14.24), witty word-play (Seneca *Controuersiae* 7.3.8), morally improving observations (Petronius *Satyrica* 55), myth rationalised as history (Catullus, quoted in the scholiast to Lucan 1.543-4), comic dance (Suetonius, quoted in Diomedes *De poematibus* = *Grammatici Latini* 1.491-2 Keil).

12. Cicero *Ad Atticum* 1.16.11 (July 61 BC): *illa contionalis hirudo aerari, misera ac ieiuna plebecula, me ab hoc Magno unice diligi putat; et hercule multa et iucunda consuetudine coniuncti inter nos sumus, usque ut nostri isti comissatores coniurationis, barbatuli*

For those who believe that the urban *plebs* took no interest in politics, this passage has to be improbably explained away.[13] It seems simpler to take it literally, and be grateful for a precious insight into how ordinary Romans expressed their views on current affairs, applauding those they approved of and whistling at those they didn't. In 61 BC any friend of Pompey's was a friend of theirs; previously, we have to suppose, they had given Cicero the whistling treatment.[14]

If we wonder why unpopular politicians would ever subject themselves to such demonstrations of disapproval, the answer must be that mostly they didn't. Consider the settings of *De oratore* and *De finibus* books 3–4: in each case the Roman gentlemen were at their Tusculan villas because the games were on in Rome.[15] The correspondence reveals that Cicero was regularly away from the city in April and May, during the sequence of *ludi Megalenses, Ceriales* and *Florales*,[16] and that senatorial business was kept to a minimum at that time, presumably because many senators were at their villas.[17] It is true, of course, that April and May were a good time to be in the country anyway; but Cicero was often away in November as well,[18] and I think that should make us curious about the *ludi plebeii*.

One question that seems never to be asked is how much difference there was between the games given by the curule aediles (*Megalenses* and *Romani*), those given by the plebeian aediles (*Ceriales, Florales* and *plebeii*), and those given by the urban praetor (*Apollinares*). Despite the absence of direct evidence, it seems at least possible that the

---

iuuenes, illum in sermonibus Cn. Ciceronem appellant. itaque et ludis et gladiatoribus mirandas ἐπισημασίας *sine ulla pastoricia fistula auferebamus.*

13. Mouritsen 2001, 40–41, adducing also Cicero *Ad Q. fratrem* 2.3.4 (*contionario illo populo*) and *De oratore* 1.118 (*haec turba et barbaria forensis*), and assuming that they refer to 'those citizens, often of higher social standing, who regularly frequented the Forum and could be relied upon to turn up for a *contio* in support of the senate'. See also Mouritsen 2017, 72–9.

14. As they did to Roscius Otho in 63 BC (Plutarch *Cicero* 13.3) and Hortensius in 51 (Caelius in Cicero *Ad familiares* 8.2.1). Cf. Cicero *Ad Atticum* 4.15.6 on applause for Cicero at the *ludi Apollinares* in 54, no doubt because of his *rapprochement* with Caesar.

15. Cicero *De oratore* 1.24, *De finibus* 3.8.

16. Cicero *Ad Atticum* 2.4-17 (59 BC); *Ad Q. fratrem* 2.6.4, *Ad Atticum* 4.7 (56 BC); *Ad Atticum* 4.6, 4.9 (55 BC); *Ad familiares* 7.18.3, 16.10, 16.13-15 (53 BC); *Ad Atticum* 14.1-15.5 (44 BC).

17. Cicero *Ad Atticum* 14.5.2 (*res prolatae*, 11 April), *Ad familiares* 3.9.4 (*discessus senatus*, spring); cf. *In Clodium et Curionem* fr. 19 Crawford (*cum Romae nihil agitur*, April). Still true a generation later: Dio Cassius 54.29.6 (spring 12 BC).

18. Cicero *Ad Atticum* 4.8a (56 BC), 4.13.1 (55 BC); *Ad Q. fratrem* 3.4.6 (54 BC); *Ad familiares* 16.24.2, *Ad Atticum* 16.8-15 (44 BC).

plebeian aediles' games were more specifically *popularis* in character than the others. Once again, the evidence is what Cicero's correspondence presupposes.

In 57 BC, two months after his return from exile, Cicero stayed in Rome in November because of the ongoing dispute about the restoration of his house. It was a matter of some ideological importance. Eighteen months earlier the house had been destroyed, and the Roman People had legislated for the consecration of the site, the demolition of the adjoining portico of Catulus, and the use of the combined site for a new portico carrying the name of their tribune Clodius.[19] This new portico contained an altar and cult image of the goddess Libertas.[20] In early October 57 the *pontifices* decided that Cicero should have his site back, and the Senate authorised the rebuilding of Catulus' portico. That meant that the new portico would be destroyed, and 'the People's Liberty' would lose her shrine.[21]

The *ludi plebeii* began on 4 November and lasted fourteen days; in 57, Clodius as aedile-elect was no doubt prominently involved. That's the background to Cicero's dramatic narrative to Atticus, written later that month:

> On 3 November the builders were driven off my site by armed men; the portico of Catulus, which was being rebuilt by decree of the Senate on the consuls' contract and had almost reached roof level, was knocked down; my brother Quintus' house was first damaged by stones thrown from my site and then set on fire by Clodius' order, with firebrands thrown in while the whole city looked on. . . . On 11 November [Clodius] pursued me with his men as I was going down the Sacra Via. Shouts, stones, clubs, swords, and all without any warning. I withdrew into Tettius Damio's forecourt. The people with me easily prevented the hired men from getting in. He himself could have been killed—but I'm starting to use diet treatment, I'm tired of surgery.[22]

19. Destruction of house: Cicero *Post reditum in senatu* 18, *De domo* 60–2, 101, 113, *De haruspicum responso* 15, *Pro Sestio* 54, *In Pisonem* 26, 52. Legislation: *De domo* 44, 47, 50–1, *Pro Sestio* 65, *In Pisonem* 30. Demolition and replacement of portico: *De domo* 102, 114, *Ad Atticum* 4.2.5, *Pro Caelio* 78. Inscription with Clodius' name: *De domo* 51, 100.

20. Cicero *De domo* 100-103, 112, 121, 136-7, *De haruspicum responso* 33. Not a temple, as is often said: for the full argument see Wiseman 2012b, 658–60.

21. Cicero *Ad Atticum* 4.2.2-5, 4.3.2; Dio Cassius 39.11, 39.20.3.

22. Cicero *Ad Atticum* 4.3.2-3 (23 November 57 BC): *armatis hominibus a.d. III Non. Nou. expulsi sunt fabri de area nostra, disturbata porticus Catuli, quae ex senatus consulto consulum locatione reficiebatur et ad tectum paene peruenerat, Quinti fratris domus primo fracta coniectu lapidum ex area nostra, deinde inflammata iussu Clodi inspectante urbe coniectis ignibus . . . a.d. III Id. Nou. cum Sacra uia descenderem, insecutus est me cum*

It would be interesting to know who exactly drew their swords on the Sacra Via. Those on one side of the fracas are called 'hired men' (*operae*), those on the other just 'the people with me'—but if killing Clodius was a real possibility, then the people with Cicero were evidently armed.

What he didn't mention, because he didn't need to, is that 11 November was the seventh day of the *ludi plebeii*. He was on his way down to the Forum,[23] where no doubt there was an *ad hoc* theatre and a big crowd enjoying the games.[24] Perhaps Clodius and his friends just wanted to make it clear that he wasn't welcome. Certainly the armed guards suggest that Cicero knew he had to take precautions. Normally he wouldn't have been in Rome at all, as letters from the two subsequent years make clear:

> Since an extra day has been added to the games, I'll spend it all the better here with Dionysius.[25]

> I see you know I got to Tusculum on 14 November.[26] Dionysius was there for me. I want to be in Rome on the 18th—well, 'want', in fact I'm obliged to be (Milo's wedding!).[27]

So even in 56 and 55, when his palinode in favour of Pompey and Caesar might have got him applause from the audience, Cicero still chose to talk literature at Tusculum with Atticus' learned freedman Dionysius rather than take his chance in Rome at the *ludi plebeii*.

What results from this close reading of the sources fits very well with Fergus Millar's view of the political role of the Roman People. But it is

---

suis. clamor, lapides, fustes, gladii; et haec improuisa omnia. discessi in uestibulum Tetti Damionis. qui erant mecum facile operas aditu prohibuerunt. ipse occidi potuit; sed ego diaeta curare incipio, chirurgiae taedet. 'Surgery' in the final phrase was a euphemism for political assassination (Wiseman 2012a).

23. *Descendere* without further explanation normally means to come down from one's house to the Forum: Catullus 112.1, Q. Cicero *Commentariolum petitionis* 36; Cicero *Pro Roscio Amerino* 133 (*de Palatio*), *Philippics* 2.15, 8.6; Horace *Epistles* 1.20.5, Seneca *Apocolocyntosis* 12.1 (*per Sacram uiam*). Cf. Cicero *Ad Atticum* 1.18.1, *De oratore* 2.267 (specifying *in forum*).

24. *Ad hoc* theatres: Varro in Servius on Virgil *Georgics* 3.24, Tacitus *Annals* 14.20.2, Dio Cassius 37.58.3-4. In the Forum: Plautus *Curculio* 462–84, with Marshall 2006, 40–43; cf. Wiseman 2009, 164–70.

25. Cicero *Ad Atticum* 4.8a.1 (c. 17 November 56 BC, from Antium or Tusculum): *ludis quidem quoniam dies est additus, eo etiam melius hic eum diem cum Dionysio conteremus.*

26. Probably from Arpinum: cf. *Ad Atticum* 16.13.1-2 for the sequence in November 44 BC.

27. Cicero *Ad Atticum* 4.13.1 (15–16 November 55 BC): *nos in Tusculum uenisse a.d. XVII Kal. Dec. uideo te scire. ibi nobis Dionysius praesto fuit. Romae a.d. XVIII Kal. uolumus esse. quod dico 'uolumus', immo uero cogimur. Milonis nuptiae.*

hard to make sense of it if you insist from the start on a 'peculiar and ingrained "depth of obedience", which seems to have been characteristic of the *populus Romanus*', and a 'collective consensus' which was 'an essential factor supporting the social coherence between the *populus Romanus* and its political class'.[28] Millar's critics see the People's political role as just selecting the winners in a competition for honours among the ruling elite.[29] But Cicero and Clodius were not rivals for office. The critics' *a priori* framework of interpretation simply fails to explain the phenomena.

6.2. *What's on the programme?*

So far, we have been using the evidence for the *ludi scaenici* to test the idea that the Roman People had neither the time nor the leisure to take an interest in politics. What has emerged is that the *ludi* offered a regular opportunity for ordinary citizens to make their opinions known, and to put pressure on those whose political attitudes they didn't like. That prompts another question that no-one ever seems to ask. Given that the magistrate responsible for each set of games was a senator with a political position and political ambitions of his own, how did he choose the programme of entertainment?

There is plenty of well-known evidence for the performance of classic tragedies and comedies, and occasions when fortuitously topical lines were emphasised by the actors or reacted to by the audience.[30] But with several consecutive days to fill, the magistrates in charge had to provide much more than just the old classics, and we should therefore expect them also to be commissioning new work from contemporary authors.[31] In fact, commissioning competitions (*commissiones ludorum*) are also well attested,[32] though the evidence seems to have escaped the notice of theatre historians.

Augustus instructed the praetors responsible for the annual games not to accept work too obviously adulatory towards himself, whereas

28. Hölkeskamp 2010, 98–9, 131; 'depth of obedience' is quoted from Simmel 1992, 340.

29. Hölkeskamp 2010.92: 'In the first place, it was the essential right and duty of the *populus Romanus* to award the *honores* in the annual elections.' Cf. Hurlet 2012, 42: 'Hölkeskamp a vu juste en faisant du people romain non pas l'organe souverain, mais l'arbitre des rivalités entre les puissants.'

30. Cicero *Ad Atticum* 2.19.3 (59 BC), *Pro Sestio* 118-23 (57 BC, section 2.3 above), Suetonius *Diuus Iulius* 84.2.

31. As Clodius tried to do from Laberius (Macrobius *Saturnalia* 2.6.6).

32. Cicero *Ad Atticum* 16.5.1, Pliny *Letters* 7.24.6, Suetonius *Diuus Augustus* 43.5, Macrobius *Saturnalia* 2.7.7-9; cf. Cicero *Ad Q. fratrem* 3.4.6 (*quo die ludi committebantur*). Not to be confused with the *commissiones* of competing declaimers in the rhetorical schools (Suetonius *De grammaticis* 17.1, *Gaius* 53.2).

Domitian evidently did the opposite.[33] Adjusting that situation to republican conditions, we may imagine hopeful authors submitting work that was complimentary to the presiding magistrate—and as it happens, Cicero's correspondence once again provides the evidence. In the summer of 43 BC he got a letter from Asinius Pollio about the behaviour of the younger Balbus, promagistrate in charge of Baetica:

> Then there were the things he did 'like Gaius Caesar', as he always boasts: at the games he put on at Gades he granted the actor Herennius Gallus the gold ring on the last day, and led him to a seat in the fourteen rows (yes, he'd got that many equestrian places) . . . But other things he didn't even have Caesar's precedent for, such as the *praetexta* he put on at the games about his own journey to try to win over L. Lentulus the proconsul—and he even wept during the performance, so moved he was by the memory of his great deeds.[34]

It is not clear whether Balbus wrote the *praetexta* himself, as is normally assumed,[35] or commissioned it from a local poet.[36] Either way, we would never have heard about it but for the accident of Pollio's indignation. How many other such ephemeral productions were played at the Roman games and then forgotten?

Before pursuing that question, it is worth looking for a moment at what Balbus did in imitation of Caesar. The precedent probably dated from the great victory games of September–October 46 BC:

> At the [theatre] games Decimus Laberius, a Roman knight, acted in his own *mimus*, was presented with 500,000 sesterces and the gold ring, and passed from the stage through the orchestra to sit in the fourteen rows.[37]

33. Suetonius *Diuus Augustus* 89.3 (*ne paterentur nomen suum commissionibus obsolefieri*), Pliny *Panegyricus* 54.1 (*cum laudes imperatorum ludis etiam et commissionibus celebrarentur*). The praetors took over responsibility for the annual *ludi* in 22 BC (Dio Cassius 54.2.3-4).

34. Cicero *Ad familiares* 10.32.2-3 (8 June 43 BC): *haec quoque fecit, ut ipse gloriari solet, eadem quae C. Caesar: ludis quos Gadibus fecit Herennium Gallum histrionem summo ludorum die anulo aureo donatum in XIIII sessum deduxit (tot enim fecerat ordines equestris loci) . . . illa uero iam ne Caesaris quidem exemplo, quod ludis praetextam de suo itinere ad L. Lentulum pro consule sollicitandum posuit, et quidem cum ageretur fleuit memoria rerum gestarum commotus.*

35. Manuwald 2001, 54–62.

36. Cf. Cicero *Pro Archia* 26 for poets in Spain (Corduba).

37. Suetonius *Diuus Iulius* 39.2: *ludis Decimus Laberius eques Romanus mimum suum egit donatusque quingentis sestertiis ei anulo aureo sessum in quattuordecim e scaena per orchestram transiit.* Sometimes attributed to the *ludi plebeii* of 47 (Schwartz 1948, 264–6), but I think unnecessarily.

Suetonius had just reported that a former senator and a man of praetorian descent fought in the gladiatorial contests, and the children of Asiatic and Bithynian aristocrats performed the Pyrrhic dance. There is no suggestion of coercion; on the contrary, Dio's report of the games specifies that Caesar *permitted* equestrians (but not senators) to fight as gladiators, implying that the initiative came from them.[38] Certainly there is ample evidence for *equites* later appearing on stage or in the arena,[39] despite repeated attempts under Augustus and Tiberius to discourage the practice.[40]

Since Balbus was clearly honouring Herennius Gallus by presenting him with the gold ring and leading him to an equestrian seat in the fourteen rows, the natural inference is that Caesar had been honouring Laberius when he did the same thing three years earlier. He was, after all, inviting him to receive the public applause of a huge audience of Roman citizens.

That is compatible with the elder Seneca's brief reference to the incident: 'Caesar at his games brought on Laberius as an actor, then restored him to the equestrian order and told him to go and sit in the equestrian seats.'[41] Aulus Gellius, however, evidently represented it as a deliberate humiliation of Laberius: the chapter-headings of his lost eighth book include 'How the poet Laberius was ignominiously treated by Gaius Caesar, with a quotation of Laberius' own words on that subject'.[42]

Fortunately Gellius' lost chapter was reproduced by Macrobius, and so we know that in this version of the story Caesar's invitation to Laberius to star in his own play was regarded as compulsion, 'as Laberius himself attests in his prologue with these verses':

> O Necessity, whose blind-side assaults many have sought to avoid—most to no avail—where have you made me fall, when I'm nearly breathing my last? No ambition, no largesse, no fear, no force, no man's prestige could make me shift my stance when I was young: now that

38. Dio Cassius 43.23.5, Suetonius *Diuus Iulius* 39.1.

39. Dio Cassius 48.43.2-3 (38 BC), 51.22.4 (a senator at Octavian's games, 29 BC), Suetonius *Diuus Augustus* 43.3 (early Augustus), Dio Cassius 53.31.3 (Marcellus' games, 23 BC), Suetonius *Nero* 4 (L. Ahenobarbus' games, 19 and 16 BC), Dio Cassius 55.10.11 (Quinctius Crispinus' games, 2 BC), 55.33.4 (AD 8), 56.25.7-8 (AD 11), 57.14.3 (AD 15), Suetonius *Tiberius* 35.2 (Tiberius, undated).

40. Suetonius *Diuus Augustus* 43.3, *Tiberius* 35.2 (undated *s.c.*), Dio Cassius 54.2.5 (22 BC), *Année Épigraphique* 1978, 145, 17–21 (*s.c.* AD 11), 1978, 145 (*s.c.* AD 19). For detailed discussion of 'Ritter, Gladiatoren und Schauspieler' see Lebek 1990, 43–58.

41. Seneca *Suasoriae* 7.3.9: *Laberium diuus Iulius ludis suis mimum produxit, deinde equestri illum ordini reddidit; iussit ire sessum in equestria.*

42. Aulus Gellius 8.15 (Loeb trans.): *quibus modis ignominiatus tractatusque sit a C. Caesare Laberius poeta; atque inibi appositi uersus super eadem re eiusdem Laberii.*

I'm old, do you see how easily I'm undone by the invitation—humble and mild—that issues from the merciful mind of the man who towers above us? Of course, for me to say 'no' to the man the very gods have denied nothing—would that not be outrageous? I, who have passed twice thirty years with not a mark against my name, left my household gods a Roman knight to return to them—a mime. Surely today I've lived one day longer than I ought.

O Fortune, who know no mean in good and bad alike, if it was your pleasure to break me at the pinnacle, in the full bloom of the fame I'd won by my glory in letters, why did you not make me bow down, to destroy my pliant self, when I still had the vigour of limbs in their prime, when I could put on a proper show for the People and the great man? *Now* you cast me down? Why? What do I bring to the stage? The beauty and dignity of a well-formed body, the mind's wit or a sweet-sounding voice? As ivy destroys the vital force of trees by creeping round them, so long passage of years is killing me. Like a tomb, I keep nothing but my name.[43]

So was it an honour or a humiliation? The question has become all the more puzzling now that Costas Panayotakis, in his edition of Laberius, has pointed out that the style and prosody of these lines are conspicuously unlike all the rest of the fragments. As he carefully puts it, 'there are serious problems with the versification of this piece, which render the attribution of the lines to L[aberius] highly suspicious'.[44]

Leaving that problem in abeyance for the moment, let's go back to Pollio's letter and the self-glorifying play put on by Balbus at his games in Gades. It was a *praetexta*, a type of drama that is now at last getting serious scholarly attention.[45] The name referred to the *toga praetexta* of the Roman magistrate, because the plays 'dramatised the business of commanders and public affairs, and brought on stage Roman kings or leaders'.[46] The subject matter might be in the distant past,[47] but could

43. Macrobius *Saturnalia* 2.7.2-3 (*unde se et Laberius a Caesare coactum in prologo testator his uersibus*); Laberius fr. 90 Panayotakis (Macrobius *Saturnalia* 2.7.3, trans. R. A. Kaster).

44. Panayotakis 2010, 455, cf. 72–6 for the metrical analysis.

45. Manuwald 2001; Wiseman 2008, 194–209; Boyle 2008, xlii–lv; Kragelund 2016, 1–126.

46. Diomedes *De poematibus* 10.3 = *Grammatici Latini* 1.489 Keil: *in quibus imperatorum negotia agebantur et publica et reges Romani uel duces inducuntur*. Evidently from Varro (fr. 306 Funaioli): section 3.2 above.

47. E.g. Manuwald 2001, 141–61, 172–9 (Romulus); 220–43 (L. Brutus); 243–8 (Aeneas).

just as easily be contemporary: the classic examples are Naevius' *Clastidium*, on M. Marcellus' victory in 222 BC, Ennius' *Ambracia*, on that of M. Nobilior in 189 BC, Pacuvius' *Paullus*, presumably on L. Paullus' conquest of Macedon in 168 BC, and the *Octavia* wrongly attributed to Seneca, on the popular rising in support of Nero's wronged wife in AD 62.[48]

The *Octavia* is particularly important for our present purpose, because the chorus of Roman citizens, witnessing Octavia's departure to the island where she will be killed, reflects on the *fauor populi* and the repeated violent deaths of the People's champions (877–98). Their view of the Gracchi, conspicuously at odds with the neo-optimate assumptions normal in early imperial literature,[49] presupposes a popular audience for whom the traditional *popularis* ideology was still a reality.[50] We know from Varro that the purpose of *fabulae praetextae* was to 'teach the People',[51] and the range of attested subjects shows that the People were learning not only about Roman history but also about public events in their own time.

So far, then, I think the evidence for the *ludi scaenici* has established at least a *prima facie* case in favour of Fergus Millar's position. At the traditional public games, which took up fifty-eight days of the year, the Roman People regularly expressed their attitude to current politics and politicians, and were entertained and instructed by performances that often had a political and topical content. And one imagines that was even more true at the *ludi Victoriae* introduced by Sulla and Caesar,[52] and at the one-off theatre games sometimes held in connection with triumphs and aristocratic funerals.[53]

So if anyone wants to argue that the Roman People had no time for, or interest in, politics, they must take on the burden of proof and show why we shouldn't believe what our sources say on the subject.

48. Manuwald 2001, 134–41 (Naevius), 162–72 (Ennius), 180–96 (Pacuvius). The idea that *Octavia* was not a *praetexta* at all (Ferri 2003, 2–3) seems to me just another example of the triumph of preconception over evidence: see Wiseman 2008, 205–9.

49. *Octavia* 882-6; contrast (e.g.) Velleius Paterculus 2.3.2, 2.6.2; Valerius Maximus 4.7.1, 7.2.6b, 9.4.1; Lucan 6.796.

50. As also implied by the Roman People's reaction to the possibility of a restored optimate republic in AD 41 (Josephus *Antiquitates* 19.227-8).

51. Varro *De lingua Latina* 6.18 (*cur hoc, togata praetexta data* †*eis*† *Apollinaribus ludis docuit populum*); Manuwald 2001, 66–71.

52. Respectively 26 October–1 November and 20–30 July.

53. Triumphs: e.g. Tacitus *Annals* 14.21.1 (145 BC). Funerals: e.g. Livy 41.28.11 (174 BC); *didascaliae* to Terence *Adelphoe* and *Hecyra* (160 BC). Both categories are unnecessarily dismissed by Flower 1995, 177–81.

6.3. Docudrama

Having got this far, I think we may take a step further. If the *ludi scaenici* normally included dramatisations of historical or contemporary events, and if, as Lucretius vividly reminds us, what one saw at the *ludi* was deeply embedded in one's memory,[54] it must follow that much of what we loosely call Roman 'cultural memory' was actually what people had seen acted out on stage before their eyes.[55] Cicero confirms as much when he identifies the sources of *opiniones* as 'parent, nurse, teacher, poet, the stage'.[56]

That in turn makes it possible that historians in the Roman world, or the sources they drew on, sometimes reported not what they knew from documentary evidence but what they already had in their mind's eye and didn't need to document. That case is often made for early Roman history,[57] but it is no less applicable to the contested politics of the late republic. When Plutarch's account of the death of Gaius Gracchus includes a histrionic scene in front of two doors (as in a *scaenae frons*),[58] when Suetonius' report of Caesar at the Rubicon features a supernatural being playing a reed pipe,[59] and when Appian adds to the credible narrative of the aftermath of Caesar's death a scene that would have been possible only on the stage,[60] then I think empirical method requires us to suggest an explanation. Just shrugging one's shoulders is hardly enough.

What is at issue here is the fictionalisation of current events, the achievement of what we may call 'instant myth'. That was something that much concerned Tacitus,[61] and his comments on the subject are worth close attention. First, on the death of Tiberius' son Drusus:

54. Lucretius 4.973-83, esp. 978-9: *per multos itaque illa dies eadem obuersantur ante oculos.*

55. See chapter 2.

56. Cicero *De legibus* 1.47.

57. It is implicit at Plutarch *Romulus* 8.7 (δραματικὸν καὶ πλασματῶδες), Dionysius of Halicarnassus *Roman Antiquities* 3.18.1 (θεατρικαῖς ἐοικότα περιπετείαις), 9.22.3 (πλάσμασιν ἔοικε θεατρικοῖς) and Livy 1.46.3 (*sceleris tragici exemplum*).

58. Plutarch *Gaius Gracchus* 14.5-15.4, with Wiseman 1998, 52–9. Acerbic disagreement: Keaveney 2003, 322–32.

59. Suetonius *Diuus Iulius* 32, with Wiseman 1998, 60–63.

60. Appian *Civil Wars* 2.121.509-122.511, with Wiseman 2009, 221–2. Polite disagreement: Beard 2013, 97–8.

61. See especially Tacitus *Annals* 3.14.2: *is finis fuit ulciscenda Germanici morte, non modo apud illos homines qui tum agebant etiam secutis temporibus uario rumore iactata. adeo maxima quaeque ambigua sunt, dum aliqui quoquo modo audita pro compertis habent, alii uerum in contrarium uertunt, et gliscit utrumque posteritate.*

> In my case the reason for transmitting and criticising the rumour was that on the basis of a resounding example I might dispel false hearsay and ask of those into whose hands my work comes that they should not be hungry to accept well publicised incredibilities nor prefer them to what is genuine and uncorrupted by the miraculous.[62]

Next, on the bigamous marriage of Messallina and Silius:

> As I am not unaware, it will seem fantastic . . . yet none of this has been compiled to promote a marvel, but I am transmitting what was heard and written by my elders.[63]

And finally, on the death of Otho:

> Just as I have taken the view that seeking out fantastic items and gratifying readers' minds with fiction is far from the gravity of the work I have undertaken, so too I would not wish to deny credibility to what has been publicised and transmitted.[64]

That same vocabulary of *fabula* and *miraculum* occurs in the two best proof texts for plays on historical subjects, Livy on the siege of Veii in 390 BC and Ovid on the arrival of the Great Mother in 204 BC:

> At this point a story is inserted. . . . It's not worth the trouble to affirm or refute these things, which are more appropriate to the show of the stage that delights in marvels than to credibility.[65]
>
> The things I shall tell are marvellous, but also attested by the stage.[66]

It is quite possible that the Tacitean examples also came from 'the stage that delights in marvels',[67] and that contemporary political events, as well as those in the distant past, were routinely shaped by dramatists to astonish the audience at the *ludi scaenici*.

62. Tacitus *Annals* 4.11.3 (trans. A. J. Woodman): *mihi tradendi arguendique rumoris causa fuit ut claro sub exemplo falsas auditiones depellerem peteremque ab iis quorum in manus cura nostra uenerit ne diuulgata atque incredibilia auide accepta ueris neque in miraculum corruptis antehabeant.*

63. Tacitus *Annals* 11.27 (trans. A. J. Woodman): *haud sum ignarus fabulosum uisum iri . . . sed nihil compositum miraculi causa, uerum audita scriptaque senioribus tradam.*

64. Tacitus *Histories* 2.50.2: *ut conquirere fabulosa et fictis oblectare legentium animos procul grauitate coepti operis crediderim, ita uulgatis traditisque demere fidem non ausim.*

65. Livy 5.21.8-9: *inseritur huic loco fabula . . . haec ad ostentationem scaenae gaudentis miraculis aptiora quam ad fidem neque adfirmare neque refellere est operae pretium.*

66. Ovid *Fasti* 4.326: *mira, sed et scaena testificata loquar.*

67. As *Annals* 14.63.2 evidently came from *Octavia* 932-57: Ferri 2003, 394, Boyle 2008, 283.

From the very beginning of ancient drama, one form of astonishment had been the appearance of a ghost on stage,[68] a fact which should draw our attention to Plutarch's narrative of the Philippi campaign:

> One night, just before the army crossed over to Greece [summer 42 BC], he was sitting alone in his tent, which was dimly lit; the hour was late, and the whole camp was wrapped in silence. In the midst of his meditations, he thought he heard someone enter the tent, and as he turned his eyes towards the entrance he caught sight of a strange and horrible apparition, a monstrous and terrifying figure standing silently by his side. Summoning up his courage to question it, he asked, 'What man or god are you, and what do you want with me?' The phantom answered, 'I am your evil spirit [*daimon*], Brutus: you shall see me at Philippi.' Brutus kept his self-control and replied, 'I shall see you then.'[69]

It is no surprise to discover that the phantom was not mentioned in the most reliable history of the campaign, the eyewitness account of Brutus' friend P. Volumnius.[70] What follows in Plutarch, a scene where Cassius expounded the Epicurean theory of sense perception and declared that no-one should believe in *daimones*,[71] is very reminiscent of the soothsayers' explanation of Tarquin's dream in Accius' *Brutus*, or the nurse's explanation of Poppaea's dream in *Octavia*.[72]

It seems to me likely that this episode was first created for the stage, and that a different author, appropriately discussing *miracula*, may even preserve the scene where Cassius discovered he was wrong:

> Gaius Cassius, who must never be named without reference to his public parricide, was standing firm and full of courage in the battle-line at Philippi when he saw Divus Iulius, more august than in human form, wearing the purple cloak of a commander and with a menacing expression, charging at him on a galloping horse. Terrified at the sight he turned his back on his enemy, having first cried out, 'What more do you have to do if killing isn't enough?'[73]

68. E.g. Aeschylus *Persae* 681 (Darius), *Eumenides* 94 (Clytemnestra), Euripides *Hecuba* 1 (Polydorus). Roman examples: e.g. Pacuvius *Iliona* (Cicero *Pro Sestio* 126, Polydorus), ps.Seneca *Octavia* 593 (Agrippina). It may be relevant that Catullus wrote a *Phasma* (Juvenal 8.186) and Laberius a *Necyomantia* (Aulus Gellius 16.7.12, 20.6.6).

69. Plutarch *Brutus* 36.5-7, trans. Ian Scott-Kilvert.

70. Plutarch *Brutus* 48.2 (*FRHist* 47 F1).

71. Plutarch *Brutus* 37.6: δαίμονας δ' οὔτ' εἶναι πιθανὸν.

72. Cicero *De diuinatione* 1.45; *Octavia* 740-55.

73. Valerius Maximus 1.8.8.

Plutarch wasn't going to report anything as sensational as that, but it's clear that this supernatural scenario affected his own view of the death of Caesar and the way it was avenged:

> His great guardian spirit [*daimon*], which had accompanied him in life, continued to avenge his murder, pursuing and tracking his killers over every land and sea, until not one remained and everyone had been punished who had any contact with the killing in thought or in execution.[74]

That should not surprise us. Even Tacitus, while insisting he was not relating falsehoods, was still willing to report an account that involved a supernatural apparition.[75]

All this circumstantial evidence for 'docudrama' supports the hypothesis that current political events, as well as properly historical ones, were regularly on the programme at the Roman theatre games, and therefore that the Roman People, for whom the games were both entertainment and instruction, were necessarily engaged in the political business of the republic.

6.4. Two hypothetical examples

At this point we can return to our problem with Laberius and Caesar. Before Aulus Gellius in the mid-second century AD, whose argument is reproduced for us by Macrobius, there is no sign that Caesar's invitation to Laberius to act his own mime was intended to humiliate him. On the contrary, the earliest evidence for it, Pollio's letter to Cicero three years later, clearly implies it was an honour, and the later accounts by the elder Seneca and Suetonius are compatible with that.[76] If Panayotakis is right to doubt the genuineness of the Laberian prologue quoted by Gellius (via Macrobius)—and there is no-one better qualified to make the judgement—then it may be that Gellius was deceived by a text in which Laberius was a character but not the author.

74. Plutarch *Caesar* 69.2 (trans. Christopher Pelling): ὁ μέντοι μέγας αὐτοῦ δαίμων, ᾧ παρὰ τὸν βίον ἐχρήσατο, καὶ τελευτήσαντος ἐπηκολούθησε τιμωρὸς τοῦ φόνου, διά τε γῆς πάσης καὶ θαλάττης ἐλαύνων καὶ ἀνιχνεύων ἄχρι τοῦ μηδένα λιπεῖν τῶν ἀπεκτονότων, ἀλλὰ καὶ τοὺς καθ' ὁτιοῦν ἢ χειρὶ τοῦ ἔργου θιγόντας ἢ γνώμης μετασχόντας ἐπεξελθεῖν.

75. Tacitus *Annals* 11.21.1 (*neque falsa prompserim*), on Curtius Rufus as a young man at Hadrumetum.

76. Cicero *Ad familiares* 10.32.2, Seneca *Suasoriae* 7.3.9, Suetonius *Diuus Iulius* 39.2.

We know the playwright died in the tenth month after the Ides of March, therefore in December 44 or January 43 BC.[77] At that time the one great polarising issue in Roman politics was what view to take of Caesar, and of his assassins. As both consul and proconsul, Antony insisted on the essential public duty of exacting vengeance for the murder.[78] For Cicero and the *optimates*, on the other hand, it was self-evident that Caesar had been a tyrant, and that the men who killed him were liberators of the republic. That was a view freely expressed by Cicero in his correspondence, and in works—like *De officiis* and the second *Philippic*—that did not receive general publicity.[79] In public, the most he allowed himself to say was that Caesar's *popularis leuitas* gained him power that a free republic could not tolerate, and that the Senate regarded his killing as lawful.[80]

What the Roman People thought of it may be inferred from Lucius Piso's speech in the Senate on the first day of 43 BC, when the immediate issue was the impending war for the control of Cisalpine Gaul:

> 'As for the governorship of Gaul, Antonius was not appointed to it by us, but by the People, who gave it by a law which was passed when Cicero himself was present, in the same way as they have often conferred other powers and indeed once gave this very governorship to Caesar. . . . If it is the law that Cicero criticises, he is criticising the People who passed it. He should have made them change their minds, not insult them after joining them in passing it. Nor should he entrust the province to Decimus, whom the People expelled as a result of the murder, and refuse to trust Antonius with what the People have granted him. Good counsellors do not quarrel with the People at times of great danger, nor do they forget that this very function, of deciding who is a friend and who a foe, used once to belong to the People. According to the ancient laws the People are the sole and sovereign authority in cases of peace and war. I hope to God they will not find a leader and understand any of this and be angry with us.'[81]

77. Jerome *Chronica* Ol. 184.2: *Laberius mimorum scriptor decimo mense post C. Caesaris interitum Puteolis moritur.*

78. Cicero *Ad familiares* 12.3.2 (October 44); *Philippics* 13.38-9, 46 (March 43).

79. Cicero *Philippics* 2.25, 114, 116-17; *De officiis* 2.23, 3.19, 82-5; for the correspondence, cf. Wiseman 2009, 201.

80. Cicero *Philippics* 5.49, 13.2; cf. 13.18 (*Caesare dominante*). These were speeches in the Senate, but as Fergus Millar rightly pointed out (1998, 183, on Asconius 44-5C), such speeches might be immediately reported outside.

81. Appian *Civil Wars* 3.55.225-9, trans. John Carter.

The same point is made in the peroration:

> 'I urge you also to be careful of the People, who very recently assaulted Caesar's murderers, in case we appear to be insulting them by giving some of the murderers provincial governorships and by commending Decimus for ignoring a law passed by the People, while we judge Antonius to be a public enemy because he received Gaul from the People.'[82]

Since Appian had good sources for this period,[83] we may be confident that the general tone of Piso's speech, if not every detail,[84] is accurately reported.

For the first half of the year, as attested by the *Philippics* and the letters to Brutus, Cicero and the *optimates* were able to maintain their position, in the misguided hope that the young Caesar would maintain his alliance with them. So if we are right to believe that the theatre games were a sounding-board for political opinion, a playwright hoping to have his work featured at *ludi* presided over by an optimate magistrate might easily have written the pseudo-Laberian prologue quoted by Gellius and Macrobius. It would have honoured the memory of a recently deceased colleague, and presented Caesar in an odious light by reinterpreting his invitation to Laberius as a deliberate humiliation.[85]

Everything changed in July, when huge crowds welcomed the young Caesar to Rome, and Cicero's withdrawal from the city marked the collapse of the optimate cause.[86] There is, I think, no reason to doubt that the young Caesar's election to the consulship on 19 August was what the great majority of the Roman People wanted, and that the subsequent confirmation of his adoption and judicial condemnation of the assassins were carried out, as our sources say, in the People's name and by due process of

82. Appian *Civil Wars* 3.60.247, trans. John Carter.

83. Primarily Pollio, no doubt. Andrew Drummond's very cautious discussion of the question rightly concludes that 'for later chroniclers of this period Pollio should have been high on their reading list, given his closeness to the events narrated, his personal involvement in a number of crucial episodes, and his access to eyewitness accounts and other primary information' (Drummond 2013, 443).

84. Cicero had not, in fact, been present when Antony was given Cisalpine Gaul as his province.

85. In 43 BC the *ludi Apollinares* were presumably the responsibility of M. Cornutus, *praetor urbanus* (Cicero *Philippics* 14.37), who not long after the games were over committed suicide when the legions he was commanding to protect the city joined the forces of Caesar's son (Appian *Civil Wars* 3.92.381).

86. Appian *Civil Wars* 3.92.378-80 (crowds), 3.93.385 (Cicero's flight).

law.[87] What is certain is that the programme of events at the *ludi Romani* in September, and the *ludi plebeii* in November, must have reflected the new situation.

With that in mind, I now turn to a puzzling passage in Appian which seems to mis-date the flight of Cicero by about three months. The context is before the battle of Mutina on 14 April:

> At Rome, in the absence of the consuls, Cicero acted like a popular leader. There were frequent meetings of the People, and he had arms manufactured by gathering the craftsmen together to work without pay, collected money, and exacted extremely heavy contributions from Antonius' supporters. The latter readily paid up to avoid damaging accusations, until Publius Ventidius, who had served under Caesar and was a friend of Antonius, could not endure Cicero's oppression any longer. He took himself off to Caesar's colonies, and being a well-known figure re-enlisted two legions for Antonius and made a rapid march on Rome to arrest Cicero. There ensued a gigantic commotion. Most of the population expected the worst and evacuated their women and children, while Cicero himself fled the city. On hearing this, Ventidius turned away to join Antonius. His way was barred by Octavian and Hirtius, so he proceeded to Picenum, recruited another legion, and awaited further developments.[88]

The march on Rome and subsequent panic are not only unhistorical, as is proved by Cicero's speeches and letters at the time; they also duplicate what happened in July, with even the same phraseology in the text.[89] It is as if Appian's source here wanted to give Ventidius credit for what in reality was later brought about by the young Caesar.

Ventidius, who was one of the praetors of the year, did indeed go to Picenum and did indeed enrol three legions to reinforce Antony at Mutina.[90] In the autumn, during the discussions between the three future triumvirs, it was agreed that the young Caesar should resign the consulship,

87. Appian *Civil Wars* 3.94.389 (adoption κατὰ νόμον κουριάτιον . . . ἐπὶ τοῦ δήμου), 3.94.390 (curiate law ἐπινομώτατος), 3.95.392 (murder court νόμῳ); Dio Cassius 46.45.3 (election πρὸς τοῦ δήμου), 46.47.4 (adoption confirmed κατὰ τὰ νομιζόμενα), 46.48.2 (murder court ἐν δίκῃ τινὶ). Cf. Augustus *Res gestae* 1.4 (*populus . . . me consulem . . . creauit*), 2.1 (*qui parentem meum interfecerunt, eos in exilium expuli iudiciis legitimis*).

88. Appian *Civil Wars* 3.66.269-71 (trans. John Carter); for the date, see Degrassi 1963, 279 (*Feriale Cumanum*); Ovid *Fasti* 4.627-8, 675-6.

89. Appian *Civil Wars* 3.66.271, 3.89.367 (θόρυβος ἄπλετος).

90. Cicero *Philippics* 12.23 (Ancona); Appian *Civil Wars* 3.72.297, 3.80.328.

and that the praetor Ventidius should be made consul in his place.[91] The triumvirs themselves were evidently elected on 27 November.[92] It is not known whether Ventidius' election was before or after that, but his candidacy would certainly have been known at the time of the *ludi plebeii*, which were held from the 4th to the 17th of the month.

All this may suggest a solution to the problem of the Appian passage. We know from Cicero's letter to Trebatius ten years earlier that the entertainment at theatre games might include satirical comment from the mime-writers on current events and individuals in the public eye.[93] Perhaps this time Cicero himself was the subject, portrayed as a domineering pseudo-*popularis* abusing his position to extort money from political opponents, and then ignominiously fleeing from the city rather than face punishment by the heroic Ventidius—who just happened to be presenting himself for election to the consulship at the time of the games.

My main point here is methodological. It seems to me a dereliction of scholarly duty to turn a blind eye to oddities in the evidence, and not even enquire how they could have come about. It is certainly odd that the transmitted text of Laberius' prologue is unlikely to be by Laberius, and that Appian's account of Ventidius' march on Rome is demonstrably unhistorical. The conjectural explanation I offer, that both these anomalies are the result of topical drama scenarios being taken as authentic historical record, is not just a 'flight of fancy'.[94] It depends on good Ciceronian evidence for what happened at the *ludi scaenici*, and good Tacitean evidence for how historians could be deceived by false versions created even at the time of the events. Of course it may not be right, but it does at least explain the phenomena.

91. Appian *Civil Wars* 4.2.6, Dio Cassius 47.15.2, Velleius Paterculus 2.65.3.

92. Degrassi 1947, 273–4 (*fasti Colotiani*).

93. Cicero *Ad familiares* 7.11.2 (n. 8).

94. Beard 2013, 101.

CHAPTER SEVEN

Tullia and the Furies

7.1. A historical drama?

In 1855 Sir George Cornewall Lewis, recently appointed Chancellor of the Exchequer in Lord Palmerston's government, published his two-volume 'inquiry into the credibility of the early Roman history'. Though largely forgotten nowadays, it is a very impressive historical argument, well worth the attention of modern readers. Reporting the traditional narrative of the death of king Servius Tullius, Lewis made a telling comment on how the king's daughter Tullia urged her second husband, Tarquin, to get rid of her father: 'In this Roman tragedy, she sustains the part of Lady Macbeth.'[1]

Lewis was well aware of the evidence for historical subjects being treated like drama,[2] and for dramatists themselves staging historical subjects,[3] but he never considered the possibility that Roman historians drew on plays as sources for their own narratives. That was an idea that became fashionable a generation later, with the work of Otto Ribbeck, Leopold von Ranke and others.[4] Given that Livy actually states that the murder of Servius Tullius was a subject for tragedy, it was surprisingly late

1. Lewis 1855, 1.504, cf. 1.228 on the murder of Servius as a 'tragic crime . . . suitable to poetry', clearly a reminiscence of Livy 1.46.3 (*sceleris tragici exemplum*).

2. Lewis 1855, 1.240–41, on Plutarch *Romulus* 8.7 (δραματικὸν καὶ πλασματῶδες) and Livy 5.21.9 (*haec ad ostentationem scaenae . . . aptiora*).

3. Lewis 1855, 1.226–7, on Aeschylus' *Persians*, Phrynichus' *Capture of Miletus* and Shakespeare's history plays.

4. E.g. Ribbeck 1875, 63–75, Ribbeck 1881, von Ranke 1883, 108–15, Meiser 1887, Schöne 1893, Soltau 1909, 17–59.

in the scholarly process that his story of Tullia, Tarquin and Servius came to be cited as evidence for a lost historical drama.[5]

The full argument was first made by an American scholar, Henry B. Wright, in a 'Festschrift' booklet in 1910. Very briefly at the end he suggested Lucius Accius as the author, on the strength of two phrases from Accius quoted by Cicero: 'One woman, of two men', and 'I see two tombs, of two bodies'.[6] Tullia's adultery with Tarquin, and the deaths of her first husband and Tarquin's wife,[7] provide a very suitable context for both of them. We know that Accius was interested in Servius Tullius, to whom he referred in his play *Brutus* as 'Tullius, who had established freedom for citizens'.[8] So there is strong circumstantial evidence for Livy having Accius in mind as he wrote the story.

But even the best ideas can be forgotten, or prematurely dismissed. Wright's unobtrusive work had no immediate impact, and even when it was picked up forty years later in an article by Agnes Kirsopp Michels,[9] that was still not enough to get it taken seriously. Henry Bardon's brilliant survey of lost Latin literature would have been the place to give it the currency it deserved, but alas, Bardon brushed aside the whole notion of plays detectable in historical narratives: 'A fine imaginative effort, a laudable desire to breathe life into phantoms—but these dreams of scholarship produce only empty shadows.'[10]

Things got even worse in 1965, with Robert Ogilvie's commentary on the early books of Livy. Ogilvie cited Wright and Michels, but did not engage with their arguments. Like Bardon, he simply delivered an *ex cathedra* judgement:

> [Livy] has not, of course, utilized an actual play as a model. He has written his own tragedy. . . . It is certain that L[ivy] does not depend upon Ennius or an unknown Roman tragedian. With a profound interest in psychology he is writing tragedy not copying it.[11]

5. Livy 1.46.3 (n. 1 in this chapter); Schöne 1893, 17, one in a list of possible examples.

6. Wright 1910, 25–47, esp. 47 on Accius frr. 655-6 Ribbeck = 699-700 Dangel (Cicero *Orator* 156, on forms of the genitive plural): *atqui dixit Accius 'uideo sepulcra duo duorum corporum', idemque 'mulier una duum uirorum'.*

7. Livy 1.46.6-9, Dionysius of Halicarnassus *Roman Antiquities* 4.28.3-30.1.

8. Quoted by Cicero *Pro Sestio* 123: *nominatim sum appellatus in Bruto: 'Tullius qui libertatem ciuibus stabiliuerat'* (Manuwald 2001, 234–5); section 2.3 above.

9. Unfortunately with the arbitrary suggestion of Asinius Pollio as the author (Michels 1951, 24); she does not mention the Accius quotations.

10. Bardon 1952, 327: 'Bel effort d'imagination, louable désir de ressusciter des fantômes: mais de ces songes philologiques ne naissent que des ombres impalpables.'

11. Ogilvie 1965, 186, 196.

That was two generations ago. Are we still content to accept dogmatic authority, or should we decide on the basis of the evidence? I think the latter is preferable.

First, the notion of prose narrative being influenced by what the author and his readers had seen on the stage is not in itself outlandish. On the contrary, it is what we should expect. The stage had a serious educational function, and its importance in forming people's opinions is attested by Cicero (section 2.1 above).[12] It was more than just popular entertainment. Notionally at least, at the *ludi scaenici* everyone was there together, including senators and equestrians in their reserved seats; the audience was the whole citizen body, *populus Romanus uniuersus*,[13] and we can certainly assume that that included Livy.

As for the Tullia and Tarquin story, there is one remarkable feature of Livy's narrative to which no serious attention has yet been paid: the prominence of the Furies (Greek *Erinyes*), the deities who avenged kin murder.[14] Historians were very cautious about attributing agency to gods or goddesses,[15] and Livy was no exception. In the entire surviving text (thirty books in total) there are only six references to the Furies, two of which are in speeches and a third is merely metaphorical;[16] the other three are all in the Tullia narrative. Why should that be so?

It can hardly be a coincidence that the Furies were a familiar sight on the Roman stage (section 2.1 above). Ennius wrote a *Eumenides*, as did Varro a century later.[17] Cicero provides evidence as explicit as one could wish, noting more than once that 'you often see in plays that those who have committed some impious or criminal act are driven in terror by the blazing torches of the Furies'.[18] Given all that, why should we *not* infer that Livy's narrative of the death of Servius Tullius was based on a stage play?

12. On the sources of *opiniones* see Cicero *De legibus* 1.47 (*parens, nutrix, magister, poeta, scaena*); for the educational purpose of drama see Cicero *Pro Rabirio Postumo* 29 (*ut . . . discamus*), Varro *De lingua Latina* 6.18 (*docuit populum*), and in general Rawson 1991, 570–81.

13. Cicero *Pro Sestio* 118, 119, 122, 124, *Philippics* 1.36, Pliny *Natural History* 36.119. Reserved seats: Livy 34.54.4-5 (senators), Asconius 78-9C (*equites*).

14. They goad both Tarquin (1.47.7) and Tullia (1.48.7) to fateful action, and they are summoned by the citizens when Tullia flees her home in the rising against Tarquin (1.59.13); briefly registered, but not exploited, by Michels 1951, 17, 19–20, 23.

15. For the issues involved see Polybius 3.47.6-9, Dionysius of Halicarnassus *Roman Antiquities* 2.68.1-2, 8.56.1, Valerius Maximus 1.8.7; Wiseman 2008, 243–70.

16. Livy 10.29.4 (metaphor), 29.18.15 (Locrians' speech), 40.10.1 (Perseus' speech).

17. Jocelyn 1969, 99–100 (Ennius); Varro *Menippean Satires* frr. 117–65 Astbury; for Varro's satire as a stage genre (*hic modus scaenatilis*, fr. 304), see Wiseman 2015, 76–8.

18. Cicero *Pro Roscio Amerino* 67 (*quem ad modum in fabulis saepenumero uidetis, eos qui aliquid impie scelerateque commiserint agitari et perterreri Furiarum taedis*

7.2. The evidence

The case in favour can best be made by a close reading of Livy 1.46-48, with running commentary. I give Livy's narrative in the excellent translation of T. J. Luce (Oxford World's Classics):

> 46 [1] Servius was no doubt *de facto* king, but from time to time the young Tarquin ventilated in public his contention that Servius ruled without the People's consent.[19] In response the king first won the goodwill of the plebeians by dividing up land captured from the enemy and giving it to them in individual allotments;[20] he then ventured to ask the People for their formal consent to his rule, which they gave with more unanimity than for any of the earlier kings.
>
> [2] But this did not stop Tarquin. Quite the contrary: he wanted the throne for himself and, when he perceived that the senators were displeased in the matter of the land distribution to the *plebs*, he saw his opportunity to worm his way into their good graces by censuring the king on the Senate floor. He was a restive and ambitious young man, to be sure, but at home he had a wife—Tullia—who inflamed that ambition still further.[21] [3] From this the Roman royal house produced a tragic spectacle to rival those of Greece,[22] in order that disgust with the kings might all the sooner usher in an era of liberty and that the last king would be one who seized the throne through crime.
>
> [4] This Lucius Tarquinius—whether he was the son or grandson of King Tarquinius Priscus is not clear,[23] but I follow the majority of

---

ardentibus); also *In Pisonem* 46 (*in scaena*), *De haruspicum responso* 39 (*in tragoediis*), *De legibus* 1.40 (*in fabulis*), *Academica* 2.89 (quoting Ennius' *Alcmeo*, Jocelyn 1969, 74). It was equally true of Athenian tragedy (Aristophanes *Ploutos* 423-5, Aeschines *In Timarchum* 190).

19. See Livy 1.41.6: Servius had assumed the kingship, with the help of queen Tanaquil, on the death of Tarquinius Priscus. The popular vote he now obtains confirms the legitimacy of his rule and removes any possible justification for Tarquin's act.

20. See Livy 1.42.2-3 for Servius' war against Veii and other Etruscan cities, which according to Dionysius of Halicarnassus (*Roman Antiquities* 4.27.1-6) went on for twenty years.

21. See Livy 1.42.1: Servius had married his two daughters, each called Tullia, to the two sons of Tarquinius Priscus, as Livy later reminds us (1.46.4-5 below).

22. Unusually, Luce's translation misses something here. *Tulit enim et Romana regia sceleris tragici exemplum* means 'The Roman royal house too produced an example of crime fit for tragedy'. The *et* does indeed refer to Greek tragedy (i.e., like the Mycenaean or Theban royal houses), but *sceleris tragici* is more than just a spectacle: the key word *scelus*, 'crime', is repeated at the end of the sentence, and at 1.47.1 (twice), 1.47.3, 1.48.5 and 1.48.7.

23. Dionysius, who took chronology seriously (*Roman Antiquities* 1.74.1-75.3), insists they were his grandsons (*Roman Antiquities* 4.6-7, 4.28.1, 4.30.2-3), thus losing Tullia's most persuasive argument.

> writers in saying he was the son—had a brother, Arruns Tarquinius, a youth of mild disposition. [5] These two had married the two Tullias, daughters of the king, as I said before, who were likewise very different in character. It happened by chance that the two of violent temperament were not married to one another—or rather, I think, it was owing to the Fortune of the Roman People, whose purpose it was that the reign of Tullius endure long enough to lay a firm foundation for the building of Rome's national character.

In a play, this background information would be given in the prologue, and Livy's reference to the purpose of Fortuna, who we know was a familiar stage character at just this time,[24] suggests that she would have spoken it. Luce is right to give her a capital letter: this is a very specific goddess, *Fortuna Publica* or *Fortuna* (*Publica*) *populi Romani Quiritium*, whose annual festivals—on 5 April, 25 May and an unknown third date, were respectively celebrated at three adjacent temples on the Quirinal next to the Colline Gate.[25]

The first of those dates coincided with the first of the annual Roman theatre games (*ludi Megalenses*, 4–10 April), a very appropriate occasion for a patriotic drama showing how the goddess looked after the Roman People.[26] Ovid refers to Fortuna 'confessing' her love for Servius, perhaps to the audience in our imagined prologue.[27] Livy's narrative too now turns to characters *speaking*:

> 46 [6] Tullia—the one who was so headstrong[28]—was greatly aggrieved because her husband did not have the stuff of manhood, neither hungry for power nor two-fisted;[29] turning from him, she set her

24. Diodorus Siculus 32.10.5: τῆς Τύχης ὥσπερ ἐν δράμασι τὸ παράδοξον τῆς περιπετείας ἀγούσης.

25. *Fortuna Publica*: Ovid *Fasti* 4.375–6, 5.729–30; *Fasti Praenestini* (Degrassi 1963, 126–7); cf. Lucan 8.686 (*Fortuna Romana*). *Fortuna P.R.Q.* or *P.P.R.Q*: *Fasti Antiates, Caeretani, Esquilini, magistrorum uici* (Degrassi 1963, 11, 67, 87, 91). Three temples: Vitruvius 3.3.2 (*Fortunae tres . . . proxime portam Collinam*).

26. See Livy 1.46.3 above for a hint of divine teleology, and 2.1.3–6 for the idea that Rome's citizens needed the 'moderate' rule of successive good kings (2.1.6 on *moderatio imperii*, 1.48.9 on Servius' *moderatum imperium*) before they could be ready for 'mature' freedom.

27. Ovid *Fasti* 6.573–4 (*dum dea furtiuos timide profitetur amores, | caelestemque homini concubuisse pudet*); Wiseman 1998, 25–30.

28. Literally 'ferocious' (*ferox*); cf. Tarquin at Livy 1.48.2, attacking Servius *ferociter*.

29. Literally 'adequate neither for desire nor for audacity' (*neque ad cupiditatem neque ad audaciam*); *audacia* recurs at the end of the sentence, applied to Tullia herself (Luce's 'backbone'), and at Livy 1.48.1 and 3 (*audere*), applied to Tarquin.

> sights on the other Tarquin, confessing her admiration for someone who was a real man, a true son of a king, while ridiculing her sister for having married such a fine specimen, while lacking the backbone a woman should have. [7] Their similar natures swiftly drew them together, as so often happens: evil attracts evil. Yet it was the woman who began the débâcle.[30] Conversing secretly with another woman's husband became normal for her: she had no scruples in damning her husband to his brother, her sister to her sister's husband; she maintained it would have been better if she had remained a spinster and he a bachelor than to be married to such unsuitable spouses: as it was, their enterprising nature was being stifled by the spinelessness of others; [8] if the gods had given a husband who was worthy of her, she would soon see in her own house the royal power she now saw in her father's. [9] It did not take long for her to fill the young man with her own recklessness. Lucius Tarquinius and the younger Tullia emptied their houses with virtual back-to-back funerals. They married, with Servius not forbidding it more than with his approval.

In what we may think of as Act I, Tullia is in charge. Dionysius, as befits a professor of rhetoric, has her deliver an elaborately formal *suasoria* speech to her brother-in-law;[31] Ovid's much briefer version omits these early moves in Tullia's plot. All three narrators, I suggest, were transcribing into their respective idioms material with which they were familiar from the stage.

Similarly, all three narrators pass very swiftly over what happened next, the murders of the respective spouses and the marriage of the guilty pair.[32] It is a striking feature of the only surviving Roman historical drama, the pseudo-Senecan *Octavia*, that Nero's marriage to the 'haughty harlot' Poppaea is mentioned in the text only in advance and in retrospect: it takes place between lines 645 (exit the Ghost of Agrippina) and 646 (enter Poppaea and her Chorus), presumably as a danced spectacle

30. Literally 'general upheaval' (*turbandi omnia*), a phrase often applied to demagogues (e.g. M. Manlius at Livy 6.14.7, M. Lepidus at Sallust *Histories* 1.67.1 Ramsey).

31. *Roman Antiquities* 4.28.3–30.1; for historians who composed speeches 'like exercises for the rhetorical school', see Polybius 12.25a.5 (on Timaeus).

32. Livy 1.46.9 (*prope continuatis funeribus cum domos uacuas nouo matrimonio fecissent*), Ovid *Fasti* 6.587 (*Tullia coniugio sceleris mercede peracto*); Dionysius *Roman Antiquities* 4.30.1 ('both died the same way'), cf. 4.79.1–2 (by poison, according to L. Brutus); the formulation in *De uiris illustribus* 7.15 (*mites seu forte seu fraude perierunt*) is similarly vague.

without dialogue.[33] We may reasonably infer a similar sequence in the putative drama of Tullia and Tarquin. Tullia speaks again as Livy's narrative proceeds.

> 47 [1] From then on Tullius' old age proved an increasing source of danger and his hold on the throne became more precarious with each passing day: the woman, having committed one crime, was now looking to commit another. Night and day she pressured her husband not to let the previous murders go for nothing. [2] What she had previously, she said, was a man to whom she could be said to be married and with whom she wordlessly served those in power; what she had not had was a man who thought himself worthy of the throne, who remembered he was the son of Tarquinius Priscus, who preferred to take the throne than to hope for it.
>
> [3] 'If you are the man whom I think I married, I salute you as husband and king. If not, my situation is worse than before, for what I now have is a criminal as well as a coward. [4] Why not arm yourself for action? You are not from Corinth or Tarquinii.[34] You do not, like your father, have to win a kingdom in a foreign land. The gods of your house and of your ancestors, the image of your father, the palace that was your home, the royal throne in that home, the very name of Tarquin—they all declare and make you king. [5] If you lack the nerve, then why disappoint everyone's expectations? Stop parading around as a prince of the blood royal. Clear out of Rome, slink back to Tarquinii or Corinth. Revert to what your family once was, more like your brother than your father!'
>
> [6] With such taunts as these she goaded the youth to act. Yet she was equally hard on herself: if a spirited woman like Tanaquil—and a foreigner as well—could act as a kingmaker twice in a row, first for her husband and then for her son-in-law,[35] then why was she, who was of royal blood, unable to make headway in making and unmaking a king?

'Act II' thus consists of two speeches by Tullia: one to Tarquin, the other a soliloquy after he has left to start his campaign for political support. Ovid

33. [Seneca] *Octavia* 125 (*superba paelex*), 593-7 (in advance), 671-3, 683-5 (in retrospect); Boyle 2008, 230–31, Wiseman 2008, 198–9.

34. See Livy 1.34.1-11 (and section 1.2 above) on his grandfather Demaratus and his father Tarquinius Priscus.

35. First for Demaratus' son Lucumo, who became Tarquinius Priscus (Livy 1.34.4-10), then for Servius Tullius, the palace slave-boy marked out by the gods (Livy 1.39.1-5, 1.41.1-6).

offers a brief version of the former, which the commentators too easily assume was no more than a précis of Livy;[36] since he puts into Tullia's mouth the aphorism 'Crime is a king's thing!', alluding to a well-known Euripidean quotation used also by Dionysius,[37] here again we may be looking at three different ways of handling the same dramatic material.

Dionysius, however, turns away from drama at this point, resuming his 'school of rhetoric' mode. He composes two set-piece senatorial speeches, one by Tarquin attacking Servius' right to rule, one by Servius defending it, and then a speech by Servius before the People to confirm the legitimacy of his government.[38] There are no such formalities in Ovid or Livy.

> 47 [7] Tarquin, goaded by the frenzied ambition of his wife,[39] went the rounds, seeking in particular the support of the senators from the lesser families:[40] he reminded them of the favour his father had done them, and now sought their support in return. He won over the younger men with gifts, and increased his influence everywhere by making extravagant promises and denouncing the king. [8] Finally, the moment to strike was at hand. Escorted by a cadre of armed men he burst into the forum.[41] When everyone was stricken with fear, he took his seat on the king's throne in the entrance to the senate-house and ordered a herald to summon the senators into the presence of King Tarquin.

'Enter Tarquin, escorted' can be taken as the start of the third act. He takes his seat in the king's place in front of the Senate-house (*in regia sede pro curia*);[42] as Livy's readers would know, and as we see later in the story, the Senate-house was on a raised podium with steps leading down

36. Ovid *Fasti* 6.587-96; Schilling 1993, 192, Littlewood 2006, 177; for a more nuanced view see Murgatroyd 2005, 201–4.

37. Ovid *Fasti* 6.595 (*regia res scelus est*); cf. Euripides *Phoenissae* 524-5 (εἴπερ γὰρ ἀδικεῖν χρή, τυραννίδος πέρι | κάλλιστον ἀδικεῖν), whence Dionysius *Roman Antiquities* 4.29.7 (καὶ γὰρ ἐὰν τἆλλα τις ἀδικεῖν ὀκνῇ, βασιλείας γε χάριν οὐ νέμεσις ἅπαντα τολμᾶν). According to Cicero, not an unbiased source, Caesar 'always had the Euripides verses on his lips' (Cicero *De officiis* 3.82, '*nam si uiolandum est ius, regnandi gratia | uiolandum est*').

38. *Roman Antiquities* 4.30.4-7 (Tarquin's conspiracy), 4.31-32 (Tarquin in the Senate), 4.33-36 (Servius in the Senate), 4.37 (Servius before the People).

39. Literally 'possessed by female Furies' (*muliebribus instinctus Furiis*), referring to the avenging deities themselves, as at Livy 1.48.7 and 1.59.13.

40. See Livy 1.35.6: the families of 100 men whom Tarquinius Priscus had made senators.

41. According to Dionysius (*Roman Antiquities* 4.38.2) his escort consisted of friends with swords under their togas and servants acting as lictors carrying axes.

42. Cf. Ovid *Fasti* 6.597-8 (*solio priuatus in alto | sederat*).

to the Comitium (place of assembly) below.[43] It is worth remembering that when the *ludi Romani* were on, the Comitium was probably used as a theatre.[44]

> 47 [9] They gathered at once, some acting on cue, others fearful that non-appearance might get them into trouble; people were dumbfounded by this brazen step: Servius, they thought, was doomed. [10] Tarquin began by attacking the king, going back to his base origin:[45] a slave born of a slave, he seized the throne after the shameful murder of Tarquin's father, without the customary interregnum, without calling the assembly, without a vote of the people, without the sanction of the senate: the throne was the gift of a woman! [11] Such was his birth, such was how he became king, a champion of the dregs of society from which he himself came; in his hatred of others' nobility he took land from the high-born and gave it to riff-raff; [12] all the burdens that once had been shared in common were now piled on the backs of the nation's leaders; he had instituted the census so that the rich might be singled out as objects of jealousy, while providing a perpetual source, whenever he wanted, of lavishing gifts upon the needy.
>
> 48 [1] In the midst of this harangue Servius burst upon the scene,[46] alerted to the alarming news. In a great voice he called out from the antechamber of the senate-house, 'Tarquin, what is the meaning of this? How dare you presume to call the senate or take my seat while I am alive?' [2] Tarquin snarled in reply that he was sitting in his father's seat; the son of a king had a far better claim to the throne than a slave; Servius had flouted his masters long enough with an insulting licence that knew no limits. An uproar arose from the supporters of each man; a crush of people pushed into the senate chamber;[47] it was clear that the victor would be king. [3] Tarquin was forced to stake everything on

43. Livy 1.48.3 (*in inferiorem partem per gradus deiecit*); Dionysius *Roman Antiquities* 4.38.5 (κατὰ τῶν κρηπίδων τοῦ βουλευτηρίου τῶν εἰς τὸ ἐκκλησιαστήριον φερουσῶν), cf. 4.39.1 (τὸν Ταρκύνιον ἐπὶ τῆς κρηπῖδος ἑστῶτα); the steps are referred to at Cicero *Ad Q. fratrem* 2.1.3 and Livy 1.36.4.

44. Livy 27.36.8 (207 BC, *comitium tectum esse memoriae proditum est et ludos Romanos semel instauratos ab aedilibus*); see Wiseman 2009, 164–70 on multiple stages at the *ludi scaenici*.

45. The speech is omitted by Dionysius (*Roman Antiquities* 4.38.2), who had worked through all the arguments in the Senate debate he had previously inserted (n. 38).

46. Literally 'when Servius intervened in this speech' (*huic orationi Seruius cum interuenisset*); but Luce's choice of phrase is a natural one.

47. The Latin is more explicit (*concursus <u>populi</u> fiebat in curiam*): this was an intervention of the Roman People.

> his next move.[48] Much younger and stronger, he seized Servius about the waist, carried him out of the room and flung him down the steps of the senate-house to the ground below. He returned to the chamber and ordered the senators to resume their places.

We have to suppose that at 47.9 the senators and Tarquin go inside the chamber, where he delivers his speech; that is the implied scene at 48.1, where Servius' voice is heard from the *uestibulum*. But at 48.1-2 it is clear that Tarquin is still sitting in the royal seat, which at 47.8 was out in front of the building. The uproar (*clamor* and *concursus*) take place inside, and Tarquin's act of 'extreme daring' at 48.3 risks becoming merely grotesque as he picks the old king up and walks out of the door with him.[49]

These inconcinnities disappear when we imagine it performed. We need a big stage with steps up from ground level, a *scaenae frons* with the columns of the Senate-house as its central entrance, and the royal seat in front of it.[50] There would be a crowd at ground level representing the Roman People, through which Tarquin and his supporters would force their way at the start of 'Act III'. They would control the crowd; he would go up the steps, take his seat and summon the senators.

The senators would enter, perhaps from the side doors of the *scaenae frons*, and take up positions on the stage and the upper steps to form an audience around Tarquin. That simple dramatic convention for presenting an 'indoor' scene was not something Livy could exploit; hence the slight oddities in his account. In performance it would have the economical effect of making Tarquin's harangue to the senators equally audible to the 'Roman People' at ground level, as well as to the real Roman People in the audience behind them.

Now enter Servius, with a much smaller escort, and this time the crowd respectfully gives way. He rushes up the steps to challenge Tarquin while the respective supporters of the usurper and the rightful king struggle for control. Eventually, in a single dramatic—and horrifying—move, Tarquin seizes Servius and hurls him bodily down the steps. In Livy he then 'returned to the chamber and ordered the senators to resume their

48. Literally 'now forced to the most extreme daring by necessity itself' (*necessitate iam ipsa cogente ultima audere*).

49. In Dionysius (*Roman Antiquities* 4.38.5) Tarquin calls his servants to help him take the old man outside.

50. Compare the thrones *in medio* imagined by Virgil at *Aeneid* 1.506 (Dido) and 7.169 (Latinus).

places',[51] but no further senatorial business is reported. I imagine Livy was remembering the end of 'Act III', the exit of Tarquin and the terrified senators through the central door of the *scaenae frons*.

> 48 [4] Servius' attendants and companions took to their heels, while Servius himself, faint from the loss of blood and close to death, headed back to the palace, assisted by some of the royal bodyguards.[52] But Tarquin had sent men after him, who caught him as he fled and cut him down. [5] Some believe that this was done at Tullia's prompting: it certainly fits in with the other terrible things she did. For all agree that she rode into the forum in a wagon and, unabashed by the presence of the males gathered there, called her husband forth from the senate-house and was the first to salute him king.[53] [6] He told her to clear out and fast, for the situation was dangerous. When she was heading back home and had reached the top of Cuprius Street (where the chapel to Diana was until recently),[54] and as she made a right turn on Urbius Street *en route* to the Esquiline hill,[55] her driver started in horror and, reining in, pointed out to his mistress the body of the slain king.

After everyone flees and Servius is helped back home (48.4), 'Act IV' begins with the arrival of Tullia in her carriage. Tarquin comes out; she hails him; he tells her to go home. Luce's 'clear out' is good: the colloquial verb *facessere* was what she had sarcastically used to him in 'Act II'.[56] Now he is in charge, but we may wonder how 'ferocious' Tullia will react to being

51. Literally 'then he went back into the Senate-house to compel the senators' (*inde ad cogendum senatum in curiam rediit*), who should have been still inside.

52. Literally 'as he was going back home with the royal escort' (*cum . . . regio comitatu domum se reciperet*); presumably the *apparitores* and *comites* who fled at the start of the sentence had now remembered their duty.

53. In Dionysius' typically longwinded version (*Roman Antiquities* 4.49.1-3), Tullia is driven to the Forum, salutes Tarquin as king while he stands on the steps, takes him aside to advise him not to let Servius live, and is driven away again. (Her *carpentum*, a lady's carriage, deserves a more polite description than Luce's 'wagon', and of course she was not driving it herself.)

54. Probably the *Dianae sacellum in Caeliculo* removed by L. Piso as consul in 58 BC (Cicero *De haruspicum responso* 32). The toponym *Caeliculum* is otherwise unknown; it is often identified (e.g. Rodríguez Almeida 1993) with the *Caeliolum* at Varro *De lingua Latina* 5.46, but there seems to be no reason to identify it as the street linking Carinae and the Caelian at 5.47, where the MS readings are *ceroniensem, cerolienses* and *cerulensis.*

55. I assume that 'made a left turn' in Luce's text is a simple slip and not a deliberate 'correction' of Livy's *flectenti carpentum dextra*; there is certainly no warrant for it in any of the manuscripts. 'Urbius Street' for *cliuus Vrbius* misses the point that it was a gradient, leading *up* to the Esquiline.

56. Livy 1.47.5; it occurs otherwise only twice in the whole of Livy (4.58.7, 6.17.8).

so brusquely ordered away.[57] Does she obey him, or does Livy's careful description of her route indicate something else?[58]

Note first that the respective exits of Servius and Tullia are described in identical terms: *cum . . . domum se reciperet* (Servius, 48.4), *cum se domum reciperet* (Tullia, 48.6). In a play, the symmetry would be visible: 'Help me home', says the old king to his attendants, and exits stage right; 'Go home', Tullia is told by her husband, and exits stage left. In Livy's time it was known where the various kings had lived.[59] Servius' house was on the Esquiline, above the *cliuus Vrbius*; that of Tarquinius Superbus was also on the Esquiline, but above the *cliuus Pullius* at the Fagutal grove.[60]

Self-evidently, the old king was returning to one address and his daughter to another.[61] So how did Tullia come upon her father's body? The answer must lie in Livy's careful naming of the streets, *uicus Cuprius* and *cliuus Vrbius*, to explain what she was doing. Instead of going 'home' to her husband's house, Tullia was now heading to the house of Servius. She was going to take possession.[62]

Livy's narrative, like those of Ovid and Dionysius,[63] naturally follows Tullia and shows her ordering the carriage to be driven over her murdered father's body. In a play, however, 'Act IV' would end with Tullia's exit; how would the audience know of her dreadful deed? Possibly from a 'messenger speech',[64] if the driver came back with the blood-stained carriage

57. Cf. *De uiris illustribus* 7.18 (*coniugem regem salutauit, a quo iussa turba decedere*), presumably from Livy.

58. Dionysius too mentions the *cliuus Vrbius*, using the alternative spelling *Orbius* (*Roman Antiquities* 4.39.5, ὁ στενωπὸς Ὄρβιος καλούμενος); cf. Varro *De lingua Latina* 5.159 for its proximity to the *uicus Cuprius*.

59. Varro *De uita populi Romani* fr. 22 Pittà (Nonius 852L); Solinus 1.21-6, evidently from Varro (Pittà 2015, 134–5).

60. Solinus 1.25-6: *Seruius Tullius Esquilinus supra cliuum Vrbium. . . . Tarquinius Superbus et ipse Esquilinus supra cliuum Pullium ad Fagutalem lucum* [MSS *lacum*]. For the grove see Varro *De lingua Latina* 5.49, Pliny *Natural History* 16.37; Coarelli 2019, 334–8.

61. *Pace* Palombi 1997, 47 ('dal Foro al Clivo Urbio dove Servio abitava . . . i due percorsi coincisero'). Palombi 1997 is the standard work on the topography of the area (superseding Terrenato 1992 and Ziółkowski 1996), but this assumption makes his reconstruction of the ancient street system very problematic.

62. Festus 450–1L (*properans in possessionem domus paternae*); cf. 196L on *Orbius cliuus* (n. 58 above), where *<po>ssessionem* survives in a very damaged text, along with the names of Tullia and Tarquin. The situation is, I think, misunderstood by Ziółkowski 1996, 133 ('Tullia rides home by the most roundabout way imaginable'), and by Coarelli 2019, 347–9, who supposes there were two rival narratives (confused by Livy?), in one of which Tullia went home, in the other to Servius' house.

63. Ovid *Fasti* 6.603-10, Dionysius of Halicarnassus *Roman Antiquities* 4.39.3-5.

64. As suggested by Michels 1951, 17.

and reported what he had been forced to do. But in that case, what had the audience been watching in the meantime? A better alternative is suggested by the way Livy goes on:

> 48 [7] She is said to have committed an appalling and barbaric crime there—and the place is a reminder of it, for they call it the Street of Crime: maddened by the avenging spirits of her sister and former husband, Tullia, so the story goes, drove the wagon over Servius' body. Spattered and defiled by the blood of her murdered father, she brought back part of it to her own household gods and those of her husband, who in their anger saw to it that the evil beginning of the reign would soon have a suitably bad ending.

'So the story goes' (*traditur*) is the sort of phrase Livy often used for narratives of divine agency, the truth of which he could not guarantee; at one point he observed of such tales that 'they are more appropriate to the ostentation of the stage, which delights in marvels, than to credibility'.[65] Our story is probably an example.

Luce's 'avenging spirits' were the Furies, as familiar on the Roman tragic stage as they were on the Athenian,[66] but in this case we have also the Penates, gods of the household, outraged by Tullia's pollution of her father's house. I suggest that 'Act V' consisted of the Furies describing what Tullia has done, followed by the Penates explaining how she will be punished.

Specifically Roman deities could appear on stage as easily as the gods of Greek tragedy. The best known examples are the *Lar familiaris* who speaks the prologue in Plautus' 'pot of gold' comedy, and Anna Perenna, the eponymous heroine of a play by Laberius.[67] The Penates would appear as two young men carrying spears, iconographically similar to Castor and Pollux.[68] Their function here, as usual with gods in Roman

65. Livy 5.21.9 (*haec ad ostentationem scenae gaudentis miraculis aptiora quam ad fidem*); see in general Levene 1993, 19–20, Wiseman 2008, 245–6.

66. Livy 1.48.7 (*agitantibus furiis sororis ac uiri*); see above, nn. 17–18. In Ennius' *Eumenides*, after the acquittal of Orestes Minerva tells them to 'clear out', using the same verb Livy conspicuously repeats in this episode (*facessite*, n. 56 above): Nonius 477L, Jocelyn 1969, 100. For the *Erinyes* in Greek tragedy see Lloyd-Jones 1990.

67. Plautus *Aulularia* 1-39 (cf. Priscian *Grammatici Latini* 2.213 Keil for a *fabula Atellana* by L. Pomponius entitled *Lar familiaris*); Aulus Gellius 16.7.10, Nonius 129L (see chapter 5).

68. Dionysius of Halicarnassus *Roman Antiquities* 1.68.2; see the coin-types of M'. Fonteius, C. Sulpicius and C. Antius C.f. Restio (Crawford 1974, 316, 320, 470, nos 307, 312.2 and 455.2), where the legends read *Dei Penates* or (*D*) *P P* for (*Dei*) *Penates publici*. They were sometimes identified as the θεοὶ μεγάλοι of Samothrace, whom Varro in turn (cited in Servius on *Aeneid* 3.12) identified as the Dioscuri.

tragedy,[69] would be to reassure the audience: justice would be done, Tullia would be driven from the house to face the Furies. Livy, I suggest, turned that promise into narrative. A few pages later, describing the uprising against Tarquin, he notes that 'in the tumult Tullia fled from her home, with men and women cursing her wherever she went and calling down on her the Furies of her kin'.[70]

All the indications point in the same direction. It seems clear that at this point in his narrative Livy deliberately, and conspicuously, based his narrative on a stage play, a classic tragedy that he knew his own audience, and later his readers, would recognise.[71] It was what Greek and Roman historians had done for centuries, adding enjoyable vividness to their narratives by exploiting the effects of drama.[72] The playwright concerned was very probably Accius, one of the three 'greats' of Roman tragedy,[73] as Wright convincingly proposed more than a century ago.

7.3. The scene in the city

Let's return to fierce Tullia in her carriage, sent home by Tarquin but changing her route to take possession of the old king's house.[74] Both Servius and Tarquin lived on the Esquiline, which covered a substantial area to the east of the Forum.[75] Servius' house was evidently on the northern side of the hill, overlooking the *uicus Patricius* (modern via Urbana) and therefore probably on the height where the church of S. Pietro in Vincoli

69. Plautus *Amphitruo* 41-4: *ut alios in tragoediis | uidi, Neptunum, Virtutem, Victoriam | Martem, Bellonam commemorare quae bona | uobis fecissent.*

70. Livy 1.59.13 (*inter hunc tumultum Tullia domo profugit exsecrantibus quacumque incedebat inuocantibusque parentum furias uiris mulieribusque*); cf. 1.59.10, Lucius Brutus' recollection of Tullia's crime and invocation of the *ultores parentum di.* On this episode, also a subject for drama, see chapter 8.

71. For historians' audiences at this time see *FRHist* 48 T1, 54 T1: respectively Horace *Satires* 1.3.86-9 (with ps.Acro *ad loc.*) on Octavius Ruso, who recited *in spectaculo*, and *Suda* K 2098 = 3.158 Adler on Cornutus, who drew crowds larger than Livy's.

72. See Moles 1993, 112–3, Morgan 1993, 184–6. The key texts are Duris of Samos *BNJ* 76 F1 (*mimesis* and pleasure), Polybius 2.56.10-12 (Phylarchus confusing the aims of tragedy and history), Cicero *Ad familiares* 5.12.6 (history as a *fabula* with successive 'acts'), Plutarch *Pericles* 28.1 (Duris turning history into tragedy); what Polybius and Plutarch disapproved of was evidently common practice.

73. Along with Ennius and Pacuvius (Cicero *De oratore* 3.27, *Orator* 36, *Academica* 1.10); for his stature see Cicero *Pro Sestio* 120 (*summi poetae ingenium*), *Pro Plancio* 59 (*grauis et ingeniosus poeta*).

74. Livy 1.48.6-7; see above, nn. 58–62.

75. It consisted of two hills, *mons Oppius* to the south-west and *mons Cispius* to the north-east (Varro *De lingua Latina* 5.50), separated by the valley of the Subura, which ran from the Argiletum to the Porta Esquilina; however, the *mons Cispius* (S. Maria Maggiore) does not concern us here.

is now.[76] Tarquin's house cannot be placed precisely, but the logic of the drama requires that the respective houses were reached by different routes from the Forum: exit Servius in one direction; exit Tullia in another. Tarquin's assassins followed Servius, so the theatre audience could have no suspicion, until it was explained to them, that Tullia would arrive at the crime scene and drive over the corpse.

That explanation leads us into a notorious complex of topographical problems.[77] To understand the relevant routes from Forum to Esquiline, four documents are essential.

The first is Dionysius' account of the Penates, who were believed to have been brought from Troy by Aeneas:

> They show you in Rome a temple built not far from the Forum in the short street that leads to Carinae; it is a small shrine, and is darkened by the height of the adjacent buildings. The place is called in the native speech 'Velia'. In this temple there are images of the Trojan gods which it is lawful for all to see, with an inscription showing them to be the Penates.[78]

The second is Dionysius' narrative of Spurius Cassius, who was executed for treason in 485 BC:

> His house was razed to the ground and to this day its site remains vacant, except for that part of it on which the state afterwards built the temple of Earth [i.e. Tellus], which stands in the street leading to Carinae.[79]

There is no reason to doubt that the same street is meant.[80]

In the third passage Dionysius refers again to 'Carinae', and also to one of the street-names in Livy's story.[81] In the reign of Tullus Hostilius the

76. Festus (Paulus) 247L; Coarelli 2019, 350–51.

77. Most recently addressed by Coarelli 2019, 315–95, who provides full bibliography.

78. Dionysius of Halicarnassus *Roman Antiquities* 1.68.1 (Loeb trans. by E. Cary): νεὼς ἐν Ῥώμῃ δείκνυται τῆς ἀγορᾶς οὐ πρόσω κατὰ τὴν ἐπὶ Καρίνας φέρουσαν ἐπίτομον ὁδὸν ὑπεροχῇ σκοτεινὸς ἱδρυμένος οὐ μέγας. λέγεται δὲ κατὰ τὴν ἐπιχώριον γλῶτταν Οὐελία [MSS ὑπ' ἐλαίως or ὑπελαίας] τὸ χωρίον. ἐν δὲ τούτῳ κεῖνται τῶν Τρωικῶν θεῶν εἰκόνες, ἃς ἅπασιν ὁρᾶν θέμις, ἐπιγραφὴν ἔχουσαι δηλοῦσαν τοὺς Πενάτας. The emendation Οὐελία is based on Varro *De lingua Latina* 5.54 and Augustus *Res gestae* 19.2 (*in Velia*).

79. Dionysius of Halicarnassus *Roman Antiquities* 8.79.3 (Loeb trans. by E. Cary): ἥ τε οἰκία κατεσκάφη, καὶ μέχρι τοῦδε ἀνεῖται ὁ τόπος αὐτῆς αἴθριος ἔξω τοῦ νεὼ τῆς Γῆς, ὃν ὑστέροις ἡ πόλις κατεσκεύασε χρόνοις ἐν μέρει τινὶ αὐτῆς κατὰ τὴν ἐπί Καρίνας φέρουσαν ὁδόν.

80. *Pace* Palombi 1997, 49–51 and Coarelli 2001, 20–21; they assume that ἐπίτομον at 1.68.1 (n. 78) is a defining adjective, meaning 'the short street as opposed to another longer one', but that is an unnecessary complication. The adjective may equally well be simply descriptive.

81. Livy 1.48.6: *ad summum Cuprium uicum . . . dextra in Vrbium cliuum ut in collem Esquiliarum eueheretur.*

hero Horatius, who had killed his sister, was purified of her death by passing under a 'yoke':

> The place in the city where they performed this expiation is regarded by all the Romans as sacred; it is in the street that leads from Carinae as one goes towards *uicus Cuprius.*[82]

One of the few things known about 'Carinae' is that it was on a hillside,[83] either the north-eastern slope of the Velia or the south-western slope of the Esquiline.

Our fourth document is the explanation of the name 'Carinae' in Varro's *De lingua Latina*:

> Perhaps from *caerimonia*, because here begins the origin of the Sacra Via, which extends from the shrine of Strenia to the *arx*, by which the sacred items are brought month by month to the *arx*, and along which the augurs normally set out from the *arx* to carry out their auguries.[84]

The site of Strenia's shrine is unknown; nevertheless, it is clear that the Sacra Via descended from 'Carinae' to the Forum,[85] and from there went up to the citadel (*arx*) on the Capitol.

What these four passages attest is the existence of two separate routes from the Forum eastwards to 'Carinae' (wherever that was) and the Esquiline (fig. 10).

The first, a 'short street', went directly over the Velia, which Dionysius elsewhere describes as a 'fairly high and steep hill overlooking the Forum'.[86] The temple of the Penates was on the summit of the hill, sup-

82. Dionysius of Halicarnassus *Roman Antiquities* 3.22.8 (Loeb trans. by E. Cary): ἐν ᾧ δὲ τῆς πόλεως χωρίῳ τὸν ἁγνισμὸν ἐποιήσατο πάντες Ῥωμαῖοι νομίζουσιν ἱερόν· ἔστι δ' ἐν τῷ στενωπῷ τῷ φέροντι ἀπὸ Καρίνης τοῖς ἐπὶ τὸν Κύπριον ἐρχομένοις στενωπόν. See also Livy 1.26.13, Festus 380L: the story was an aetiology of the *tigillum sororium*, an ancient cult site at the *compitum Acilium* (*Fasti Arualium*, Degrassi 1963, 36–7).

83. As implied by Varro *De lingua Latina* 5.48 (the *pagus Succusanus* so called *quod succurrit Carinis*) and Festus 476L (*mons Oppius* so called because Opiter Oppius, a Tusculan ally of Tullus Hostilius, settled *in Carinis*).

84. Varro *De lingua Latina* 5.47: *Carinae pote a caerimonia, quod hinc oritur caput Sacrae uiae ab Streniae sacello quae pertinet in arcem, qua sacra quotquot mensibus feruntur in arcem et per quam augures ex arce profecti solent inaugurare.* So too Festus 372L.

85. For *descendere in forum* see Cicero *Pro Plancio* 17, Horace *Satires* 1.9.1 and 35, Ovid *Tristia* 3.1.27-30, Pliny *Natural History* 19.23, Plutarch *Cicero* 22.1.

86. C–D in fig. 10. Dionysius of Halicarnassus *Roman Antiquities* 5.19.1 (λόφον ὑπερκείμενον τῆς ἀγόρας ὑψηλὸν ἐπιεικῶς καί περίτομον), the site of the house of P. Valerius Publicola; cf. Cicero *De republica* 2.53 (*in excelsiore loco*), Livy 2.7.6 (*alto atque munito loco*), Plutarch *Publicola* 10.2 (ἐπικεκραμένην τῇ ἀγορᾷ καὶ καθορῶσαν ἐξ ὕψους ἅπαντα).

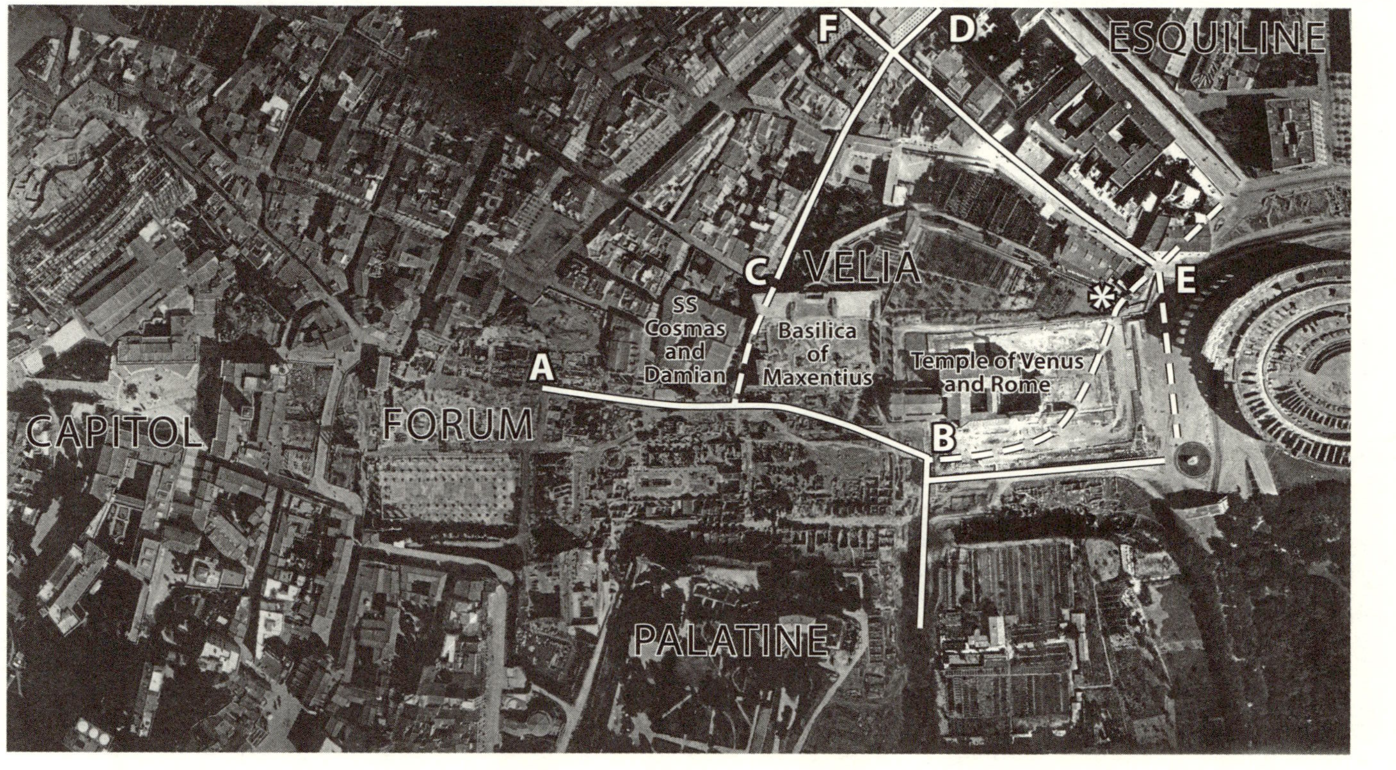

FIGURE 10. Vertical view of the historic centre of Rome from the Colosseum to the piazza del Campidoglio, from a mosaic of aerial photographs taken by Giacomo Boni in 1908: Aerofototeca Nazionale ICCD, GM_1908_150_MOS-T_0 33221 0 (detail). Known Roman streets are marked as follows:
A–B: the Sacra Via, as excavated by Boni in 1899; for its continuation, see Ziółkowski 2004.
C–D: via del Tempio di Pace > via di S. Pietro in Vincoli (now via Frangipani): Lanciani 1990, tavv. 22, 29.
E–F: via del Colosseo > via Cardello: Lanciani 1990, tavv. 22, 29.
The asterisk marks the site of the *compitum Acilium*, discovered in 1932.

posedly on the site of the house of Tullus Hostilius;[87] the temple of Tellus, on the other hand, may have been on the north-eastern slope of the Velia, out of sight of the Forum but evidently not out of earshot.[88] The profile of the hill was much altered by the construction of Vespasian's *templum Pacis* and the Basilica of Maxentius, and practically all of what remained was dug away in 1932 for the construction of Mussolini's 'via dell'Impero', the road now called 'via dei Fori Imperiali'.[89]

The second route was the Sacra Via, a processional way with a less steep gradient, used for triumphs.[90] To reach the same place ('Carinae') as the direct route, it must have rounded the Velia to the south-east. We must assume that that was the way Tullia's carriage was imagined as going, whereas the wounded Servius was taken by the direct route, past the temple of the Penates who would in due course avenge him.

Each of these routes is archaeologically attested at the western end. The first begins immediately above the so-called Temple of Romulus, where paving survives of a street leading north-east between Vespasian's *templum Pacis* complex (now the church of SS. Cosmas and Damian) and the Basilica of Maxentius.[91] The second route is the Sacra Via, of which the pre-Neronian paving was exposed in 1899 from the Forum piazza up as far as the great platform of the Hadrianic temple of Venus and Rome; from there it must have curved round to the left behind the Velia towards 'Carinae' by a route now untraceable.[92]

A new element was added to the topographical problem by the discovery in 1932, during the destruction of the eastern Velia to make room for the new road, of the cross-road shrine known as *compitum Acilium*.[93]

87. Solinus 1.22 (*Tullus Hostilius in Velia, ubi postea deum Penatium aedes facta est*); Cicero *De republica* 2.53 (*ubi rex Tullus habitauerat*), thereafter the house of Publicola (n. 86). This evidence is, I think, wrongly discounted by Ziółkowski 1996, 140–41.

88. See n. 79 above, with Appian *Civil Wars* 2.131.547, where Lepidus, outside the temple of Tellus, is called down to the Forum.

89. Details in Manacorda and Tamassia 1985, 181–94; excellent illustrations in Palombi 1997, figs 13 and 44, tavv. I-VI.

90. A–B in fig. 10. Horace *Epodes* 7.7-8 (*intactus ut Britannus ut descenderet | Sacra catenatus uia*), *Odes* 4.2.34-6 (*quandoque trahet feroces | per Sacrum cliuum merita decorus | fronde Sugambros*).

91. Coarelli 1983, 45–9.

92. B–E in fig. 10. Palombi 1997, fig. 31; details and discussion in Ziółkowski 2004. The traditional notion that the Arch of Titus stood over the Sacra Via is wholly without foundation; the platform it stood on covered the paving of a street leading from the Sacra Via to the Palatine.

93. Marked with an asterisk in fig. 10. Pisani Sartorio 1993; Lott 2004, 148–52, 188; Coarelli 2019, 342–4.

FIGURE 11. Oblique aerial photograph of c. 1910, looking north-northwest from the Colosseum (bottom right) to the piazza di Venezia (top left). The lines mark the suggested routes of Servius (dots) and Tullia (dashes); the asterisk marks the find-spot of the frieze attributed to the temple of Tellus (fig. 12).

That was known to be close to the *tigillum sororium* where Horatius was purified after the killing of his sister, 'in the street that leads from Carinae as one goes towards *uicus Cuprius*'.[94] Assuming that that refers to people coming from the Forum,[95] the site of the *compitum* makes it likely that 'Carinae' was on the slope of the Velia, not of the Esquiline. The passage may also imply that the *uicus Cuprius* was a major thoroughfare.

With the help of figures 10 and 11, we can now try to map the positions and relationships of the relevant streets. Figure 11 is based on an aerial photograph of the area taken early in the twentieth century,[96] before its historic topography was devastated by Mussolini's grandiose road project. The new broad streets of post-1870 *Roma capitale* are much in evidence,[97] but the underlying medieval and early-modern urban structure, including some street-lines surviving from Roman times, is still clearly visible. And though a bird's-eye view inevitably flattens out the gradients, it enables us to imagine the ancient topography in a way the modern city makes impossible.

The next stage of the argument involves the elusive neighbourhood called 'Carinae', which featured, I suggest, in the respective routes of both Servius and Tullia in Livy's story.[98]

7.4. Tellus and the Giants

In Livy's time, and perhaps already in that of Accius, 'Carinae' was a fashionable part of the city, a place where senators lived conveniently close to the Forum.[99] It was dominated by the temple of Tellus ('Earth'), a structure big enough to house a meeting of the Senate.[100] Although neither

94. Dionysius of Halicarnassus *Roman Antiquities* 3.22.8 (n. 82), with Degrassi 1963, 36–7 (*Fasti Arualium*): *tigillo soror(io) ad compitum Acili(um)*.

95. Rightly stressed by Coarelli 2001, 22: 'Se la direzione indicata fosse quella verso il Foro, si sarebbe evidentemente citato quest'ultimo, tra l'altro assai più noto. Se si è scelto il *vicus Cuprius* è perché era questo l'unico elemento suscettibile di indicare la direzione.'

96. The print was bought in a Rome street market many years ago, with no indication of provenance; since it shows the Victor Emmanuel monument already clad in bright Brescia marble, it must post-date Giacomo Boni's pioneering aerial photography programmes (1899–1909: Fortini 2014, 57).

97. Via Cavour running west to east, via dei Serpenti > via degli Annibaldi running north to south.

98. Coarelli 2001, 18–23; 2019, 342–59.

99. Virgil *Aeneid* 8.361 (*lautis Carinis*); Cicero *Ad Q. fratrem* 2.3.7 (house of Q. Cicero); Cicero *De haruspicum responso* 49, Suetonius *De grammaticis* 15.1 (house of Pompey); Horace *Epistles* 1.7.48-9 (house of Marcius Philippus).

100. Cicero *Philippics* 1.31, Appian *Civil Wars* 1.126.525-6, Dio Cassius 44.22.3 (17 March 44 BC). The temple was effectively synonymous with the Carinae: see Suetonius *De grammaticis* 15.1 (*in Carinis ad Telluris*), ps.Acro on Horace *Epistles* 1.7.46 (*Carinae* . . .

Tellus nor Carinae is mentioned in Livy's narrative, his audience and his Roman readers would have known exactly where the doomed old king was going and how his daughter got to where he was killed. In particular, I think, they would realise that Tellus, like the Penates,[101] was a witness of the crime.

The remains of the temple of Tellus were discovered in the mid-sixteenth century, and fortunately reported and described (by Pirro Ligorio and Onofrio Panvinio) before being dispersed for reuse.[102] The temple evidently featured a sculptured frieze showing the battle of the gods against the Giants, of which four substantial fragments were later discovered nearby, two in 1693 and two more in 1887.[103] The find-spot was close to where Tullia's carriage turned right to go up the *cliuus Vrbius*,[104] and one of the fragmentary panels shows a Fury with her burning torch (fig. 12).

This seems to be the only representation of them in Roman art,[105] and it is very different from the horrifying figures that pursued Orestes.[106] In particular, there is no sign of the snakes in the hair that define the Furies in all the poets from Aeschylus onwards.[107] The Furies portrayed here are not figures of madness but the implacable punishers of wrongdoing who were known in Athens as 'the solemn goddesses'.[108] That conception of them was well understood in Rome, as is made clear by the *pontifex* Gaius Cotta in Cicero's dialogue on the nature of the gods:

> If the *Eumenides* are goddesses, since in Athens they have a temple and here the 'Grove of Furina' (as I interpret it), then the Furies are

---

est locus ad Tellurem), Servius on Virgil *Aeneid* 8.361 (*Carinae sunt aedificia . . . quae erant circa templum Telluris*); medieval sources refer to the area as *in Tellure* (De Spirito 1999).

101. See n. 78.

102. Ziółkowski 1992, 156–61; Carandini and Carafa 2017, tab. 105; Coarelli 2019, 364–7.

103. Vian 1988, 241, no. 484; Coarelli 2019, 370–75.

104. Coarelli 2019, 371: 'lungo il tratto di Via del Colosseo adiacente alla Villa Rivaldi, poco prima dell'incrocio con l'attuale Via Frangipane.' Marked with an asterisk in fig. 11.

105. Coarelli 2019, 370, figs 142–3; neither this nor any other Roman example is cited in the standard work on the iconography of the *Erinyes* (Sarian 1986).

106. Aeschylus *Choephori* 1048-50, *Eumenides* 46-59; see Sarian 1986, 841–2 for the Aeschylean presentation used by Athenian vase-painters and imitated by south-Italian and Etruscan artists.

107. Aeschylus *Choephori* 1049-50 (innovating, according to Pausanias 1.28.6); Catullus 64.193, Horace *Odes* 2.13.35-6, Tibullus 1.3.69, Propertius 3.5.40, Virgil *Georgics* 4.482-3, *Aeneid* 6.571, 7.329, 7.346-53, 7.447-50, 12.848.

108. Homer *Iliad* 19.259-60 (αἵ θ' ὑπὸ γαῖαν | ἀνθρώπους τίνυνται ὅτις κ' ἐπίορκον ὀμόσσῃ). Σεμναὶ θεαί (Lloyd-Jones 1990): Aeschylus *Eumenides* 1041, Sophocles *Oedipus at Colonus* 89-90, 458, Pausanias 1.28.6.

FIGURE 12. Fragment of a marble frieze, found in 1887 near the Villa Rivaldi. The torch identifies the right-hand figure as a Fury (*Erinys*); the figure on the left may be one too. Roma, Musei Capitolini, Centrale Montemartini (inv. MC 1570): Archivio Fotografico dei Musei Capitolini. © Roma, Sovrintendenza Capitolina ai Beni Culturali.

> goddesses in their role as investigators and punishers of crime and wickedness.[109]

It is also implied in Varro's *Eumenides*, where the three Furies are seen punishing avarice and ambition:

> The third of the Punishers was Infamy, standing with all her weight [like an incubus] on the chest of the crowd, her undressed hair streaming, her clothes unwashed, her face stern.[110]

109. Cicero *De natura deorum* 3.46: *quae si deae sunt, quarum et Athenis fanum est et apud nos, ut ego interpretor, lucus Furinae, Furiae deae sunt, speculatrices credo et uindices facinorum et sceleris.* Cf. Plutarch *C. Gracchus* 17.2, *De uiris illustribus* 65.5 for *lucus Furinae* as ἄλσος Ἐριννύων.

110. Varro *Menippean Satires* 117 Astbury (*uidemus populum Furiis instinctum tribus*), with Wiseman 2009, 148. Varro *Menippean Satires* 123 Astbury: *tertia Poenarum | Infamia stans nixa in uulgi | pectore, flutanti intonsa coma, | sordida uestitu, ore seuero.*

That describes well enough the goddess portrayed on the Gigantomachy frieze from the temple of Tellus.

The Furies in the Aeschylean tradition are nightmare figures, appropriately the daughters of Night.[111] In Hesiod's *Theogony*, however, their mother is Earth, Γῆ or Γαῖα in Greek, Tellus in Latin.[112] That might account for their appearance on the frieze of the Tellus temple, punishing the rebellious Giants; but since the Giants were also Earth's offspring,[113] it cannot be quite that simple.

The story of the Giants as dangerous insurgents could carry a political message. In 63 BC Cicero as consul revealed an attempted coup by Catiline and his allies; controversially, on the authority of the Senate alone, he put those responsible to death without trial. Thereafter he had to justify his action against serious criticism, and one of the ways he did it can be seen in his defence of Publius Sulla the following year:

> Do not think, gentlemen of the jury, that that attempted attack was the work of human beings. There was never any race so barbarous, so monstrous, as to produce so cruel an enemy of our native land—even one, let alone so many! They appeared as a sort of bestiality, savage and portentous monsters clothed in human form. Look into it again and again, gentlemen, for there is nothing in this case that can be urged more forcefully. Look deep into the minds of Catiline, Autronius, Cethegus, Lentulus and the rest. What lusts you will find there, what crimes, what foulness, what audacity, what incredible madness, what stains of their misdeeds, what proofs of kin-murder, what accumulations of crime! That violence erupted suddenly out of serious, long-standing and now desperate diseases of the republic, in such a way that only when it was done with and ejected could the citizen body finally regain its strength and be healed. While those malignant elements remained within the republic, it is impossible to believe that survival was possible. Thus Furies drove them—not to commit their crime, but to pay their punishment to the republic.[114]

111. Aeschylus *Eumenides* 321-2, 416, 745, 821-2, 843-4, 1034; Virgil *Aeneid* 7.331, 12.846, 12.860, Ovid *Metamorphoses* 4.451-2.

112. Hesiod *Theogony* 184-5; cf. Homer *Iliad* 19.259 (n. 108 ὑπὸ γαῖαν).

113. Hesiod *Theogony* 185-6, Virgil *Georgics* 1.278-83, Horace *Odes* 3.4.73-5.

114. Cicero *Pro Sulla* 76: *nolite, iudices, arbitrari hominum illum impetum et conatum fuisse; neque enim ulla gens tam barbara aut tam immanis umquam fuit in qua non modo tot, sed unus tam crudelis hostis patriae sit inuentus. beluae quaedam illae ex portentis immanes ac ferae forma hominum indutae exstiterunt. perspicite etiam atque etiam iudices—nihil enim est quod in hac causa dici possit uehementius—penitus introspicite Catilinae, Autroni, Cethegi, Lentuli ceterorumque mentis; quas uos in his libidines, quae flagitia, quas turpitudines, quantas audacias, quam incredibilis furores, quas*

In the same vein for a wider audience, in 60 BC Cicero wrote an epic poem,[115] in which, exploiting the generic convention of divine agency, he represented himself as summoned to the council of the gods and deputed by Jupiter to protect Rome from danger.[116] Since Cicero was regarded at the time as a major poet,[117] it may well have been from him that Virgil took the picture of Catiline hanging from a cliff in Tartarus, menaced by the Furies.[118]

The house in which Cicero lived up to 62 BC, and his brother Quintus thereafter, was in Carinae close to the temple of Tellus.[119] We happen to know that Cicero had taken on responsibility for the upkeep of the temple, a task that certainly included furnishing it with works of art.[120] The fragments of the frieze belong to the temple as it was rebuilt after the great fire of AD 64, but its design evidently replicated an earlier one that can be dated to the first century BC.[121] The stern Furies in the battle against the Giants may even have been Cicero's own choice of subject.

The Gigantomachy was always a myth of order against chaos, civilisation against barbarism. The most spectacular exploitation of it was the Great Altar at Pergamum, set up by Eumenes II in the 180s BC in honour of his father Attalus' victory over the Gauls.[122] In Augustan Rome the theme was applied to internal enemies: the monstrous Giants were the assassins of Caesar, defeated at Philippi by Caesar's adopted son.[123]

---

notas facinorum, quae indicia parricidiorum, quantos aceruos scelerum reperietis! ex magnis et diuturnis et iam desperatis rei publicae morbis ista repente uis erupit, ut ea confecta et eiecta conualescere aliquando et sanari ciuitas posset; neque enim est quisquam qui arbitretur illis inclusis in re publica pestibus diutius haec stare potuisse. itaque eos non ad perficiendum scelus, sed ad luendas rei publicae poenas Furiae quaedam incitauerunt.

115. Courtney 1993, 156–73: dated by Cicero *Ad Atticum* 1.19.10 (March), 2.3.4 (December).

116. Ps.Sallust *In Ciceronem* 3, Quintilian 11.1.24 (*secutus quaedam Graecorum exempla*).

117. Plutarch *Cicero* 2.4 (ἔδοξε . . . ποιητὴς ἄριστος εἶναι Ῥωμαίων); the derision came later (Seneca *De ira* 3.37, Tacitus *Dialogus* 21.6, Juvenal 10.122-6).

118. Virgil *Aeneid* 8.668-9: *et te, Catilina, minaci | pendentem scopulo Furiarumque ora trementem.*

119. Plutarch *Cicero* 8.3, Cicero *Ad Q. fratrem* 2.3.7.

120. Cicero *De haruspicum responso* 31 (*aedes Telluris est curationis meae*), *Ad Q. fratrem* 3.1.14 (statue of Quintus).

121. Coarelli 2019, 374–5, comparing a fragment in Basel and drawing attention to Cicero's *curatio.*

122. For the date see Coarelli 2016, 143–58. Attalus himself exploited the Gigantomachy in his victory offering at Athens (Pausanias 1.4.5-6, 1.25.2).

123. Horace *Odes* 3.4.37-80 (on the settlement of the veterans who fought there), Ovid *Fasti* 5.555-6 (on the temple of Mars Ultor, 'worthy of trophies of the Giants'); for the

Cicero, who rejoiced at Caesar's murder,[124] would also have used the myth as a political allegory, but from just the opposite viewpoint.

Cicero was consul at a time of acute economic hardship in Italy, culminating in a 'peasants' revolt' supposedly orchestrated by Catiline (who eventually left Rome in order to lead it).[125] The political rhetoric of the time was ideologically polarised between the poor and the rich,[126] *populares* and *optimates*,[127] reforming tribunes and reactionary consuls.[128] Defeated at first, the *populares* made a spectacular comeback in 59–58 BC (Caesar as consul, Clodius as tribune, Cicero in exile); but then their opponents regained the upper hand.

Recalled from exile and enjoying a short-lived spell of political confidence, Cicero announced that all citizens except criminals, madmen and bankrupts were natural *optimates*.[129] But they had to stand firm:

> In such a large body of citizens there is a great multitude of men who either (*a*) fearing punishment and conscious of their own crimes, seek to cause new risings and revolutionary changes, or (*b*) because of a sort of inborn madness of mind, feed on civic discord and sedition, or (*c*) thanks to the chaotic state of their own finances, prefer to be burned up in a general conflagration, not just their own.[130]

---

enemy at Philippi see also Ovid *Fasti* 3.705-6 (*nefas ausi, prohibente deorum numine*), 5.575 (*scelerato sanguine*).

124. Cicero *Ad Atticum* 14.9.2 (*eius interfecti morte laetamur*), 12.1 (*laetitia*), 13.2 (*laetitiam autem apertissime tulimus omnes*), 14.4 (*laetitiam quam oculis cepi iusto interitu tyranni*), 22.2 (*nam aperte laetati sumus*): April–May 44 BC.

125. Details in Wiseman 1994b, 346–58: see especially Sallust *Catiline* 32.3-34.1 (complaints of violent exploitation met with the empty assurance that 'the Senate of the Roman People has always been merciful and compassionate'), Cicero *Pro Murena* 50 (Catiline as *dux et signifer calamitosorum*).

126. E.g. Sallust *Catiline* 33.1 (*miseri egentes*), Cicero *Pro Murena* 50 (Catiline as *miserorum defensor*), *Ad Atticum* 1.16.11 (the *misera ac ieiuna plebecula* as the 'bloodsucker of the treasury'), 1.19.4 (Cicero as leader of the *locupletes*).

127. E.g. Cicero *In Catilinam* 4.9-10 (Caesar and Crassus as *populares*), *De lege agraria* 2.6-10 (Cicero claiming to be *popularis*), *Ad Atticum* 1.20.3 (Cicero following *hanc uiam optimatem*); Plutarch *Cicero* 22.1 (the execution of the conspirators as a demonstration of ἀριστοκρατικῆς τινος ἐξουσίας).

128. E.g. Cicero *Pro Rabirio* 22 (*tribunicium furorem an consularem auctoritatem?*), *De lege agraria* 2.10-14 (land distribution), Dio Cassius 37.25.3-4 (debt relief etc).

129. Cicero *Pro Sestio* 97: *omnes optimates sunt qui neque nocentes sunt nec natura improbi nec furiosi nec malis domesticis impediti.*

130. Cicero *Pro Sestio* 99: *etenim in tanto ciuium numero magna multitudo est eorum qui aut propter metum poenae peccatorum suorum conscii nouos motus conuersionesque rei publicae quaerant, aut qui propter insitum quendam animi furorem discordiis ciuium ac seditione pascantur, aut qui propter implicationem rei familiaris communi incendio malint quam suo deflagrare.*

Behind such ideological stereotyping lay the dangerous reality of senatorial landowners faced with desperate rebellion by their own tenants.[131] It is not hard to see how Cicero, safely restored to public life in 57 BC, might have chosen to decorate the temple for which he was responsible with the great myth of order and authority defeating 'savage and portentous monsters'.[132]

The gods' agents were the Furies with their blazing torches, driving the rebel Giants into the underground dungeon where they would be tortured.[133] Ovid shows us the scene in book 4 of his *Metamorphoses*, when Juno visits the Underworld to engage the Furies in a project she wants to pursue:

> She called the stern and implacable power, the sisters born of Night. In front of the prison doors, barred with adamant, they were seated, combing the black snakes from their hair; the goddesses rose as soon as they recognised her in the shadows of darkness. It is called the House of Crime.[134]

The House of Crime, *sedes Scelerata*; the Street of Crime, *uicus Sceleratus*.[135] What links the stern Furies with the site of Tullia's horrendous act is a threefold argument: about a neighbourhood ('Carinae') not named by Livy but recognisable to his readers; about a temple (of Tellus) that overlooked the route Tullia took; and about a political allegory (the Giants) expressed not only in prose and poetry but also in the temple's sculptured frieze.

7.5. Accius and the optimates

If Cicero and his optimate allies portrayed themselves as Olympians and the *populares* as rebel Giants, it turned out that the Gigantomachy was not over. In 49 BC civil war broke out over that classic issue of Roman

131. Catiline's forces were armed mainly with hunting spears and sharpened stakes (Sallust *Catiline* 56.3); but they fought for life and liberty against 'the power of the few' (ibid. 58.11).

132. As he described the Catilinarians (*Pro Sulla* 76, n. 114).

133. Horace *Odes* 3.4.73-80, Virgil *Aeneid* 6.570-2, Pausanias 10.29.3; the same fate awaited their real-life analogues (Livy 2.23.6, *ductum . . . in ergastulum et carnificinam*), which is why Catiline's forces fought to the last rather than be taken alive (Sallust *Catiline* 61.1-5).

134. Ovid *Metamorphoses* 4.451-4: *illa sorores | Nocte uocat genitas, graue et implacabile numen; | carceris ante fores clausas adamante sedebant | deque suis atros pectebant crinibus angues. | quam simul agnorunt inter caliginis umbras, | surrexere deae. sedes Scelerata uocatur.* See also *Ibis* 77-8 (*quasque ferunt torto uittatis angue capillis | carceris obscuras ante sedere sedes*), and Allecto at Virgil *Aeneid* 7.454 ('*adsum dirarum ab sede sororum*').

135. Varro *De lingua Latina* 5.159, Livy 1.48.7, Festus 450-1L.

political ideology, the rights and powers of the People's tribunes.[136] As the *popularis* Caesar marched towards the city, the *optimates* fled abroad with Pompey, and the Roman People welcomed their champion.[137] Three years later, cautiously back in an unsympathetic Rome,[138] Cicero resumed his literary output with a dialogue on the history of Roman oratory addressed to Marcus Brutus.

Now that optimate rhetoric was effectively silenced,[139] he consoled himself by remembering the great men of the past that he had known himself or heard of from others. One of his sources was the dramatist Accius:

> As I used to hear from his good friend Lucius Accius the poet, your ancestor Decimus Brutus, son of Marcus, was accustomed to give speeches in an educated style, and by the standards of the time was well-read in literature both Latin and Greek. Accius paid that tribute to Quintus [Fabius] Maximus, grandson of Lucius Paullus, as well—and even before Maximus he used to say that Scipio—the one who as a private citizen led the killing of Tiberius Gracchus—was as vigorous in speaking as he was forceful in everything else.[140]

Cicero was sixty-four years younger than Accius.[141] An ambitious young orator eager to learn from the past, he must have talked to the old man at the very high point of optimate success, when Sulla's 'victory of the aristocracy' had emasculated the tribunate and effectively cancelled the popular gains made by the 'struggle of the orders' three centuries before.[142]

136. The tribunes M. Antonius and Q. Cassius were forced out of the city by the consuls in order to prevent them from exercising their legitimate power of veto (Caesar *De bello ciuili* 1.2-7, 1.22.5, Cicero *Ad Atticum* 11.7.1).

137. Even Cicero grudgingly recognised the *populi studium* (*Ad Atticum* 10.4.8, cf. 7.3.5, 7.7.6, 8.3.4); see also Appian *Civil Wars* 1.4.16-17 (Caesar as δημοτικώτατος), Florus 2.13.91 (Caesar honoured *non ingratis ciuibus*).

138. Cicero *Brutus* 2 (*alienissimo rei publicae tempore*), 330 (*in hanc rei publicae noctem*), 331 (*misera fortuna rei publicae*), 332 (*haec importuna clades ciuitatis*).

139. Cicero *Brutus* 324: *perterritum armis hoc studium, Brute, nostrum conticuit subito et obmutuit.* (A *suggestio falsi*: the war was overseas, and Rome itself was peaceful.)

140. Cicero *Brutus* 107: *uester etiam D. Brutus M. filius, ut ex familiari eius L. Accio poeta sum audire solitus, et dicere non inculte solebat et erat cum litteris Latinis tum etiam Graecis ut temporibus illis eruditus. quae tribuebat idem Accius etiam Q. Maximo L. Paulli nepoti; et uero ante Maximum illum Scipionem, quo duce priuato Ti. Gracchus occisus esset, cum omnibus in rebus uehementem tum acrem aiebat in dicendo fuisse.*

141. Accius was born in 170 BC (Jerome *Chronica* Ol. 160.2), Cicero in 106 (Aulus Gellius 15.28.3).

142. Cicero *Pro Sex. Roscio* 135-6, 141-2 (*causa nobilitatis, uictoria nobilium*, 80 BC); Appian *Civil Wars* 1.59.266-7 (legislation of 88 BC).

Accius' choice of admired orators was certainly in the spirit of the times. The murder of Tiberius Gracchus was an epochal event—if not the actual origin of the ideological divide in Roman politics, at least the moment when it became toxic.[143] Scipio Nasica and his band of senators deliberately beat to death a tribune presiding over a popular assembly, and no-one was ever put on trial for it. Cicero's position is clear: elsewhere in the dialogue he states that the republic itself killed Gracchus, because of his 'turbulent' tribunate, and that Scipio freed the Roman People from his 'domination'.[144] His informant probably took the same view.

A few months after the murder, Accius' aristocratic friend Decimus Brutus held a triumph over the Gallaeci of northern Spain, and set about building a grand temple of Mars in the Circus Flaminius, paid for from the spoils of war and adorned with verses by Accius himself.[145] It was Brutus who took the lead in the military operation against Gaius Gracchus and his supporters in 121 BC. The younger Gracchus had resumed his brother's reform programme in 123 BC, but this time the reactionary opposition had been more careful; they waited till he was out of office, and they got authorisation from the Senate to do whatever they thought necessary (an expedient later used by Cicero in 63 BC and the optimate consuls in 49).[146] Gracchus fled to the grove of Furina on the Janiculum, and there took his own life.[147] One of the consuls that year was Q. Fabius Maximus, the third of the admirable speakers recalled by Accius in conversation with the young Cicero.

Fur(r)ina was a deity who had her own *flamen*, and her own day, *Fur(r)inalia*, in the archaic Roman calendar.[148] Later evidence attests a

143. Cicero *De republica* 1.31 (*diuisit populum unum in duas partes*), Velleius Paterculus 2.3.3 (*hoc initium in urbe Roma ciuilis sanguinis*), Plutarch *Ti. Gracchus* 20.1 (ταύτην πρώτην ἱστοροῦσιν ἐν Ῥώμῃ στάσιν . . . αἵματι καὶ φόνῳ πολιτῶν διακριθῆναι), Appian *Civil Wars* 1.1.4, 1.17.71-2; Wiseman 2009, 177–87.

144. Cicero *Brutus* 103 (*propter turbulentissimum tribunatum . . . ab ipsa re publica est interfectus*), 212 (*qui ex dominatu Ti. Gracchi priuatus in libertatem rem publicam uindicauit*); similarly *De officiis* 1.109, *Philippics* 8.13.

145. Eutropius 4.19, Degrassi 1947, 558 (triumph); Cornelius Nepos *FRHist* 45 F11, Pliny *Natural History* 36.26 (temple); Cicero *Pro Archia* 27, Scholia Bobiensia 179 Stangl (Accius' verses).

146. Orosius 5.12.7 (D. Brutus); Cicero *In Catilinam* 1.4, *Philippics* 8.14, Livy *Epitome* 61 (action *ex senatus consulto*); Caesar *De bello ciuili* 1.5.3-4 (49 BC); for this very contentious procedure, 'an encouragement to the magistrates to use force against fellow-citizens without concerning themselves with the strict legality of what they did', see Lintott 1999, 89–93.

147. *De uiris illustribus* 65.5-6; cf. Appian *Civil Wars* 1.26.117 (ἐς ἄλσος τι), Plutarch *C. Gracchus* 17.2 (εἰς ἱερὸν ἄλσος Ἐριννύων).

148. Varro *De lingua Latina* 5.84, 6.19, 7.45; Festus (Paulus) 78L.

collective of Forinae or Forrines, evidently nymphs.[149] Nothing is known about her (or them), but Cicero puts into the mouth of Gaius Cotta, a man from the heart of the optimate faction, the view that the grove of Furina belonged to the Furies.[150] Since Plutarch reports Gaius Gracchus' suicide in 'the grove of the Erinyes',[151] it looks as if this too is evidence for the tendentious doctrine that *popularis* politicians were doomed to punishment in the underworld.

Plutarch's assertion is consistent with the conspicuously dramatic style of his narrative of Gaius Gracchus' last hours. That phenomenon was noted long ago by Karl Meiser, who used it as one of his examples of material from drama surviving in later historical narratives (section 7.1 above).[152] It was objected by Wilhelm Soltau that a drama on a subject as contentious as the death of Gaius Gracchus would never have been allowed at the Roman theatre games,[153] and so Meiser's intelligent suggestion was forgotten. Revived in 1998, it was dismissed again, by a scholar very much on his high horse as the spokesman of orthodoxy.[154]

The fact remains, however, that contemporary and controversial events *were* presented on the Roman stage, as the pseudo-Senecan *Octavia* is enough to show.[155] The orthodoxy has now shifted:

> The Roman theatre of the mid- to late republic was intensely political. The *fabula praetexta*, especially, and even tragedy often served expressly partisan purposes, promoting the causes of particular members of Rome's elite (such as the Marcelli with Naevius' *Clastidium*, or Fulvius Nobilior with Ennius' *Ambracia*) or attacking populist revolutionaries (such as Tiberius Gracchus with Accius' *Atreus*).[156]

It is quite possible that Accius or some other dramatist wrote a *praetexta* on the death of Gaius Gracchus. Of course there is no direct evidence for

149. *CIL* 6.422 (*genio Forinarum*), 10200 (*ad ar*[*am*] *Forinar*[*um*]), 36802 (νύμφες Φορρίνες).

150. Cicero *De natura deorum* 3.46 (n. 109); cf. Sallust *Histories* 3.15.8 Ramsey (*C. Cotta, ex factione media consul*).

151. Plutarch *C. Gracchus* 17.2 (n. 147).

152. Meiser 1887, 32–6.

153. Soltau 1909, 53–4; so too Wright 1910, 29 n. 2.

154. Wiseman 1998, 52–9; Keaveney 2003, 322 ('it might lead some of us to ask'), 323 ('it will come as something of a surprise to some of us'), 325 ('so some of us at least just doubt a little'), 329 ('some of us, at least, do require a higher standard of proof'), 330 ('some of us might just prefer to believe').

155. See Kragelund 2016, 286–7 (approval of the Gracchi at lines 882–6), 297–360 (time of writing).

156. Boyle 2008, xxvii–iii.

it; but I believe that the contrasting house-doors of Gracchus and Fulvius in Plutarch's narrative are best explained by the hypothesis that his source was an author who had seen the events on stage.[157] That would fit with the attribution of Furina's grove to the avenging Furies, easily explicable as a dramatist's tendentious invention.

The friendship between Decimus Brutus, supposedly descended from the first consul of the republic, and Lucius Accius, the son or grandson of freed slaves, was of course based on mutual advantage.[158] Brutus had the authority to get Accius' plays shown at the *ludi scaenici*; Accius had the talent to make Brutus' family history part of the living experience of the Roman People. He did that with a *praetexta* on the first consul himself, Lucius Brutus, who had led the rising that expelled Tarquin.[159] The date of its first production is unknown, though 138 BC (D. Brutus' consulship) and 133 BC (his triumph) are obvious possibilities.

More important is the play's afterlife in the politics of the late republic. It was presented at the consul's games in 57 BC (section 2.3 above), when the *optimates* were using every means at their disposal to reverse the People's decision of the previous year and bring Cicero back from exile. The message was first conveyed by Aesopus' performance in Accius' *Eurysaces*, pleading the case of the banished Teucer and making it clear to the audience whom they should have in mind.[160] The following year, now restored, Cicero himself described the scene:

> The actor, as he pleaded my cause with such emotion, wept so often for what happened to me that that splendid voice of his was choked with tears; the poets, whose genius I have always loved, did not fail me when I needed them; and the Roman People showed its approval not only by its applause but even by its audible distress. So if the Roman people had been at liberty, was it proper that it should be Aesopus or Accius speaking so on my behalf, or that it should be the leaders of the state? In the *Brutus* I was mentioned by name—'Tullius, who had established freedom for the citizens'—and it was encored time after time. Wasn't that enough to show that in the Roman People's judgement the thing

157. Wiseman 1998, 53–5, on Plutarch *C. Gracchus* 14.5.

158. Accius: Jerome *Chronica* Ol. 160.2 (*parentibus libertinis*). Brutus: Posidonius *FGrH* 87 F40, Cicero *Tusculan Disputations* 4.2, Plutarch *Brutus* 1.1.

159. Fragments and discussion in Manuwald 2001, 220–37.

160. Cicero *Pro Sestio* 120-2, with Scholia Bobiensia 136-7 Stangl. Lentulus' games for Honos and Virtus took place in late May or early June (Kaster 2006, 400 n. 25); the bill for Cicero's recall was passed on 4 August (Cicero *Ad Atticum* 4.1.4).

> depraved citizens accused me of overthrowing was established by the Senate and myself?[161]

In the play, of course, Tullius was Servius Tullius, who set up the original voting assembly, the *comitia centuriata*. The *optimates* approved of it because it was biased towards the rich, and now they would use it to get Cicero recalled.[162] When Sulla had marched on Rome thirty years before, he had announced his intention to restrict all voting to the centuriate assembly, 'as king Tullius ordained'.[163]

Long dead at the time of the play's action, Servius Tullius can have been only a peripheral figure in the *Brutus*. But the main theme, the ending of Tarquin's tyrannical reign, was equally congenial to the *optimates*, who consistently accused their *popularis* opponents of Tarquin-like tyranny.[164] During Caesar's consulship in 59 BC Cicero was reported to have said 'What we need is a Brutus';[165] a few years later, when Cato was denouncing as 'tyranny' the second consulships of Pompey and Crassus, Brutus the 'liberator' was conspicuously portrayed on the coins of Cato's nephew Marcus Brutus.[166] Before long a new *Brutus* play would be written, by a poet who was one of Caesar's assassins.[167]

161. Cicero *Pro Sestio* 123: *histrio casum meum totiens conlacrimauit, cum ita dolenter ageret causam meam, ut uox eius illa praeclara lacrimis impediretur; neque poetae, quorum ego semper ingenia dilexi, tempori meo defuerunt; eaque populus Romanus non solum plausu sed etiam gemitu suo comprobauit. utrum igitur haec Aesopus potius pro me aut Accium dicere oportuit, si populus Romanus liber esset, an principes ciuitatis? nominatim sum appellatus in Bruto: 'Tullius, qui libertatem ciuibus stabiliuerat.' miliens reuocatum est. parumne uidebatur populus Romanus iudicare id a me et a senatu esse constitutum, quod perditi ciues sublatum per nos criminabantur?*

162. Cicero *De republica* 2.39 (*ut suffragia non in multitudinis sed in locupletium potestate essent*); Livy 1.43.10 (*ut . . . uis omnis penes primores ciuitatis esset*); Dionysius of Halicarnassus *Roman Antiquities* 4.20.3 (ἐπὶ τοὺς πλουσίους μετέθηκε τὸ τῶν ψήφων κράτος). The *comitia centuriata* met in the Campus Martius, where the vote for Cicero's return took place (Cicero *De domo* 90).

163. Appian *Civil Wars* 1.59.266 (ὡς Τύλλιος βασιλεὺς ἔταξε).

164. E.g. Cicero *De amicitia* 41, Sallust *Jugurthine War* 31.7, Plutarch *Ti. Gracchus* 19.2-3 (Ti. Gracchus as *rex* or *tyrannus*); Appian *Civil Wars* 1.59.267 (Sulla on the 'tyrannical' power of *popularis* tribunes); Cicero *Ad Atticum* 2.8.1, 2.12.1, 2.13.2, 2.14.1, 2.17.1, *Ad Q. fratrem* 1.2.16 (Caesar and Pompey in 59 as *reges* or *tyranni*); Cicero *Pro Milone* 43, 80 (Clodius as *rex* or *tyrannus*).

165. Cicero *Ad Atticum* 2.24.3 (*Brutum opus esse reperire*).

166. Plutarch *Pompey* 52.1, *Crassus* 15.2 (cf. *Brutus* 2.1 for the relationship); Crawford 1974, 455–6 (no. 433), dated to 54 BC, but that was more probably the year of Brutus' quaestorship in Cilicia.

167. Cassius of Parma (Porphyrio on Horace *Epistles* 1.4.3): fragments and discussion in Manuwald 2001, 237–43. For the likely date see section 8.6 below.

Accius, meanwhile, retained his classic status. In July 46 BC, Cicero was exchanging Accius quotations with his correspondents, no doubt from plays just seen at the *ludi Apollinares*,[168] and examples taken from Accius are very numerous in the philosophical works he wrote in the next two years.[169]

Caesar won the civil war, but in the *optimates*' prejudiced view he was necessarily a tyrant, however un-tyrannically he behaved.[170] Even his spectacular demonstration, at the Lupercalia in February 44 BC, that 'there is no king in Rome but Jupiter', was twisted by his opponents to prove that he really wanted to be king himself;[171] and a month later, when the conspirators under Marcus Brutus killed him for it, Accius' *Brutus* and the tyranny of Tarquin provided the jubilant *optimates* with a perfect historical analogy.

The play was due to be performed at the *ludi Apollinares* of 44 BC, just four months after the murder, with Marcus Brutus himself presiding as urban praetor. That would have made a powerful statement, but Caesar's adopted son was now in Rome and the *optimates* were becoming anxious;[172] so Brutus stayed away, and his representatives put on Accius' *Tereus* instead.[173] But Cicero made the most of Tarquin and Lucius Brutus as he tried to rally the *optimates* in the autumn of that year,[174] and predictably it was Accius who came to mind as he damned 'king' Caesar's memory in the *De officiis*.[175]

168. Cicero *Ad familiares* 7.33.1 (to Volumnius, quoting Accius' *Philoctetes*), 9.16.4-7 (to Paetus, quoting Accius' *Oenomaus*).

169. Cicero *De finibus* 2.94, 4.68, 5.32; *Tusculan Disputations* 1.68, 1.105, 2.13, 2.19, 2.23, 2.33, 3.62, 4.55, 4.77, 5.52; *De natura deorum* 1.119, 2.89, 3.41, 3.68, 3.90; *De diuinatione* 1.43-5; *De officiis* 1.97, 3.84, 3.102, 3.106; many of the unassigned quotations may be from Accius too.

170. Cicero *Ad Atticum* 7.11.1, 7.20.2, 8.2.4, 9.4.2, 9.13.4, 10.1.3, 10.4.2, 10.8.6, 10.12a.1 (January–May 49 BC), *Ad familiares* 9.16.6 (July 46 BC); for the prejudice see Wiseman 2009, 191–207.

171. Nicolaus of Damascus *BNJ* 90 F130.21.73 (Toher 2017, 108–11), Suetonius *Diuus Iulius* 79.2, Dio Cassius 44.11.3; details in Wiseman 2009, 170–75.

172. Octavius in Rome: Cicero *Ad Atticum* 14.20.5, 14.21.4, 15.2.3. Anxiety: *Ad Atticum* 15.18.2 (*prorsus non mihi uideor esse tutus*), 15.20.2.

173. Cicero *Ad Atticum* 15.10 (*ludos uero non facere!*), 15.11.1 (Brutus not safe in Rome), 15.11.2 (*ut ludi absente se fierent suo nomine*), 15.12.1 (*ludos enim absens facere malebat*), 15.18.2 (*ludorum curam et administrationem*), 15.26.1, 15.28, 15.29.1, 16.5.1 (*de Tereo Acci*), 16.2.3 (*delectari mihi Tereo uidebatur*), *Philippics* 1.37.

174. Cicero *De officiis* 3.40, *Philippics* 1.13, 2.26, 2.85, 2.114, 3.8-11, 5.17.

175. Cicero *De officiis* 3.83-4 (quotation probably from the *Atreus*, as at 1.97, 3.102, 3.106).

Not just an author to be read but a classic dramatist whose plays were still performed at the *ludi scaenici*, in the forties BC Accius was a significant influence in Roman culture, and a continued inspiration to those on one side of the political divide. That is something to bear in mind when we think about Livy's formative years.

7.6. The young Livy

Suetonius wrote a biography of Livy in his lost work *De uiris illustribus*, which was used by Jerome for the chronicle he compiled in AD 380. One of Jerome's entries for 59–58 BC reads: 'Birth of the orator Messalla Corvinus and of the historical writer Titus Livius of Patavium.'[176] Since that seems too late for Messalla, who held a senior position under Brutus and Cassius in 43–42 BC,[177] it has been doubted for Livy too: perhaps the consular date *Caesare et Figulo* (64 BC) was misread as *Caesare et Bibulo* (59 BC)?[178] But Jerome will have found the two men in different parts of Suetonius' work, and it is too much to assume that he made the same mistake twice. The date for Livy should be accepted.

When did Livy come to Rome? We know nothing of his early life, but the case of his younger contemporary Ovid, for whom we have first-hand information, should give us an idea what to expect. Ovid and his brother (a year older) were born in Paelignian Sulmo, but 'we began our education young, and thanks to our father's care we attended teachers in Rome well known in the art [of rhetoric]'.[179] Livy certainly had a first-rate rhetorical education,[180] and despite what is often said, there is no good reason to think he got it anywhere but Rome.[181] If, like Ovid, he started his education young, he may have been there as early as 46 or 45 BC. It seemed at that point that the civil war was over, and for a youth with talent, energy

176. Jerome *Chronica* Ol. 180.2: *Messalla Coruinus orator nascitur et Titus Liuius Patauinus scriptor historicus*. Livy's death at Patavium is listed under Olympiad 199.1 (AD 17–18).

177. Cicero *Ad M. Brutum* 1.12.1, 1.15.1; Velleius Paterculus 2.71.1.

178. Syme 1959, 40 = 1979, 414; followed (wrongly, I think) by Luce 1965, 231–2.

179. Ovid *Tristia* 4.10.15-16: *protinus excolimur teneri curaque parentis | imus ad insignes urbis ab arte uiros*.

180. Seneca *Epistulae* 100.9 (one of the *eloquentissimi*), *De ira* 1.20.6 (*disertissimus*); Quintilian 8.1.3 (*mirae facundiae*), 10.1.101 (*supra quam enarrari potest eloquens*); Tacitus *Agricola* 10.3 (*eloquentissimus*), *Annals* 4.34.3 (*eloquentiae praeclarus imprimis*).

181. *Pace* Syme 1959, 51 = 1979, 426 ('Livy may have come late to Rome') and Walsh 1961, 2 ('Livy almost certainly received his education in Patavium and not in Rome').

and ambition, all three of which Livy clearly had in abundance, Rome was the only place to be.[182]

Although Livy was a generous author who liked to see the best in the great men he wrote about,[183] he was certainly not blind to their failings. A friend of Augustus in later years, he still reported doubts about whether the birth of Julius Caesar (now deified) had really been beneficial to Rome.[184] A whole-hearted admirer of Cicero's oratory, he was still aware that Cicero would have been as cruel as the triumvirs if the optimate cause had prevailed in 43 BC.[185] He saw his history as a public duty of education, presenting not just admirable behaviour to be imitated but also deeds to be avoided, 'foul in inception and foul in outcome', of which Tullia's 'foul and inhuman crime' was explicitly an example.[186]

The stage too was public education, in the Roman world as in the Greek.[187] Livy took a serious interest in the *ludi scaenici*, recording their origins and development from the time of the kings right down to the extravagant spectacles of his own day.[188] During his formative years he had plenty of opportunity to see Roman politics and Roman history presented

182. For the ambition and energy see for instance Livy pref. 1-5, Pliny *Natural History* pref. 16. I see no grounds for the view of Walsh 1961, 2–3: 'He was only a schoolboy when Julius Caesar precipitated the Civil War by invading Italy; it would have been madness for responsible guardians to expose a young boy to the considerable physical and moral dangers which both the journey and the disordered life in the capital might produce.' There is no reason to think he was unprotected; compare Ovid again ('thanks to our father's care').

183. Seneca *Suasoriae* 6.21-2: *T. Liuius benignus . . . natura candidissimus omnium magnorum ingeniorum aestimator*.

184. Seneca *Naturales quaestiones* 5.18.4 (*de Caesare maiore uulgo dictitatum est et a T. Liuio positum, in incerto esse utrum illum magis nasci reipublicae profuerit an non nasci*); cf. Tacitus *Annals* 4.34.3 for Augustus' *amicitia*.

185. Quintilian 10.1.39 (*apud Liuium . . . legendos Demosthenem et Ciceronem, tum ita ut quisque esset Demostheni et Ciceroni simillimus*); Seneca *Suasoriae* 6.22 (*a uictore inimico <nihil> crudelius passus erat quam quod eiusdem fortunae conpos ipse fecisset*).

186. Livy pref. 10 (*inde tibi tuaeque rei publicae quod imitere capias, inde foedum inceptu foedum exitu quod uites*), 1.48.7 (*foedum inhumanumque inde traditur scelus*).

187. See n. 12, and compare Aristophanes *Acharnians* 649-58, *Wasps* 1010-14, *Frogs* 686-7 (comedy); *Frogs* 1008-10, 1418-19, 1500-503 (tragedy); Pausanias 1.3.3 (learning 'from choruses and tragedies'), Libanius *Oratio* 64.112 (tragedians as κοινοὶ διδάσκαλοι τοῖς δήμοις).

188. Livy 1.35.9 (*ludi Romani* instituted by Tarquinius Priscus), 6.42.12-13 (origin of curule aediles' responsibility), 7.2.3-13 (origin of *ludi scaenici*, contrast with current 'insane' extravagance); 25.12.1-15, 27.23.5-7 (origin of *ludi Apollinares*); 29.10.4-11.8, 29.14.5-14, 34.54.3, 36.36.4 (origin of *ludi Megalenses*); 34.54.5-7 (senators' reserved seats a threat to *concordia* and *libertas aequa*); *Epitome* 115 (*spectacula* at Caesar's triumph in 46 BC), fr. 56 = Censorinus *De die natali* 17.9 (17 BC, *ludos saeculares Caesar ingenti adparatu fecit*); cf. Censorinus 17.10 for Livy's reporting of *ludi saeculares* in 249 and 149 BC.

on stage in many different styles, from the mime-actors' satirical comments on current events to classic plays exploited for a topical message.[189] In the tense time between Caesar's murder and the deaths of the assassins, there could be nothing more topical than plays about kings.

Caesar was killed 'because he wanted to be king',[190] and by that the *optimates* meant he wanted to be a king like Tarquin. But not all kings were tyrants, and the Roman People may have preferred Caesar as king to renewed domination by the optimate oligarchy from which he had freed them five years before.[191] Livy himself argued that the Roman monarchy was a valuable institution preventing the otherwise inevitable conflict of rich against poor, *plebs* against *patres*.[192] In that context, the historical figure of Servius Tullius, 'with whom just and legitimate reigns came to an end',[193] was worthy of particular attention.

The *populares* of the late republic claimed Servius Tullius as one of their own. He relieved the burden of debt, as the tribunes of 63 BC had tried to do; he divided up public land among the poor, like Tiberius Gracchus in 133 BC; his power was granted directly by the People against the opposition of the Senate, as Caesar's *imperium* was in 59 and 55 BC; he was a 'democratic king', who would have abolished the monarchy if a conspiracy of patricians had not plotted against him.[194] Carefully non-

189. Mime-actors: Cicero *Ad Atticum* 14.2.1, 14.3.2 (18–19 April 44 BC); cf. *Ad familiares* 7.11.2 (53 BC). Classic plays: Suetonius *Diuus Iulius* 84.2 (Caesar's funeral games); cf. Cicero *Ad Atticum* 2.19.3 (59 BC), *Pro Sestio* 118-23 (57 BC).

190. Cicero *De officiis* 3.83: *qui rex populi Romani dominusque omnium gentium esse concupiuerat idque perfecerit*. For how the issue came to a head in January–March 44 BC, see Livy *Epitome* 116, Nicolaus of Damascus *BNJ* 90 F130.69-75, Velleius Paterculus 2.68.4-5, Suetonius *Diuus Iulius* 79, Plutarch *Caesar* 60–62, *Brutus* 9.5-8, *Antony* 12, Dio Cassius 44.9-12.

191. Caesar *De bello ciuili* 1.23.3: *se . . . ex prouincia egressum . . . ut se et populum Romanum factione paucorum oppressum in libertatem uindicaret.*

192. Livy 2.1.4-5: *quid enim futurum fuit, si illa pastorum conuenarumque plebs . . . soluta regio metu agitari coepta esset tribuniciis procellis et in aliena urbe cum patribus serere certamina?* It was only after the death of Tarquin that the patricians began to exploit and abuse the plebeians: Sallust *Histories* 1.10.3 Ramsey (*dein seruili imperio patres plebem exercere*), Livy 2.21.6 (*iniuriae a primoribus fieri coepere*).

193. Livy 1.48.8: *cum illo simul iusta ac legitima regna occiderunt.*

194. Dionysius of Halicarnassus *Roman Antiquities* 4.10.2 (debts, cf. Dio Cassius 37.25.4), 4.10.3, 4.13.1 (*ager publicus*), 4.12.3 (παραλαμβάνει τότε τὴν ἀρχὴν παρὰ τοῦ δημοτικοῦ πλήθους πολλὰ χαίρειν τῇ βουλῇ φράσας); 5.75.3 (δημοτικώτατος βασιλεύς), cf. 4.10.1, 4.25.1 (δημοτικός), with 4.8.3 and 4.40.1 for the hostile version; 4.40.3-4 (would have changed τὸ σχῆμα τῆς πολιτείας εἰς δημοκρατίαν but for the conspiracy). This tradition is presupposed by Ovid *Fasti* 6.575-8 and 773-6, Plutarch *Moralia* 322c and 323d, Festus (Paulus) 247L.

partisan, Livy uses this tradition without endorsing it:[195] it is enough for him that Servius was a good king and Tarquin a bad one. But the fact that he knew the tendentious version shows what sort of material was being read, listened to or seen on stage,[196] at a time when the history of Rome was coming under more urgent scrutiny than ever before.[197]

It is easy to imagine a play on the killing of the good king, whether by Accius or some other dramatist, finding a sympathetic audience at the *ludi scaenici* at any time after the Ides of March. Since Caesar had been *parens patriae*,[198] the theme of Tullia's patricidal plot, and pursuit by the Furies, would be particularly appropriate. So too the assassins of Caesar were condemned as parricides, and pursued to their deaths by an avenging *daimon*.[199]

It is now generally agreed that Livy's preface, and most if not all of the first pentad, were written in the late 30s BC, before the end of the civil wars.[200] The historian was therefore in his mid- to late twenties, and his years of preparation for the great work had been among the most tormented in the whole of Roman history. He attributed the 'ancestral curse' of lust for power even to the founder himself, and pointed out that at the time of writing most people believed that Romulus killed his brother with his own hand.[201] And when he came to the death of Servius Tullius, he used what he had seen on stage to make his moral lesson as vivid as he could.

It is true that there is no direct attestation of Livy's dramatic source for Tullia and the Furies. All the evidence is circumstantial, but in its cumulative effect I think it is proof enough.

195. Livy 1.46.1 (division of land), 1.48.9 (unfulfilled *liberandae patriae consilia*).

196. For 'hearing or reading' history see Cicero *De finibus* 5.52 (*res gestas audire et legere*), *De senectute* 20 (*legere aut audire*), Caelius in Cicero *Ad familiares* 8.15.1 (*aut audisti aut legisti*), Sallust *Catiline* 53.2 (*mihi multa legenti multa audienti*), *Jugurthine War* 85.13 (*audire aut legere*), [Sallust] *Ad Caesarem* 2.10.3 (*legendo atque audiendo*), Dio Cassius 53.19.6 (ὧν ἀνέγνων ἢ καὶ ἤκουσα).

197. Varro's *De uita populi Romani* was evidently written in 44–43 BC (Arnobius 5.8 on the consulship of Hirtius and Pansa dates the companion piece *De gente*); Sallust's two monographs date from about 42–40 BC, and his *Histories* not long after; the histories of Q. Tubero and Asinius Pollio (*FRHist* 38 and 56) were probably begun in the 30s.

198. Degrassi 1947, 182–3 (*Fasti Ostienses* on 44 BC): *Caesar pare[ns patriae occisus]*. Full details in Weinstock 1971, 200–205.

199. Valerius Maximus 1.8.8, 3.1.3, 6.4.5, 6.8.4, Tacitus *Annals* 4.34.3 (*parricidae*); Suetonius *Diuus Iulius* 88 (*placuit Idus Martias Parricidium nominari*); Valerius Maximus 1.7.7, Plutarch *Brutus* 36.5-7, *Caesar* 69.2 (δαίμων).

200. Luce 1965; Woodman 1988, 128–35; Oakley 1997, 109–10: the 'Augustan' passages at 1.19.3 and 4.20.5-11 are later 'addenda and corrigenda' inserted between 27 and 25 BC; at 9.19.17 peace is recent and precarious.

201. Livy 1.6.4 (*auitum malum, regni cupido*), 1.7.2 (*uolgatior fama est . . . Remum . . . ab irato Romulo . . . interfectum*); cf. Horace *Epodes* 7 (probably 32 BC).

CHAPTER EIGHT

Brutus the Liberator

THE END of Tarquin's reign, like its beginning, was a subject for dramatists, and once again the details of Livy's historical narrative may give us an insight into how and why the story was put on the stage.

8.1. A puzzle in Livy

After the rape and suicide of Lucretia, Livy presents Lucius Brutus in the Roman Forum, urging the citizens to rebel against Tarquin. Here is the historian's summary of his speech:

> He spoke of the violence and lust of Sextus Tarquin, of the unspeakable rape of Lucretia and her wretched death, of the bereavement of Lucretius Tricipitinus and the cause of his daughter's death, which for him was more unworthy and more pitiable than the death itself. He mentioned also the arrogance of the king himself and how the *plebs* had been forced underground to dig out trenches and sewers: the men of Rome, victorious over all their neighbours, had been turned into drudges and quarry slaves, warriors no longer. He recalled the appalling murder of King Servius Tullius and how his daughter had driven over her father's body in that accursed wagon, and he invoked her ancestral gods as avengers.[1]

1. Livy 1.59.8-10 (trans. T. J. Luce): *de ui ac libidine Sex. Tarquini, de stupro infando Lucretiae et miserabili caede, de orbitate Tricipitini cui morte filiae causa mortis indignior ac miserabilior esset. addita superbia ipsius regis miseriaeque et labores plebis in fossas cloacasque exhauriendas demersae; Romanos homines, uictores omnium circa populorum, opifices ac lapicidas pro bellatoribus factos. indigna Ser. Tulli regis memorata caedes et inuecta corpori patris nefando uehiculo filia, inuocatique ultores parentum di.*

There must have been more, but Livy does not report it:

> After saying these things and, I am sure, even more shocking ones prompted by his outrage of the moment, which are not easy for writers to capture on paper, he brought his listeners to such a pitch of fury that they revoked the king's power and ordered the exile of Lucius Tarquinius, together with his wife and children.[2]

What did Livy mean by *haudquaquam relatu scriptoribus facilia*? If Luce's translation 'not easy for writers to capture on paper' seems too far from the Latin, Aubrey de Sélincourt in the Penguin Classics version has 'but a mere historian can hardly record them', and R. M. Ogilvie in his commentary offers 'which historians find it embarrassing to recount'.[3]

It is true that *scriptores* in Livy are always historians;[4] but far from being embarrassed, historians in the Greek and Roman world relished the chance to report impassioned speeches.[5] Since Livy has just summarised most of what Brutus is supposed to have said, it is not obvious why he feels he has to break off here. What exactly was his problem?

I think the plural *scriptores* is significant. He is evidently not deciding how much *he* is prepared to relate, as de Sélincourt's translation implies, but offering an explanation for lack of material in the previous writers whose work he used.[6] That is: Livy is putting on record his belief (*credo*) that Brutus' indignation prompted him to make still more dreadful accusations against the Tarquins, even though they weren't in his written sources. The question is, *why* did he believe that? If there was nothing in the written sources (*scriptores*), how else could he have access to a speech given nearly five hundred years before?

2. Livy 1.59.11 (trans. T. J. Luce): *his atrocioribusque, credo, aliis, quae praesens rerum indignitas haudquaquam relatu scriptoribus facilia subiecit, memoratis incensam multitudinem perpulit ut imperium regi abrogaret exsulesque esse iuberet L. Tarquinium cum coniuge et liberis.*

3. Ogilvie 1965, 228.

4. Livy pref. 2 and 3, 1.44.2, 3.23.7, 4.23.2, 8.30.7, 9.18.5, 23.6.8, 26.11.10, 29.14.9, 33.36.15, 45.44.19. More specifically *scriptores rerum*: 21.1.1, 38.56.5, 39.50.10. In the singular, Valerius Antias is twice referred to as a *scriptor* (36.38.7, 38.55.8).

5. As Lucian observed (*Historia* 58), 'if you have to bring on someone to make a speech . . . then you're allowed to be oratorical and show off your skill with words'.

6. So 3.48.8, cited for comparison in the commentary of Weissenborn and Müller, is no real parallel: Livy there may be simply summarising an emotional speech found in his source.

8.2. An uneasy narrative

It is worth looking more closely at Livy's narrative of these events. There are at least three oddities in it that may turn out to be revealing.

First, Brutus is giving this speech in an official capacity, as *tribunus celerum*, 'a post that he chanced to be holding at that moment'.[7] But Livy has already told the famous story of how the young Lucius Iunius, after his father and brother were murdered by Tarquin, pretended to be an idiot, and was kept in the king's house as an object of mockery; that of course was why he was called *brutus* ('stupid').[8] But the *tribunus celerum* was the king's deputy, commander of his cavalry, later equated with the Prefect of the Praetorian Guard.[9] How could Tarquin have entrusted his safety to a man he believed to be an idiot?

The same paradox appears in the somewhat different narrative of Dionysius of Halicarnassus, and in his painstaking way Dionysius does at least try to explain it. His Brutus, having thrown off his idiot's disguise at the death of Lucretia, is conferring with her father and husband and Publius Valerius about how they should effect the overthrow of the Tarquins. When he proposes that they summon the People to the Forum, Valerius asks which of them will do it, 'for that's a magistrate's business, and none of us holds a magistracy'. 'I shall,' replies Brutus:

> 'for I am the commander of the *celeres*, and empowered by law to call an assembly when I wish. The tyrant gave me this office, important though it is, in the belief that as an idiot I wouldn't know what its powers are, or if I did know I wouldn't use them.'[10]

Even if one could believe that, one might wonder why Valerius didn't know. So desperate an expedient is a clear sign of a historian combining two mutually inconsistent accounts. Livy, faced with the same problem,

7. Livy 1.59.7 (*in quo tum magistratu forte Brutus erat*), trans. T. J. Luce.

8. Livy 1.56.7-12, esp. 8 (*Bruti quoque haud abnuit cognomen*).

9. Pomponius in *Digest* 1.2.2.15 and 19: *is autem erat qui equitibus praeerat et ueluti secundum locum a regibus optinebat, quo in numero fuit Iunius Brutus qui auctor fuit regis eiciendi . . . quod officium fere tale erat quale hodie praefectorum praetorio.* For the *celeres* see Livy 1.15.8 (king's bodyguard), Pliny *Natural History* 33.35 (*equites*).

10. Dionysius of Halicarnassus *Roman Antiquities* 4.71.5-6: ἄρχοντι γὰρ ἀποδέδοται τοῦτο πράττειν· ἡμῶν δὲ οὐδεὶς οὐδεμίαν ἀρχὴν ἔχει. ὁ δ' ὑποτυχών, ἐγώ φησίν, ὦ Οὐαλέριε. τῶν γὰρ κελερίων ἄρχων εἰμί, καὶ ἀποδέδοταί μοι κατὰ νόμους ἐκκλησίαν, ὅτε βουλοίμην, συγκαλεῖν. ἔδωκε δέ μοι τὴν ἀρχὴν ὁ τύραννος μεγίστην οὖσαν ὡς ἠλιθίῳ οὔτ' εἰσομένῳ τὴν δύναμιν αὐτῆς οὔτ' εἰ γνοίην, χρησομένῳ. (Cf. 4.68-9 for the 'idiot' story).

knew better than to try to explain; he just mentions the office in passing and hopes his readers won't notice as the narrative sweeps on.

In the story Cicero knew, mentioned in *De republica* (51 BC), Brutus leads the rebellion as a private citizen. As Ogilvie rightly pointed out, that must be the original version, presupposing the feigned-idiocy legend.[11]

The second oddity in Livy's story is the way Brutus arrives in the Forum. The death of Lucretia took place at Collatia, where she had summoned her father and husband after the rape.[12] In Dionysius' variant Lucretia has to go to Rome, to her father's house, to tell her story and then kill herself; that is more convenient for the sequel, since her body can be displayed in the Roman Forum to help rouse the citizens to act.[13] But Livy keeps to the more usual version, which means that the display of the body takes place in the market-place at Collatia, and it is there that Brutus first urges action.[14]

In response to his call, 'all the fiercest young men' take up arms.[15] Guards are posted at the gates of Collatia, to prevent news getting out to Tarquin. And then:

> Brutus led the rest of the warriors to Rome. The arrival of a large group of armed men caused fear and commotion wherever it went; on the other hand, the sight of the nation's leaders at the forefront made people think that whatever was afoot there must be good reason for it.[16]

No other account of the end of the monarchy makes any mention of these armed men and the panic they caused. It's not as if they were the *celeres*, of whom Brutus was supposedly in command; Livy makes it clear they were a volunteer force, and the Roman People evidently regarded them as a private army with no obvious business to be carrying weapons in the city.

11. Cicero *De republica* 2.46 (*qui cum priuatus esset . . . quo auctore et principe concitata ciuitas*); Ogilvie 1965, 228.

12. Diodorus Siculus 10.20.3, Livy 1.58.5-6, Ovid *Fasti* 2.813-16, Dio Cassius 2.11.18, *De uiris illustribus* 9.4-5, Servius on *Aeneid* 8.646, Zonaras 7.11; some of these sources have others present too (see section 8.5 below).

13. Dionysius of Halicarnassus *Roman Antiquities* 4.66-7, 70–84.

14. Livy 1.59.3-4: *elatum domo Lucretiae corpus in forum deferunt . . . Brutus castigator lacrimarum atque inertium querellarum auctorque, quod uiros, quod Romanos deceret, arma capiendi.*

15. Livy 1.59.5: *ferocissimus quisque iuuenum cum armis uoluntarius adest; sequitur et cetera iuuentus.*

16. Livy 1.59.5-6 (trans. T. J. Luce): *ceteri armati duce Bruto Romam profecti. ubi eo uentum est, quacumque incedit armata multitudo, pauorem ac tumultum facit; rursus ubi anteire primores ciuitatis uident, quidquid sit haud temere esse rentur.*

They cannot be a Livian invention: they don't help his narrative, and he immediately cancels out the effect of their appearance by reporting the reassuring presence of 'the nation's leaders' (*primores ciuitatis*). But they must have been important to someone earlier, whose version of the events is reflected in Livy.

Finally, what about Lucretia, whose body was last seen in the market-place at Collatia (1.59.3)? If the *primores ciuitatis* are Brutus, Collatinus, Spurius Lucretius and Publius Valerius (and it's hard to see who else they could be), then Lucretia's husband and father must have left her there unburied. It is evident that Livy has combined, with less than complete success, two separate narratives of the rousing of the citizens against Tarquin: first, the more usual version, set in Collatia, in which Brutus spoke over Lucretia's body at her funeral;[17] and second, a scene set in the Roman Forum, where Brutus was a magistrate with an armed escort holding a formal *contio* before the People.

It is in connection with the second scenario that Livy seems to be conscious of things Brutus said which his written sources did not record.

8.3. A recent parallel

When Livy wrote book 1, it was little more than a decade since the traumatic day of 'fear and commotion' when a magistrate called Brutus, with an armed escort, held a public meeting in the Roman Forum in which he urged the Roman People to seize its liberty after the overthrow of a 'tyrant'.[18] It was the afternoon of the Ides of March 44 BC, and although on that occasion the armed men were gladiators and the citizen audience was shocked and silent, the parallels with the Livian scenario are much too close to be accidental.

The alleged descent of Marcus Brutus, praetor in 44 BC, from Lucius Brutus the liberator, already advertised on the coins he issued ten years earlier, had been exploited by opponents of Caesar's regime in anonymous messages urging Brutus to act like his ancestor.[19] To the assassins' surprise and dismay, the Roman People soon made it clear that they saw the

17. Livy 1.59.3, Ovid *Fasti* 2.847-50 (*fertur in exsequias*, 847), Zonaras 7.11 (ὁ Βροῦτος . . . τὴν γυναῖκα πολλοῖς τῶν τοῦ δήμου κειμένην ὑπέδειξε); cf. Dionysius of Halicarnassus *Roman Antiquities* 4.76.3, the same scene shifted to Rome.

18. Nicolaus of Damascus *BNJ* 90 F130.26.98-100, Appian *Civil Wars* 2.122.512-4.

19. Crawford 1974, 455, no. 433; Plutarch *Brutus* 9.6-7, *Caesar* 62.1 and 4, Suetonius *Diuus Iulius* 80.3, Appian *Civil Wars* 2.112.469, Dio Cassius 44.12.1-3.

death of Caesar not as tyrannicide but as murder and sacrilege;[20] however, after the amnesty of 17 March and Cicero's revival of the optimate cause in the autumn of 44, the parallel between the old Brutus and the new one could still be drawn, though now it was a bitterly controversial issue.[21]

How was the controversy played out during those long months of desperate strife, between the Ides of March and Brutus' suicide at Philippi on 23 October 42 BC? The short answer is that we don't know, but it may be possible to offer a more interesting longer answer, inevitably conjectural.[22]

Not surprisingly, Lucius Brutus and the expulsion of the Tarquins were a subject for the Roman stage. Two *fabulae praetextae* are attested with the title *Brutus*: Lucius Accius' classic drama of the late second century BC, and a play by 'Cassius', twice cited by Varro in *De lingua Latina*.[23] There may have been more. We know from casual comments in our sources that in Livy's lifetime plays on Roman subjects were a regular part of contemporary drama;[24] among the examples that happen to be referred to are one on the capture of Corinth in 146 BC, and another on the arrival of the Magna Mater in 204.[25]

Marcus Brutus should have been in charge of the *ludi Apollinares* in 44 BC, but circumstances made it necessary for a deputy to preside on his behalf.[26] We know from Cicero's correspondence that Brutus was expecting Accius' play about his ancestor to be put on; though that didn't happen, it illustrates how politically relevant even plays from three generations earlier could be made to be.[27] However, classic revivals were not the only way of making political points.

20. Appian *Civil Wars* 2.119.501 (τοῦ δήμου δὲ αὐτοῖς οὐ προσθέοντος ἠπόρουν καὶ ἐδεδοίκεσαν), 143.596-147.614 (popular reaction at funeral).

21. E.g. Cicero *Philippics* 2.26. Controversy: see Plutarch *Brutus* 1.6 on οἱ διὰ τὸν Καίσαρος φόνον ἔχθραν τινὰ καὶ δυσμένειαν ἀποδεικνύμενοι πρὸς Βροῦτον (Richardson 2020, 191–3).

22. For a sceptical view, see Keaveney 2006.

23. Fragments and discussion in Manuwald 2001, 220-37 (Accius), 237–43 (Cassius); see section 8.6 below on Cassius.

24. Horace *Ars poetica* 285-8; Manilius *Astronomica* 5.282 (with G. P. Goold's ordering of the text in the Loeb edition).

25. Horace *Epistles* 2.1.187-93, Manuwald 2001, 71–5; Ovid *Fasti* 4.326 (*mira sed et scaena testificata loquar*).

26. Appian *Civil Wars* 3.23.87 (C. Antonius).

27. Cicero *Ad Atticum* 16.5.1, cf. 2.3. The *locus classicus* for contemporary political allusions is Cicero *Pro Sestio* 118-23 (see section 2.3 above).

Topical comments were a regular feature of the mimes,[28] but not necessarily restricted to them. In the early principate, performances at the *ludi scaenici* regularly dealt with contemporary themes; normally, of course, it was loyal praise of the emperor, always in danger of descending into mere flattery,[29] but the pseudo-Senecan play *Octavia* suggests that on the right occasion it was possible to deal with more contentious subjects. I think it is more likely than not that under the republic, and especially at periods of acute tension like 44–42 BC, the aediles and praetors responsible for the theatre games would have made sure that the performances reflected their own political attitudes.

8.4. A solution to the puzzle

To return to Livy: his Lucius Brutus, invoking the gods who avenge kin-murder, reminds the citizens of the killing of Servius Tullius and the guilt of his daughter, Tarquin's queen.[30] Livy had reported that story with the theatre in mind—'the Roman royal house produced a tragic spectacle to rival those of Greece'—and now he concludes it with the citizens calling down the avenging Furies against the murderous Tullia.[31] As we know from Cicero (section 2.1 above), the Furies pursuing the guilty were a familiar sight on the Roman stage.[32]

Livy's version of Brutus' speech also makes much of the suffering of the plebeians, who allegedly had to work underground digging trenches and sewers for Tarquin's engineering projects.[33] But that brutal exploitation of the citizen body is elsewhere attributed to Tarquinius *Priscus*, and his construction of the Cloaca Maxima two generations earlier.[34] Why should it be brought up now? Although it can be no more than a guess, I think we should remember the huge building and engineering works put in train by

28. Cicero *Ad familiares* 7.11.2 (53 BC), *Ad Atticum* 14.3.2 (44 BC).

29. Phaedrus 5.7.16-27; Suetonius *Diuus Augustus* 89.3 (cf. 43.5 and Cicero *Ad Atticum* 16.5.1 for *commissio* referring to *ludi scaenici*); Pliny *Panegyricus* 54.1-2.

30. Livy 1.59.10 (*inuocatique ultores parentum di*); see chapter 7.

31. Livy 1.46.3 (*tulit enim et Romana regia sceleris tragici exemplum*), trans. T. J. Luce; Livy 1.59.13 (*inuocantibusque parentum furias uiris mulieribusque*).

32. Cicero *In Pisonem* 46 (*ut in scaena uidetis*), *De legibus* 1.40 (*sicut in fabulis*), *Academica* 2.89 (tragedy); cf. *De haruspicum responso* 39 (*in tragoediis*) on the Furies and madness.

33. 1.59.9 (*miseriaeque et labores plebis in fossas cloacasque exhauriendas demersae*), previously reported at 1.56.2.

34. Pliny *Natural History* 36.107-8, cf. Livy 1.38.6; Dionysius (*Roman Antiquities* 3.67.5, 4.44.1-2) achieves a spurious consistency by making Superbus finish what Priscus had started.

Caesar and paid for out of his Gallic booty.[35] They included not only the creation of what later became the Forum Iulium, but also the excavation of a system of passages underneath the Roman Forum itself; it has been convincingly suggested that they were designed to enable the Forum to be used for wild-beast shows, as it was for Caesar's great triumphal games in 46 BC.[36]

The hypothesis I propose—by its nature unprovable, but I hope adequate to explain the phenomena—is that not long after the Ides of March someone produced a drama about the end of the monarchy which presented Lucius Brutus and Tarquin in a way deliberately reminiscent of Marcus Brutus and Caesar.[37] As we saw in the previous chapter (section 7.6), in the tense time between Caesar's murder and the deaths of the assassins, there could be nothing more topical than plays about kings; Livy was in his teens at that time,[38] and could easily have seen a performance that stuck in his mind and influenced the way he thought about the events.

Cicero tells us that the stage was a source of information; Varro tells us that plays at the *ludi scaenici* taught the Roman People about history; Plutarch tells us that a playwright's version of events could be regarded as accurate if not contradicted by a historian's.[39] The very unexpectedness of those passages is a good reason for taking them seriously as evidence for how the Romans understood historical drama.

Livy was well aware of the ways playwrights could distort history. There is a famous passage in book 5 where he refuses to endorse a story about the fall of Veii which seemed to him 'more appropriate to the show of the stage that delights in marvels'.[40] But Livy was not making any such fundamental objection in the passage we are concerned with. If, as we have argued, he had in his head the memory of a play about the end of the monarchy, no doubt he found it perfectly credible that Brutus should have given a speech in the Forum, and he was able to make it compatible

35. Cicero *Ad Atticum* 4.16.8, cf. Plutarch *Caesar* 29.2-3.

36. Welch 2007, 38–42; Dio Cassius 43.22.3-23.3 on Caesar's 'hunting theatre' in the Forum; cf. Pliny *Natural History* 15.78 (altar removed), 19.23 (awnings over the whole Forum).

37. Perhaps the death of Servius Tullius was adduced as analogous to the death of Pompey, which was cited in March 44 as an example of Caesar's 'tyranny' (Appian *Civil Wars* 3.127.533).

38. Born in 59 BC, according to Jerome (*Chronica* Ol. 180.2).

39. Cicero *De legibus* 1.47 (*scaena* among sources of *opiniones*); Varro *De lingua Latina* 6.18 (*togata praetexta data †eis† Apollinaribus ludis docuit populum*); Plutarch *Theseus* 28.2 (on Phaedra and Hippolytus).

40. Livy 5.21.9: *ad ostentationem scaenae gaudentis miraculis aptiora quam ad fidem.*

(just) with what earlier historians reported about a speech over Lucretia's body at Collatia.

However, the stage speech he remembered may have included material that was not reconcilable with what Livy found in the *scriptores*. If that was the case, he just used what he could and excused himself from reporting the rest: the other items were *haudquaquam relatu scriptoribus facilia* (section 8.1 above). Livy uses the verb *referre* very frequently, but the supine form *relatu* occurs nowhere else in the whole huge extent of the surviving text. As a unique passage, it requires a very particular explanation, and the hypothesis of an influential play on the subject provides one.

8.5. The bloody knife

An earlier oddity in Livy's narrative may have come from the same source. The morning after the rape,

> Lucretia, stricken to the heart at the disgrace, sent the same messenger to her father in Rome and husband in Ardea: each was to come with one trustworthy friend; it must be done this way and done quickly; a terrible thing had happened. Spurius Lucretius arrived with Publius Valerius son of Volesus, Collatinus with Lucius Brutus, in whose company he was travelling *en route* to Rome when his wife's messenger chanced to meet him. They found Lucretia seated downcast in her bedchamber.[41]

She tells them what has happened, and makes a very specific demand: 'Pledge with your right hands and swear that the adulterer will not go unpunished.'[42] Then she draws the knife she has concealed and plunges it into her heart. Her father and husband cry out together:

> While they were taken up with lamentation, Brutus pulled the knife dripping with blood from Lucretia's body. Holding it before him he cried, 'By this blood, so pure before defilement by prince Tarquin, I hereby swear—and you, O deities, I make my witnesses—that I will drive out Lucius Tarquinius Superbus together with his criminal wife and all his progeny with sword, fire, and whatever force I can muster,

41. Livy 1.58.5-6 (trans. T. J. Luce): *Lucretia maesta tanto malo nuntium Romam eundem ad patrem Ardeamque ad uirum mittit, ut cum singulis fidelibus amicis ueniant; ita facto maturatoque opus esse; rem atrocem incidisse. Sp. Lucretius cum P. Valerio Volesi filio, Collatinus cum L. Iunio Bruto uenit, cum quo forte Romam rediens ab nuntio uxoris erat conuentus. Lucretiam sedentem maestam in cubiculo inueniunt.*

42. Livy 1.58.7 (trans. T. J. Luce): *'date dexteras fidemque haud impune adultero fore'.*

> nor will I allow them or anyone else to be king at Rome.' He then handed the dagger to Collatinus, and next to Lucretius and Valerius, who stood amazed at the miraculous change that had come over him. They repeated the oath after him.[43]

Once again, the swift dramatic narrative discourages awkward questions. Of course Lucretia needs her father and her husband with her, but why must each of them bring a friend? Of course she demands punishment for the rapist Sextus, so why does Brutus swear to drive out Sextus' parents?

The only evidence for the form of the story before Livy comes in a Byzantine epitome of Diodorus Siculus:

> But when the day came and Sextus departed, she summoned her kinsmen and asked them not to allow the man to go unpunished who had sinned against the laws both of hospitality and of kinship. As for herself, she said, it was not proper for the victim of a deed of such wanton insolence to look upon the sun, and plunging a dagger into her breast she slew herself.[44]

That the 'kinsmen' were her husband Collatinus and her father Spurius Lucretius is made explicit in other sources.[45] The presence of Brutus and Valerius is not required, yet Livy makes a point of getting them there right from the start,[46] and by doing so he achieves that dramatic scene of the four men swearing their oath on the bloody knife.

43. Livy 1.58.11-59.2 (trans T. J. Luce): *conclamat uir paterque. Brutus illis luctu occupatis cultrum ex uolnere Lucretiae extractum manante cruore prae se tenens, 'Per hunc' inquit 'castissimum ante regiam iniuriam sanguinem iuro, uosque, di, testes facio me L. Tarquinium Superbum cum scelerata coniuge et omni liberorum stirpe ferro igni quacumque dehinc ui possim exsecuturum, nec illos nec alium quemquam regnare Romae passurum.' cultrum deinde Collatino tradit, inde Lucretio ac Valerio, stupentibus miraculo rei unde nouum in Bruti pectore ingenium. ut praeceptum erat iurant.*

44. Diodorus 10.20.3 (trans. C. H. Oldfather): ἡμέρας δὲ γενομένης ὁ Σέξτος ἐχωρίσθη· ἡ δὲ ἐκάλεσε τοὺς οἰκείους καὶ ἠξίου μὴ περιιδεῖν ἀτιμώρητον τὸν ἀσεβήσαντα εἰς ξενίαν ἅμα καὶ συγγένειαν. ἑαυτῇ δὲ φήσασα μὴ προσήκειν ἐφορᾶν τὸν ἥλιον τηλικαύτης ὕβρεως πεπειραμένην, ξιφιδίῳ πατάξασα τὸ στῆθος ἑαυτῆς ἐτελεύτησεν.

45. Ovid *Fasti* 2.815-6 (*grandaeuumque patrem fido cum coniuge castris | euocat*), Dio Cassius 2.11.18 (μετεπέμψατο τόν τε ἄνδρα καὶ τὸν πατέρα), *De uiris illustribus* 9.4 (*aduocatis patre et coniuge*). In one late source (Servius on Virgil *Aeneid* 8.646) Lucretia also summons Brutus, supposedly her maternal uncle.

46. In Dionysius (*Roman Antiquities* 4.66.1), Lucretia goes to Rome to her father's house, where some other unspecified relatives 'happen to be present'; her father then summons 'the most prominent men' (4.67.1), among whom were Brutus and Valerius. Ovid, whose narrative is closest to Livy's, suddenly introduces Brutus in mid-scene (*Fasti* 2.837: *Brutus adest*), but doesn't say how he got there. Zonaras (7.11) has Brutus and Valerius both present, following Livy but with no explanation.

The Romans believed that the expulsion of the Tarquins was brought about by a popular rising under the leadership of Lucius Brutus: he and he alone was their liberator from tyranny.[47] So why should Livy go out of his way to present a four-man team bound by a common oath?

The play we have suggested he saw as a boy offers a likely answer. If it gave Lucius Brutus the legendary liberator a speech in the Forum like that of Marcus Brutus the real-life assassin on the Ides of March, in an earlier scene it might well have presented the liberator doing what the assassin had done, collecting and motivating like-minded allies. Swearing an oath created a *coniuratio*, a conspiracy.[48]

There was a difference: Tarquin and his family were expelled from Rome, not killed. Lucius Brutus and his friends were not assassins, whereas Marcus Brutus and the Ides of March conspirators ran from the scene of the killing to the Capitol waving bloodstained daggers. At the time, it caused panic and terror,[49] but later the conspirators used it as a badge of honour: coins struck for Brutus in the Philippi campaign showed two daggers with a cap of liberty between them.[50] Whoever first presented the story of Lucius Brutus as a conspiracy sworn on a blood-stained dagger may have wanted to justify Brutus the contemporary conspirator by making him look like Brutus the old-time liberator.

It is easy to imagine how the oath scene could be played on stage (fig. 13), and what an impact it would have had on a young spectator.

8.6. Cassius' Brutus

One of the Ides of March assassins, Cassius Parmensis, was a playwright,[51] and it is normally, and reasonably, assumed that he was the Cassius whose *Brutus* was twice quoted by Varro.[52] If Livy's narrative was indeed

47. [Cicero] *Rhetorica ad Herennium* 4.66 (*'ego reges eieci . . . patriam liberaui'*); Cicero *De finibus* 2.66 (*duce et auctore Bruto*), *De republica* 2.46 (*uir ingenio et uirtute praestans*); cf. *De oratore* 2.225, *Pro Plancio* 60, *Brutus* 53, *Philippics* 1.13 (*populum/ciuitatem/rem publicam dominatu regio liberauit*).

48. *De uiris illustribus* 9.5 (Collatinus and Sp. Lucretius Tricipitinus *in exitium regum coniurarunt*), 10.4 (L. Brutus *cum Tricipitino et Collatino in exitium regum coniurauit*).

49. Nicolaus of Damascus *BNJ* 90 F130.25.91 (τὰ ἐγχειρίδια ᾑμαγμένα ἔχοντες), 92–4; Appian *Civil Wars* 2.118.494-5, 119.494 (τὰ ξίφη μετὰ τοῦ αἵματος ἔχοντες); Plutarch *Brutus* 18.7-8, *Caesar* 77.1-2.

50. Crawford 1974, 518, no. 508: *BRVT. IMP. / EID. MAR.*

51. Porphyrio on Horace *Epistles* 1.4.3 refers to his *multae tragoediae*; the 'poems in various genres' (e.g. elegy and epigram) attributed to him by the 'pseudo-Acro' scholia may just be guesswork based on Horace's reference to his *opuscula*.

52. Varro *De lingua Latina* 6.7 (*in Bruto Cassii*), 7.72 (*apud Cassium*); Manuwald 2001, 239–40, cf. Stothard 2020, 59–62.

FIGURE 13. Jacques-Antoine Beaufort, *The Oath of Brutus* (1771): Musée municipal Frederic Blandin, Nevers. Wikimedia Commons. Gavin Hamilton's slightly earlier treatment of the same scene, equally melodramatic, is in the Yale Center for British Art, New Haven (Paul Mellon Collection).

influenced by the memory of a play, that play must surely have been Cassius' *Brutus*. But when could he have seen it performed?

The assassins benefited from the amnesty agreed in the Senate on 17 March 44 BC, but had to keep out of Rome to avoid the hostility of the populace.[53] By the summer, however, they and their optimate allies were hopeful that their position could be strengthened by a formal agreement of impunity.[54] It is not known where Cassius Parmensis was living at the time, but we can be sure that as a playwright he was looking ahead to the *ludi Romani*, which began on 5 September. The curule aediles in charge of them may have been sympathetic to the assassins,[55] since Antony as consul

53. See Appian *Civil Wars* 2.126-35 (Senate meeting), 143–8 (popular anger at the funeral), esp. 2.127.528 (most of the senators favoured the assassins) and 2.148.615 (assassins' flight from Rome).

54. Cicero *Ad Atticum* 16.7.1-5, *Philippics* 1.1, 1.7-10.

55. It is not known who they were (*pace* Broughton 1952, 322): the Antonian Trebellius who was evidently aedile that year (Cicero *Philippics* 13.26) may not have been curule,

chose to retire to his Tiburtine villa for the duration of the games.[56] It is an easy guess that one of the plays they put on was Cassius Parmensis' *Brutus*, recently composed and with a point to make about heroic conspirators.

Varro's citations of the play come in books 6 and 7 of *De lingua Latina*, which were dedicated to Cicero.[57] Those books were evidently written between June 45 BC, when the dedicatee politely prompted Varro to get on with it, and the death of Cicero in December 43.[58] The chronology is tight but workable, if we assume that Varro, having seen or read the play in September 44, cited two lines from it in books that were written and published within the next year or so.

As for Cassius Parmensis himself, in late August or September 43 BC he and all his fellow conspirators were condemned for the murder of Caesar.[59] Since he lived the rest of his life as an outlaw,[60] it is highly unlikely that his play would have been performed again in public, though written copies could have circulated privately. If Livy saw it, it must have been as an impressionable fifteen-year-old in 44 BC.

---

and the inscription of the curule aediles L. Trebellius and Varro Murena (*ILLRP* 704) is undatable.

56. Cicero *Ad familiares* 12.2.1, *Philippics* 5.20: he used the time to work on his speech (attacking Cicero) for the Senate meeting on 19 September, immediately after the games.

57. See n. 52, with Varro *De lingua Latina* 5.1 for the dedication of books 5–7.

58. Cicero *Ad familiares* 9.8.1, Tacitus *Dialogus* 17.2.

59. Augustus *Res gestae* 2, Livy *Epitome* 120, Velleius Paterculus 2.69.5, Appian *Civil Wars* 3.95.392-3, Dio Cassius 46.48.1-4.

60. He was the last of the assassins to be executed, probably in 30 BC (Velleius Paterculus 2.87.3).

CHAPTER NINE

Velleius and the Games

ANCIENT TEXTS provide us with two quite different categories of evidence. There is what the author himself wants his readers to know, which in the case of a historian is obviously a large category; and there is also what we can infer from his work, irrespective of his own intention, about the world in which it was written. The latter type of evidence is particularly valuable because the author was unaware he was providing it. As an example, this chapter looks at what Velleius Paterculus' world history in two volumes may imply about the history and conditions of Roman theatre.

9.1. Chronological markers

Among Velleius' most noticeable characteristics as a historian are, first, an insistence on precise chronology, particularly in numbering the years before Marcus Vinicius' consulship; second, a serious interest in the foundation of cities, noticeable especially in the fragmentary first book; third, an instinct to collect together similar items, whether events or people, into groups and lists; and fourth, a weakness for sudden and unexpected digressions from the narrative. All four of these features are conspicuously present in the lengthy passage (1.14-15) with which he marks the transition from the first part of his work to the second.[1]

1. Velleius Paterculus 1.14.1 (Loeb trans.): 'Inasmuch as related facts make more impression upon the mind and eye when grouped together than when they are given separately in their chronological sequence, I have decided to separate the first part of this work from the second by a useful summary, and to insert in this place an account, with the date, of each colony founded by order of the Senate since the capture of Rome by the Gauls. . . . And it will perhaps not seem out of place if in this connection we weave into our history the various extensions of the citizenship and the growth of the Roman name through granting to others a share in its privileges.' The sudden essay at 1.16-17 on 'the most distinguished

It consists of a list of all the colonies founded by the Romans from the capture of the city by the Gauls down to the sixth consulship of Marius in 100 BC, with the addition, in the same chronological sequence, of those Italian communities which were granted the privilege of Roman citizenship. It was a subject of interest not only to Velleius, who came from Campania, but also to Marcus Vinicius himself, whose home town was the Latin colony of Cales, just north of Capua.[2] Both the historian and his dedicatee were a part of the expansion of Rome (*auctum Romanum nomen*, 1.14.1), and this passage at the turning-point of his narrative discreetly indicates the fact.

Fifty-six cities and communities are named in the list, under thirty-seven separate dates. The chronology is mainly relative ('the following year', 'three years later', etc), but absolute dates are provided as well—by consular pairs (ten examples), by 'years before the present' (six examples), and in seven cases by reference to other events. This last group is particularly valuable, as indicating which chronological fixed points were so significant to Velleius, or to his readers, that he could use them to pin down particular items in his long list.

The first one is obvious, the Gallic sack itself: the colony at Sutrium was founded seven years after the Gauls took the city (1.14.2). More interesting are two items which link Rome with events in the wider world: Fundi and Formiae were granted Roman citizenship in the year Alexandria was founded (1.14.3), and colonies were established at Minturnae and Sinuessa in the year Pyrrhus became king in Epirus (1.14.6). The loss of most of the first book makes it easy to forget that Velleius' subject was not confined to Rome, and that one of his themes was the succession of monarchical power (*imperium*) in Asia and Greece.[3] The wars with Carthage provide more obvious chronological markers: the colonies at Firmum and

---

minds in each branch of human achievement' (*eminentissima cuiusque professionis ingenia*, 1.16.2), and its appendix on famous cities at 1.18, are explicitly detached from the structure of the work as a whole. See 1.16.1 (Loeb trans.): 'Although this portion of my work has already, as it were, outgrown my plan, . . . yet I cannot refrain from noting a subject which has often occupied my thoughts.'

2. 1.7.2 (foundation of Capua as 'domestic business', *res domestica*), 2.76.1 (grandfather C. Velleius 'a man second to none in Campania'); Tacitus *Annals* 6.15.1 (Vinicius from Cales). At 1.14.3 Velleius notes the grant of citizenship without the vote to the Campanians and the foundation of Cales; cf. also 2.44.4 and 45.2 (Capua's rights restored by Caesar's land settlements), 2.81.1 (further colonists sent by Augustus). The 'military colonies' referred to at 1.14.1 and 15.5 presumably include the veteran settlements in Campania.

3. 1.1.2 (Agamemnon as king of kings), 1.2.1 (Heraclidae as 'leaders in the recovery of *imperium*'), 1.6.1 (*imperium* of Asia passes from Assyrians to Medes); cf. 1.6.6, the interpolated passage from Aemilius Sura on successive empires.

Castrum were founded at the start of the First Punic War, and those at Cremona and Placentia just before Hannibal came into Italy (1.14.8).

The remaining two items are, to put it mildly, surprising. Three years after the consulship of Torquatus and Sempronius (244 BC), the colony at Spoletium was founded 'in the year when the games of Flora began'.[4] And the colony at Auximum in Picenum was founded '187 years ago' (158 BC),

> three years before Cassius the censor began the construction of a theatre from the Lupercal towards the Palatine; in building it he was then resisted by the remarkable strictness of the citizen body and by Caepio [?] the consul, which I would number among the most splendid proofs of the will of the People.[5]

In the second case something is wrong with the chronology: C. Cassius Longinus was censor in 154 BC, whereas Cn. and Q. Servilii Caepiones were consuls in 141 and 140 BC. The consul's name was emended to 'Scipio' in the Aldine edition of 1571, but the second consulship of P. Scipio Nasica was in 155 BC, the year *before* Cassius' censorship.

9.2. Dangerous games

Velleius' approving comment about the opposition to Cassius' new theatre must have been made with an eye on his own time. In AD 23 Tiberius had suppressed *theatralis seditio* (2.126.2), the riotous behaviour of actors' and dancers' fan clubs, by the ruthless expedient of banishing all public stage performers from Italy.[6] But that makes it all the more remarkable that Velleius should use two items from the history of the Roman theatre games as chronological markers of the same status as the foundation of Alexandria and the First Punic War, particularly in the case of Cassius' abortive theatre, which wasn't even started in the year the historian wants to identify.

We may find an explanation by turning to Velleius' contemporary Valerius Maximus, who devoted the second book of his collection of *exempla*

4. 1.14.8: *et post triennium Spoletium, quo anno Floralium ludorum factum est initium.* Cf. Pliny *Natural History* 18.236 for the *ludi Florales* instituted 'in the year of the city 516' (238 BC).

5. 1.15.3: *ante triennium quam Cassius censor a Lupercali in Palatium uersus theatrum facere instituit, cui inde moliendo eximia ciuitatis seueritas et consul †cepio† restitere, quod ego inter clarissima publicae uoluntatis argumenta numerauerim.* (*inde moliendo* is the Budé editor's emendation for *in demoliendo.*)

6. Tacitus *Annals* 4.14.3, Suetonius *Tiberius* 37.2, Dio Cassius 57.21.3.

to 'ancient and memorable institutions'.[7] The fourth item in his list of ten, perhaps surprisingly, is the theatre:

> From military institutions the next step to take is to the fortresses of the city, that is, the theatres, since they too have frequently drawn up fierce battle lines. They were invented for the worship of the gods and the delight of men, but to the shame of peace they have stained pleasure and religion with the blood of citizens, for the sake of the monstrosities of the stage.
>
> This began in the censorship of Messalla and Cassius [154 BC].[8] On the proposal of P. Scipio Nasica, however, it was decided to auction off all the equipment of the craft. It was also forbidden by senatorial decree that anyone in the city or within a mile of it should set up benches or watch the games sitting down, no doubt with the intention of linking mental enjoyment with the virility of a standing posture appropriate to the Roman race.[9]

Already in the 20s BC Livy had referred disapprovingly to the contrast between the humble origins of the *ludi scaenici* and the theatrical extravagance of his own time (section 3.1 above), 'to show the sober origins of something which has now reached this state of insanity, hardly tolerable in wealthy monarchies'.[10] It is not known whether he expanded on the subject when he reached the Scipio Nasica story, since the epitome of his forty-eighth book reports only this:

> When a theatre contracted by the censors was under construction, it was destroyed by decree of the Senate on the proposal of P. Scipio

7. Valerius Maximus 2.pref: he will turn his pen to *priscis et memorabilibus institutis*.

8. Does *quae* ('these') refer back to *theatra*, or *portenta*? Shackleton Bailey (2000, 151 n. 4) notes that *eorum* in the next sentence 'seems to be the actors, though the nearest antecedent is *quae* (*theatra*)'; I think it is more likely that Valerius meant *quae portenta* ('these monstrosities'), referring to the actors themselves.

9. Valerius Maximus 2.4.1-2: *proximus <a> militaribus institutis ad urbana castra, id est theatra, gradus faciendus est, quoniam haec quoque saepenumero animosas acies instruxerunt, excogitataque cultus deorum et hominum delectationis causa non sine aliquo pacis rubore uoluptatem et religionem ciuili sanguine scaenicorum portentorum gratia macularunt. quae incohata quidem sunt a Messalla et Cassio censoribus. ceterum auctore P. Scipione Nasica omnem apparatum operis eorum subiectum hastae uenire placuit, atque etiam senatus consulto cautum est ne quis in urbe propiusue passus mille subsellia posuisse sedensue ludos spectare uellet, ut scilicet remissioni animorum standi uirilitas propria Romanae gentis iuncta esset.*

10. Livy 7.2.13 (on 364 BC): *ut appareret quam ab sano initio res in hanc uix opulentis regnis tolerabilem insaniam uenerit.* Livy was writing at about the time Augustus transferred responsibility for the games from the aediles to the praetors (n. 17); *pace* Oakley 1998, 71, I do not think the point was the number of days devoted to games.

> Nasica, as something of no value and harmful to public morals, and for some time after that the populace stood to watch the games.[11]

(How long after, we are not told, but a ban even on benches for *ad hoc* stages can hardly have lasted for long.)

So we may infer a growing unease about the theatre throughout the Augustan period, no doubt connected with the spectacular success of Pylades and Bathyllus and the new style of dramatic dance. Augustus at one point banished Pylades for *seditio*, and the dancer is said to have told him 'It's in your interests, Caesar, that the People should spend their leisure time on us instead'.[12] There were outbreaks of serious violence in AD 14 and 15,[13] and eventually Tiberius reversed Augustus' policy of tolerance and took his drastic action.

I think we may assume that the historical precedents were thoroughly rehearsed in the Senate in AD 23—not only the famous one of Cassius' censorship in 154 but also a later attempt to construct a permanent theatre, evidently frustrated by Q. Caepio the consul of 106 BC.[14] That no doubt accounts for Velleius' treatment of Cassius' censorship as a historical milestone; and it may also be the reason for his confused reference to 'Caepio the consul', if his memory was running together two separate occasions in the ongoing struggle between the theatre and old-fashioned moral standards.

It is possible that the other surprising date in the list of colonies has a similar explanation. The games of Flora were instituted in the third century BC at the same time as her new temple, next to that of Liber, Libera and Ceres on the slope of the Aventine.[15] It must have been burned down along with the Liber temple in 31 BC, and since the two buildings were rededicated only in AD 17, it is clear that Augustus decided to replace them very late in his principate, perhaps in response to the disastrous famine of AD 5–8.[16]

Velleius proudly tells us of the praetorships he and his brother obtained on the commendation of Augustus himself (2.124.4). They held office in

11. Livy *Epitome* 48: *cum locatum a censoribus theatrum exstrueretur, P. Cornelio Nasica auctore tamquam inutile et nociturum publicis moribus ex senatus consulto destructum est, populusque aliquamdiu stans ludos spectauit.*

12. Dio Cassius 54.17.4-5: 'συμφέρει σοι, Καῖσαρ, περὶ ἡμᾶς τὸν δῆμον ἀποδιατρίβεσθαι'.

13. Tacitus *Annals* 1.54.2, 1.74.2, 1.77.1-3; Dio Cassius 56.47.2.

14. Appian *Civil Wars* 1.28.125, with North 1992.

15. Tacitus *Annals* 2.49.1 (temple), Ovid *Fasti* 5.287-92 (games), paid for by the aediles L. and M. Publicii.

16. Dio Cassius 50.10.3 (31 BC fire); 55.22.3, 26.1-3, 27.1, 31.3-4, 33.4 (famine); Tacitus *Annals* 2.49.1 (dedication of rebuilt temples).

AD 15, at a time when the long-delayed rebuilding of Flora's temple was well under way. Ever since 22 BC, the *ludi scaenici* had been one of the praetors' responsibilities,[17] and it is quite possible that in the spring of AD 15 Velleius was himself organising the *ludi Florales*. If so, he would have been particularly aware of the goddess's return to favour, and it would not be surprising if the date of the foundation of both games and temple were prominent in his mind.

9.3. A subject for history

Whether or not there was a particular reason for it, Velleius' interest in public entertainments is manifest throughout his work.

He relates the institution of the Olympic games, that most famous of all competitions (*clarissimum omnium ludicrum certamen*), and then adds the tradition that they were originally begun 'about 1250 years ago' by Atreus in honour of his father Pelops, with Hercules winning every event (1.8.1-2). Much later, he concludes his account of the civil war of 83–2 BC with the games commemorating the battle of the Colline Gate:

> Sulla honoured the good fortune of the day on which the army of Telesinus and the Samnites was defeated with a permanent memory in the form of the Circus games that are celebrated under his name as the games of the Sullan Victory.[18]

He reports the final victory of Caesar's civil wars by listing the splendid shows put on before the triumph (*magnificentissima spectacula*, 2.56.1); his account of the death of Marcellus in 23 BC draws attention to the games the young man celebrated as aedile (*magnificentissimum munus aedilitatis*, 2.93.1); when referring to the turning-point of Augustus' principate in 2 BC, he contrasts the spectacular shows (*magnificentissima spectacula*)—gladiators and naval battle, like Caesar's—with the disaster of Julia's disgrace (2.100.2). And he makes a point of the fact that Augustus died in Campania because the Neapolitans had invited him to an athletic competition (*athletarum certaminis ludicrum*, 2.123.1).

17. Dio Cassius 54.2.3-4 (previously the aediles' responsibility); the change may well have been to make control of the games easier.

18. Velleius 2.27.6: *felicitatem diei quo Samnitium Telesinique pulsus est exercitus Sulla perpetua ludorum circensium honorauit memoria, qui sub eius nomine Sullanae Victoriae celebrantur.*

The theatre in particular mattered to him. It is not self-evidently obvious why a historian who insists on the brevity and selectivity of his work should find room for the law of the tribune Roscius in 67 BC reserving places in the theatre for the *equites* (2.32.3),[19] or that of the tribunes Ampius and Labienus in 63 BC giving Pompey the right to wear a golden crown and triumphal regalia at the *ludi circenses* and *scaenici* (2.40.4), especially as Pompey only used the privilege once; or that when referring to the death of Sextus Pompeius he should add that the man responsible for it was later driven out of Pompey's theatre when presiding over the games there (2.79.6).[20] Moreover, Pompey's theatre complex is mentioned twice elsewhere—once as marking the high point of its constructor's fame (2.48.2), and again as evidence for Tiberius' magnanimity in rebuilding it (2.80.1).

In his digression on great cultural figures (*eminentissima ingenia*), dramatic authors feature prominently, taking pride of place over authors in other literary forms: three authors each for Athenian tragedy, Old Comedy and New Comedy (1.16.3), Accius alone for Roman tragedy, Caecilius, Terence and Afranius for Roman comedy (1.17.1). Again in book 2 he notes the dramatists, as well as the orators and historians, who flourished in the late second century BC: Afranius in comedy, Pacuvius and Accius in tragedy (2.9.3), and even Pomponius, 'to be commended for the novelty of the genre he invented', namely the *Atellana* (2.9.6).

One of the most interesting of Velleius' dramatic references is the first of all. It comes in a methodological digression attached to the account of the origin of Thessaly, previously the land of the Myrmidons but now named after Thessalus, who conquered it about two generations after the Trojan War:

> On this point, astonishment is appropriate that those who write the events at Troy refer to this region as Thessaly. Although others do it, it is the tragic poets who do it most often, and they are the ones least entitled to; for they do not speak at all in the character of the poet, but entirely in that of people living at the time.[21]

19. Velleius refers to it as the 'restoration' of equestrian places, which may imply unusually precise information: cf. Cicero *Pro Murena* 40 (*L. Otho . . . equestri ordini restituit . . . dignitatem*) with Wiseman 1987, 79–80.

20. I wonder if Velleius was told that story by Sex. Pompeius Sex.f., consul in AD 14.

21. Velleius 1.3.2: *quo nomine mirari conuenit eos qui Iliaca componentes tempora de ea regione ut Thessalia commemorant. quod cum alii faciant, tragici frequentissime*

That is, one might condone the anachronism in the voice of a narrator, but not in that of contemporary characters; a few sentences later Velleius notes that while Homer refers to Corinth, he does so only in his own person (*ex persona poetae*, 1.3.3).

What is striking here is the casual assumption that tragedians come under the heading of 'those who write the events at Troy', as if they too should be expected to provide accurate historical evidence. Plutarch offers a similar perspective in his life of Theseus: where the tragic poets are not specifically contradicted by the historians, one is entitled to accept their version as a reliable account of what happened.[22] The traditions of early Rome were similarly transmitted via dramatic performances;[23] the most explicit evidence is that of Livy on the bringing of Juno Regina from Veii,[24] and that of Ovid on the Great Mother's vindication of Q. Claudia in 204 BC.[25] But since we have nothing of Velleius' Roman history between the rape of the Sabine women and the Third Macedonian War, we cannot know whether he himself used such material.

What we can know, I think, is that like Augustus but unlike Tiberius,[26] Velleius enjoyed the games and regarded them as an important part of Roman life. And it may even be that the *ludi scaenici* helped to shape him as a historian. What he does best is convey the vividness and excitement of scenes he witnessed himself when serving as an equestrian officer under Tiberius. He describes himself as a *spectator* of Tiberius' achievements,[27] a word normally used of the audience at the games. That sense of the word is confirmed, I think, by Velleius' phraseology in two of his most dramatic

---

faciunt, quibus minime id concedendum est; nihil enim ex persona poetae sed omnia sub eorum qui illo tempore uixerunt disserunt.

22. Plutarch *Theseus* 28.2, on Phaedra and Hippolytus.

23. As shown by Plutarch *Romulus* 8.7 (Romulus story like drama or fiction, δραματικὸν καὶ πλασματῶδες), Dionysius of Halicarnassus *Roman Antiquities* 3.18.1 (Alban triplets story like theatrical changes of fortune, θεατρικαῖς ἐοικότα περιπετείαις), 9.22.3 (story of the Fabii at the Cremera like theatrical fiction, πλάσμασιν ἔοικε θεατρικοῖς), and Livy 1.46.3 (death of Servius Tullius a crime appropriate to tragedy, *tragicum scelus*).

24. Livy 5.21.3-4: *ad ostentationem scaenae gaudentis miraculis aptiora.*

25. Ovid *Fasti* 4.326: *mira, sed et scaena testificata loquar.*

26. Tacitus *Annals* 1.54.2 (trans. A. J. Woodman): 'And in fact he [Augustus] personally did not shrink from such enthusiasms and deemed it citizenlike to blend in with the pleasures of the public. Tiberius' way of behaving was otherwise.' Cf. Suetonius *Diuus Augustus* 45.1 (Loeb trans.) on Augustus' 'interest and pleasure in the spectacle, which he never denied and often frankly confessed'.

27. Velleius 2.104.3: 'For nine continuous years, as prefect or legate, I was a *spectator* of his superhuman achievements.'

scenes, the meeting of Gaius Caesar with the Parthian king and the return of Tiberius to the command of Germany. In each case he describes the event as a *spectaculum*.[28]

To be present when history is being made was like being present at the games, watching the actors on the stage. And it was more than just a metaphor: as the Romans saw it, what the actors presented on the stage often *was* history, the events at Troy (in tragedy), or dramatic episodes from the history of Rome itself.

28. Velleius 2.101.1-2 (*quod spectaculum*), 104.3 (*illi spectaculo*), in each case referring to his own presence.

CHAPTER TEN

Phaedrus and his Fables

PRACTICALLY ALL we know about Phaedrus is what we can infer from his text. He introduces himself as a mere mouthpiece for Aesop, translating the master's work and dressing it up in iambic *senarii*.[1] In his second book, however, he says he will include new material 'in the old man's style',[2] and sure enough, item 2.5 satirises contemporary Roman obsequiousness with a story set in the garden of Tiberius Caesar's villa at Misenum.[3] From this point on, we learn quite a lot about Phaedrus himself.

10.1. The exile

Already in the epilogue to book 2, hoping that Latin speakers will appreciate his work,[4] he is seriously worried about its reception:

> If my work comes to educated ears, and opinion understands that fables are invented by art, good fortune removes any offence. But if my literary labour runs into those ranters hostile nature gave birth to, who can't do anything but criticise their betters, I shall bear fated exile with a hardened heart, till Fortune is ashamed of her accusation.[5]

1. Phaedrus 1.prol.1-2: *Aesopus auctor quam materiem repperit | hanc ego poliui uersibus senariis.*

2. 2.prol.8 (*morem seruabo senis*), cf. 4.prol.12-13 (*usus uetusto genere sed rebus nouis*).

3. 2.5.1 (*est ardalionum quaedam Romae natio*), 2.5.7-8 (*Tiberius Caesar cum petens Neapolim | in Misenensem uillam uenisset suam*). For a commentary on 2.5 see Henderson 2001, 9–31.

4. 2.ep. 8–9: *quodsi labori fauerit Latium meo, | plures habebit quos opponat Graeciae.*

5. 2.ep.12-19: *si nostrum studium ad aures cultas peruenit | et arte fictas animus sentit fabulas, | omnem querelam submouet felicitas. | sin autem rabulis doctus occurrit labor, |*

A very specific situation is envisaged.[6] The *rabulae* ('ranters') he was afraid of were aggressive prosecutors;[7] the accusation and exile he refers to were real possibilities, if some powerful person *did* take offence at fables 'invented by art', and thought they were directed at himself.

At the time of writing that was a particularly acute danger. Because Tiberius was unpopular, traditional free speech about contemporary life could easily be presented as disloyalty and brought before the law as a way of currying favour with the emperor.[8] Tiberius, like his predecessor, dismissed such charges,[9] but in AD 26 he retired to Capri, leaving Rome in the hands of Sejanus, the Praetorian Prefect, who encouraged prosecutions and filled the city with terror.[10] 'The more uncompromising the accuser, the more privileged he seemed to be; it was people without power or status who suffered punishment.'[11] One such was Attalus, a Greek teacher of philosophy whose Stoic austerity was evidently not appreciated; Sejanus had him banished.[12]

Phaedrus too was a teacher, in his way: his little book, he said, didn't just make people laugh, it gave them good advice on how to live.[13] It began with the fable of the wolf and the lamb, 'written because of those who oppress the innocent with invented charges',[14] followed by the fable of King Log, a very political story set in the Athens of Pisistratus but in terms all too

---

sinistra quos in lucem natura extulit | nec quidquam possunt nisi meliores carpere, | fatale exilium corde durato feram | donec Fortunam criminis pudeat sui.

6. *Pace* Champlin 2005, 101 ('nothing about a trial . . . the whole context is literary') and Geue 2019, 122 ('*exile?!* This is "just" a metaphor here, of course').

7. The word was almost a technical term: Cicero *De oratore* 1.202 (*causidicum . . . clamatorem aut rabulam*), *Brutus* 180, 226 (orators as *rabulae*), *Orator* 47 (*rabula de foro*); Quintilian 12.9.12 (*rabula latratorque*, 'concerned not to win over the judge but to convey his client's bad temper'); Festus 354-5L (*causidicus pugnaciter loquens*).

8. Free speech: e.g. Tacitus *Annals* 3.75.2 (Labeo's *incorrupta libertas*), Dio Cassius 58.1.1-2 (παρρησία).

9. Tacitus *Annals* 1.73.1-4 (AD 15), 2.50.1-2 (AD 17); cf. Seneca *De beneficiis* 3.27.1, Suetonius *Diuus Augustus* 54–5 (Augustus).

10. Seneca *De beneficiis* 3.26.1 (*accusandi frequens et paene publica rabies*), Tacitus *Annals* 4.69.3 (*non alias magis anxia et pauens ciuitas*, AD 28).

11. Tacitus *Annals* 4.36.9: *ut quis destrictior accusator, uelut sacrosanctus erat; leues ignobiles poenis adficiebantur.*

12. Seneca *Suasoriae* 2.12 (*a Seiano circumscriptus*); Seneca *Epistles* 108.13-14, 110.14-20.

13. Phaedrus 1.prol.3-4: *duplex libelli dos est: quod risum mouet | et quod prudenti uitam consilio monet.*

14. 1.1.14-15: *haec propter illos scripta est homines fabula | qui fictis causis innocentes opprimunt.*

applicable to Rome.[15] Phaedrus too was without power or status, once a slave of the imperial house,[16] now trying to find influential supporters,[17] and what happened to Attalus seems to have happened to him.

In October AD 31 Sejanus was deposed and executed. There was chaos in Rome as furious crowds hunted down his accomplices and hangers-on; the Senate voted to erect a statue of *Libertas* in the Forum.[18] Could those wrongfully condemned for free speech now hope to regain their position? That appears to be the situation presupposed in Phaedrus' third book.

I know you're a busy man, he says to Eutychus in the prologue, but you ought to find time to read my work if you care about literature.[19] Why was that? He goes on to explain:

> My mother gave birth to me on the Pierian ridge where holy Mnemosyne, nine times pregnant, bore to Jupiter Thunderer the chorus of the arts.[20] Although I was practically born in the *schola* itself,[21] and have wholly erased from my heart any care for wealth and devoted myself to this life with the blessing of Pallas, yet I am admitted to the company only with distaste. . . .
>
> I made a road in place of [Aesop's] footpath. I made up more themes than those he'd left to us, some of them chosen to my own disaster. If the accuser, the witness and the judge had been anyone other than Sejanus, I'd admit I deserve such evils and not try to mitigate pain with these remedies. If anyone is led astray by his own suspicion, applies to himself what is common to all and stupidly reveals his own bad conscience, all the same I'd ask him to excuse *me*. My

15. *Aequis legibus* (Phaedrus 1.2.1); 'equal laws' were what defined the Roman republic (Livy 3.56.9, 3.61.6, 3.63.10, 3.67.9). *Procax libertas* (1.2.2); cf. Cicero *De republica* 1.68 on popular *libertas* leading to tyranny, with Pisistratus as an example. *Tyrannus . . . Pisistratus* (1.2.5): cf. Cicero *Ad Atticum* 7.20.2, 8.16.2 on Caesar as Pisistratus, *De officiis* 2.23, 3.19 on Caesar as a *tyrannus*.

16. The ninth-century MSS *P* and *R* present his book as *Phaedri Augusti liberti liber fabularum*; despite modern scepticism (e.g. Champlin 2005, 99), there is no good reason to reject the statement.

17. Namely Eutychus (3.prol.2), Particulo (4.prol.10) and Philetus (5.10.10), all unknown and possibly pseudonymous.

18. Dio Cassius 58.3.2-4, cf. Juvenal 10.56-89.

19. Phaedrus 3.prol.1-16: *Phaedri libellos legere si desideras* | . . . *intrare si Musarum limen cogitas.*

20. The reference is of course to the nine Muses.

21. Usually, but wrongly, translated as 'although I was all but born in a school' (e.g. Champlin 2005, 102, repudiated as 'fatuous' at 105). The meaning of the passage is discussed below.

> intention is not to stigmatise individuals, but to show life itself and the way people behave.[22]

He ended his pitch with a very specific request: 'You're known for candour, so I ask you to deliver an honest judgement on me.'[23] What sort of judgement (*iudicium*) did he mean?

10.2. Getting on the programme

Modern scholarship evades the question,[24] but an answer can be found if we listen to what the evidence says. Phaedrus returned to his subject in the epilogue to book 3:

> An accused man who's confessed has often received pardon; how much more justly should it be given to an innocent man? It's up to you. Before, it was up to others; later, the turn of others will come as it goes round again. Give the verdict that duty and good faith allow, so I may be glad to stay standing thanks to your judgement.[25]
>
> My feelings have exceeded the limit I set myself, but it's hard for one's spirit to hold back when it is conscious of pure integrity but oppressed by the insolence of guilty men. Who are they, you ask? In time, they will be seen. There's a saying I read as a child long ago: 'For a plebeian, muttering openly has to be expiated.' As long as my sense stays sound I'll take care to remember that.[26]

22. 3.prol.17-23, 38-50: *ego quem Pierio mater enixa est iugo, | in quo Tonanti sancta Mnemosyne Ioui | fecunda nouies artium peperit chorum, | quamuis in ipsa paene natus sim schola | curamque habendi penitus corde eraserim | nec Pallade hanc inuita in uitam incubuerim, | fastidiose tamen in coetu recipior. | . . . ego illius pro semita feci uiam | et cogitaui plura quam reliquerat, | in calamitatem deligens quaedam meam. | quodsi accusator alius Seiano foret, | si testis alius, iudex alius denique, | dignum faterer esse me tantis malis | nec his dolorem delenirem remediis. | suspicione siquis errabit sua | et rapiens ad se quod erit commune omnium | stulte nudabit animi conscientiam, | huic excusatum me uelim nihilo minus. | neque enim notare singulos mens est mihi, | uerum ipsam uitam et mores hominum ostendere.*

23. 3.prol.62-3: *sincerum mihi | candore noto reddas iudicium peto.*

24. See for instance Henderson 2001, 92, Champlin 2005, 108, Geue 2019, 125–6.

25. *Stare* ('stay standing') in the sense of 'succeed, hold one's own' was a phrase particularly appropriate to public performance: it meant being still there to take the applause, not having been shouted off the stage (Terence *Andria* 27, *Hecyra* 15, *Phormio* 9-10, Horace *Epistles* 2.1.76).

26. 3.ep.22-35: *saepe impetrauit ueniam confessus reus: | quanto innocenti iustius debet dari? | tuae sunt partes, fuerunt aliorum prius, | dein simili gyro uenient aliorum uices. | decerne quod religio, quod patitur fides, | ut gratuler me stare iudicio tuo. | excedit animus quem proposui terminum, | sed difficulter continetur spiritus, | integritatis qui*

At this particular moment Eutychus had the responsibility of delivering a formal judgement (*iudicium*) for or against Phaedrus. It was not a legal judgement on the poet's banishment—a disaster, as he says in the prologue, that this appeal could only 'mitigate'—but a professional judgement on his work. I think Eutychus' job was to accept it or reject it for performance at a public festival.

Of all genres, Aesopic fable required a popular audience; it was not primarily aimed at those who could read it for themselves on expensively hand-written papyrus.[27] Aesop himself was imagined as telling his stories to whole citizen bodies, assembled in the theatre or some other public place.[28] The equivalent scene at Rome was the public *ludi*, for which the praetors were responsible in Phaedrus' time,[29] or a show put on by some grandee at his own expense.[30] The entertainments could include poetic recitals,[31] and for the public games, at least, there was fierce competition to get selected.[32] The best evidence comes from Horace, who was able to avoid it:

> These things I play about with aren't meant to resound in the temple,
> in a competition with Tarpa as judge, or to come back again and again
> as theatre shows.[33]

> I don't see fit to canvass literary constituencies and stages. That's the problem. If I say 'I'm ashamed to recite my unworthy writings

---

sincerae conscius | a noxiorum premitur insolentiis. | qui sint, requiris? apparebunt tempore.| ego, quondam legi quam puer sententiam | 'palam muttire plebeio piaculum est', | dum sanitas constabit, pulchre meminero.

27. See Wiseman 2015, 4–6 on the cost of books; fables appealed particularly to a lower-class audience (*rustici et imperiti*, Quintilian 5.11.19).

28. E.g. the Samians (Aristotle *Rhetoric* 2.20.6), the Delphians (Callimachus *Iambi* 2.15-17 Pf), the Athenians (Phaedrus 1.2.6-9 and 29-31, cf. 4.5.27-32). Theatre: *Life of Aesop* 16 (Samos).

29. Dio Cassius 54.2.3-4 (from 22 BC); previously, all but the *ludi Apollinares* had been provided by the aediles.

30. *ILLRP* 803.10 (*quae modo nobilium ludos decoraui choro*); Phaedrus 5.5.4 (*facturus ludos diues quidam nobilis*), 5.7.16 (*erat facturus ludos quidam nobilis*).

31. As implied by Ovid *Fasti* 5.190 (*hoc quoque cum circi munere carmen eat*); recitations to the *populus* (Ovid *Tristia* 4.10.57, Persius 1.13-21) or in the theatre (Petronius *Satyrica* 90.5, Statius *Siluae* 5.2.160-3) were probably at the *ludi*.

32. The competitions were called *commissiones*: see Cicero *Ad Atticum* 15.26.1, 16.5.1 (*ludi Apollinares*); Suetonius *Diuus Augustus* 89.3 (under the praetor's authority); Seneca *Letters* 84.10, Pliny *Letters* 7.24.6, *Panegyricus* 54.1.

33. Horace *Satires* 1.10.37-9: *haec ego ludo | quae neque in aede sonent certantia iudice Tarpa | nec redeant iterum atque iterum spectanda theatris.*

> in crowded theatres and add weight to trifles', then someone replies: 'You're laughing—you keep your stuff for the ears of Jove.'[34]

Tarpa was evidently a man of authority (*iudex*),[35] and he exercised his judgement at 'the temple of the Muses, where poets used to gather to recite their works to a large audience'.[36] So at least the ancient commentators on Horace say, offering various explanations, one of which is probably correct: 'because Tarpa used to decide which works were to be taken to the stage'.[37]

In fact the temple was that of Hercules and the Muses, founded in 187 BC and famous for its statues of the nine goddesses, looted from Ambracia in north-west Greece (section 3.6 above).[38] It was rebuilt about 30 BC and surrounded by a colonnade, the *porticus Philippi*,[39] which was probably where the competitions were held. At this point we must remember something Phaedrus says about himself:

> My mother gave birth to me on the Pierian ridge where holy Mnemosyne, nine times pregnant, bore to Jupiter Thunderer the chorus of the arts. . . . I was practically born in the *schola* itself.[40]

Elsewhere Phaedrus says he was born in Thrace, and thus able to claim Linus and Orpheus among his forebears.[41] Here he stretches the point to

34. Horace *Epistles* 1.19.39-44: *non ego . . . | grammaticas ambire tribus et pulpita dignor. | hinc illae lacrimae. 'spissis indigna theatris | scripta pudet recitare et nugis addere pondus' | si dixi, 'rides' ait 'et Iouis auribus ista | seruas.'* The phrase *ambire tribus* is a metaphor from electoral canvassing (Wiseman 2015, 142–3): in prose the phrase was *tribus circumire* (Livy 3.72.2, 8.37.9, Suetonius *Diuus Augustus* 56.1).

35. Cf. Horace *Ars poetica* 387 (*Maeci . . . iudicis*); since Tarpa's name is given as 'Maetius Tarpa' by Porphyrio on *Satires* 1.10.37-8, he is often identified as the Sp. Maecius who had chosen the programme for Pompey's famous *ludi* in 55 BC (Cicero *Ad familiares* 7.1.1), though the dates are far apart. Valerius Cato evidently did a similar job in the 40s BC: see Cornelius Gallus 2.8-9 Courtney (*non ego, . . . Kato, iudice te uereor*), Furius Bibaculus 6.2 Courtney (*qui solus legit ac facit poetas*).

36. Ps.Acro on Horace *Satires* 1.10.38 (*in aede Musarum ait, quo solebant poetae conuenire et dicta sua multis audientibus recitare*), cf. Porphyrio on the same line (*in aede Musarum, ubi poetae carmina sua recitabant*).

37. Ps.Acro on Horace *Satires* 1.10.38: *uel quod Tarpa probare consueuisset quae ad scaenam deferenda essent.*

38. Servius *auctus* on *Aeneid* 1.8, Cicero *Pro Archia* 27, Pliny *Natural History* 35.66, *Forma urbis Romae* fr. 31; Wiseman 2004, 184, fig. 71. Phaedrus' 'threshold of the Muses' at 3.prol.16 may refer to the temple (Champlin 2005, 105).

39. Ovid *Fasti* 6.799-812, Suetonius *Diuus Augustus* 29.5; Coarelli 1997, 452–84, Heslin 2015, 197–254.

40. 3 prol.17-20 (n. 22).

41. 3.prol.54-9; the allusion is to Virgil *Eclogues* 4.55-9, which is all about poetic competition.

bring in the Muses, whose birthplace Pieria was in neighbouring Macedonia, and thus makes a particular claim, however far-fetched, on the place of competition.[42]

A *schola* was a seating area (*exedra*), usually in a portico, 'where philosophers, rhetoricians and other lovers of literature might sit and debate'.[43] This one was no doubt the *schola poetarum* frequented by Martial and his friends, the place where Phaedrus the freedman was admitted only with distaste.[44] We are, I think, entitled to identify it as the place in the portico round the Muses' temple where Eutychus, that year's equivalent of Horace's Tarpa, was the judge whose *iudicium* decided which of the competing poets' works would go on the programme at the *ludi*.

If, as he says, Phaedrus was prosecuted under Sejanus' reign of terror and banished from Rome, the long prologue and epilogue addressed to Eutychus are easily explained. Unable to present his work in person, Phaedrus could only send book 3 to Eutychus and hope for the best. Hence his concluding plea:

> Have I induced you to read it? You're known for candour, so I ask you to deliver an honest judgement on me.[45]

But he didn't. Knowing all about malicious opposition and disapproval of 'plebeians muttering openly',[46] Phaedrus probably wasn't surprised at the outcome. There would be no grand public performance of his fables. Few people would even know of their existence.[47]

42. Champlin (2005, 105–6) infers that the author was really born in Rome, near the temple, and that his birth in Pieria (or Thrace) was all part of a fictional persona; that is because Champlin thinks Phaedrus 'was a member of the Roman élite, masquerading as a man of the people' (117), 'his true life obscured by an elaborate mask' (108). Whatever one thinks of that idea, the choice of which 'birth' to take literally seems an arbitrary one.

43. Vitruvius 5.11.2 on *palaestra* design: *constituantur autem in tribus porticibus exedrae spatiosae habentes sedes in quibus philosophi, rhetores reliquique qui studiis delectantur sedentes disputare possint*. Cf. Cicero *Pro Caelio* 41, Varro *Antiquitates diuinae* fr. 8 Cardauns (philosophers in *scholae*).

44. Martial 3.20.8 (*otiosus in schola poetarum*), 4.61.3-4 (*in schola poetarum | dum fabulamur*), with Coarelli 1997, 465–6; Phaedrus 3.prol.23 (*fastidiose tamen in coetum recipior*). Champlin 2005, 105 takes it as the seat of the *collegium poetarum* attested for the first century BC (Valerius Maximus 3.7.11, *Année Épigraphique* 1959, 147), but the connection is very tenuous; see Caldelli 2012, 134–41 for a sober assessment of the evidence and modern bibliography.

45. 3.prol.62-3: *induxi te ad legendum? sincerum mihi | candore noto reddas iudicium peto*.

46. 2.ep.10 (*liuor*), 3.prol.60 (*liuor*), 3.ep.31 (*insolentiae*), 3.ep.34 (*palam muttire plebeio piaculum est*).

47. Writing in or about AD 43, Seneca described Aesopic fable as 'a genre unattempted by Roman talents' (*Ad Polybium* 8.3); I think Champlin 2005, 101 is too hasty in taking that as proof that Phaedrus had not yet *written*.

Book 4, addressed to 'Particulo', another busy man, reveals the disappointed author's fall-back position:

> You'll read this fourth book when you have the time. If malice wants to criticise, as long as it can't imitate, then let it criticise. I've already won praise for it, because you and others like you copy my words on to your own paper and judge it worthy to be long remembered. I don't need the applause of the illiterate.[48]

That must be sour grapes.[49] Distributing written copies was a poor second best: as Ovid said of his own banishment, writing poetry with no audience to hear it was like dancing in darkness.[50] But at least Phaedrus' work might now be read, as it was by Martial, who imagined one of the habitués of the *schola poetarum* imitating 'the fables of deplorable Phaedrus'.[51] Having kept him out in his lifetime, they were evidently taking his credit fifty years later.

10.3. In the theatre

There are just ten fables in the fifth book, and the meaning of the last one, about an old dog losing his strength, was self-explanatory.[52] As it happens, two of these last ten concern stage games, the milieu Phaedrus himself wasn't able to exploit.

The story of fable 5.5 begins with 'a certain wealthy aristocrat about to put on games',[53] who issued an invitation to all, with a prize, to come forward with some novel entertainment. Among the professionals who entered this competition for fame was a stand-up comic (*scurra*), 'well known for his city wit', who claimed to have a type of act never before presented in a theatre.[54] What follows gives us a rare eyewitness glimpse:

48. 4.prol.14-20: *quartum libellum cum uacaris perleges. | hunc obtrectare si uolet malignitas, | imitari dum non posit, obtrectet licet. | mihi parta laus est quod tu, quod similes tui | uestras in chartas uerba transfertis mea, | dignumque longa iudicatis memoria. | inlitteratum plausum nec desidero.*

49. As in fable 4.3.

50. Ovid *Ex Ponto* 4.2.33-4 (*in tenebris numerosos ponere gestus, | quodque legas nulli scribere carmen, idem est*); cf. *Tristia* 3.1.77 (*nec enim mihi turba roganda est*).

51. Martial 3.20.5 (cf. n. 44): *an aemulatur improbi* λόγους *Phaedri?* No other reference till Avianus in the fifth century.

52. 'You can see perfectly well why I've written this, Philetus' (4.10.10); the addressee is mentioned nowhere else.

53. Phaedrus 5.5.4: *facturus ludos diues quidam nobilis.*

54. 5.5.8-10: *quos inter scurra notus urbano sale | habere dixit se genus spectaculi | quod in theatro numquam prolatum foret.*

> When the word spreads, it brings all the citizens together. Seats that had been vacant are now not enough for the crowd. When at last he took his position on the stage—alone, without props, no supporting cast—the expectation itself brought about silence.[55]

It turned out he did animal noises, his pig impression receiving great praise and applause. But a countryman in the audience stood up and said he could do it better. Next day there was an even bigger crowd, eager to mock the bumpkin's attempt. The comic did his turn again; the countryman did his, by pulling the ear of the real piglet he had under his tunic; the audience shouted that the comic's version was far better, and the countryman should be chucked out. He pulled out the piglet and shouted back: 'That shows what sort of judges *you* are!'[56]

Phaedrus told that story as an example of 'dishonest partisanship',[57] something he had evidently suffered from himself. The moral of his other 'showbiz' fable was equally pointed:

> When an empty mind, caught by a worthless breath of favour, has grabbed an arrogant self-confidence, its foolish triviality is easily brought to derision.[58]

The derision in this tale was directed at a pipe-player called Princeps, who worked as a stage accompanist for the 'all-mime' dancer Bathyllus in the time of Augustus.[59]

'At some games, I don't remember which',[60] Princeps was flying above the stage on a crane when he fell and broke his leg. Recovery took a long time, but eventually he was able to walk with a stick. At that point (again) 'a certain aristocrat about to put on games' begged him, and paid him, to

55. 5.5.11-15: *dispersus rumor ciuitatem concitat. | paulo ante uacua turbam deficiunt loca. | in scaena uero postquam solus constitit | sine apparatu nullis adiutoribus, | silentium ipsa fecit exspectatio.*

56. 5.5.38: *'en hic declarat quales sitis iudices!'*

57. 5.5.1 (*prauo fauore*), cf. 5.5.25 on the theatre audience (*iam fauor mentes tenet*).

58. 5.7.1-3: *ubi uanus animus aura captus friuola | arripuit insolentem sibi fiduciam, | facile ad derisum stulta leuitas ducitur.*

59. 5.7.5 (*operam Bathyllo solitus in scaena dare*); for Bathyllus, freedman and lover of Maecenas, see Tacitus *Annals* 1.54.2, Dio 54.17.5, Crinagoras 39 Gow-Page (*Anthologia Palatina* 9.542), Seneca *Controuersiae* 3.pref.16, 10.pref.8, Athenaeus 1.20d. The *tibicen* was probably L. Cassius Princeps, known from the tomb-inscription of his daughter at Ameria just north of Rome (*CIL* 11.4424, with Buecheler 1882, 333).

60. 5.7.5 (*is forte ludis, non satis memini quibus*); cf. 3.10.8 and 39 for Phaedrus' memory of events under Augustus.

make an appearance on the day of the *ludi*.[61] And again we get the scene in the auditorium:

> When the day comes, the theatre's buzzing with talk about the pipe-player: some say he's dead, others that he's going to appear any moment. The curtain came down,[62] the thunders were rolled,[63] and the gods spoke in the traditional way. Then the chorus came in loudly with a song unfamiliar to the man who'd just come back:[64] 'Rejoice, Rome, safe in the safety of the *princeps*.' The audience stood up and applauded.[65]

Princeps the pipe-player thought it was for him, and came out to blow kisses to his public. 'The equestrian order realises his stupid mistake'; they burst out laughing and called for an encore.[66] The chorus sang it again, with Princeps practically prostrating himself on stage in an ecstasy of appreciation.[67] Eventually the entire audience, each of the wedge-shaped sections into which the theatre was divided,[68] caught on to what was happening. In his snow-white costume and snow-white shoes, Princeps was claiming the honour meant for 'the divine house'. 'He was thrown out head-first by the whole audience.'[69]

That is, he suffered what the countryman suffered in the other tale,[70] but this time the spectators got it right. Phaedrus' criticism was aimed at stage professionals (*artifices*): the comic with his reputation and his mindless fans ('dishonest partisanship'), and the musician with his ludicrous

61. 5.7.16-19: *erat facturus ludos quidam nobilis* [cf. n. 53]. | *is, ut incipiebat Princeps ad baculum ingredi,* | *perducit pretio precibus ut tantummodo* | *ipse ludorum ostenderet sese die.*

62. For the show to start: the curtain was kept down during the performance (Horace *Epistles* 2.1.189) and raised at the end of it (Cicero *Pro Caelio* 65).

63. Apparently vessels filled with stones, rolled behind the stage (Festus [Paulus] 50L); for their use cf. Sallust *Histories* 3.10.3 Ramsey, Vitruvius 5.6.8.

64. Because it was topical (either Augustus' return from abroad or his recovery from illness), and Princeps' broken leg had kept him away from the theatre.

65. 5.7.20-8: *qui simul aduenit, rumor de tibicine* | *fremit in theatro: quidam adfirmant mortuum,* | *quidam in conspectum proditurum sine mora.* | *aulaeo misso deuolutis tonitribus* | *di sunt locuti more translaticio.* | *tunc chorus ignotum modo reducto canticum* | *insonuit, cuius haec fuit sententia:* | *'laetare incolumis Roma saluo principe'.*

66. 5.7.30-1: *equester ordo stultum errorem intellegit* | *magnoque risu canticum repeti iubet.*

67. 5.7.32-3: *se in pulpito* | *totum prosternit.*

68. 5.7.35 (*ut uero cuneis notuit res omnibus*); cf. Virgil *Aeneid* 5.664 (*cuneosque theatri*), Vitruvius 5.6.2 (*cunei spectaculorum in theatro*), Statius *Siluae* 5.2.162 (*cuneosque per omnes*).

69. 5.7.37-9: *niueisque tunicis, niueis etiam calcibus,* | *superbiens honore diuinae domus,* | *ab uniuersis capite est protrusus foras.*

70. 5.5.33-4: *adclamat populus . . . et cogit rusticum trudi foras.*

sense of his own importance ('arrogant self-confidence').[71] Given the evidence we have pieced together about his own struggles, particularly the recognition of Eutychus in book 3 as a gate-keeper for the public games, it is easy to see how the disappointments of a would-be performer could create such resentment towards the arrogant and successful.

10.4. Phaedrus as evidence

'The applause of the illiterate' was what Phaedrus wanted.[72] He never got it, but in trying to achieve it he has left us with precious information about the realities of Roman 'theatre games' as seen from one particular point of view. Four points are worth particular notice.

Firstly, Phaedrus shows no interest in the particular theatrical occasion. His pig-squealing comic and self-important pipe-player could have been performing at the *ludi Megalenses* (April), *Ceriales* (April), *Florales* (April–May), *Apollinares* (July), *Victoriae* (July), *Romani* (September) or *plebeii* (November), the regular annual theatre festivals, for each of which one of the praetors would be in charge;[73] or it could have been at the annual votive games for Augustus' safety, provided on a four-year cycle by each of the main colleges of priests;[74] or it could have been at some *ad hoc* show for a particular occasion.[75] All that mattered to Phaedrus was that 'some aristocrat' was in charge, that he needed acts to put on stage, and that he had the money to pay for them.[76]

The second striking feature of 'Phaedrus on theatre' is the range of entertainment that might be on offer. The performance where Princeps made his untimely entrance featured the chorus whose song he took as his cue, the musicians who must have accompanied them, the actors who played the gods,[77] and the stage-hands behind the scenes 'rolling the thunders'; that was the kind of elaborate staging needed for the 'all-mime'

71. 5.5.7 (*uenere artifices laudis ad certamina*), 5.5.1 (*prauo fauore*), 5.7.2 (*insolentem sibi fiduciam*).

72. Cf. 4.prol.20 (n. 48).

73. For their respective histories see Bernstein 1998, with corrections at Wiseman 2008, 167–74.

74. Dio Cassius 51.19.2, 53.1.4-6 (first held in 28 BC); Augustus *Res gestae* 9 ([*sacerdotu*]*m quattuor amplissima colle*[*gia*]), Suetonius *Diuus Augustus* 44.3 (*pontificalibus ludis*), Pliny *Natural History* 7.158 (*pro salute diui Augusti*, AD 9). Note the words of the song at Princeps' disastrous come-back (5.7.27, *saluo principe*).

75. Cf. Claudius' *spectacula commenticia* (Suetonius *Diuus Claudius* 21.1).

76. 5.5.4, 5.7.16 (*quidam nobilis*); 5.5.5 (*proposito praemio*), 5.7.18 (*pretio*).

77. 5.7.4 (*di sunt locuti more translaticio*), on which see further below.

spectacle of Bathyllus and Pylades.[78] The pig-impressionist, on the other hand, was conspicuously on his own, the absence of assistance all part of his act. Presumably Phaedrus too would have appeared solo, if Eutychus had given that honest judgement and booked a performer who told Aesopic stories in the metre of Roman comedy.

Thirdly, we may note the internal dynamics of the audience—acting as one in applauding the pig-squeak,[79] but interestingly differentiated in its reaction to Princeps' intervention. The front fourteen rows were where members of the equestrian order had their seats, a privilege resented by their fellow-citizens.[80] The *equites* could see immediately who it was who had come out to take a bow, and laughed and applauded in mocking encouragement; the rest of the audience thought he was part of the show, not realising at first what had happened.[81] Two passages in Horace illustrate this social dissonance:

> What often frightens even a bold poet off is the fact that the unlearned and stupid are in the majority; though inferior in worth and rank, they're ready to make a fight of it if the *equites* don't agree with them, and shout for bear-baiting or boxers even while the arias are being sung.[82]

> 'It's enough for me if the *equites* applaud', as bold Arbuscula said, scornful of the rest, as she was shouted off the stage.[83]

Princeps didn't even have Arbuscula's satisfaction. In his case the *equites* were just setting him up; then they joined the rest of the audience in getting rid of him. At least, that's what Phaedrus' story says.

The final detail worth noticing is what happened right at the start of the performance commandeered by Princeps. After the rolls of thunder, 'the gods spoke in the traditional way'.[84] The phraseology suggests

78. Manilius 5.483-5 (chorus), Lucian *Saltatio* 30 (singers), 68 (musicians, actors, singers), Jerome *Chronica* Ol. 189.3 (chorus and *fistula*); full *testimonia* in Hall and Wyles 2008, 378–419.

79. 5.5.34 (*adclamat populus*); the audience at the *ludi* was the *populus Romanus uniuersus* (Cicero *Pro Sestio* 122–5, *Philippics* 1.36, Pliny *Natural History* 36.119).

80. Plutarch *Cicero* 13.2-3, Pliny *Natural History* 7.117, Juvenal 3.153-9, Appian *Civil Wars* 5.15.62.

81. 5.7.33-4: *plaudit inludens eques; | rogare populus hunc choro ueniam aestimat.*

82. Horace *Epistles* 2.1.182-6: *saepe etiam audacem fugat hoc terretque poetam, | quod numero plures, uirtute et honore minores, | indocti stolidique et depugnare parati | si discordet eques, media inter carmina poscunt | aut ursum aut pugiles.*

83. Horace *Satires* 1.10.76-7: *satis est equitem mihi plaudere, ut audax | contemptis aliis explosa Arbuscula dixit.*

84. 5.7.24: *di sunt locuti more translaticio.*

something more than just an opening dialogue on stage: one would expect gods to comment on the action from above.[85]

Evidence from about a century and a half after Phaedrus confirms that expectation. The *Onomasticon* of Julius Pollux, addressed to the emperor Commodus, includes a section on stage terminology (4.95-154), one item of which runs as follows: 'Gods appear from the *theologeion*, which is on high above the stage: for example, Zeus and company in *The Weighing of Souls*.'[86] At about the same time, Lucian was producing comic stage libretti in which gods conversed at the high level before 'coming down' to join in the action on the stage.[87] And by great good fortune, we even have an illustration of how it could be arranged in the theatre.

Precisely in the time of Commodus, and continuing for another century or so, there was a flourishing tradition of appliqué-relief pottery in the province of Gallia Narbonensis.[88] A fine early example, evidently from Arles, shows a scene in a theatre, complete with two iambic lines from the play's dialogue (fig. 14). The plot is taken from an archaic story of Greek mythology, one largely ignored in the Roman tradition but newly topical in the age of Commodus 'the Roman Hercules'.[89] On the stage Mars confronts Hercules, who has just killed his son Cycnus in a duel and is evidently claiming the victor's prize. 'Believe it: I am present, as my son's avenger.' 'Unconquered valour,' replies the hero, 'can nowise be affrighted.'[90] Between them is Jupiter's eagle, symbolising the thunderbolt that prevented a combat between two of Jupiter's sons.[91]

85. As Apollo does for Iullus at a dramatic moment in Virgil's *Aeneid* (9.639, *desuper*); cf. *Aeneid* 8.705, the same adverb used for when Apollo drew his bow for Augustus at Actium.

86. Pollux 4.130: ἀπὸ δὲ τοῦ θεολογείου ὄντος ὑπὲρ τὴν σκηνὴν ἐν ὕψει ἐπιφαίνονται θεοί, ὡς ὁ Ζεὺς καὶ οἱ περὶ αὐτον ἐν Ψυχοστασίᾳ. The plot of Aeschylus' play was the weighing of the souls of Achilles and Memnon by Zeus, in the presence of the two heroes' respective mothers, Thetis and Eos.

87. Lucian *Bis accusatus* 9, *Dearum iudicium* 5 (ἐπεὶ καταβεβήκαμεν), with Wiseman 2015, 172–5 on 'Lucian in the theatre'.

88. Wuilleumier and Audin 1952, 13–14: 'Il semble donc que la fabrication a commencé dans le dernier tiers du IIe siècle et qu'elle a durée une centaine d'années.'

89. Hesiod *Scutum* 57-471, Apollodorus 2.5.11, Hyginus *Fabulae* 31; Cambitoglou and Paspalas 1994.979 (no. 140), cf. 987 on 'the iconographic revival of the subject after such a long gap'. For Commodus as *Hercules Romanus* see Historia Augusta *Commodus* 8.5-9, 9.2, 11.8-14, Herodian 1.14.8-9; there is a superb bust of Commodus as Hercules in the Palazzo dei Conservatori (Musei Capitolini inv. MC 1120).

90. Wuilleumier and Audin 1952, 223 (no. 1): *adesse ultorem nati m*[*e*] *credas mei.*—[*inuic*]*ta uirtus nusqua*[*m*] *terreri potest.* Hercules carries the victor's palm-branch.

91. Hyginus *Fabulae* 31.3.

FIGURE 14. Appliqué medallion from a Gallo-Roman beaker, late second century AD: British Museum (inv. M 131: 1904,0204.441). Found at Orange (?) according to the museum catalogue and *CIL* 12.5687.4; near Arles according to Wuilleumier and Audin 1952, 22–3. © The Trustees of the British Museum.

As for Jupiter himself, he sits above, flanked by winged Victoria and helmeted Minerva, on the *theologeion* from where 'the gods speak in the traditional way'. Behind the scene, the stage hands are rolling the thunder.

CHAPTER ELEVEN

Suetonius and the Origin of Pantomime

SUETONIUS IS best known as a biographer of the Caesars, but he was also a scholar whose curiosity and erudition covered many different subjects. The scope and detail that make the *Lives* so interesting came from a deep knowledge of the social and cultural history of the Greco-Roman world. The known titles of his extensive output are listed in section 3.3 above, and given the importance of the games in Roman culture, the second item in the list (*On Roman Shows and Competitions*, two volumes) is a particularly regrettable loss. However, a few traces of it can be detected in surviving authors, and I think it is worth investigating them. One result, I believe, will be a surprising addition to our knowledge about the history of Roman theatre.

11.1. Suetonius on stage games and circus games

According to the *Suda*, the two volumes concerned were περὶ τῶν παρὰ Ῥωμαίοις θεωριῶν καὶ ἀγώνων. What was the Latin title? Possibly *De spectaculis et certaminibus*, since Suetonius elsewhere refers to Greek *agones* (competitions) as *certamina*.[1] However, there may be a better alternative. Varro in his *Antiquitates diuinae* also had two books on the Roman games, and he evidently divided them as 'On circus games' (*de ludis circensibus*) and 'On stage games' (*de ludis scaenicis*);[2] and if, as is likely,

1. Suetonius *Nero* 12.3, *Domitian* 4.4.

2. See Augustine *City of God* 6.3 on the structure of the *Antiquitates diuinae*: three books *de hominibus*, three *de locis*, three *de temporibus*, three *de sacris*, three *de dis*. The *de temporibus* books (8–10) were *de feriis*, *de ludis circensibus* and *de ludis scaenicis*.

Aulus Gellius was referring to this work when he cited 'the first book of Suetonius' *ludicra historia*', then *ludi* probably featured in Suetonius' title too.[3] Since the Greek phraseology implies an order different from Varro's, I suggest the title was *De ludis scaenicis et circensibus*.

The structure of the work can be inferred from Tertullian's *De spectaculis*, the source for which is described as 'Suetonius, or those from whom he took the information'.[4] Tertullian carefully enumerates the five headings under which he discusses the different types of spectacle:[5] they are 'origins', 'titles', 'apparatus', 'sites' and 'skills'. The types of spectacle themselves are circus games, stage games, athletic competitions (*agones*) and gladiatorial shows (*munera*),[6] repeated in order in his rhetorical treatment of the circus, the theatre, the stadium and the amphitheatre, each with its particular form of temptation to sin.[7] That is consistent with how Suetonius organised his material in the 'shows' chapters of his imperial biographies,[8] and I think it is very likely that Tertullian's five headings go back to him.

The equal status granted not only to circus and theatre but also to stadium and amphitheatre would be appropriate to a work composed after the construction of the Flavian amphitheatre and Domitian's stadium. It is important to remember that when Varro wrote about the games in his *Antiquitates*, probably in the late 50s BC, even a permanent theatre was a very recent phenomenon at Rome. A passage in Servius' commentary on Virgil's *Georgics* is relevant here:

3. Aulus Gellius 9.7.3 (on how the winter solstice affects the sound of the lyre); see Funaioli 1932, 627 and Taillardat 1967, 30–31 for the attribution, which is doubted by Wardle 1993, 92–6.

4. Tertullian *De spectaculis* 5.8 (on the games founded by Romulus and his successors): *positum est apud Suetonium Tranquillum uel a quibus Tranquillus accepit.* Roth 1858, 278–9 prints *De spectaculis* 5.2-8 as a Suetonian 'fragment'; Reifferscheid 1860, 332–45 offers a much more generous selection from *De spectaculis* 4-13 as his 'fragments 184–194'; see Wallace-Hadrill 1983, 41–2 on the two editors and their respective methods.

5. Tertullian *De spectaculis* 4.4, 13.1.

6. Tertullian *De spectaculis* 5-12, arranged as follows: *origines* (5) and *tituli* (6) of circus and theatre games together; *apparatus* (7), *loca* (8) and *artificium* (9) of circus games; *origo* and *tituli* (10.1), *apparatus* (10.2), *loca* (10.3-7) and *artes* (10.8-13) of stage games; *origo* (11.1), *tituli* (11.2), *apparatus* (11.3), *loca* and *artes* (11.4-5) of athletic competitions; *origo* (12.1-4), *tituli* (12.5), *apparatus* (12.6) and *loca* (12.7) of gladiatorial shows.

7. Tertullian *De spectaculis* 16 (circus), 17 (theatre), 18 (stadium), 19 (amphitheatre), and then 20.5 on the frenzy of the circus, the immorality of the stage, the impropriety of the stadium and the cruelty of the amphitheatre.

8. Suetonius *Diuus Iulius* 39, *Diuus Augustus* 43–5, *Tiberius* 34.1, *Gaius* 18–20, *Diuus Claudius* 21, *Nero* 53, *Domitian* 4. *Spectacula* are a regular 'rubric' in the *Lives*.

> In our ancestors' time, 'theatres' were just steps.[9] The scene-set was built of wood for each occasion, whence even today the custom has survived of scaffolds being constructed by those responsible for putting on theatre games.[10] The scene-set that was made was either 'turnable' or 'pullable': it was 'turnable' when it was suddenly revolved in its entirety by a special mechanism and showed a different painted scene;[11] it was 'pullable' when panels were drawn to one side and the other and a painted scene was revealed within. So [Virgil] has cleverly alluded to both by saying 'separates as the panels turn', including each item with each word. Varro and Suetonius record this.[12]

The final sentence suggests that Suetonius may have cited Varro for his account of the situation that existed before the great theatres and arenas were constructed.

Ad hoc wooden structures did not inhibit the ambitious politicians of the late republic from lavishing conspicuous expenditure on the theatre games for which they were responsible. Valerius Maximus and the elder Pliny give us a list of extravagant innovators—who first provided awnings, who first decorated the stage-set in silver or gold or ivory, and so forth—which they probably got from Varro himself.[13] But once the theatre of Pompey was opened in 55 BC, Caesar's monumental Circus Maximus in 46 BC, the amphitheatre of Statilius Taurus in 29 BC, the theatre of Balbus in 13 BC, and the theatre of Marcellus in 11 BC,[14] magnificent display was

9. Either literally, the steps of temples (see Goldberg 1998), or in the sense of terraces of stepped seats (e.g. Vitruvius 5.6.3).

10. *Pegma* can refer to any wooden construction; it might be used of the crane that enabled actors to 'fly' (e.g. Phaedrus 5.7.7, Juvenal 4.122), but here it is evidently the equivalent of *pulpitum*, a raised platform (Martial 5.25.7-8, 8.33.3-4): see Strabo 6.2.6 (C273) for its use in a punitive wild-beast show in the Roman Forum.

11. As described in Vitruvius 5.6.8; cf. also Valerius Maximus 2.4.6, Pollux 4.126.

12. Servius on Virgil *Georgics* 3.24 (Roth 1858, 279–80, Reifferscheid 1860, 341): *apud maiores theatri gradus tantum fuerunt, nam scaena de lignis ad tempus fiebat, unde hodieque consuetudo permansit ut componantur pegmata a ludorum theatralium editoribus. scaena autem quae fiebat aut uersilis erat aut ductilis: uersilis tunc erat, cum subito tota machinis quibusdam conuertebatur et aliam picturae faciem ostendebat; ductilis tunc, cum tractis tabulatis hac atque illac species picturae nudabatur interior: unde perite utrumque tetigit dicens 'uersis discedat frontibus', singula singulis complectens sermonibus. quod Varro et Suetonius commemorant.*

13. Valerius Maximus 2.4.6, Pliny *Natural History* 19.23, 21.6, 33.53, 35.27, 36.117, accepted as Varro frr. 309-14 Funaioli. For the awnings (of which Lucretius 4.75-83 is a wonderful eyewitness description), see Varro *Antiquitates diuinae* fr. 82 Cardauns = Macrobius *Saturnalia* 6.4.8.

14. Asconius 1C (Pompey); Dio Cassius 51.23.1 (Taurus), 54.25.2 (Balbus); Pliny *Natural History* 8.65 (Marcellus); Pliny *Natural History* 36.102, Suetonius *Diuus Iulius* 39.2 (Caesar).

possible at quite a different level. In his seventh book, written no doubt in the twenties BC, Livy described the show business of his own time as an insanity hardly tolerable in wealthy monarchies.[15]

In 22 BC Augustus transferred responsibility for the annual *ludi* from the aediles to the praetors.[16] Magistrates with *imperium* (the power of military command) were evidently needed for what was increasingly becoming a public order problem. A new form of dance introduced by Bathyllus and Pylades—sometimes called *pantomimus*—gave rise to violent rivalry among the performers' respective fans, and by the end of Augustus' principate it had reached a stage of serious bloodshed which even the Praetorian Guard found hard to control.[17]

Less indulgent than Augustus, Tiberius banished all public performers from Italy in AD 23,[18] in an atmosphere for which Valerius Maximus provides good contemporary evidence (section 9.2 above). In his section on the ancient institutions of Rome, Valerius makes a transition from the army to the theatre in these terms:

> From military institutions the next step to take is to the fortresses of the city, that is, the theatres, since they too have frequently drawn up fierce battle lines. They were invented for the worship of the gods and the delight of men, but to the shame of peace they have stained pleasure and religion with the blood of citizens, for the sake of the monstrosities of the stage.[19]

Not surprisingly, the history and development of the *ludi scaenici* were of particular interest in Tiberius' time.[20] But that was nothing compared with the high profile that Roman show business came to enjoy in the next

15. Livy 7.2.13, cf. Seneca *De clementia* 1.26.2 (n. 25); Jory 1981, 153–5.

16. Dio Cassius 54.2.3-4, cf. Dionysius of Halicarnassus *Roman Antiquities* 2.19.4.

17. Bathyllus as the innovator: Athenaeus 1.20d. Pylades as the innovator: Jerome *Chronica* Ol. 189.3 (22–21 BC), Macrobius *Saturnalia* 2.7.18. Pylades and 'sedition': Dio Cassius 54.17.4-5, Macrobius *Saturnalia* 2.7.19. Riots: Tacitus *Annals* 1.54.2, Dio Cassius 56.47.2 (AD 14); Tacitus *Annals* 1.77.1 (AD 15); Velleius Paterculus 2.126.2 ('the sedition of the theatre').

18. Suetonius *Tiberius* 37.2, Tacitus *Annals* 4.14.3 (cf. 1.74.2), Dio Cassius 57.21.3 (cf. 59.2.5, ban revoked by Gaius).

19. Valerius Maximus 2.4.1: *proximus <a> militaribus institutis ad urbana castra, id est theatra, gradus faciendus est, quoniam haec quoque saepenumero animosas acies instruxerunt, excogitataque cultus deorum et hominum delectationis causa non sine aliquo pacis rubore uoluptatem et religionem ciuili sanguine scaenicorum portentorum gratia macularunt.*

20. For Velleius, see chapter 9.

generation, with Gaius, who loved performing,[21] and the 'actor-emperor' Nero.[22]

Gaius built a new circus in the Vatican district; Nero built a new amphitheatre in the Campus Martius; Vespasian outdid it with his own 'new amphitheatre', the Colosseum; Domitian built a stadium for athletic games.[23] It was an almost continuous 150-year sequence from Pompey to the Flavians, interrupted only by the austerity of Tiberius; and even he had to rebuild Pompey's theatre when it was damaged by fire.[24]

If Suetonius did indeed use the categories later employed by Tertullian, we can see how much he would have to record under 'sites' (*loca*). The lavish decoration of the buildings would be among his material for 'apparatus',[25] along with all the mechanical marvels that astonished the audience—'constructions that rise of their own accord, floors that silently lift into the air, things that fit together and then fall apart, things that are separate and then join together, things that stand upright and then gradually subside'.[26] And in the sphere of 'skills' (*artes*), the main innovation that had taken place since Varro's classic account of the *ludi* was the new style of dance performance introduced under Augustus by Bathyllus and Pylades.[27]

That was certainly discussed by Suetonius, but in which of his works? The nineteenth-century editors disagreed: Carl Roth attributed the relevant fragment to the work on the *ludi*, August Reifferscheid to the *De poetis*.[28] I think Roth was right, but what matters more is to get a proper understanding of the text that transmits the information.

21. Philo *De legatione* 42, 78-9, 96; Seneca *De ira* 1.20.8; Suetonius *Gaius* 11, 52, 54; Dio Cassius 59.5.4-5, 59.26.5-10; Josephus *Antiquitates* 19.30, Aurelius Victor *De Caesaribus* 3.12.

22. Pliny *Panegyricus* 46.4 (*scaenicus imperator*); Champlin 2003b, 53–83.

23. Pliny *Natural History* 16.201, 36.74 (Gaius); Tacitus *Annals* 13.31.1, Pliny *Natural History* 16.200, 19.24 (Nero); *CIL* 6.40454a (Vespasian's *amphitheatrum nouum*); Suetonius *Domitian* 5, Jerome *Chronica* on Ol. 217.1-2 (Domitian).

24. Velleius Paterculus 2.130.1, Tacitus *Annals* 3.72.2, Seneca *Consolatio ad Marciam* 22.4. With the temple of Divus Augustus, it was the only public building he undertook—and he never came to Rome to dedicate either of them (Suetonius *Tiberius* 47, *Gaius* 21).

25. Seneca *De clementia* 1.26.2, on shows (*spectacula*) as an opportunity for informers: 'they can be equipped (*apparentur*) at great expense with regal magnificence (*regiis opibus*) and the choicest names of artists, but what good are games (*ludi*) when you're in jail?'

26. Seneca *Epistles* 88.22, on the art of the *machinatores*; cf. Dio Cassius 62.12.2 (collapsible ship).

27. See n. 17.

28. Roth 1858, 280; Reifferscheid 1860, 11–12.

11.2. Diomedes on comedy

The grammarian Diomedes, whom we met in sections 3.2 and 4.3 above, declared in the third book of his *Ars grammatica*[29] that there are three kinds of poem:[30] first, dramatic or mimetic, in which characters speak without any intervention in the poet's voice (Virgil's *Eclogues* 1 and 9 are the examples he gives); second, narrative or expository, in which the poet speaks without any intervention in other characters' voices (his examples are Virgil *Georgics* 1–3, the first part of *Georgics* 4, and Lucretius); and third, a mixture of the two, in which the poet both speaks in his own voice and brings on characters speaking in theirs (for instance Homer's *Iliad* and *Odyssey* and Virgil's *Aeneid*).[31] The particular poetic genres are then discussed in turn:[32] epic, elegy, iambus, epodes, satire, bucolic, tragedy, comedy.

The study of this interesting text was blown off course at an early stage by a largely spurious argument about Diomedes' supposed source. Otto Jahn started it in 1854 with a brief suggestion that the *De poematibus* chapter was taken from Suetonius, and indeed from his lost work on *ludi*.[33] Reifferscheid agreed it was Suetonian, but attributed it to the *De poetis*, and included large chunks of it among his fragments of that work.[34] Later scholars preferred Valerius Probus as the source, or Remmius Palaemon.[35] But all these theories were based on a false premise, since there is not the slightest reason to believe in a single exclusive source for *De poematibus*. Diomedes' *Ars grammatica* is a patchwork, its material evidently stitched together from many of his predecessors' books. As Robert Kaster puts it, 'Diomedes wished to produce a wide-ranging collection of excerpts from earlier works', creating 'a mosaic, in which the junctures between the individual pieces remain visible while the pieces combine to form a coherent pattern'.[36]

29. Kaster 1988, 270–2. The full text is in Keil 1857, 297–529; the relevant part was edited by Friedrich Leo in Kaibel 1899, 53–61: I shall cite it by Leo's section numbers followed by the Keil page number.

30. *De poematibus* 1.2-3 = *Grammatici Latini* 1.482 Keil.

31. For the theoretical tradition Diomedes exploits here, see Janko 1984, 128–33. Diomedes extends his treatment at *De poematibus* 1.4-6 = *Grammatici Latini* 1.482-3 Keil, giving further examples of the three kinds (including drama proper for the first), clearly from a new source.

32. *De poematibus* 3-14 = *Grammatici Latini* 1.483-92 Keil.

33. Jahn 1854, 629–30, followed by Keil 1857, liv–lv, Roth 1858, 280.

34. Reifferscheid 1860, 4–22, 370–77.

35. Respectively Buchholz 1897 and Koett 1904, 41–50.

36. Kaster, 1988, 148.

Diomedes' treatment of comedy is as long as that of all the other genres put together,[37] incorporating as it does Varro's schematic categorisation of Greek dramatic forms and their supposed Roman equivalents (section 2.2 above).[38] It concludes with a remarkable passage, some at least of which was taken from Suetonius, on the constituent parts of comedy:

> The constituent parts of comedies are three in number: *diuerbium*, *canticum* and *chorus*. (The constituent parts of a comedy [in the sense of 'acts']{39} are different, but confined to a specific number between five and ten.) *Diuerbia* are the parts of comedies in which the characters of various people are involved; the characters in *diuerbia* ought to be two or three or rarely four, and it is not permitted to increase the number. In *cantica* there should be only one character, or if there are two it should be that one listens from out of sight and doesn't speak to the other but only, if necessary, to himself. In *chori*, of course, there is no specific number of characters, since they should all speak together as if creating a single character by merging their voices and singing as one. Latin comedies, therefore, have no chorus, but consist of just two elements, *diuerbium* and *canticum*.
>
> Originally, as Tranquillus asserts, everything that [now] happens on stage was performed in comedy. For the *pantomimus*, the *pythaules* and the *choraules* used to sing in comedy. But because not everything could be equally excellent in the performance of everyone, those among the comedy performers who had greater ability and skill each claimed the artistic primacy for himself. So it came about that the *mimi* were unwilling to yield to the others in their own speciality, and so there was a split from the rest. For since, being more skilled, they were not prepared to serve the less skilled in the work they shared, they separated themselves from comedy; and so it happened that once the precedent had been established, the practice of each speciality began to follow suit, and not appear in comedy.
>
> Evidence for this is provided by the old comedies, in which we find 'Performed on equal pipes' or 'unequal pipes' or 'Tyrian pipes'. For when the chorus sang, the performer accompanied them on choral pipes, i.e. *choraulicae*, whereas in a *canticum* he responded on *pythaulicae*. As for the 'equal' or 'unequal pipes' that we find written, that means that

37. *De poematibus* 9-14 = *Grammatici Latini* 1.488-92 Keil.

38. *De poematibus* 10 = *Grammatici Latini* 1.489-90 Keil (Varro fr. 306 Funaioli); for the limitations of Varro's scheme, see Wiseman 2008, 194–9.

39. Thus Leo (in Kaibel 1899, 61, *app. crit.*), surely rightly.

> when he was performing for a *monodium*[40] he blew into one pipe, and when for a *synodium* into both.[41]

It was noted long ago that this particular passage in Diomedes is more concerned with the history of drama than with *poemata* as such,[42] and so I think we may safely attribute it to Suetonius' work on the Roman *ludi*.

11.3. A new dance genre

It is a curious fact that in all the excellent work that has recently appeared on the subject of '*pantomimus*', this important text has been either briefly dismissed or completely ignored.[43] But if historians of drama find it hard to fit into their conceptual framework, perhaps that framework itself is part of the problem.

40. *Monodium* (solo song) is presumably the same as *canticum*, as *synodium* must be the same as *chorus*; the different terminology may imply a change of source between *De poematibus* 14.4 and 14.5.

41. *De poematibus* 14 = *Grammatici Latini* 1.491-2 Keil: [14.1] *membra comoediarum sunt tria: diuerbium canticum chorus. membra comoediae diuersa sunt, definito tamen numero continentur a quinque usque ad decem.* [14.2] *diuerbia sunt partes comoediarum in quis diuersorum personae uersantur; personae autem diuerbiorum aut duae aut tres aut raro quattuor esse debent, ultra augere numerum non licet.* [14.3] *in canticis autem una tantum debet esse persona aut, si duae fuerint, ita esse debent ut ex occulto una audiat nec conloquatur, sed secum, si opus fuerit, uerba faciat.* [14.4] *in choris uero numerus personarum definitus non est, quippe iunctim omnes loqui debent quasi uoce confuse et concentu in unam personam reformantes. Latinae igitur comoediae chorum non habent, sed duobus membris tantum constant, diuerbio et cantico.* [14.5] *primis autem temporibus, sic uti adserit Tranquillus, omnia quae in scaena uersantur in comoedia agebantur. nam et pantomimus et pythaules et choraules in comoedia canebant. sed quia non poterant omnia simul apud omnes artifices pariter excellere, siqui erant inter actores comoediarum pro facultate et arte potiores, principatum <sui> sibi artificii uindicabant. sic factum est <ut>, nolentibus cedere mimis in artificio suo ceteris, separatio fieret reliquorum. nam dum potiores inferioribus qui in communi ergasterio erant seruire dedignantur, se ipsos a comoedia separauerunt, ac sic factum est ut exemplo semel sumpto usus quisque artis suae rem exequi coeperit neque in comoediam uenire. cuius rei indicia produnt nobis antiquae comoediae, in quibus inuenimus 'acta tibiis paribus aut imparibus aut Sarranis'. quando enim chorus canebat, choricis tibiis id est choraulicis artifex concinebant, in cantico autem pythaulicis responsabat. nam quod 'paribus tibiis uel imparibus' inuenimus scriptum, hoc significat quod, siquando monodio agebat, unam tibiam inflabat, siquando synodio, utrasque.*

42. Usener 1892, 618 = 1913, 293; Buchholz 1897, 127; Funaioli 1932, 601.

43. There is no mention at all in Jory 2004, Lada-Richards 2007, Hall and Wyles 2008, Webb 2008, or Slater 2010. Garelli 2007, 151 refers briefly to the passage, assuming that when Diomedes-Suetonius refers to *comoedia* he means *mimus*; this improbable idea is falsely attributed to Jory 1981, whose paragraph on the passage is at 1981, 156.

Of course there had always been dancers on the Roman stage. For Varro and Lucretius no less than for Propertius and Ovid, dancers were precisely what you thought of when you thought of the theatre.[44] When Augustus asked Pylades what exactly was new about the new style, he replied with a quote from Homer: 'the cry of flutes and pipes and the hubbub of men'.[45] What did he mean?

To find an answer we need to go forward two hundred years, to Lucian's wonderful essay on dance (*Saltatio*).[46] Of course all art forms develop, and we cannot know how far the performances Lucian was familiar with differed from those of Pylades and his contemporaries. But since he states explicitly that 'dance as it now is . . . began mainly under Augustus',[47] I think we may, with proper caution, accept his evidence at least for the basics.[48] For instance, he points out that the dancer's mask has a closed mouth, unlike the open-mouth masks of tragedy and comedy, because that is 'appropriate to the action involved':

> For [the dancer] has many people raising their voices on his behalf. In the past, they themselves both danced and sang, but later, because their heavy breathing as they moved disturbed the singing, it seemed better that others should sing as accompaniment for them.[49]

He also helpfully enumerates the dancer's support team—'the pipe, the flute, the foot-clappers, the clash of cymbals, the fine voice of an actor, the combined voice of singers'.[50]

So Pylades' Homeric definition evidently referred not only to wind instruments but also to choral singing ('raising their voices', 'combined voice') as elements essential to the performance. Both are attested in the Augustan period: Bathyllus' piper used to 'fly' above the stage on the crane, until he fell off and broke his leg, and Manilius refers to performers

44. Varro *Menippean Satires* fr. 513 Astbury, Lucretius 4.973-83; Propertius 2.22.3-6, Ovid *Remedia amoris* 751-5. See in general Jory 2004, 147–8, Lada-Richards 2007, 20–22, Wiseman 2023, 110–16.

45. Macrobius *Saturnalia* 2.7.18, quoting Homer *Iliad* 10.13.

46. At vol. 5, pp. 209–89 of the Loeb edition.

47. Lucian *Saltatio* 34; see Jory 2004, 151–2, Lada-Richards 2007.

48. Pylades' own book on dance (σύγγραμμα περὶ ὀρχήσεως, Athenaeus 1.20d)—no doubt one of Lucian's sources—may have helped to keep the rules of the form relatively stable; see Jory 1981, 150–51 on its likely influence.

49. Lucian *Saltatio* 29 (τῷ ὑποκειμένῳ δράματι ἐοικός), 30: ἔχει γὰρ πολλοὺς τοὺς ὑπὲρ αὐτοῦ βοῶντας. πάλαι μὲν γὰρ αὐτοὶ καὶ ᾖδον καὶ ὠρχοῦντο· εἶτ' ἐπειδὴ κινουμένων τὸ ᾆσθμα τὴν ᾠδὴν ἐπετάραττεν, ἄμεινον ἔδοξεν ἄλλους αὐτοῖς ὑπᾴδειν.

50. Lucian *Saltatio* 68: αὐλόν, σύριγγα, ποδῶν κτύπον, κυμβάλου ψόφον, ὑποκριτοῦ εὐφωνίαν, ᾀδοντων ὁμοφωνίαν.

whose gestures 'match the songs of the chorus'.[51] Both are mentioned in Jerome's note on Pylades, which was surely taken from Suetonius:

> Pylades, Cilician *pantomimus*: although the ancients used to dance and sing themselves, he was the first at Rome to have a chorus and pipe music accompany him.[52]

And both are implicit in Diomedes *De poematibus* 14.4-5,[53] where the passage containing the Suetonius citation arises from the presence or absence of a chorus, and ends with the use of different sorts of pipes.

Diomedes' whole discussion is in the context of comedy. For Lucian the dancer's subjects are essentially tragic,[54] but that may be a later development. We know from contemporary evidence that Pylades specialised in tragedy, Bathyllus in comedy;[55] and although the learned Athenaeus attributes to Bathyllus the invention of 'the tragic dance', he says that he did it by applying not only the *emmeleia* dance appropriate to tragedy but also the *kordax* of comedy and the *sikinnis* of satyr-play.[56] So it is quite possible that Suetonius, like Diomedes, discussed the origins of the new dance performance as part of the development of comedy. But is what Diomedes attributes to him credible?

11.4. Greek theatre and Italian theatre

Throughout the *De poematibus* chapter, Diomedes uses Latin and Greek authors alike for his examples and quotations. Even in his section on satire, where there were no Greek authors to cite, he adduces Old Comedy and a possible derivation from satyrs.[57] So too in his treatment of comedy he gives a version of the Athenian 'Old, Middle and New Comedy'

51. Phaedrus 5.7.4-9 (section 10.3 above); Manilius 5.483-5, cf. Phaedrus 5.7.25.

52. Jerome *Chronica* Ol. 189.3: *Pylades Cilix pantomimus, cum ueteres ipsi canerent atque saltarent, primus Romae chorum et fistulam sibi praecinere fecit.* Cf. pref. 4 on Jerome's 'careful excerpts from Tranquillus and other well-known historians'; Jory 1981, 148. Jerome was no doubt using the *De uiris illustribus*, but Suetonius may have made the point in his work on *ludi* as well.

53. See n. 41.

54. E.g. Lucian *Saltatio* 31, cf. 27 for tragedy as the *comparandum*. See Jory 2004, 154–6, Lada-Richards 2007, 32–7.

55. Seneca *Controuersiae* 3.pref.10: 'Pylades in comedy and Bathyllus in tragedy are out of their normal range'.

56. Athenaeus 1.20d, from Aristonicus of Alexandria; cf. 1.20e for Pylades' style as bombastic (ὀγκώδης), Bathyllus' as more cheerful (ἱλαρωτέρα); Jory 1981, 149–50. The three genre-specific dances are mentioned also by Lucian *Saltatio* 26.

57. Diomedes *De poematibus* 6 = *Grammatici Latini* 1.485-6 Keil (section 3.3 above).

scheme, in order to derive Roman comedy from the last of these.[58] But there was plenty of Greek comedy other than Athenian, and plenty of Latin comedy other than the 'plays in Greek costume' (*fabulae palliatae*) of Plautus and Terence.

For Plato and Theocritus, the inventor of comedy was Epicharmus of Syracuse; Aristotle adds that according to the Sicilians Epicharmus was 'much earlier than Chionides and Magnes', the pioneers of Athenian comedy in the 480s and 470s BC.[59] Other Sicilian comic poets are little more than names to us,[60] but there is plentiful evidence from vase-painting for a very widespread and varied tradition of comic and burlesque drama all over south Italy and Sicily in the fourth century BC (section 1.4 above).[61] The next known names are playwrights of 'Italian comedy' (as Athenaeus defines it)—Rhinthon, who was either Syracusan or Tarentine and was active soon after 300 BC; Skiras, who was certainly Tarentine; and a Campanian, Blaisos of Capri.[62]

Two points are worth emphasising about this important but neglected theatrical tradition.

First, it was not restricted to Greek-speaking communities.[63] Two fine mid-fourth-century cups from the inland Etruscan city of Clusium show naked showgirls, first with a dancing satyr, then performing Leda and the swan in the version known from Euripides.[64] Similar scenes of naked girl

58. *De poematibus* 9.4-5 = *Grammatici Latini* 1.488-9 Keil. For Hellenistic scholarship on Attic comedy see Janko 1984, 46–7.

59. Plato *Theaetetus* 152e, Theocritus in *Anthologia Palatina* 9.600 (Gow and Page 1965, 1.188); Aristotle *Poetics* 1448a.32-5 (according to *Suda* E 2766 = 2.393 Adler, Epicharmus was active in Syracuse 'six years before the Persian wars'). Diomedes too was aware of this tradition (*De poematibus* 9.6 = *Grammatici Latini* 1.489 Keil). See Olson 2007, 6–11.

60. See Kassel and Austin 2001, 174–83 for Phormis and Dinolochos.

61. Dearden 2004 on Sicily, Robinson 2004 on S. Italy. Excellent collection of material in Todisco 2002; mythological burlesque is well illustrated in Walsh 2009, esp. figs 16, 26, 34, 36, 39, 42, 50, 79, 89 for scenes explicitly on stage.

62. Athenaeus 9.402b (τῆς Ἰταλικῆς καλουμένης κωμῳδίας); cf. Lydus *De magistratibus* 1.41, who describes the three as Pythagoreans. Rhinthon: Nossis in *Anthologia Palatina* 7.414 (Gow and Page 1965, 1.153), Syracusan; *Suda* R 171 = 4.295 Adler, Tarentine 'in the time of Ptolemy I'. Skiras: Athenaeus 9.402b. Blaisos: Stephanus Byzantinus 357.1. See sections 2.6, 3.4 and 4.4 above: full testimonia and fragments in Kassel and Austin 2001, 260–74; see also Olson 2007, 13–16, and Taplin 1993, 49–52 on Rhinthon.

63. Cf. Taplin 1993, 40–41 for an Oscan-speaking vase owner, Taplin 2007, 21–2 on 'Hellenized non-Greeks', 2007, 32 on the Pronomos vase from Apulian Ruvo. My only reservation about Taplin's two ground-breaking books is the impression they give that this phenomenon is an anomaly requiring special explanation.

64. Vatican, Museo Gregoriano Etrusco, inv. 14962–18212; Musée d'art et d'histoire, Geneva, inv. 23471 (where the eagle implies the version in Euripides *Helen* 17-21); Martelli

performers with dancing and pipe-playing satyrs are known from fourth-century bronze caskets (*cistae*) from Latium; one of them, as we saw in the first chapter (fig. 4), is clearly a version of Iphigeneia at Aulis.[65]

Authors of the early empire believed, rightly or wrongly, that stage games were first introduced to Rome from Etruria in the fourth century, and as proof they pointed to the fact that the Latin *histrio* (actor) was an Etruscan loan-word.[66] In an important article in 1975 Oswald Szemerényi argued that it was originally *histōr* (ἵστωρ), a Greek loan-word in Etruscan, and that *scaena* (stage), *persona* (mask, character) and *ludio* (player) had likewise come into Latin from Greek via Etruscan.[67] It may help his case that one of the fourth-century bronze caskets from Latium shows a character labelled *(h)istor* taking part in a scene that also featured a young Silenus, Laodameia, Ajax and Agamemnon.[68]

This should not surprise us. Horace's patronising vision of the Latins as mere peasants, with no idea of Greek drama until after the Punic wars, is a demonstrable absurdity.[69] Already in the archaic world Hesiod (or pseudo-Hesiod) knew Latinos, ruler of the far-famed Tyrrhenians, as a son of Odysseus and Circe;[70] by the fourth century BC Aristotle and Heraclides Ponticus could think of Rome as 'a Greek city';[71] two generations later Callimachus used a Roman hero as an example of *pan-Hellas*.[72]

Some of the best evidence for the comic stage of fourth-century Italy is provided by the brilliant school of red-figure vase painters that flourished at Paestum in northern Lucania.[73] Once Greek Poseidonia, Paestum had been conquered by the Lucanians some time about 400 BC, so the

---

1987, 331, Wiseman 2008, 111–13; colour illustrations in Wiseman 2004, plate 8. For naked actresses on the Tarentine comic stage, see Hughes 1997 on Konnakis.

65. Battaglia and Emiliozzi 1979, nos 45, 51–2; 1990, no. 82 (Iphigeneia); Wiseman 2008, 111–17. Iphigeneia at Aulis was the subject of one of Rhinthon's 'cheerful tragedies' (*PCG* F 5, Pollux 7.90).

66. Livy 7.2.4-6 (364 BC), Valerius Maximus 2.4.4; section 3.1 above. Cf. Adams 2003, 165 for possible linguistic evidence of 'a time when there were Etruscan actors at Rome'.

67. Szemerényi 1975, 307–19: *persona* ultimately from πρόσωπον, *ludio* ultimately from αὐλῳδός.

68. Battaglia and Emiliozzi 1979, no. 45 (*Silanus, Ladumeda, Aiax Ilios, Acmemeno*); Wiseman 2004, 109–10, fig. 46.

69. See Wiseman 2008, 231–3 on Horace *Epistles* 2.1.156-63.

70. Hesiod *Theogony* 1011-16.

71. Plutarch *Camillus* 22.2 = Heraclides Ponticus fr. 102 Wehrli (πόλις Ἑλληνίς); Dionysius of Halicarnassus *Roman Antiquities* 1.72.3-4 = Aristotle fr. 609 Rose (Achaeans).

72. Callimachus *Aetia* 4.106 Pfeiffer, with the *diegesis*.

73. Trendall 1987, 433 (index) for 'vases with theatrical subjects', e.g. figs 6 and 7 here; see in general Green 1994, 89–99, Green 1995, 107–12 and plates 9–11, Robinson 2004, 209–10.

witty and elegant work of Asteas, Python and their colleagues represents the culture of a community that had not been Greek for fifty years.[74] A century or so later, the Campanian playwright Blaisos came from Greek-speaking Capri, a dependency of Naples; but his neighbours spoke Oscan, and there is no reason to doubt that the distinctive comic drama of Oscan-speaking Atella was already flourishing in his time.[75] In northern Campania they spoke Latin (the Latin colonies at Cales and Suessa date from 334 and 313 respectively), and Blaisos' tragi-comic *Satournos* carried the name of the Latin god whose story was an aetiology of Latium itself.[76] Elizabeth Rawson acutely noted that the Samnite Nysius who wrote popular philosophy in Greek in the second century BC may well have done so for the stage; the great theatre at Pietrabbondante amply confirms Strabo's description of the Samnites as philhellenes.[77]

The second thing to emphasise about this multifarious Italian stage tradition is that it evidently did not recognise the generic boundaries of Athenian drama.[78] Dinolochus of Syracuse in the fifth century BC wrote a *Comoedotragoedia*; Rhinthon was credited with the invention of 'cheerful tragedy' and comedy in hexameters; the works of Blaisos of Capri were simultaneously serious and comic (*spoudogeloia*).[79] Two early Paestan pots show comic actors sharing the stage with female acrobats or tumblers performing nearly naked.[80] The ubiquity of satyrs in the iconographic

74. For the 'barbarization' of Poseidonia, represented as a cultural tragedy for the 'enslaved' Greeks, see Aristoxenus of Tarentum in Athenaeus 14.632a.

75. Livy 7.2.12, Strabo 5.3.6 C233, Diomedes *De poematibus* 10.5 = *Grammatici Latini* 1.490 Keil, Cicero *Ad familiares* 7.1.3, 9.16.7, Varro *De lingua Latina* 7.29, 95; Frassinetti 1967, 1–8.

76. Athenaeus 11.487c (Blaisos *PCG* F 2), with Rawson 1985, 103 = 1991, 475; Virgil *Aeneid* 8.319-23, Ovid *Fasti* 1.233-8 (Latium *a Saturno latente*); Velleius Paterculus 1.14.3-4 (dates of colonies).

77. Rawson 1985, 101 = 1991, 474 on *Index Stoicorum Herculanensis* (*PHerc* 1018) 75 Traversa, which names Nysius the 'parodist of serious subjects' (σπουδαιοπάρῳδος); Strabo 5.4.12 C250; Sear 2006, 153 for the Pietrabbondante theatre, Wallace-Hadrill 2008, 72–143 on the Italo-Greek cultural background.

78. Well noted by Dearden 1995, 85–6, who concludes that fourth-century Italians 'saw drama of whatever genre in a comprehensive light'.

79. *Antiatticista* 111'.29 (Dinolochus *PCG* F 3) for Dinolochus. *Suda* R 171 = 4.295 Adler for Rhinthon's ἱλαροτραγῳδία; Stephanus Byzantinus 357, 603 for Blaisos as a poet of σπουδογελοίων and Rhinthon as 'transforming tragedy into the laughable' (τὰ τραγικὰ μεταρρυθμίζων ἐς τὸ γελοῖον); Lydus *De magistratibus* 1.41 for Rhinthon's comedy in hexameters; see section 1.6 above. For possible local Italian influence on Rhinthon, see Robinson 2004, 209–11.

80. Trendall 1987, 46, 69 (nos 1/99, 2/33, plates 12f, 24f); Dearden 1995. One of them (1/99, fig. 6 here) comes from Lipari, where the theatrical tradition was clearly very strong: see Bernabó Brea 2001.

evidence (section 4.5 above) brings to mind the definition of satyr-play as mixing the serious with the playful.[81] However, the Italian tradition evidently did not keep the satyrs attached to tragedies, as in Athens, but had them performing with dancing girls, often naked, who look like the *mimae* (actresses) we know from Roman literary texts; the *ludi Florales*, where the *mimae* traditionally performed naked, were introduced at about the same time that Andronicus of Tarentum produced the first of his plays in Latin at Rome.[82]

With Livius Andronicus, to give him his Roman citizen name, we come within range of the Roman antiquarian tradition, and texts Suetonius could have read. It is important to realise that the Italian theatrical traditions sketched above did not come to an end when red-figure vase-painting and the engraving of bronze *cistae* went out of fashion: they continued to develop, and aspects of them can still be identified in our literary sources on republican Rome.

Plautus plays with the idea of *tragicomoedia* in the prologue to *Amphitruo*;[83] his own name seems to allude to the Oscan comedy of Atella;[84] his younger contemporary Caecilius Statius used material more appropriate to mime in his versions of Menander.[85] Cicero quotes Rhinthon (section 2.6 above), and the later grammarians' inclusion of *Rhinthonica* among Roman comic genres may go back to Suetonius.[86] The un-Athenian mixture of serious and comic is reflected in Varro's own Menippean satires, written for the stage, and also in the Sibyl's instructions for the Secular Games of 17 BC.[87]

81. Demetrius *On Style* 168-9 ('playful tragedy'), Horace *Ars poetica* 226 ('turning serious matters to play'); Griffith 2008, 76. For Dionysiac initiates performing as satyrs, see Turner 2004, 101–3.

82. Wiseman 2008, 86–124 on satyrs and dancing girls, 175–86 on the *ludi Florales*, 194–9 on fluid categories; Valerius Maximus 2.10.8 for the nakedness at Flora's games as an old comic tradition (*priscus mos iocorum*). Livius Andronicus' first production in 240 BC: Cicero *Brutus* 72-3 (from Atticus), *Tusculan Disputations* 1.3, Aulus Gellius 17.21.42 (probably from Varro); see section 1.1 above. *Ludi Florales* introduced in 241 or 238 BC: Velleius Paterculus 1.14.8, Pliny *Natural History* 18.236.

83. Plautus *Amphitruo* 50-63.

84. Plautus *Asinaria* 11 ('translated by Maccus'); Diomedes *De poematibus* 10.9 = *Grammatici Latini* 1.490 Keil ('Oscan characters in Atellan plays, like Maccus').

85. Aulus Gellius 2.23.12; cf. 15.24.1 (Volcacius Sedigitus fr. 1 Courtney), where *mimico* is a probable emendation.

86. Cicero *Ad Atticum* 1.20.3 (Rhinthon *PCG* F 12); Evanthius *De comoedia.* 4.1, Donatus *De comoedia* 6.1, Lydus *De magistratibus* 40 (sections 3.3 and 3.4 above).

87. Strabo 16.2.29 C759 for Menippus as a σπουδογέλοιος (cf. nn. 77 and 79 on Nysius the Samnite and Blaisos of Capri); Wiseman 2009, 131–9 on Varro's *Menippeans*, esp. frr.

Certainly the world of the theatre was still widespread and multilingual.[88] Actors in the second and first centuries BC thought of themselves as 'wandering round Italy' or 'touring the towns',[89] and we need not suppose that it mattered much whether the towns were primarily Greek-, Oscan- or Latin-speaking. So too at Rome the theatre festivals provided *ludi Graeci* and *ludi Osci*, evidently as a regular thing (section 2.4 above).[90] It is possible that there were *ludi Etrusci* as well, since Varro mentions a writer of Etruscan tragedies in the first century BC.[91] When Suetonius reports 'actors in all languages' at the games of Caesar and Augustus, his point is not that such performances were unusual in themselves, but that on these great occasions they were put on throughout the city, and not just on one particular stage.[92]

11.5. How did he know?

Suetonius was a learned man, and had at his disposal an extensive late-republican and Augustan literature on theatre history—not only the two relevant books of Varro's *Antiquitates*, but also Varro's *De scaenicis originibus* and *De actionibus scaenicis* (three volumes each), and the *Libri spectaculorum* of Sinnius Capito, who certainly predated Verrius Flaccus.[93] He was well placed to have good information about the origin of what his Greek contemporaries called 'the Italian dance'.[94]

---

218 (theatre audience addressed) and 304 ('this stage style'); Sibylline oracle in Phlegon of Tralles *BNJ* 257 F37 ('let seriousness be mixed with laughter').

88. See Rawson 1985 = 1991, 468–87, who consciously corrects the sources' Romanocentric bias.

89. Diodorus Siculus 37.12.3 on the Latin Sannio at Asculum in 91 BC; Lucilius 1034 Marx, with Rawson 1985, 105–6 = 1991, 478–9; Macrobius *Saturnalia* 2.7.7 on Publilius Syrus in 46 BC.

90. Cicero *Ad familiares* 7.1.3 ('I don't suppose you miss the Greek and Oscan *ludi*'), on the dedication games for Pompey's theatre in 55 BC. *Ludi Graeci*: Plutarch *Marius* 2.2 (triumph games 101 BC), Nicolaus of Damascus *FGrH* 90 F127.9.19 (triumph games 46 BC), Cicero *Ad Atticum* 16.5.1 (*ludi Apollinares* 44 BC), *CIL* 6.32323.156-61 (*ludi saeculares* 17 BC); *CIL* 1^2.1214.13 ('on the Greek stage'). *Ludi Osci*: Strabo 5.3.6 (C233); see Wallace-Hadrill 2008, 88–96 on the use of Oscan as a statement of identity.

91. Volnius: Varro *De linga Latina* 5.55, where 'he used to say' (*dicebat*) implies a contemporary. Cf. Harris 1971, 169–84 on the not yet extinct Etruscan language.

92. Suetonius *Diuus Iulius* 39.1, *Diuus Augustus* 43.1 (*omnium linguarum histriones*).

93. Varro frr. 70–86 Funaioli; n. 2 for the *Antiquitates*. Sinnius Capito: Lactantius *Diuina institutio* 6.20.35; date inferred from Festus 438L (Verrius Flaccus was the tutor of Augustus' grandsons about 10 BC). See Wallace-Hadrill 1983, 53–7 for Suetonius' expertise in late-republican and Augustan writings.

94. Athenaeus 1.20e (τὴν Ἰταλικὴν ὄρχησιν).

I suspect that what has caused his evidence to be dismissed or ignored is the natural tendency of classicists to be over-influenced by classic texts. If we choose to think of 'comedy' as just 'Plautus and Terence', we may prefer not to engage with an argument based on the premise that 'everything that happens on stage was performed in comedy'. But if instead we try to do justice to the complex evidence for the history of comic theatre in Sicily and Italy from the late sixth century onwards, when tragedy merged with comedy, as it did for Dinolochus and Rhinthon, or with erotic dance, as it evidently did for the fourth-century Etruscans and Latins, then Suetonius' account of the dancers' and musicians' declaration of independence may make some kind of sense.

At the very least, we should not assume that we are better informed than he was. On the contrary, Suetonius' wide-ranging erudition puts to shame our compartmentalised modern scholarship, where specialists on ancient drama and specialists on Roman history too rarely venture beyond their self-imposed boundaries.

CHAPTER TWELVE

The Lupercalia as a Spectacle

The fourth Sibyl is the Italian one. It was her lot to spend her life in the wilderness of Italy; her son was Euandros, who founded the cult-place of Pan in Rome, which is called Luperkon. Eratosthenes wrote about her.

THAT LACONIC note from an ancient commentator on Plato provides our earliest textual evidence for the Roman cult of Pan, the Lupercalia.[1]

Eratosthenes, the commentator's source, was writing a century or so after the bronze mirror was made that showed the twin Lares suckled by the she-wolf at the Lupercal (fig. 8). The mirror presented Pan Lykaios, the shepherd-god of Arcadia, naked but for a goatskin knotted round his shoulders, just like the Luperci themselves, the fellowship (*sodalitas*) of young men who ran naked at his festival on 15 February striking anyone in their way with strips of raw goat-hide.[2]

The Lupercalia cult is important for the history of theatre because the Luperci were thought of as performers (*ludii*) presenting a spectacle.[3]

1. Eratosthenes (reference missing at *BNJ* 241 F26), quoted in the *scholia* to Plato *Phaedrus* 244b: τετάρτη Ἰταλική. ἡ ἐν ἐρημίᾳ τῆς Ἰταλίας τὴν διατριβὴν λαχοῦσα, ἧς υἱός ἐγένετο Εὔανδρος, ὁ τὸ ἐν Ῥώμῃ τοῦ Πανὸς ἱερόν, τὸ καλούμενον Λούπερκον, κτίσας. περὶ ἧς ἔγραψεν Ἐρατοσθένης. For Evander as the founder see also Livy 1.5.1-2, Dionysius of Halicarnassus *Roman Antiquities* 1.32.3, Ovid *Fasti* 2.267-82, Plutarch *Romulus* 21.3, Clement of Alexandria *Stromateis* 1.10.3, Justin 43.1.6-7, Servius on Virgil *Aeneid* 8.343.

2. Pompeius Trogus in Justin 43.1.7: *ipsum dei simulacrum nudum caprina pelle amictum est, quo habitu nunc Romae Lupercalibus decurritur.* For the Luperci see Cicero *Pro Caelio* 26 (*sodalitas*), Nicolaus of Damascus *BNJ* 90 F130.71 (αἰγείοις δοραῖς), cf. Ovid *Fasti* 2.445-6 (*pellibus exsectis*), Festus (Paulus) 76L (*pelle caprina*); Wiseman 2023, 121–3, fig. 6.2.

3. Varro *Antiquitates diuinae* fr. 80 Cardauns = Tertullian *De spectaculis* 5.3 (*Lupercos ludios appellabant, quod ludendo discurrant*), Livy 1.5.1 (*ludicrum*), Valerius Maximus 2.2.9 (*spectaculo sui*).

No doubt they were mainly showing off their athletic prowess,[4] but it must be significant that in 154 BC the Lupercal was the chosen site for the construction of a permanent theatre,[5] and though that building was soon demolished, an *ad hoc* wooden theatre may have been set up there each year.[6] When Ovid explains why the Luperci were naked, the story he tells looks very much like a stage performance.[7]

The evidence, as always, is scattered and haphazard, requiring conjecture (guesswork, if you prefer) to make historical sense of it. In this final investigation the idea of performance and spectacle at the Lupercalia is applied first to visual evidence from the third century AD and then to a papal manifesto from the late fifth century AD, three generations after Christian Rome had put an end to the cult of the traditional gods.

12.1. The sarcophagus of Aelia Afanacia

The 'catacomb of Praetextatus' on the Via Appia Pignatelli originated in the second century AD as an aristocratic burial ground, which later seems to have become imperial property;[8] from the fourth century onwards it was used for Christian burials, including that of Aelia Afanacia in a reused sarcophagus first made a century or so earlier.[9] The original occupier, whose name has not survived, had ordered a very particular scene to be sculpted on it (fig. 15). Its iconography only became intelligible in 1961, with the publication of an elaborate floor mosaic from a Roman house at el-Djem in Tunisia: the scenes show each of the months of the year, and February is represented by the Lupercalia, which took place on the 15th of the month (fig. 16).[10] On the mosaic, as on the sarcophagus, what is shown is a woman being held in position by two men for a third man to whip her exposed rump. The man with the whip is a Lupercus, the other two are his attendants.

4. As in the Romulus legend (Ovid *Fasti* 2.365-8, *Origo gentis Romanae* 22.2).

5. Velleius Paterculus 1.15.3: *Cassius censor a Lupercali in Palatium uersus theatrum facere instituit.*

6. Livy *Epitome* 48: *theatrum . . . ex senatus consulto destructum est, populusque aliquamdiu stans ludos spectauit.* In a great storm in 60 BC, 'the wooden bridge was destroyed, and a theatre constructed from timbers [?] for some festival was overthrown' (Dio Cassius 37.58.3-4); the Lupercal was of course close to the Tiber bank.

7. Ovid *Fasti* 2.303-58 (Faunus, Omphale and Hercules), with Wiseman 2023, 120–25.

8. It contains the sarcophagus of Balbinus, who reigned briefly in AD 238; the 'villa of Maxentius' is nearby.

9. Schumacher 1968–9; Tortorella 2000, 253–4; North and McLynn 2008, 179 and plate 4.

10. Stern 1968; Schumacher, 1968–9, 67–8 and plate 11a; Tortorella 2000, 245–6, 252.

FIGURE 15. Fragmentary marble sarcophagus, third century AD: Rome, Museo Classico delle Catacombe di Pretestato (inv. PCAS Pre 273). © German Archaeological Institute: detail of D-DAI-ROM 68.970, photo M. Hutzel.

FIGURE 16. Detail of floor mosaic from Thysdrus (el-Djem), third century AD: Tunisia, Musée de Sousse. © Ad Meskens / Wikimedia Commons.

We know what the Lupercalia were like in the last years of the Roman republic, when the young men running naked, masked or smeared with mud, are attested both textually and iconographically.[11] Augustus 'revived'

11. Lactantius *Diuinae institutiones* 1.21.46 (*qui nudi uncti coronati aut personati aut luto obliti currunt*), clearly taken from Cicero *Philippics* 3.12 and other late-republican sources: see *Diuinae institutiones* 1.22.9-11 for Lactantius' use of Varro, Gavius Bassus and

the ritual,[12] perhaps after only a short period of inactivity, and it was probably at this stage that the Luperci started wearing goatskin loincloths, thus making masks unnecessary.[13] Their social standing had not been high in the late republic,[14] but after Augustus they were always of equestrian rank; symbolically, when the *ordo equester* wanted to honour Drusus Caesar in AD 23 they put up their statue of him at the Lupercal.[15] It is clear that under the principate the Luperci were characterised less by athletic high spirits than by the conscious dignity of their equestrian status.[16]

We know that in Augustus' time the flagellation of females was a significant part of the ritual and the spectacle, as it had been probably since 276 BC, when it was introduced as an aid to conception.[17] But the sexy game of naked young men chasing young women, as our sources describe the republican Lupercalia,[18] was perhaps less fitting for the dignified Luperci of the imperial period. Certainly by the time of Hadrian they wore a costume more decorous than a goatskin loincloth,[19] and the scenes on the mosaic and the sarcophagus are probably about 100–150 years later than that. The Lupercus on the mosaic seems to be dressed in the Hadrianic fashion, but on the sarcophagus a further stage in Lupercan uniform may

---

Sextus Clodius. For the visual evidence see Wiseman 2023, 121–3, fig. 6.2; they were not 'masked like wolves', as imagined by Hopkins 2017, 318.

12. Suetonius *Diuus Augustus* 31.4: he put a ban on boys before the age of puberty taking part.

13. Ovid *Fasti* 5.101 (*cinctuti*), Dionysius of Halicarnassus *Roman Antiquities* 1.80.1 (ὑπεζωσμένους τὴν αἰδῶ); cf. Valerius Maximus 2.2.9 *(cincti*), Plutarch *Romulus* 21.5 (ἐν περιζώσμασι).

14. Cicero *Ad Atticum* 12.5.1; see *ILLRP* 696 and Pliny *Natural History* 34.11-12 for a freedman as *magister Lupercorum*. Rüpke 2008, 979 provides a list of all known Luperci.

15. Crawford 1996, 544–5 (*CIL* 6.31200.b-c).

16. Pliny *Natural History* 34.18 on statues *Lupercorum habitu*, with Tortorella 2000, 248 for an example. On a Hadrianic grave altar in the Vatican (*CIL* 6.3512: Tortorella 2000, 249 and McLynn 2008, 168 and plate 3), young Ti. Claudius Liberalis was portrayed first as a mounted *eques Romanus* escorted by a man carrying a symbolic military flag (*uexillum*), as on the sarcophagus, and then as a whip-carrying Lupercus escorted by two attendants, who would presumably do the job of the two men in the mosaic and sarcophagus scenes.

17. Ovid *Fasti* 2.425-52, esp. 445-6 (*iussae sua terga puellae . . . percutienda dabant*), cf. the scholiast on Juvenal 2.142 (*aut catomus* [i.e. κατ' ὤμους] *leuabantur aut a manibus uapulabant*). For the date see Livy fr. 63 = Gelasius *Aduersus Andromachum* 12 (section 12.3 below), Orosius 4.2.2.

18. Livy 1.5.2 (*per lusum atque lasciuiam*), Valerius Maximus 2.2.9 (*iocantes*), Plutarch *Caesar* 61.2 (ἐπὶ παιδιᾷ καὶ γέλωτι), Dio Cassius 46.19.4 (ἐν τῷ παιγνιώδει τῶν γιγνομένων).

19. See n. 13: Claudius Liberalis' 'dress uniform' (North and McLynn 2008, 180) was a sort of wrap worn low on the hips but covering the thighs, 'folded in the shape of bermuda-shorts' (Graf 2015, 164).

be detected, with the nakedness now limited to the shoulders and upper chest. It all seems very formal.[20]

Our first reaction to the scene on the sarcophagus (fig. 15) is likely to be one of distaste: here is a woman being publicly humiliated before an audience of men. Historians, however, must try to make sense of what was going on, and the point of this chapter is to see what can be discovered from the scrutiny of details.

Look first at the male figures in the background of the flagellation scene. At the far right is the Lupercus' equestrian flag-bearer,[21] and behind him someone carrying the branch of a tree: that might be the god Silvanus, often so portrayed, who was sometimes identified as either Faunus or Pan, the presiding deities of the Lupercal.[22] But the other five figures are more puzzling. Why is the man between 'Silvanus' and the Lupercus restraining the attendant who holds the woman's legs? What is the clean-shaven young man behind the other attendant carrying on his shoulder? Why are the two men to the left of him carrying candles? Was this happening after dark, like the erotic games of Flora?[23] Certainly there is much that we don't know.

12.2. *Licensed sadism*

Now we must turn to the flagellation itself, suspending distaste for the sake of objectivity. In attempting a reconstruction of the scene we shall call the lady Valeria, for strength and courage; the Lupercus can be Caeso, and his two attendants Tenax and Crurifer.

The first thing to notice is how Valeria was being held. If you wanted to present someone's buttocks for a flogging, there was a perfectly easy way of doing it, known not only in Roman schools but also in English ones as late as the mid-nineteenth century. You hoisted the victim on someone else's back, as illustrated in a wall-painting of a school in the forum at

20. The attribution of 'drunken hilarity' to the men in the mosaic scene (Hopkins 2017, 317) seems to be a false inference from conditions that had applied two or three centuries earlier (Cicero *Philippics* 3.12, 13.31, Valerius Maximus 2.2.9).

21. See n. 16.

22. *Origo gentis Romanae* 4.6, Servius *auctus* on *Georgics* 1.20; cf. Livy 2.7.2 (with Dionysius of Halicarnassus *Roman Antiquities* 5.16.3). The deities were regularly associated with each other (Virgil *Eclogues* 10.24-7, *Georgics* 1.16-20, 2.494, Grattius 17-20, Ovid *Metamorphoses* 1.192-3); see Dorcey 1992, 17–19 (iconography with tree-branch), 33–42 (Faunus and Pan).

23. Ovid *Fasti* 5.361-8, Dio Cassius 58.19.1-2.

Pompeii.[24] There is good ancient evidence that that method could be used on women (even goddesses) as well as schoolboys.[25] So why was Tenax holding Valeria face to face? The position is confirmed by the scene on the mosaic.[26] There must have been a reason for it.

In order to end up in that position, Valeria had to co-operate. She must have been standing with Tenax facing her, closer than she would normally permit, and Crurifer down on one knee immediately behind her. She would need to lift her dress high enough for Crurifer to take hold of each of her legs just below the knee, then raise her arms to grasp Tenax's shoulders (as on the mosaic) or forearms (as on the sarcophagus), and allow him to hold her firmly by the midriff.

We must assume that when the Lupercus gave the signal Tenax stepped back, pulling Valeria with him, and that as she fell forward Crurifer lifted her legs off the ground and stood up between them.[27] They could then hold her suspended as Caeso raised her dress to the waist. That is the situation presented in the two art works. The attendants could of course take advantage, Tenax by shifting his grip, Crurifer by edging forward. It may be that on the sarcophagus Crurifer was being warned not to do so; nevertheless, it is hard to avoid the suspicion that that opportunity was why this elaborate method of holding the woman was devised in the first place.

'Whatever else this might be, it is presented as a spectacle.'[28] The onlookers were watching a lady of quality being half-stripped in public and intimately handled by two lower-class men, in a position where she must keep her head up and show her face.[29] After the flagellation the Lupercus could keep her on display for as long as he chose, or as long as the audience demanded, before ordering his attendants to set her on her feet and let her dress cover her again. And what happened next? Did Caeso and his men go off to look for another lady? Or was the next lady already waiting her turn?

24. Beard 2008, 77, fig. 29 (from the *praedia* of Julia Felix).

25. Scholiast on Juvenal 2.142 (n. 17), Tertullian *Apologeticus* 15.1 (*Diana flagellata* as a mime-plot); for Venus punished on a gilt-bronze mirror in Boston (MFA no. 095, 1986.750) see Wiseman 2023, 134–5, fig. 6.7.

26. The notion that there she was being held face upwards (Tortorella 2000, 245 and 252, Hopkins 2017, 317) is surely mistaken: the artist was trying to portray her looking back over her left shoulder.

27. The mosaic shows him standing; on the sarcophagus he is still on one knee.

28. North and McLynn 2008, 179.

29. Always an important consideration: cf. Suetonius *Vitellius* 17.1 (*ut uisendam praeberet faciem*), Pliny *Panegyricus* 34.3 (*intueri . . . supina ora retortasque ceruices*).

Two and a half centuries had passed since the time of the athletic running Luperci, cheerfully lashing whomever they happened to encounter.[30] Here in the third century AD the ritual performance looks very static, and it may be that it now took place at a single fixed venue, a sort of theatre of licensed sadism. The ritual had demonstrably changed over time, and it would change again.

12.3. Pope Gelasius' polemic

Another two and a half centuries pass before we have our next evidence, part of a war of words between Pope Gelasius and Andromachus, probably the City Prefect, in or about AD 495.[31] By then the Lupercalia as a religious ritual had been obsolete for three generations, as had the Luperci as a public priesthood;[32] when Servius wrote his commentary on Virgil some time in the early fifth century, the naked running was a thing of the past.[33] Even so, Gelasius' attack on Andromachus makes it clear that the Lupercalia were still celebrated by the city magistrates,[34] who by this date would of course be Christians. What they provided was a performance of some kind, described by Gelasius as 'foul songs' attributing crimes and sexual misbehaviour to named individuals.[35]

30. Valerius Maximus 2.2.9 (*obuios iocantes petiuerunt*); Plutarch *Romulus* 21.5-6 (τὸν ἐμποδὼν παίοντες . . . ἐμποδίους τύπτοντας), *Caesar* 61.2 (τοὺς ἐμποδὼν ἐπὶ παιδιᾷ καὶ γέλωτι παίοντες), *Antony* 12.1 (καθικνούμενοι μετὰ παιδιᾶς τῶν ἐντυγχανόντων); *Origo gentis Romanae* 22.1 (*occursantes quosque sibimet uerberantes*).

31. Gelasius *Aduersus Andromachum* (CSEL 35.1); see McLynn 2008 and Graf 2015, 166–75 for reconstruction of the dispute.

32. *Codex Theodosianus* 16.10.20.1 (funding of public cults withdrawn in 382), 16.10.10 (animal sacrifice banned in 391); see Cameron 2011, 163–72 for the decline of priestly colleges. 'By 480 it had been the best part of a century since anyone had seen an authentic pagan festival in Rome' (Cameron 2004, 512).

33. Past tenses in Servius on *Aeneid* 8.663 (*consuetudo permansit ut nudi Lupercalia celebrarent*); contrast Servius *auctus* on *Aeneid* 8.343 (*id in morem uersum, ut hodieque nudi currunt . . . et puellae de loro capri caeduntur*), probably from Aelius Donatus, who was active about AD 354 (Jerome *Chronica* Ol. 283.2); see Cameron 2011, 573–80. However, Donatus quoted his sources verbatim (*Vita Vergilii* preface: *maluimus optima fide quorum res fuerant eorum etiam uerba seruare*), so the present-tense formulation may be that of an earlier commentary, e.g. Asper in the third century AD (Cameron 2011, 574).

34. Gelasius *Aduersus Andromachum* 16 (*uos ipsi qui Lupercalia defenditis et agenda proponitis*), 19 (*Lupercaliorum patroni . . . digni magistri uesaniae*).

35. Ibid. 19 (*cantilenarum turpium . . . obscaenitatum et flagitiorum uocibus*), 20 (*facinora uniuscuiusque uulgando . . . criminum decantationibus*). He called it *ludibria* (ibid. 17, 19, 20, 24), obviously in the sense of 'mockery, insult' (*Oxford Latin Dictionary s.u.* 3).

Gelasius wanted this public naming and shaming to be discontinued, and if he had personal reasons for that he did not reveal them. His tactic was to use his historical learning (he quotes Livy) to mock Andromachus and his colleagues for not putting on the *real* Lupercalia:[36] why didn't they run naked through the streets, as had been done in the past? Instead, they had handed the proceedings over to contemptible characters of the lowest class, mere street-corner performers.[37] In their forefathers' time, he says, it was respectable married women who were stripped and whipped.[38] His disingenuous argument was that nowadays, with just professional performers involved, there was no point doing it at all. It was just a charade, 'street theatre'.[39]

It is clear from Gelasius' polemic that the magistrates continued to celebrate the Lupercalia festival because it was believed to protect the city from plague.[40] A tiny piece of evidence about that is provided by one of his learned contemporaries, a man called Iunius Philargyrius who wrote a commentary on Virgil. Here is Philargyrius's annotation on a line in the first *Eclogue*, where the rustic Tityrus mentions the city of Rome:

> Even before Romulus there was Roma, and [the city] took its name from her, as Marianus, poet of the Lupercalia, shows as follows:
>
> The goddess fair and beautiful,
> Roma, Aesculapius' daughter,
> Made for Latium a new name.
> Everyone now calls it Rome,
> After her name who founded it.[41]

36. Ibid. 11-12 (*Liuius in secunda decade*), 16-17 (*more maiorum*); the Livy reference (n. 17) is to an event of 276 BC.

37. Ibid. 16 (*ad uiles triuialesque personas, abiectos et infimos*); *persona* implies performance, as *triuialis* often does too (e.g. Juvenal 7.55, Suetonius *Diuus Augustus* 74, *De rhetoribus* 30.2, Calpurnius Siculus 1.28, Apuleius *Metamorphoses* 8.24.2); songs (*carmina*) at the *triuia* were familiar in Virgil's time (*Eclogues* 3.26-7). See McLynn 2008, 170, who points out that in late antiquity actors were described as *uiles* (*Codex Theodosianus* 15.7.4, 12, cf. Ammianus Marcellinus 28.4.32).

38. Ibid. 16: *apud illos . . . matronae nudato corpore uapulabant.*

39. I borrow the terms from Cameron (2004, 512; 2011, 170) and North and McLynn (2008, 180).

40. Gelasius *Aduersus Andromachum* 11 (*pestilentia*), 12 (*propter morbos inhibendos*), 13 (*morbos et pestilentiam*).

41. Philargyrius on Virgil *Eclogues* 1.19 (Courtney 1993, 405): *Roma et ante Romulum fuit et ab ea sibi nomen acquisisse Marianus Lupercaliorum poeta sic ostendit: Sed diua flaua et candida | Roma, Aesculapi filia, | nomen nouum Latio facit, | quod conditoris nomine | Romam sub ipso omnes uocant.* The MSS read *Lupercanorum*: Courtney emends to *Lupercorum*, which may be right.

Otherwise unattested, Marianus may belong to the second or third century AD, a time when Rome was visited by repeated outbreaks of deadly plague;[42] it was because of plague, half a millennium earlier in 292 BC, that the cult of the healing god Aesculapius had been brought to Rome.[43]

What did it mean to be a 'poet of the Lupercalia'? The metre Marianus used gives us the answer, as Alan Cameron explains:

> Two centuries later, through St Ambrose, it was to become the standard meter of Christian Latin hymnography. . . . Iambic dimeters were peculiarly well suited to short, simple verses designed to be sung.[44]

What Philargyrius has preserved seems to be part of a hymn, to be sung at the Lupercal festival on 15 February every year. Such hymns were a normal part of Roman public religion, and the quasi-historical content of Marianus' piece is consistent with what little we know about them.[45] In this case, however, Gelasius' complaint about 'foul songs' suggests that hymnodists at the Lupercalia could be satirical too.

Remembering the plague may help to account for the contrast between the cheerful excitement of the republican Lupercalia, with the young men making an exhibition of themselves and trying to get the young women to do the same,[46] and the stiff formality of the scene on Aelia Afanacia's sarcophagus. The traditional purpose of the Lupercalia was to purify the city,[47] and it is easy to imagine that by the third century AD that had become a much more serious business. One wonders whether the three men at the left of the sarcophagus scene were using *suffimenta*, materials for purification carried in a box and burned as 'candles'.[48]

42. The first of them began in AD 166, 'not only perhaps the first pandemic in human history, but also a moment of rupture in the story of the Roman Empire' (Harper 2017, 24).

43. Livy 10.47.6-7, Ovid *Metamorphoses* 15.622-744, Valerius Maximus 1.8.2, Plutarch *Quaestiones Romanae* 94 (*Moralia* 286d), Lactantius *Institutio diuina* 2.7.13, *De uiris illustribus* 22.

44. Cameron 1980, 147, cf. 146 for what little can be said about Marianus.

45. Dionysius of Halicarnassus 1.31.2 (on Faunus), 1.79.10 (on Romulus and Remus), 5.25.1 (on Horatius Cocles), 8.62.3 (on Marcius 'Coriolanus'). Faunus, identified as Pan Lykaios (n. 22), was the god of the Lupercal (Ovid *Fasti* 2.424); Romulus and Remus were suckled by a she-wolf at the Lupercal (Ovid *Fasti* 2.381-422, Servius on Virgil *Aeneid* 8.343).

46. Valerius Maximus 2.2.9 (*spectaculo sui*), cf. Ovid *Fasti* 2.445-6 (*iussae sua terga puellae . . . dabant*).

47. Varro *De lingua Latina* 6.13, 6.34, Ovid *Fasti* 2.19-36, 5.101-2, Plutarch *Quaestiones Romanae* 68 (*Moralia* 280b), *Romulus* 21.3, *Numa* 19.5, Festus (Paulus) 75–6L, Censorinus *De die natali* 22.15.

48. Compare the *suffimenta* handed out to the citizens at the *ludi saeculares* (*CIL* 6.32323.48 and 76, 32327.25-7).

12.4. The lost history of Roman theatre

Century after century, through fundamental changes in the life of Rome, it remained necessary to celebrate the Lupercalia. Of course our understanding can never be complete, but it still helps to pay attention to the detail of what evidence there is. Aelia Afanacia's reused sarcophagus and Pope Gelasius' sarcastic pamphlet are classic examples, not just of how opaque such items can be, but also of what can be got out of them by careful close reading. Throughout this book we have been puzzling over such specific bits of surviving evidence, trying to work out what they presuppose about the experience of theatre in the once living world of ancient Rome. In this case, Gelasius' contemptuous reference to low-class street-corner performers reminds us that Varro, half a millennium earlier, had called the naked Luperci *ludii*, as if they were actors.[49]

'Theatre' doesn't have to have an auditorium, just public space and an audience. At the scene shown on the sarcophagus, presumably taking place at the Lupercal, there might have been spectators seated on benches (the sculptor would have no reason to include them), but even if they were just standing in the piazza it still counts as theatre. Whether it was theatre of the same kind as in Varro's time is a quite separate question; but I think we can identify four distinct characteristics of the Lupercalia in the third to fifth centuries AD that imply a genuine continuity with the Roman stage in what was by then the very distant past.

First, the performance was not just entertainment. Whether we think of the solemn third-century Lupercus on the sarcophagus, with his elaborately formal procedure, or Andromachus the fifth-century city magistrate, unkindly mocked by Gelasius, the Lupercalia festival was a public responsibility. Similarly, from the fall of the Tarquins (section 1.4 above) to the time of Augustus, the annual theatre festivals of Rome were guaranteed by public funding and organised by elected magistrates: the curule aediles for the *ludi Romani* and *Megalenses*, the plebeian aediles for the *ludi plebeii*, *Florales* and *Ceriales*, the urban praetor for the *ludi Apollinares* (section 6.1 above); from Augustus onwards the praetors, like Velleius Paterculus in AD 15 (section 9.2 above), took care of all of them. The Lupercalia too was a fixed annual festival, the ritual necessarily performed by a public priesthood, the *sodalitas Lupercorum*.[50]

49. Varro *Antiquitates diuinae* fr. 80 Cardauns (n. 3); in his day they were still masked (n. 11).

50. Evidently under the supervision of the *flamen Dialis* (Ovid *Fasti* 2.282).

Second, the purpose of the performance was to secure divine favour, in this case 'purifying' the city and protecting it from plague. Theatre festivals had the same purpose, as Cicero made clear on his election as plebeian aedile for 70 BC:

> I think carefully about the task the Roman People has laid upon me. I shall have to put on, with all possible care and ceremony, the most sacred games of Ceres, Liber and Libera; I shall have to secure the goodwill of Mother Flora for the People and *plebs* of Rome by the popularity of her games; and for Jupiter, Juno and Minerva, with the utmost dignity and religious piety, I shall have to put on the very ancient games that were first called 'Roman'.[51]

Naturally, the magistrate emphasised the dignity of his duty to the gods, without prejudice to the wide range of entertainment he would hope to provide for the Roman People. The Lupercal festival of Pan, not organised by a senatorial magistrate as impresario but performed by the Luperci themselves, was at the very edge of what Roman decorum found acceptable;[52] it was not targeted by the hellenophobe reformers who emasculated the cult of Liber/Dionysus in 186 BC (section 3.6 above), but in 154 BC the project of a permanent theatre at the Lupercal was aborted by order of the Senate.[53] Nevertheless, in his Roman guise as Faunus the god of the Lupercal continued to be honoured for many more centuries, and the performance at his festival continued to matter to the city even after Christian Rome had abolished his public cult along with those of all the other gods.

The third point of interest is Gelasius' complaint about attacks on contemporary individuals' reputations.[54] Topical comment was equally a feature of the stage festivals, often with very specific political reference; the evidence is explicit in Cicero's letters and speeches (sections 2.2–3 and 6.1 above), and detectable even in some of Livy's historical narratives (sections 7.4–5 and 8.4–6 above). Satirical remarks about the behaviour

51. Cicero *In Verrem* 5.36: *habeo rationem quid a populo Romano acceperim; mihi ludos sanctissimos maxima cum cura et caerimonia Cereri Libero Liberaeque faciundos, mihi Floram matrem populo plebique Romanae ludorum celebritate placandam, mihi ludos antiquissimos qui primi Romani appellati sunt cum dignitate maxima et religione Ioui Iunoni Mineruaeque esse faciundos.* The final reference was to the *ludi plebeii*, supposedly founded very soon after the expulsion of the Tarquins (ps.Asconius 217 Stangl).

52. See for instance Cicero *Ad Atticum* 12.5.1, disapproving of his nephew becoming a Lupercus.

53. Velleius Paterculus 1.15.3, Livy *Epitome* 48 (nn. 5–6).

54. Gelasius *Aduersus Andromachum* 20 (n. 35).

of individuals, which may have been what got Phaedrus banished (section 10.1 above), were ubiquitous in the stage-performance genre called *satura* that we explored in chapter 4.

The last point is the musical element implied by Gelasius' reference to 'foul songs' and the hymnic metre of the 'poet of the Lupercalia' Marianus.[55] Alas, the music that accompanied performance in ancient Italy is something that cannot be documented. What tune was the bearded satyr playing as Iphigeneia stripped off for her big scene (fig. 4)? What was the opening note that told the experts in Cicero's time (section 2.2 above) whether the tragedy on the programme was *Antiopa* or *Andromacha*? What did Ovid have in mind when he made 'theatre' synonymous with 'citharas, pipes and lyres, voices and arms that move to their own measures, love stories forever danced to music'?[56] Inevitably, that whole dimension of experience is lost to us, whether at the Lupercalia ritual or on stage at the *ludi scaenici*.

We began this chapter with Eratosthenes' evidence, precariously transmitted in a marginal note on a dialogue of Plato, that 'Euandros, son of the Italian Sibyl, founded the cult-place of Pan in Rome, which is called Luperkon'.[57] The origin of the cult was thus part of Rome's earliest foundation-legend, in which exiled Euandros ('Evander') and his fellow-Arcadians were settled on the Palatine in time to welcome Herakles as he drove the cattle home in Stesichorus' story in the sixth century BC. A story composed to be sung at festivals (section 1.3 above), it was already three centuries old when Eratosthenes was writing, and over a thousand years old by the time Pope Gelasius quarrelled with Rome's civic authorities about performances at the Lupercalia.

The long historical perspective is made possible by removing 240 BC from its traditional position as the *terminus post quem* of Roman theatre and taking proper account of archaeological evidence for the wealth and ambition of 'Tarquin's Rome' (section 1.1 above). I have argued that the origin of Roman theatre was part of the origin of the Roman city-state, brought about by Lucumo son of Demaratos (alias Lucius Tarquinius '*Priscus*') the hugely wealthy Corinthian entrepreneur who created the Roman Forum, the Circus Maximus and the 'Roman games' (section 1.2). That

55. Gelasius *Aduersus Andromachum* 19 (n. 35), Philargyrius on Virgil *Eclogues* 1.19 (n. 41).

56. Ovid *Remedia amoris* 753-5 (*citharae lotosque lyraeque | et uox et numeris bracchia mota suis. | illic adsidue ficti saltantur amores*), cf. Lucretius 4.978-83, Propertius 2.22.4-6; see Wiseman 2023, 110–16 and section 11.3 above.

57. Eratosthenes in *scholia* to Plato *Phaedrus* 244b (n. 1).

may well have been the moment when the Arcadian cult of Pan Lykaios was introduced, at the place called 'Lupercal' at the foot of the Palatine between the river harbour and the Circus fairground.[58]

Finally, we can step back to consider the main theme of this book. The long perspective allows us to see that Roman theatre didn't 'come after' Greek theatre: it was contemporary with it, right from the start. The insight is a liberating one. Dionysiac iconography in fourth-century BC Latium is no longer paradoxical (sections 1.4–7); Pythagorean Rhinthon and his effect on Rome turn out not to be Byzantine make-believe (section 4.4); 'Menippean satire' can be rescued from its current status as an embarrassing anomaly (section 4.7). We still don't know enough to write a *connected* history of Roman theatre, but at least there is now a defensible historical framework into which all those scattered bits of evidence can be made to fit.

58. For the topography see Wiseman 2019, 69, fig. 30. For the god of the Lupercal as specifically *Lycaeus* see Livy 1.5.2, Ovid *Fasti* 2.424, Justin 43.1.7, Servius on Virgil *Aeneid* 8.34, Dionysius of Halicarnassus *Roman Antiquities* 1.32.3, 1.80.1.

APPENDIX

The Greek Quotations in Cicero's Correspondence

THIS IS THE body of evidence on which the argument in section 2.5 above is based: Greek authors quoted in Cicero's letters in the original language. The list does not include the many Greek passages he quoted elsewhere in Latin translation, for a general audience or readership.[1]

I. Homer

1.	*Iliad* 1.343 = *Od.* 24.452	*Fam.* 13.15.2
2.	1.174f	*Fam.* 3.7.6
3.	2.298	*Att.* 6.5.2
4–5.	4.182/8.150	*Att.* 9.9.3, *Q Fr.* 3.7.1
6.	5.428f	*Att.* 14.13.2
7.	6.181	*Att.* 2.16.4
8–9.	6.208 = 11.784	*Q Fr.* 3.5.4, *Fam.* 13.15.2
10.	6.236	*Att.* 6.1.22
11–16.	6.442 = 22.105	*Att.* 2.5.1, 7.1.4, 7.12.3, 8.16.2, 13.13.2, 13.24.1
17.	8.355	*Q Fr.* 3.7.2
18.	9.228-30	*Att.* 14.13.1
19.	9.524	*Att.* 7.11.3
20.	10.93f	*Att.* 9.6.4
21–2.	10.224	*Att.* 9.6.6, *Fam.* 9.7.1
23.	11.654	*Att.* 13.25.3
24.	12.243	*Att.* 2.3.4
25.	16.112	*Att.* 1.16.5.
26.	16.385-8	*Q Fr.* 3.5.8

1. See the lists at Čulík-Baird 2022, 273–6.

27.	17.280	*Att.* 16.5.5
28.	18.96-9	*Att.* 9.5.3
29–30.	18.112 = 19.65	*Att.* 7.1.9, 10.12a.1
31.	18.309	*Att.* 7.8.4
32.	20.308	*Att.* 16.11.1
33–4.	22.100	*Att.* 2.5.1, 7.1.4
35.	22.159	*Att.* 1.1.4
36.	22.268	*Att.* 1.15.1
37.	22.304f	*Fam.* 13.15.2
38.	23.322	*Att.* 4.15.7
39.	24.369 = *Od.* 16.72 = 21.133	*Att.* 2.9.3
40.	*Odyssey* 1.302	*Fam.* 13.15.1
41.	3.22	*Att.* 9.8.2
42.	3.26	*Att.* 9.15.4
43–4.	3.169	*Att.* 16.6.1, 16.13.1
45.	3.171f	*Att.* 16.13.2
46–7.	7.258 = 9.33	*Att.* 7.1.2, *Fam.* 13.15.2
48.	9.27f	*Att.* 2.11.2
49.	9.513	*Q Fr.* 1.2.1
50.	10.82	*Att.* 2.13.2
51.	11.634	*Att.* 9.7.3
52.	12.309	*Att.* 7.6.2
53.	17.488 = 20.384	*Att.* 4.7.3
54.	20.18	*Att.* 9.15.3
55.	22.412	*Att.* 4.7.2
56.	24.315	*Fam.* 13.15.1

II. Drama

57.	Aeschylus *Agamemnon* 375–6	*Q Fr.* 3.4.6
58.	*Prometheus* 682	*Att.* 14.10.1
59.	*Prometheus* 750	*Q Fr.* 1.2.13
60.	Aristophanes *Wasps* 1431	*Att.* 5.10.3
61.	Epicharmus *PCG* fr. 218	*Att.* 1.19.8
62.	*PCG* fr. 252	*Q Fr.* 3.1.23
63–4.	Euripides *Andromache* 448	*Att.* 2.25.1, 15.1.3
65.	*Hippolytus* 436	*Q Fr.* 3.1.18
66.	*Ion* 585	*Att.* 13.11.1
67.	*Medea* 410	*Att.* 15.4.1
68.	*Philoctetes TrGF* fr. 796	*Att.* 6.8.5
69.	*Phoenissae* 393	*Att.* 2.25.1
70.	*Phoenissae* 506	*Att.* 7.11.1
71.	*Supplices* 119	*Q Fr.* 2.14.4

72.	*Troades* 455	*Att.* 7.3.5
73.	*fab. inc. TrGF* fr. 905	*Fam.* 13.15.2
74.	*TrGF* fr. 906	*Fam.* 16.8.2
75–6.	*TrGF* fr. 918	*Att.* 6.1.8, 8.8.2
77.	*TrGF* fr. 958	*Att.* 9.2a.2
78.	*TrGF* fr. 973	*Att.* 7.13.4
79.	Menander *Epitr.* fr. 2	*Att.* 4.11.2
80.	Rhinthon *PCG* fr. 12	*Att.* 1.20.3
81.	Sophocles *Tympanistai TrGF* fr. 636	*Att.* 2.7.4
82.	*Tyro TrGF* fr. 662	*Att.* 4.8.1
83.	*fab. inc. TrGF* fr. 768	*Att.* 2.16.2
84.	*TrGF* fr. 962	*Q Fr.* 2.9.2
85.	*adesp. com. PCG* fr. 128	*Att.* 4.8a.2
86.	*PCG* fr. 129	*Att.* 13.42.1
87.	*PCG* fr. *131	*Att.* 16.15.3
88.	*anon. Dor. PCG* fr. 7	*Att.* 5.11.5
89.	*adesp. trag.* fr. 104N	*Att.* 6.4.3
90.	fr. 105N	*Att.* 14.22.2
91–2.	fr. 106N = *PCG* fr. 130	*Att.* 15.11.3, 16.6.2
93.	fr. 107N	*Fam.* 9.7.2
94	fr. 320N	*Att.* 1.12.1
95.	fr. 411N	*Fam.* 12.14.7

III. Other poetry

96.	Archilochus, fr. 56.2 Diehl	*Att.* 5.12.1
97.	Callimachus *Epigr.* 32.2 Pf	*Att.* 6.9.3
98.	fr. 732 Pf	*Att.* 8.5.1
99.	Hesiod *Op.* 289	*Fam.* 6.18.5
100.	*Op.* 350	*Att.* 13.12.3
101.	fr. 338 M-W	*Att.* 7.17.4
102–4.	Leonidas *Anth. Pal.* 10.1.1 (G-P 2490)	*Att.* 9.7.5, 9.18.3, 10.2.1
105.	Phocylides	*Att.* 4.9.1
106.	Pindar *Nem.* 1.1	*Att.* 12.5.1
107.	fr. 215 Snell	*Att.* 13.38.2
108.	Stesichorus fr. 11 Diehl	*Att.* 9.13.1
109.	*adesp. iamb.* fr. 2 West	*Att.* 6.3.1
110.	Delphic oracle (Herodotus 1.66.2)	*Att.* 10.5.2
111.	*Corpus Paroem. Gr.* 1.42	*Att.* 2.19.1
112.	1.116	*Att.* 13.20.4
113.	1.307	*Att.* 4.6.2
114.	1.314	*Att.* 1.19.10
115.	2.573	*Att.* 1.19.2

IV. Prose

116.	Epicurus ap. Diog. Laert. 10.22	*Fam.* 7.26.1
117.	10.132	*Fam.* 15.19.2
118.	Heraclitus fr. 49 Diels	*Att.* 16.11.1
119.	Plato *Ep.* 7.329d	*Att.* 9.13.4
120.	Thucydides 1.97.2	*Att.* 7.1.6
121.	1.138.3	*Att.* 10.8.7
122.	*Corpus Paroem. Gr.* 1.300	*Att.* 5.20.3
123.	1.421	*Att.* 13.42.3

The line between quotation and proverb is not an easy one to draw, and my inclusion of nos 111–15 and 122–3 as quotations is essentially guesswork.[2] (English speakers who say 'the course of true love never did run smooth' or 'fools rush in where angels fear to tread' may not know they are quoting Shakespeare or Pope, though in each case the metre suggests it's a quotation.) Similarly, some of the attributed quotations may themselves have been proverbial: it is quite likely, for instance, that Cicero used no. 60, no. 97 and no. 118 merely as proverbs, without any thought of Aristophanes, Callimachus or Heraclitus.

Scholars who have discussed these quotations seem determined to be unimpressed. Here for instance is B. S. Steele at the turn of the twentieth century:

> The range of quotations is not great, nor are there indications of an extensive acquaintance with Greek literature. All that was proverbial may be held to have had a place in the current of social communication, and to this indefinite source may likewise be assigned a few passages which, because of their prominence, were quoted by other writers. Longer quotations may represent an intimate acquaintance with the works from which they come; they may have been gleaned from 'Choice Selections' or may represent a cursory reading for quotation purposes; but, in the absence of any statement by Cicero bearing on the question, no definite answer can be given.[3]

Seventy years later, H. D. Jocelyn took much the same view:

> Cicero won notoriety in his youth for Greek learning and Atticus, seven years his elder, lived in Athens between the years 88 and 65, taking an active part in Athenian life. Both men must have possessed considerable skill in using Greek and some knowledge of the classics of Greek poetry. The seventy or so quotations in Cicero's letters need not, however, imply the deep knowledge of the original poems which enthusiasts often claim for him. Some are clearly requoted from Atticus' own letters while most are of a gnomic character, as likely to come from the cultural ambience as from the poems themselves.[4]

2. For an extensive list of Cicero's Greek proverbs, see Steele 1900, 400–403.

3. Steele 1900, 410.

4. Jocelyn 1973, 64, citing for the first sentence Plutarch *Cicero* 5 and Nepos *Atticus* 2-4. As the list above shows, 'seventy or so' was a serious understatement.

Nicholas Horsfall was even more dismissive, tacitly endorsing Steele's unsupported idea of a 'Choice Selections' handbook: 'The multitudinous quotations in Cicero's letters reveal error and misunderstanding; his reading was indeed wide but his plumes were often borrowed.'[5] Nor did Barry Baldwin's discussion, limited to the *Ad familiares* and *Ad Q. fratrem* collections, do much to counter this trend: 'On balance, the deployment of Greek in Cicero's letters to and from his friends and brother may partly confirm and partly temper Horsfall's somewhat downbeat view of Roman knowledge of Greek and Greek literature, especially poetry.'[6] It is as if Cicero were being marked on a Greek literature paper, with the examiners not disposed to give a borderline candidate the benefit of the doubt.

A more sophisticated analysis was provided by J. N. Adams in his magisterial treatment of bilingualism, but he too was censorious, in a different way:

> This is the sort of game which takes place between two members of a self-conscious literary élite. If there is an intimacy here, it is the intimacy of a shared cultural background and not merely of mutual affection, and at issue as well is membership of an in-group. . . . Unflagged quotations of Greek literature (which are very common in Cicero's letters) may be a way of flattering the recipient by assuming his knowledge of Greek literature, particularly if the quotation is unfinished and needs to be completed by the reader if the full point is to be understood; but they have another function, because they allow the writer to display his easy mastery of the classics and put pressure on the addressee to recognise the allusion. In-group membership is again at issue.[7]

At least Cicero is allowed (if ironically) an 'easy mastery of the classics'. 'In-group membership', however, seems to be just a pejorative description of what Steele called 'the current of social communication', and Jocelyn 'the cultural ambience'.

Leaving value-judgements aside, what matters for the argument of this volume is the nature of that 'cultural ambience'. How much of it came from formal literary education that only the well-off could afford, and how much from regular attendance at theatre festivals that were open to Roman citizens of every rank and station?

5. Horsfall 1979, 87. No examples of error or misunderstanding were offered.

6. Baldwin 1992, 13, cf. 2 for his aim 'to observe the breadth, depth, and dissemination of Greek amongst educated Roman gentlemen of the late Republic'.

7. Adams 2003, 312, 318; the first sentence refers to Cicero *Ad Atticum* 13.42.1 (no. 86 in the list above).

BIBLIOGRAPHY

Adams 2003: J. N. Adams, *Bilingualism and the Latin Language*. Cambridge: Cambridge University Press.

Ammerman 1990: Albert J. Ammerman, 'On the Origins of the Roman Forum', *American Journal of Archaeology* 94: 627–45.

Ammerman et al. 2008: Albert J. Ammerman, Ioannis Iliopoulos, Federica Bondioli, Dunia Filippi, Jill Hilditch, Alessandra Manfredini, Licio Pennisi and Nancy A. Winter, 'The clay beds in the Velabrum and the earliest tiles in Rome', *Journal of Roman Archaeology* 21: 7–30.

Ampolo 2013: Carmine Ampolo, 'Il problema delle origini di Roma rivisitato: concordismo, ipertradizionalismo acritico, contesti', *Annali della Scuola normale di Pisa* 5.1: 217–84.

Assmann 1992: Jan Assmann, *Das kulturelle Gedächtnis: Schrift, Erinnerung, und politische Identität in frühen Hochkulturen*. München: C.H. Beck.

Astin 1978: Alan E. Astin, *Cato the Censor*. Oxford: Clarendon Press.

Azzarello 2008: Giuseppina Azzarello, 'Sprecherhinweise in homerischen Papyri', in Sandra Lippert and Maren Schentuleit (eds), *Graeco-Roman Fayum—Texts and Archaeology* (Wiesbaden: Harrassowitz): 27–44.

Baldwin 1992: Barry Baldwin, 'Greek in Cicero's Letters', *Acta Classica* 35: 1–17.

Bandy 1992: Anastasius C. Bandy, *Ioannes Lydus: On Powers or The Magistracies of the Roman State*. Philadelphia: American Philosophical Society.

Barchiesi 1997: Alessandro Barchiesi, *The Poet and the Prince: Ovid and Augustan Discourse*. Berkeley and Los Angeles: University of California Press.

Bardon 1952: Henry Bardon, *La literature latine inconnue I: L'époque républicaine*. Paris: Klincksieck.

Battaglia and Emiliozzi 1979: Gabriella Bordenache Battaglia and Adriana Emiliozzi, *Le ciste prenestine*, I Corpus: 1.1. Rome: Consiglio nazionale delle ricerche.

Battaglia and Emiliozzi 1990: Gabriella Bordenache Battaglia and Adriana Emiliozzi, *Le ciste prenestine*, I Corpus: 1.2. Rome: Consiglio nazionale delle ricerche.

Baumbach and Bär 2012: Manuel Baumbach and Silvio Bär (eds), *Brill's Companion to Greek and Latin Epyllion and its Reception*. Leiden: Brill.

Beacham 2007: Richard C. Beacham, 'Playing Places: The Temporary and the Permanent', in Marianne McDonald and J. Michael Walton (eds), *The Cambridge Companion to Greek and Roman Theatre* (Cambridge: Cambridge University Press): 202–26.

Beacham and Denard 2023: Richard C. Beacham and Hugh Denard, *Living Theatre in the Ancient Roman House: Theatricalism in the Domestic Sphere*. Cambridge: Cambridge University Press.

Beard 2008: Mary Beard, *Pompeii: The Life of a Roman Town*. London: Profile Books.

Beard 2013: Mary Beard, *Confronting the Classics: Traditions, Adventures and Innovations*. London: Profile Books.

Beazley 1947: J. D. Beazley, *Etruscan Vase-Painting*. Oxford: Clarendon Press.

Beazley 1949: J. D. Beazley, 'The World of the Etruscan Mirror', *Journal of Hellenic Studies* 69: 1–17.

Benoist 2012: Stéphane Benoist, 'Fergus Millar, un historien dans la cité', in Stéphane Benoist (ed.), *Rome, A City and Its Empire in Perspective / Rome, une cité impériale en jeu* (Leiden: Brill): 1–17.

Bernabò Brea 2001: Luigi Bernabò Brea, *Maschere e personaggi del teatro Greco nelle terracotte liparesi* (Bibliotheca archeologica 32). Rome: L'Erma di Bretschneider.

Bernstein 1998: Frank Bernstein, *Ludi publici: Untersuchungen zur Entstehung und Entwicklung der öffentlichen Spiele im republikanischen Rom* (Historia Einzelschriften 119). Stuttgart: Franz Steiner.

Bernstein 2007: Frank Bernstein, 'Complex Rituals: Games and Processions in Republican Rome', in Jörg Rüpke (ed.), *A Companion to Roman Religion* (Malden MA and Oxford: Blackwell): 222–34.

Biffi 1988: Nicola Biffi, *L'Italia di Strabone: Testo, traduzione e commento dei libri V e VI della Geografia*. Genoa: D.AR.FI.CL.ET.

Blakeway 1935: Alan Blakeway, '"Demaratus"', *Journal of Roman Studies* 25: 129–49.

Blennow 2019: Anna Blennow, 'Instability and Permanence in Ceremonial Epigraphy: The Example of Anna Perenna', in McIntyre and McCallum 2019: 94–110.

Bonaria 1965: Marius Bonaria (ed.), *Romani mimi*. Rome: Edizioni dell'Ateneo.

Bosher 2012: Kathryn Bosher (ed.), *Theater Outside Athens: Drama in Greek Sicily and South Italy*. Cambridge: Cambridge University Press.

Boyle 2008: A. J. Boyle (ed.), *Octavia: Attributed to Seneca*. Oxford: Oxford University Press.

Bradley 2020: Guy Bradley, *Early Rome to 290 BC: The Beginnings of the City and the Rise of the Republic*. Edinburgh: Edinburgh University Press.

Bringmann and Wiegandt 2008: Klaus Bringmann and Dirk Wiegandt (eds), *Augustus: Schriften, Reden und Aussprüche* (Texte zur Forschung 91). Darmstadt: Wissenschaftliche Buchgesellschaft.

Brink 1963: C. O. Brink, *Horace on Poetry: Prolegomena to the Literary Epistles*. Cambridge: Cambridge University Press.

Briscoe 2013: J(ohn) B(riscoe), 'L. Cassius Hemina', in T. J. Cornell (ed.), *The Fragments of the Roman Historians*, vol. 3. (Oxford: Oxford University Press): 160–84.

Brommer 1978: Frank Brommer, *Hephaistos: Der Schmiedegott in der antiken Kunst*. Mainz: von Zabern.

Broughton 1952: T. Robert S. Broughton, *The Magistrates of the Roman Republic*, vol. 2. New York: American Philological Association.

Brugnoli 1995: Giorgio Brugnoli (ed.), *Curiosissimus Excerptor: Gli "Additamenta" di Girolamo ai "Chronica" di Eusebio* (Testi e studi di cultura classica 12). Pisa: Edizioni ETS.

Buchholz 1897: A. Buchholz, 'Über die Abhandlung des *De poematibus* des Diomedes', *Neue Jahrbücher für Philologie und Pädagogik* 155: 127–44.

Buecheler 1882: Franciscus Buecheler, 'Coniectanea', *Rheinisches Museum* 37: 321–42.

Bundrick 2019: Sheramy D. Bundrick, *Athens, Etruria, and the Many Lives of Greek Figured Pottery*. Madison: Wisconsin University Press.

Caldelli 2012: Maria Letizia Caldelli, 'Associazioni di artisti a Roma: una messa a punto', in Kathleen Coleman and Jocelyne Nelis-Clément (eds), *L'organisation des spectacles dans le monde romain* (Entretiens 58, Vandoeuvres-Genève: Fondation Hardt): 131–71.

Cambitoglou and Paspalas 1994: Alexander Cambitoglou and Stavros A. Paspalas, 'Kyknos I', *Lexicon Iconographicum Mythologiae Classicae* 7.1: 970–91.

Cameron 1980: Alan Cameron, 'Poetae Novelli', *Harvard Studies in Classical Philology* 84: 127–75.

Cameron 1995: Alan Cameron, *Callimachus and his Critics*. Princeton: Princeton University Press.

Cameron 2004: Alan Cameron, 'Vergil Illustrated between Pagans and Christians', *Journal of Roman Archaeology* 17: 502–25.

Cameron 2011: Alan Cameron, *The Last Pagans of Rome*. New York: Oxford University Press.

Carandini and Cappelli 2000: Andrea Carandini and Rosanna Capelli (eds), *Roma: Romolo, Remo e la fondazione della città*. Milan: Electa.

Carandini and Carafa 2017: Andrea Carandini with Paolo Carafa, *The Atlas of Ancent Rome: Biography and Portraits of the City*. Princeton: Princeton University Press.

Carpenter 2007: Thomas H. Carpenter, 'Introduction', in Eric Csapo and Margaret C. Miller (eds), *The Origins of Theater in Ancient Greece and Beyond: From Ritual to Drama* (New York: Cambridge University Press): 41–7.

Champlin 2003a: Edward Champlin, 'Agamemnon at Rome: Roman Dynasts and Greek Heroes', in David Braund and Christopher Gill (eds), *Myth, History and Culture in Republican Rome* (Exeter: University of Exeter Press): 295–319.

Champlin 2003b: Edward Champlin, *Nero*. Cambridge MA: Harvard University Press.

Champlin 2005: Edward Champlin, 'Phaedrus the Fabulous', *Journal of Roman Studies* 95: 97–123.

Coarelli 1983: Filippo Coarelli, *Il Foro Romano: periodo archaico*. Rome: Quasar.

Coarelli 1988: Filippo Coarelli, *Il Foro Boario dalle origini alla fine della repubblica*. Rome: Quasar.

Coarelli 1997: Filippo Coarelli, *Il Campo Marzio dalle origini alla fine della repubblica*. Rome: Quasar.

Coarelli 2001: Filippo Coarelli, 'Il sepolcro e la casa di Servio Tullio', *Eutopia* 1.1–2: 7–43.

Coarelli 2011: Filippo Coarelli, *Le origini di Roma: la cultura artistica dalle origini al III secolo a.C.* Milan: Jaca Book.

Coarelli 2013: Filippo Coarelli, Argentum signatum*: Le origini della moneta d'argento a Roma* (Studi e materiali 15). Rome: Istituto Italiano di Numismatica.

Coarelli 2016: Filippo Coarelli, *Pergamo e il re: Forma e funzioni di una capitale ellenistica* (Studi Ellenistici Supp. 3). Pisa: Fabrizio Serra.

Coarelli 2019: Filippo Coarelli, *Statio: I luoghi dell'ammistrazione nell'antica Roma*. Rome: Quasar.

Coffey 1976: Michael Coffey, *Roman Satire*. London: Methuen.

Connolly 2014: Joy Connolly, *The Life of Roman Republicanism*. Princeton: Princeton University Press.

Cornell 1995: T. J. Cornell, *The Beginnings of Rome: Italy and Rome from the Bronze Age to the Punic Wars (c.1000–264 BC)*. London: Routledge.

Cornell 2014: Timothy Cornell, 'Livy's Narrative of the Regal Period and Historical and Archaeological Facts', in Bernard Mineo (ed.), *A Companion to Livy* (Chichester: Wiley Blackwell): 245–58.

Courtney 1993: Edward Courtney (ed.), *The Fragmentary Latin Poets*. Oxford: Clarendon Press.

Crawford 1974: Michael H. Crawford, *Roman Republican Coinage*. Cambridge: Cambridge University Press.

Crawford 1996: M. H. Crawford (ed.), *Roman Statutes* (BICS Supplement 64), 2 vols. London: Institute of Classical Studies.

Cristofani 1990: Mauro Cristofani (ed.), *La grande Roma dei Tarquinii: catalogo della mostra*. Rome: L'Erma di Bretschneider.

Csapo and Wilson 2020: Eric Csapo and Peter Wilson, *A Social and Economic History of the Theatre to 300 BC*, vol. 2: *Theatre beyond Athens: Documents with Translation and Commentary*. Cambridge: Cambridge University Press.

Čulík-Baird 2022: Hannah Čulík-Baird, *Cicero and the Early Latin Poets*. Cambridge: Cambridge University Press.

Damiani and Parisi Presicce 2019: Isabella Damiani and Claudio Parisi Presicce (eds), *La Roma dei Re: Il racconto dell'archeologia*. Rome: Gangemi.

Davies and Finglass 2014: M. Davies and P.J. Finglass (eds), *Stesichorus: The Poems* (Cambridge Classical Texts and Commentaries 54). Cambridge: Cambridge University Press.

Dearden 1995: C. W. Dearden, 'Pots, Tumblers and Phlyax Vases', in Alan Griffiths (ed.), *Stage Directions: Essays in Ancient Drama in Honour of E.W. Handley* (BICS Supplement 66, London: Institute of Classical Studies): 81–7.

Dearden 2004: Chris Dearden, 'Sicily and Rome: The Greek Context for Roman Drama', *Mediterranean Archaeology* 17: 121–30.

Degrassi 1947: Atilius Degrassi (ed.), *Inscriptiones Italiae*, vol. 13 *Fasti et elogia*, fasc. 1 *Fasti consulares et triumphales*. Rome: Libreria dello stato.

Degrassi 1963: Atilius Degrassi (ed.), *Inscriptiones Italiae*, vol. 13 *Fasti et elogia*, fasc. 2 *Fasti anni Numani et Iuliani*. Rome: Istituto poligrafico dello stato.

Delz 1987: Iosephus Delz (ed.), *Sili Italici Punica*. Stuttgart: Teubner.

De Melo 2019: Wolfgang David Cirilo de Melo, *Varro: De lingua Latina: Introduction, Text, Translation, and Commentary*. Oxford: Oxford University Press.

De Spirito 1999: G. De Spirito, 'Tellus, templum (in fonti agiografiche)', in Eva Margareta Steinby (ed.), *Lexicon Topographicum Urbis Romae*, vol. 5: T–Z (Rome: Quasar): 25–6.

Dorcey 1992: Peter F. Dorcey, *The Cult of Silvanus: A Study in Roman Folk Religion* (Columbia Studies in the Classical Tradition 20). Leiden: Brill.

Dover 1968: K. J. Dover (ed.), *Aristophanes Clouds*. Oxford: Clarendon Press.

Drummond 2013: A(ndrew) D(rummond), 'C. Asinius Pollio', in T. J. Cornell (ed.), *The Fragments of the Roman Historians*, vol. 1. (Oxford: Oxford University Press): 430–45.

Dubuisson 1992: Michel Dubuisson, 'Le grec à Rome à l'époque de Cicéron', *Annales E.S.C.* 47: 187–206.

Duff and Duff 1934: J. Wight Duff and Arnold J. Duff (eds), *Minor Latin Poets* (Loeb Classical Library 284). Cambridge MA: Harvard University Press.

Dyck 2004: Andrew R. Dyck, *A Commentary on Cicero,* De Legibus. Ann Arbor: University of Michigan Press.

Eden 1984: P. T. Eden (ed.), *Seneca Apocolocyntosis* (Cambridge Greek and Latin Classics). Cambridge: Cambridge University Press.

Emiliozzi and Maggiani 2002: Adriana Emiliozzi and Adriano Maggiani (eds), *Caelatores: incisori di specchi e ciste tra Lazio ed Etruria* (Quaderni di archeologia etrusco-italica 27). Rome: Consiglio Nazionale delle Ricerche.

Fedeli 2024: Giacomo Fedeli, 'Ancient Histories of Satire(s): Horace as an Appropriator, Innovator and Source', in Giacomo Fedeli and Henry Spelman (eds), *Writing Literary History in the Greek and Roman World* (Cambridge: Cambridge University Press): 62–84.

Feeney 2016: Denis Feeney, *Beyond Greek: The Beginnings of Latin Literature*. Cambridge MA: Harvard University Press.

Feeney 2017: Denis Feeney, review of Wiseman 2015, *Gnomon* 89: 412–18.

Ferri 2003: Rolando Ferri (ed.), *Octavia: A Play Attributed to Seneca* (Cambridge Classical Texts and Commentaries 41). Cambridge: Cambridge University Press.

Ferriss-Hill 2022: Jennifer Ferriss-Hill, *Roman Satire*. Leiden and Boston: Brill.

Flower 1995: Harriet I. Flower, '*Fabulae Praetextae* in Context: When Were Plays on Contemporary Subjects Performed in Republican Rome?', *Classical Quarterly* 45: 170–190.

Flower 1996: Harriet I. Flower, *Ancestor Masks and Aristocratic Power in Roman Culture*. Oxford: Clarendon Press.

Forsythe 2005: Gary Forsythe, *A Critical History of Early Rome: From Prehistory to the First Punic War*. Berkeley and Los Angeles: University of California Press.

Fortini 2021: Patrizia Fortini, 'Gli scavi al Foro Romano e il Museo', in Alfonsina Russo, Roberta Alteri and Andrea Paribeni (eds), *Giacomo Boni: L'Alba della Modernità* (Verona: Electa): 46–59.

Frassinetti 1967: Paolo Frassinetti (ed.), *Atellanae fabulae*. Rome: Ateneo.

Fulkerson and Tatum 2024: Laurel Fulkerson and Jeffrey Tatum, *A History of Latin Literature from its Beginnings to the Age of Augustus*. Cambridge: Cambridge University Press.

Funaioli 1907: Hyginus Funaioli (ed.), *Grammaticae Romanae fragmenta*. Leipzig: Teubner.

Funaioli 1932: G. Funaioli, 'C. Suetonius Tranquillus', *Paulys Real-Encyclopädie* 4A: 593–641.

Gantz 1993: Timothy Gantz, *Early Greek Myth: a Guide to Literary and Artistic Sources*. Baltimore MD: Johns Hopkins University Press.

Garelli 2007: Marie-Hélène Garelli, *Danser le mythe: la pantomime et sa reception dans la culture antique* (Bibliothèque d'Études Classiques 51). Louvain: Peeters.

Geue 2019: Tom Geue, *Author Unknown: The Power of Anonymity in Ancient Rome*. Cambridge MA: Harvard University Press.

Giacchero 1974: Marta Giacchero (ed.), *Edictum Diocletiani et collegarum de pretiis rerum venalium* (Pubblicazioni dell'Istituto di storia antica e scienze ausiliarie dell'Università di Genova 8). Genova: Istituto di storia antica.

Giancotti 1967: Francesco Giancotti, *Mimo e gnome: studio su Decimo Laberio e Publilio Siro* (Biblioteca di cultura contemporanea 98). Messina: G. D'Anna.

Goldberg 1995: Sander M. Goldberg, *Epic in Republican Rome*. New York: Oxford University Press.

Goldberg 1998: Sander M. Goldberg, 'Plautus on the Palatine', *Journal of Roman Studies* 88: 1–20.

Goldberg 2005: Sander M. Goldberg, *Constructing Literature in the Roman Republic: Poetry and its Reception*. New York: Cambridge University Press.

Goldberg 2011: Sander M. Goldberg, 'Roman Comedy Gets Back to Basics', *Journal of Roman Studies* 101: 206–21.

Goldberg and Manuwald 2018: Sander M. Goldberg and Gesine Manuwald (eds), *Fragmentary Republican Latin II: Ennius: Dramatic Fragments, Minor Works* (Loeb Classical Library 537). Cambridge MA: Harvard University Press.

Goodyear 1965: F.R.D. Goodyear, *Incerti auctoris* Aetna (Cambridge Classical Texts and Commentaries 2). Cambridge: Cambridge University Press.

Goold 1956: G. P. Goold, 'Observationes in codicem Matritensem M.31: De Silii et Statii Silvarum scripta memoria', *Rheinisches Museum* 99: 9–17.

Gordon 1983: Arthur E. Gordon, *Illustrated Introduction to Latin Epigraphy*. Berkeley and Los Angeles: University of California Press.

Gow and Page 1965: A.S.F. Gow and D. L. Page (eds), *The Greek Anthology: Hellenistic Epigrams*. Cambridge: Cambridge University Press.

Gowers 2012: Emily Gowers (ed.), *Horace Satires Book I* (Cambridge Greek and Latin Classics). Cambridge: Cambridge University Press.

Graf 2015: Fritz Graf, *Roman Festivals in the Greek East from the Early Empire to the Middle Byzantine Era*. Cambridge: Cambridge University Press.

Grandazzi 2008: Alexandre Grandazzi, *Alba Longa: Histoire d'une légende* (BEFAR 336). Rome: École française de Rome.

Gratwick 1982: A. S. Gratwick, 'The Satires of Ennius and Lucilius', in E.J. Kenney (ed.), *The Cambridge History of Classical Literature II.1: The Early Republic* (Cambridge University Press): 156–71.

Green 1994: J. R. Green, *Theatre in Ancient Greek Society*. London: Routledge.

Green 1995: J. R. Green, 'Theatrical Motifs in Non-Theatrical Contexts on Vases of the Later Fifth and Fourth Centuries', in Alan Griffiths (ed.), *Stage Directions: Essays in Ancient Drama in Honour of E.W. Handley* (BICS Supplement 66, London: Institute of Classical Studies): 93–121.

Griffith 2007: Mark Griffith, '"Telling the Tale": A Performing Tradition from Homer to Pantomime', in Marianne McDonald and J. Michael Walton (eds), *The Cambridge Companion to Greek and Roman Theatre* (Cambridge: Cambridge University Press): 13–35.

Griffith 2008: Mark Griffith, 'Greek Middlebrow Drama (Something to do with Aphrodite?)', in Martin Revermann and Peter Wilson (eds), *Performance, Iconography, Reception: Studies in Honour of Oliver Taplin* (Oxford: Oxford University Press): 59–87.

Guardí 1984: Tommaso Guardí (ed.), *Titinio e Atta: Fabula togata: I frammenti*. Milan: Jaca Book.

Guthrie 1962: W.K.C. Guthrie, *The History of Greek Philosophy*, vol. 1: *The Earlier Presocratics and the Pythagoreans*. Cambridge: Cambridge University Press.

Hall and Wyles 2008: Edith Hall and Rosie Wyles (eds), *New Directions in Ancient Pantomime*. Oxford: Oxford University Press.

Hanson 1959: John A. Hanson, *Roman Theater-Temples* (Princeton Monographs in Art and Archaeology 33). Princeton: Princeton University Press.

Harper 2017: Kyle Harper, *The Fate of Rome: Climate, Disease, and the End of an Empire*. Princeton: Princeton University Press.

Harris 1971: W. V. Harris, *Rome in Etruria and Umbria*. Oxford: Clarendon Press.

Harris 1989: William V. Harris, *Ancient Literacy*. Cambridge MA: Harvard University Press.

Hart 2010: Mary Louise Hart, *The Art of Greek Theatre*. Los Angeles: J. Paul Getty Museum.

Heitland 1896: W. E. Heitland, 'The "Great Lacuna" in the Eighth Book of Silius Italicus', *Journal of Philology* 24: 188–211.

Henderson 2001: John Henderson, *Telling Tales on Caesar: Roman Stories from Phaedrus*. Oxford: Oxford University Press.

Herington 1967: C. J. Herington, 'Aeschylus in Sicily', *Journal of Hellenic Studies* 87: 74-85.

Herington 1985: John Herington, *Poetry into Drama: Early Tragedy and the Greek Poetic Tradition* (Sather Classical Lectures 49). Berkeley and Los Angeles: University of California Press.

Heslin 2015: Peter Heslin, *The Museum of Augustus: The Temple of Apollo in Pompeii, the Portico of Philippus in Rome, and Latin Poetry*. Los Angeles: J. Paul Getty Museum.

Heurgon 1953: Jacques Heurgon, 'Tarquitius Priscus et l'organisation de l'ordre des haruspices sous l'empereur Claude', *Latomus* 12: 402–17.

Heyworth 2019: S. J. Heyworth (ed.), *Ovid Fasti Book III* (Cambridge Greek and Latin Classics). Cambridge: Cambridge University Press.

Hölkeskamp 2004: Karl-J. Hölkeskamp, *Rekonstruktionen einer Republik: Die politische Kultur des antiken Rom und die Forschung der letzten Jahrzehnten* (Historische Zeitschrift Beiheft 38). München: Oldenbourg.

Hölkeskamp 2006: Karl-J. Hölkeskamp, 'History and Collective Memory in the Middle Republic', in Nathan Rosenstein and Robert Morstein-Marx (eds), *A Companion to the Roman Republic* (Malden MA and Oxford: Blackwell): 478–95.

Hölkeskamp 2010: Karl-J. Hölkeskamp, *Reconstructing the Roman Republic: An Ancient Political Culture and Modern Research*. Princeton: Princeton University Press.

Hölkeskamp 2014: Karl-J. Hölkeskamp, 'In Defense of Concepts, Categories and Other Abstractions: Remarks on a Theory of Memory (in the making)', in Karl Galinsky (ed.), *Memoria Romana: Memory in Rome and Rome in Memory* (MAAR Supplement 10, Ann Arbor: University of Michigan Press): 63–70.

Hollis 1990: A. S. Hollis, *Callimachus:* Hecale. Oxford: Clarendon Press.

Hollis 2007: Adrian S. Hollis, *Fragments of Roman Poetry c.60 BC—AD 20*. Oxford: Oxford University Press.

Hölscher 1988: Tonio Hölscher, 'Historische Reliefs', in *Kaiser Augustus und die verlorene Republik* (Mainz: von Zabern): 351–400.

Hooker 2017: Mischa Hooker, *John Lydus: On the months (De mensibus)*, second edition. N.p.: opensource [John-Lydus-On-the-Months-tr.-Hooker-2nd-ed.-2017-1].

Hopkins 2016: John North Hopkins, *The Genesis of Roman Architecture*. New Haven and London: Yale University Press.

Hopkins 2017: Keith Hopkins, *Sociological Studies in Roman History*. Cambridge: Cambridge University Press.

Hopkins 2022: John North Hopkins, 'Engagements in and beyond Rome in the 5th c. BCE: Architectural remains as evidence for action across geo-temporal boundaries', *Journal of Roman Archaeology* 35: 655–83.

Hornblower 2015: Simon Hornblower, *Lycophron Alexandra: Greek Text, Translation, Commentary, and Introduction*. Oxford: Oxford University Press.

Horsfall 1979: Nicholas Horsfall, '*Doctus sermones utriusque linguae?*', *Echos du monde classique/ Classical News and Views* 23.3: 79–95.

Horsfall 1985: Nicholas Horsfall, 'CIL VI 37965 = CLE 1988 (Epitaph of Allia Potestas): a commentary', *Zeitschrift für Papyrologie und Epigraphik* 61: 251–72.

Houston 2014: George W. Houston, *Inside Roman Libraries: Book Collections and their Management in Antiquity*. Chapel Hill: University of North Carolina Press.

Hughes 1997: Alan Hughes, 'KONNAKIS: A Scene from the Comic Theatre', *Echos du monde classique* 41: 237–46.

Hurlet 2012: 'Démocratie à Rome? Quelle démocratie? En relisant Millar (et Hölkeskamp)', in Stéphane Benoist (ed.), *Rome, A City and Its Empire in Perspective / Rome, une cité impériale en jeu* (Leiden: Brill): 1–17.

Hutchinson 1998: G. O. Hutchinson, *Cicero's Correspondence: A Literary Study*. Oxford: Clarendon Press.

Jahn 1854: Otto Jahn, 'Vermischtes', *Rheinisches Museum* 9: 625–30.

Janko 1984: Richard Janko, *Aristotle on Comedy: Towards a Reconstruction of* Poetics *II*. London: Duckworth.

Jocelyn 1969: H. D. Jocelyn (ed.), *The Tragedies of Ennius* (Cambridge Classical Texts and Commentaries 10). Cambridge: Cambridge University Press.

Jocelyn 1973: H. D. Jocelyn, 'Greek Poetry in Cicero's Prose Writing', *Yale Classical Studies* 23: 61–111.

Jones 1986: C. P. Jones, *Culture and Society in Lucian*. Cambridge MA: Harvard University Press.

Jory 1981: E. J. Jory, 'The Literary Evidence for the Beginnings of Imperial Pantomime', *Bulletin of the Institute of Classical Studies* 28: 157–61.

Jory 2004: E. J. Jory, 'Pylades, Pantomime, and the Preservation of Tragedy', *Mediterranean Archaeology* 17: 147–56.

Kaibel 1899: Georgius Kaibel (ed.), *Comicorum Graecorum fragmenta* 1.1: *Doriensium comoedia mimi phlyaces*. Berlin: Weidmann.

Kassel and Austin 2001: R. Kassel and C. Austin (eds), *Poetae comici Graeci (PCG)*, vol. 1: *Comoedia Dorica mimi phlyaces*. Berlin and New York: De Gruyter.

Kaster 1988: Robert A. Kaster, *Guardians of Language: The Grammarian and Society in Late Antiquity*. Berkeley and Los Angeles: University of California Press.

Kaster 1995: Robert A. Kaster, *C. Suetonius Tranquillus: De Grammaticis et Rhetoribus*. Oxford: Clarendon Press.

Keaveney 2003: Arthur Keaveney, 'The Tragedy of Gaius Gracchus: Ancient Melodrama or Modern Farce?', *Klio* 85: 322–32.

Keaveney 2006: Arthur Keaveney, 'Livy and the Theatre: Reflections on the Theory of Peter Wiseman', *Klio* 88: 510–15.

Keil 1857: Heinrich Keil (ed.), *Grammatici Latini*, vol. 1. Leipzig: Teubner.

Koch 1975: Guntram Koch, *Die mythologischen Sarkophage 6: Meleager*. Berlin: Mann.

Koett 1904: Engelbert Koett, *De Diomedis artis poeticae fontibus*. Jena: Nevenhahn.

Kowalzig 2008: Barbara Kowalzig, 'Nothing to Do with Demeter? Something to Do with Sicily! Theatre and Society in the Early Fifth-Century West', in Martin Revermann and Peter Wilson (eds), *Performance, Iconography, Reception: Studies in Honour of Oliver Taplin* (Oxford: Oxford University Press): 128–57.

Kragelund 2016: Patrick Kragelund, *Roman Historical Drama: The* Octavia *in Antiquity and Beyond*. Oxford: Oxford University Press.

Kraus 1994: Christina Shuttleworth Kraus (ed.), *Livy Ab Urbe Condita Book VI* (Cambridge Greek and Latin Classics). Cambridge: Cambridge University Press.

Lada-Richards 2007: Ismene Lada-Richards, *Silent Eloquence: Lucian and Pantomime Dancing*. London: Duckworth.

Lada-Richards 2008: Ismene Lada-Richards, 'Was Pantomime "good to think with" in the Ancient World?', in Hall and Wyles 2008: 285–313.

Lanciani 1990: Rodolfo Lanciani, *Forma Urbis Romae*. Rome: Quasar.

Lane 2014: Melissa Lane, *Greek and Roman Political Ideas: A Pelican Introduction*. London: Pelican Books.

La Rocca 2020: Eugenio La Rocca, 'Il linguaggio artistico di Roma e del Lazio in età medio repubblicana: la ricezione dell'arte greca e la formazione della *koiné* italiana', in Alessandro D'Alessio, Mirella Serlorenzi, Christopher J. Smith and Rita Volpe (eds), *Roma medio repubblicana dalla conquista di Veio alla battaglia di Zama* (Rome: Quasar): 357–410.

Lebek 1990: Wolfgang Dieter Lebek, 'Standeswürde und Berufsverbot unter Tiberius: Das SC der Tabula Larinas', *Zeitschrift für Papyrologie und Epigraphik* 81: 37–96.

Levene 1993: D. S. Levene, *Religion in Livy* (Mnemosyne Supplement 127). Leiden: Brill.

Levick 2010: Barbara Levick, *Augustus: Image and Substance*. Harlow: Longman.

Lewis 1855: Sir George Cornewall Lewis, *An Inquiry into the Credibility of the Early Roman History*. London: Parker and Son.

Lintott 1999: Andrew Lintott, *The Constitution of the Roman Republic*. Oxford: Clarendon Press.

Littlewood 2006: R. Joy Littlewood (ed.), *A Commentary on Ovid's* Fasti, *Book VI*. Oxford: Oxford University Press.

Lloyd-Jones 1990: Hugh Lloyd-Jones, 'Erinyes, Semnai Theai, Eumenides', in E. M. Craik (ed.), *'Owls to Athens': Essays on Classical Subjects Presented to Sir Kenneth Dover* (Oxford: Clarendon Press): 203–11.

Lott 2004: J. Bert Lott, *The Neighbourhoods of Augustan Rome*. Cambridge: Cambridge University Press.

Luce 1965: T. J. Luce, 'The Dating of Livy's First Decade', *Transactions of the American Philological Association* 96: 209–40.

Lulof 2000: Patricia S. Lulof, 'Archaic terracotta acroteria representing Athena and Heracles: manifestations of power in central Italy', *Journal of Roman Archaeology* 13: 207–19.

Maas 1992: Michael Maas, *John Lydus and the Roman Past: Antiquarianism and Politics in the Age of Justinian*. London: Routledge.

Manacorda and Tamassia 1985: Daniele Manacorda and Renato Tamassia, *Il piccone del regime*. Rome: Armando Curcio.

Manuwald 2001: Gesine Manuwald, *Fabulae praetextae: Spuren einer literarischen Gattung der Römer* (Zetemata 108). Munich: C.H. Beck.

Manuwald 2011: Gesine Manuwald, *Roman Republican Theatre*. Cambridge: Cambridge University Press.

Marconi 2006: Clemente Marconi, 'I *Theōroi* di Eschilo e le antefisse sileniche siceliote', *Sicilia Antiqua* 2, 75–93.

Marshall 2006: C. W. Marshall, *The Stagecraft and Performance of Roman Comedy*. Cambridge: Cambridge University Press.

Martelli 1987: Marina Martelli, *La ceramica degli Etruschi*. Novara: De Agostini.

Mason 1974: Hugh J. Mason, *Greek Terms for Roman Institutions: A Lexicon and Analysis* (American Studies in Papyrology 13). Toronto: Hakkert.

Mastandrea 1979: Paolo Mastandrea, *Un neoplatonico latino: Cornelio Labeone* (EPRO 77). Leiden: Brill.

McIntyre and McCallum 2019: Gwynaeth McIntyre and Sarah McCallum (eds), *Uncovering Anna Perenna: A Focused Study of Roman Myth and Culture*. London: Bloomsbury.

McLynn 2008: Neil McLynn, 'Crying Wolf: The Pope and the Lupercalia', *Journal of Roman Studies* 98: 161–75.

Meiser 1887: Karl Meiser, *Ueber historische Dramen der Römer*. Munich: Verlag der k. b. Akademie.

Menichetti 1995: Mauro Menichetti, *Quoius forma virtutei parisuma fuit . . . Ciste prenestine e cultura di Roma medio-repubblicana* (Archeologia Perusina 12), Rome: Giorgio Bretschneider.

Michels 1951: Agnes Kirsopp Michels, 'The Drama of the Tarquins', *Latomus* 10: 13–24.

Michels 1967: Agnes Kirsopp Michels, *The Calendar of the Roman Republic*. Princeton: Princeton University Press.

Millar 1973: Fergus Millar, 'Triumvirate and Principate', *Journal of Roman Studies* 63: 50–67.

Millar 1998: Fergus Millar, *The Crowd in Rome in the Late Republic* (Jerome Lectures 22). Ann Arbor: University of Michigan Press.

Moles 1993: J. L. Moles, 'Truth and Untruth in Herodotus and Thucydides', in Christopher Gill and T. P. Wiseman (eds), *Lies and Fiction in the Ancient World* (Exeter: University of Exeter Press): 88–121.

Moore 1991: Timothy J. Moore, '*Palliata togata*: Plautus, *Curculio* 462–86', *American Journal of Philology* 112: 343–62.

Morgan 1993: J.R. Morgan, 'Make-believe and Make Believe: The Fictionality of the Greek Novels', in Christopher Gill and T. P. Wiseman (eds), *Lies and Fiction in the Ancient World* (Exeter: University of Exeter Press): 175–229.

Mouritsen 2001: Henrik Mouritsen, Plebs *and Politics in the Late Roman Republic.* Cambridge: Cambridge University Press.

Mouritsen 2017: Henrik Mouritsen, *Politics in the Roman Republic.* Cambridge: Cambridge University Press.

Murgatroyd 2005: Paul Murgatroyd, *Mythical and Legendary Narrative in Ovid's* Fasti (Mnemosyne Supplement 263). Leiden: Brill.

Noguera, Valdés and Ble 2022: Jaume Noguera, Pau Valdés and Eduard Ble, 'New Perspectives on the Sertorian War in Northeastern Hispania: Archaeological Surveys of the Roman Camps of the Lower River Ebro', *Journal of Roman Archaeology* 35: 1–32.

Nora 1984: Pierre Nora (ed.), *Les lieux de mémoire*, vol. 1. Paris: Gallimard.

Nora 1996: Pierre Nora (ed.), *Realms of Memory: Rethinking the French Past*, vol. 1. New York: Columbia University Press.

North 1992: J. A. North, 'Deconstructing Stone Theatres', in *Apodosis: Essays presented to Dr. W.W. Cruickshank to mark his Eightieth Birthday* (London, St Paul's School): 75–83.

North 2008: J. A. North, 'Caesar at the Lupercalia', *Journal of Roman Studies* 98: 144–60.

North and McLynn 2008: J. A. North and Neil McLynn, 'Postscript to the Lupercalia: from Caesar to Andromachus', *Journal of Roman Studies* 98: 176–81.

Nünlist 2009: René Nünlist, *The Ancient Critic at Work: Terms and Concepts of Literary Criticism in Greek Scholia.* Cambridge: Cambridge University Press.

Oakley 1997: S. P. Oakley, *A Commentary on Livy Books VI–X*, vol. 1. Oxford: Clarendon Press.

Oakley 1998: S. P. Oakley, *A Commentary on Livy Books VI–X*, vol. 2. Oxford: Clarendon Press.

Ogden 2001: Daniel Ogden, *Greek and Roman Necromancy.* Princeton: Princeton University Press.

Ogilvie 1965: R. M. Ogilvie, *A Commentary on Livy Books 1–5.* Oxford: Clarendon Press.

Olson 2007: S. Douglas Olson (ed.), *Broken Laughter: Select Fragments of Greek Comedy.* Oxford: Oxford University Press.

O'Sullivan and Collard 2013: Patrick O'Sullivan and Christopher Collard, *Euripides Cyclops and Major Fragments of Greek Satyric Drama.* Oxford: Aris and Phillips.

Pailler 1988: Jean-Marie Pailler, *Bacchanalia: La répression de 186 av. J.-C. à Rome et en Italie* (BEFAR 270). Rome: École française de Rome.

Pairault Massa 1992: Françoise-Hélène Pairault Massa, *Iconologia e politica nell'Italia antica: Roma, Lazio, Etruria dal VII al I secolo a.C.* (Biblioteca di Archeologia 18). Milan: Longanesi.

Pais 1908: Ettore Pais, *Ancient Italy: Historical and Geographical Investigations in Central Italy, Magna Graecia, Sicily, and Sardinia.* Chicago: University of Chicago Press.

Palombi 1996: D. Palombi, 'Honos et Virtus, aedes Mariana', in Eva Margareta Steinby (ed.), *Lexicon Topographicum Urbis Romae*, vol. 3: H–O (Rome: Quasar): 33–5.

Palombi 1997: Domenico Palombi, *Tra Palatino ed Esquilino: Velia, Carinae, Fagutal* (RINASA Suppl. 1). Rome: Istituto Nazionale d'Archeologia e Storia dell'Arte.

Panayotakis 2010: Costas Panayotakis (ed.), *Decimus Laberius: The Fragments* (Cambridge Classical Texts and Commentaries 46). Cambridge: Cambridge University Press.

Paris, Bruni and Roghi 2014: Rita Paris, Silvia Bruni and Miria Roghi (eds.), *Rivoluzione Augusto: L'imperatore che riscrisse il tempo e la città*. Milan: Electa.

Pearson 1987: Lionel Pearson, *The Greek Historians of the West: Timaeus and his Predecessors* (Philological Monographs of the A.P.A. vol. 35). Atlanta: Scholars Press.

Pelling 1996: Christopher Pelling. 'The Triumviral Period', in Alan K. Bowman, Edward Champlin and Andrew Lintott (eds), *The Cambridge Ancient History*, 2nd edn, vol. 10 (Cambridge: Cambridge University Press): 1–69.

Pfeiffer 1949: Rudolf Pfeiffer, *Callimachus*, vol. 1. Oxford: Clarendon Press.

Pfeiffer 1968: Rudolf Pfeiffer, *History of Classical Scholarship: From the Beginnings to the End of the Hellenistic Age*. Oxford: Clarendon Press.

Pisani Sartorio 1993: G. Pisani Sartorio, 'Compitum Acilium', in Eva Margareta Steinby (ed.), *Lexicon Topographicum Urbis Romae*, vol. 1: A–C (Rome: Quasar): 314–5.

Pittà 2015: Antonino Pittà, *M. Terenzio Varrone,* de vita populi Romani*: Introduzione e commento.* Pisa: Pisa University Press.

Powell 2008: Anton Powell, *Virgil the Partisan: A Study in the Re-integration of Classics*. Swansea: Classical Press of Wales.

Power 2014: Tristan Power, 'Introduction: The Originality of Suetonius', in Tristan Power and Roy K. Gibson (eds), *Suetonius the Biographer: Studies in Roman Lives* (Oxford: Oxford University Press): 1–18.

Rawson 1978: Elizabeth Rawson, 'The Identity Problems of Q. Cornificius', *Classical Quarterly* 28: 188–201.

Rawson 1985: Elizabeth Rawson, 'Theatrical Life in Republican Rome and Italy', *Papers of the British School at Rome* 53: 97–113.

Rawson 1991: Elizabeth Rawson, *Roman Culture and Society: Collected Papers*. Oxford: Clarendon Press.

Reeve 1983: M.D. R(eeve), 'Silius Italicus', in L. D. Reynolds (ed.), *Texts and Transmission: A Survey of the Latin Classics* (Oxford: Clarendon Press): 389–91.

Reifferscheid 1860: August Reifferscheid (ed.), *C. Suetoni Tranquilli praeter Caesarum libros reliquiae*. Leipzig: Teubner.

Reusser 1999: Ch. Reusser, 'Tropaea Marii', in Eva Margareta Steinby (ed.), *Lexicon Topographicum Urbis Romae*, vol. 5: T–Z (Rome: Quasar): 91.

Ribbeck 1875: Otto Ribbeck, *Die römische Tragödie im Zeitalter der Republik*. Leipzig: Teubner.

Ribbeck 1881: Otto Ribbeck, 'Ein historisches Drama', *Rheinisches Museum* 36: 321–2.

Rich 2018: John Rich, 'Fabius Pictor, Ennius, and the Origins of Roman Annalistic Historiography', in Kaj Sandberg and Christopher Smith (eds), *Omnium Annalium Monumenta: Historical Writing and Historical Evidence in Republican Rome* (Leiden: Brill): 17–65.

Richardson 2020: James H. Richardson, *Kings and Consuls: Eight Essays on Roman History, Historiography and Political Thought*. Oxford: Peter Lang.

Ritschl 1857: F. Ritschl, 'Litterarhistorisches', *Rheinisches Museum* 12: 147–54.

Robinson 2004: E.G.D. Robinson, 'Reception of Comic Theatre amongst the Indigenous South Italians', *Mediterranean Archaeology* 17: 193–212.

Robinson 2011: Matthew Robinson, *Ovid* Fasti *Book 2*. Oxford: Oxford University Press.

Rodríguez Almeida 1993: E. Rodríguez Almeida, 'Caeliolus (-um), Caeliculus (-um)', in Eva Margareta Steinby (ed.), *Lexicon Topographicum Urbis Romae*, vol. 1, A–C (Rome: Quasar): 208.

Rose 1921: H. J. Rose, 'The Greek of Cicero', *Journal of Hellenic Studies* 41: 91–116.

Rosen and Farrell 1986: Ralph M. Rosen and Joseph Farrell, 'Acontius, Milanion, and Gallus: Vergil, *Ecl.* 10.52-61', *Transactions of the American Philological Association* 116: 241–54.

Roth 1858: Carolus Ludovicus Roth (ed.), *C. Suetoni Tranquilli quae supersunt omnia*. Leipzig: Teubner.

Rudd 1966: Niall Rudd, *The Satires of Horace*. Cambridge: Cambridge University Press.

Rüpke 2008: Jörg Rüpke, *Fasti sacerdotum: A Prosopography of Pagan, Jewish and Christian Religious Officials in the City of Rome, 300 BC to AD 499*. Oxford: Oxford University Press.

Rüpke 2011: Jörg Rüpke, *The Roman Calendar from Numa to Constantine: Time, History, and the* Fasti. Chichester: Wiley-Blackwell.

Rüpke 2012: Jörg Rüpke, *Religion in Republican Rome: Rationalization and Ritual Change*. Philadelphia: University of Pennsylvania Press.

Russell and Winterbottom 1972: D. A. Russell and M. Winterbottom (eds), *Ancient Literary Criticism: The Principal Texts in New Translations*. Oxford: Clarendon Press.

Sarian 1986: Haiganuch Sarian, 'Erinys', *Lexicon Iconographicum Mythologiae Classicae* 3.1: 825–43.

Sauron 1987: Gilles Sauron, 'Le complexe pompéien du Champ de Mars: nouveauté urbanistique à finalité idéologique', in *L'Urbs: Espace urbain et histoire (Ier siècle av. J.C.—IIIe siècle ap. J.C.)* (Collection de l'École française de Rome 98, Rome: École française de Rome): 457–73.

Schilling 1993: Robert Schilling (ed.), *Ovide: Les Fastes*, vol. 2 (Collection Budé). Paris: Les Belles Lettres.

Schmeling and Setaioli 2011: Gareth Schmeling with Aldo Setaioli, *A Commentary on the* Satyrica *of Petronius*. New York: Oxford University Press.

Schmidt 1997: Eva Maria Schmidt, 'Venus', *Lexicon Iconographicum Mythologiae Classicae* 8.1: 192–230.

Schöne 1893: Alfred Schöne, *Das historische Nationaldrama der Römer: die Fabula praetexta*. Kiel: Universitäts Buchhandlung.

Schumacher 1968–9: Walter N. Schumacher, 'Antikes and Christliches zur Auspeitschung der Elia Afanacia', *Jahrbuch für Antike und Christentum* 11–12: 65–75.

Schwartz 1948: J. Schwartz, 'Sur quelques anecdotes concernant César et Cicéron', *Revue des études anciennes* 50: 264–71.

Schwegler 1853: A. Schwegler, *Römische Geschichte im Zeitalter der Könige*. Tübingen: Laupp.

Sear 2006: Frank Sear, *Roman Theatres: An Architectural Study*. Oxford: Oxford University Press.

Semerényi 1975: O. Semerényi, 'The Origins of Roman Drama and Greek Tragedy', *Hermes* 103: 300–32.

Shackleton Bailey 2000: D. R. Shackleton Bailey (ed.), *Valerius Maximus: Memorable Deeds and Sayings, Books I–V* (Loeb Classical Library 492). Cambridge MA: Harvard University Press.

Shaw 2014: Carl A. Shaw, *Satyric Play: The Evolution of Greek Comedy and Satyr Drama.* Oxford: Oxford University Press.

Simmel 1992: Georg Simmel, *Soziologie: Untersuchungen über die Formen der Vergesellschaftung*, vol. 11. Frankfurt: Duncker & Humblot.

Skutsch 1985: Otto Skutsch, *The* Annals *of Quintus Ennius.* Oxford: Clarendon Press.

Slater 2010: William Slater, 'Sorting out Pantomime (and Mime) from Top to Bottom', *Journal of Roman Archaeology* 23: 533–41.

Solin 1983: Heikki Solin, 'Varia onomastica: V. Κλεῖκλος', *Zeitschrift für Papyrologie und Epigraphik* 51: 180–2.

Soltau 1909: Wilhelm Soltau, *Die Anfänge der Roemischen Geschichtsschreibung.* Leipzig: H. Haessel.

Steele 1900: R. B. Steele, 'The Greek in Cicero's Epistles', *American Journal of Philology*: 387–410.

Stern 1968: Henri Stern, 'Un calendrier romain illustré de Thysdrus (Tunisie)', in *Tardo Antico e Alto Medioevo: La forma artistica nel passaggio dall'antichità al medioevo* (Rome: Accademia dei Lincei): 177–200.

Stothard 2010: Peter Stothard, *The Last Assassin: The Hunt for the Killers of Julius Caesar*. London: Weidenfeld and Nicolson.

Sutherland 1984: C.H.V. Sutherland, *The Roman Imperial Coinage*, 2nd edn, vol. 1. London: Spink.

Swoboda 1889: Antonius Swoboda, *P. Nigidii Figuli operum reliquiae*. Vienna: Tempsky.

Syme 1959: Ronald Syme, 'Livy and Augustus', *Harvard Studies in Classical Philology* 64: 27–87.

Syme 1979: Ronald Syme, *Roman Papers*, vol. 1. Oxford: Clarendon Press.

Syme 1991: Ronald Syme, *Roman Papers*, vol. 6. Oxford: Clarendon Press.

Syme 2016: Ronald Syme, *Approaching the Roman Revolution: Papers on Republican History*. Oxford: Oxford University Press.

Taillardat 1967: Jean Taillardat (ed.), *Suétone,* περὶ βλασφημιῶν, περὶ παιδιῶν *(extraits Byzantins)*. Paris: Les belles lettres.

Taplin 1993: Oliver Taplin, *Comic Angels and Other Approaches to Greek Drama through Vase-Paintings*. Oxford: Clarendon Press.

Taplin 2007: Oliver Taplin, *Pots and Plays: Interactions between Tragedy and Greek Vase-Painting of the Fourth Century B.C.* Los Angeles: J. Paul Getty Museum.

Taplin 2020: Oliver Taplin, 'Comic Vases and the First Spread of Greek Comedy into Italy', in Almut Fries and Dimitrios Kanellakis (eds), *Ancient Greek Comedy: Genre—Texts—Reception* (Trends in Classics Supplementary Volume 101, Berlin and Boston: De Gruyter): 253–66.

Taplin and Wyles 2010: Oliver Taplin and Rosie Wyles (eds), *The Pronomos Vase and its Context*. Oxford: Oxford University Press.

Terrenato 1992: Nicola Terrenato, '*Velia* and *Carinae*: Some Observations on an Area of Archaic Rome', in Edward Herring, Ruth Whitehouse and John Wilkins (eds), *Papers of the Fourth Conference of Italian Archaeology* 3–4 (London: Accordia): 31–47.

Todisco 2002: Luigi Todisco, *Teatro e spettacolo in Magna Grecia e Sicilia: testi immagini architettura* (Biblioteca di archeologia 32). Milan: Longanesi.

Todisco 2020: Luigi Todisco, *Figure mascherate e maschere comiche nella ceramica italiota e siceliota* (Studia archeologica 242). Rome and Bristol CT: L' Erma di Bretschneider.

Toher 2017: Mark Toher (ed.), *Nicolaus of Damascus:* The Life of Augustus *and* The Autobiography. Cambridge: Cambridge University Press.

Torelli 1982: Mario Torelli, *Typology and Structure of Roman Historical Reliefs* (Jerome Lectures 14). Ann Arbor: University of Michigan Press.

Tortorella 2000: Stefano Tortorella, 'L'adolescenza dei gemelli, la festa dei *Lupercalia* e l'uccisione di Amulio', in Carandini and Capelli 2000: 244–55.

Trendall 1959: A. D. Trendall, *Phlyax Vases* (BICS Supplement 8). London: Institute of Classical Studies.

Trendall 1987: A. D. Trendall, *The Red-Figured Vases of Paestum*. London: The British School at Rome.

Trendall 1989: A. D. Trendall, *Red Figure Vases of South Italy and Sicily*. London: Thames and Hudson.

Trimble 2012: Gail Trimble, 'Catullus 64: The Perfect Epyllion?', in Baumbach and Bär 2012: 55–79.

Turner 2004: Michael Turner, 'Hamilton and Dionysus: Modern Provenance, Ancient Context', *Mediterranean Archaeology* 17: 93–103.

Usener 1892: Hermann Usener, 'Ein altes Lehregebäude der Philologie', *Sitzungsberichte Bayerische Akademie der Wissenschaften (philos.-philol. und hist. Klasse)* 4: 582–648.

Usener 1913: Hermann Usener, *Kleine Schriften*, vol. 2. Leipzig: Teubner.

Vermeule and Comstock 1988: Cornelius C. Vermeule III and Mary Comstock, *Sculpture in Stone and Bronze in the Museum of Fine Arts, Boston: Additions to the Collections of Greek, Etruscan and Roman Art, 1971–1988*. Boston: MFA.

Vian 1988: Francis Vian, 'Gigantes', *Lexicon Iconographicum Mythologiae Classicae* 4.1: 191–270.

Viscogliosi 1996: A. Viscogliosi, 'Neptunus, aedes in Circo', in Eva Margareta Steinby (ed.), *Lexicon Topographicum Urbis Romae*, vol. 3: H–O (Rome: Quasar): 341–2.

Volk 2015: Katharina Volk, 'Roman Pythagoras', in Gareth D. Williams and Katharina Volk (eds), *Roman Reflections: Studies in Latin Philosophy* (New York: Oxford University Press): 33–49.

Volk 2021: Katharina Volk, *The Roman Republic of Letters: Scholarship, Philosophy, and Politics in the Age of Cicero and Caesar*. Princeton: Princeton University Press.

Volk 2024: Katharina Volk (ed.), *Nigidius Figulus: Roman Polymath* (CSCT 47). Leiden: Brill.

Von Ranke 1883: Leopold von Ranke, *Analekten: Kritische Erörterungen zur alten Geschichte*. Leipzig: Duncker u. Humblot.

Von Rohden and Winnefeld 1911: H. von Rohden and H. Winnefeld, *Architektonische römische Tonreliefs der Kaiserzeit*. Berlin and Stuttgart: W. Spemann.

Wallace-Hadrill 1983: Andrew Wallace-Hadrill, *Suetonius: The Scholar and his Caesars*. London: Duckworth.

Wallace-Hadrill 2008: Andrew Wallace-Hadrill, *Rome's Cultural Revolution*. Cambridge: Cambridge University Press.

Walsh 2009: David Walsh, *Distorted Ideals: The World of Mythological Burlesque*. Cambridge: Cambridge University Press.

Walsh 1961: P. G. Walsh, *Livy: His Historical Aims and Methods*. Cambridge: Cambridge University Press.

Wardle 1993: D. Wardle, 'Did Suetonius Write in Greek?', *Acta Classica* 36: 91–103.

Warmington 1936: E. H. Warmington (ed.), *Remains of Old Latin II: Livius Andronicus, Naevius, Pacuvius and Accius* (Loeb Classical Library 314). Cambridge MA; Harvard University Press.

Waszink 1971: J. H. Waszink (ed.), *Desiderii Erasmi Roterodami Opera omnia*, vol. 1.2. Amsterdam: North-Holland Publishing.

Webb 2008: Ruth Webb, *Demons and Dancers: Performance in Late Antiquity*. Cambridge MA: Harvard University Press.

Webster 1948: T.B.L. Webster, 'South Italian Vases and Attic Drama', *Classical Quarterly* 42: 15–21.

Weinbrot 2005: Howard D. Weinbrot, *Menippean Satire Reconsidered: From Antiquity to the Eighteenth Century*. Baltimore MD: Johns Hopkins University Press.

Weinstock 1950: Stefan Weinstock, 'C. Fonteius Capito and the *libri Tagetici*', *Papers of the British School at Rome* 18: 44–49.

Weinstock 1971: Stefan Weinstock, *Divus Julius*. Oxford: Clarendon Press.

Welch 2007: Katherine E. Welch, *The Roman Amphitheatre: From its Origins to the Colosseum*. New York: Cambridge University Press.

West 1989: Martin West, 'The Early Chronology of Attic Tragedy', *Classical Quarterly* 39: 251–4.

West 2015: M. L. West, 'Epic, Lyric, and Lyric Epic', in P. J. Finglass and Adrian Kelly (eds), *Stesichorus in Context* (Cambridge: Cambridge University Press): 63–80.

White 2010: Peter White, *Cicero in Letters: Epistolary Relations of the Late Republic*. New York: Oxford University Press.

Wilkins and Hill 1994: John Wilkins and Shaun Hill, *Archestratus: The Life of Luxury*. Totnes: Prospect Books.

Wilson 2000: Peter Wilson, *The Athenian Institution of the* Khoregia*: The Chorus, the City and the Stage*. Cambridge: Cambridge University Press.

Winter 2009: Nancy A. Winter, *Symbols of Wealth and Power: Architectural Terracotta Decoration in Etruria and Central Italy, 640–510 BC* (MAAR Supplement 9). Ann Arbor: University of Michigan Press.

Winter et al. 2009: Nancy A. Winter, Ioannis Iliopoulos and Albert J. Ammerman, 'New light on the production of decorated roofs of the 6th c. B.C. at sites in and around Rome', *Journal of Roman Archaeology* 22: 7–28.

Wiseman 1985: T. P. Wiseman, *Catullus and his World*. Cambridge: Cambridge University Press.

Wiseman 1986: T. P. Wiseman, 'Monuments and the Roman Annalists', in I. S. Moxon, J. D. Smart and A. J. Woodman (eds), *Past Perspectives: Studies in Greek and Roman Historical Writing* (Cambridge: Cambridge University Press): 87–101.

Wiseman 1987: T. P. Wiseman, *Roman Studies Literary and Historical.* Liverpool: Francis Cairns.

Wiseman 1988: T. P. Wiseman, 'Satyrs in Rome? The Background to Horace's *Ars poetica*', *Journal of Roman Studies* 78: 1–13.

Wiseman 1994a: T. P. Wiseman, *Historiography and Imagination: Eight Essays on Roman Culture.* Exeter: University of Exeter Press.

Wiseman 1994b: T. P. Wiseman, 'The Senate and the *Populares*, 69–60 BC', in J. A. Crook, Andrew Lintott and Elizabeth Rawson (eds), *The Cambridge Ancient History*, 2nd edn, vol. 9 (Cambridge: Cambridge University Press): 327–67.

Wiseman 1995: T. P. Wiseman, *Remus: A Roman Myth.* Cambridge: Cambridge University Press.

Wiseman 1998: T. P. Wiseman, *Roman Drama and Roman History.* Exeter: University of Exeter Press.

Wiseman 1999: T. P. Wiseman, 'Democracy *alla romana*', *Journal of Roman Archaeology* 12: 537–40.

Wiseman 2004: T. P. Wiseman, *The Myths of Rome.* Exeter: University of Exeter Press.

Wiseman 2006: T. P. Wiseman, 'The Cult Site of Anna Perenna: Documentation, Visualization, Imagination', in Lothar Haselberger and John Humphrey (eds), *Imaging Ancient Rome: Documentation—Visualization—Imagination* (*JRA* Supplement 61, Portsmouth RI): 51–61.

Wiseman 2007: T. P. Wiseman, 'Names Remembered, Names Suppressed', *Journal of Roman Archaeology* 20: 421–8.

Wiseman 2008: T. P. Wiseman, *Unwritten Rome.* Exeter: University of Exeter Press.

Wiseman 2009: T. P. Wiseman, *Remembering the Roman People: Essays on Late-Republican Politics and Literature.* Oxford: Oxford University Press.

Wiseman 2012a: T. P. Wiseman, 'Cicero and the Body Politic', *Politica antica* 2: 133–40.

Wiseman 2012b: T. P. Wiseman, 'Where did they live (e.g. Cicero, Octavius, Augustus)?', *Journal of Roman Archaeology* 25: 656–72.

Wiseman 2015: T. P. Wiseman, *The Roman Audience: Classical Literature as Social History.* Oxford: Oxford University Press.

Wiseman 2016: T. P. Wiseman, 'Varro's Biography of the Roman People': *Histos* 10: cxi–cxviii.

Wiseman 2017: T. P. Wiseman, 'Life in the Street, or Why Historians Should Read the Poets', *Syllecta Classica* 28: 81–110.

Wiseman 2018: T. P. Wiseman, 'Writing Rome's Past', *Histos* 12: i–xxiii.

Wiseman 2019: T. P. Wiseman, *The House of Augustus: A Historical Detective Story.* Princeton: Princeton University Press.

Wiseman 2022: T. P. Wiseman, 'Horace as a Public Poet: The Evidence of *Odes* 3.6', *Cambridge Classical Journal* 68: 231–43.

Wiseman 2023: T. P. Wiseman, *Catullan Questions Revisited.* Cambridge: Cambridge University Press.

Wiseman 2024: T. P. Wiseman, 'Before Naevius: Poetry and History in Early Rome', in Francis Cairns and Trevor Luke (eds), *Roman History in Roman Poetry* (Tallahassee FA: Francis Cairns): 1–36.

Woodman 1988: A. J. Woodman, *Rhetoric in Classical Historiography*. London: Croom Helm.

Woodman 2007: A. J. Woodman, *Sallust: Catiline's War, The Jugurthine War, Histories*. London: Penguin.

Wrede 1995: Henning Wrede, 'Der Venus Felix peinvolles Schicksal im Lupercal', *Römische Mitteilungen* 102: 345–8.

Wright 1910: Henry B. Wright, *The Recovery of a Lost Roman Tragedy: A Study in Honor of Bernadotte Perrin, PhD LLD, Professor in Yale University 1893–1909*. New Haven: Yale University Press.

Wright 2016: Matthew Wright, *The Lost Plays of Greek Tragedy, volume 1: Neglected Authors*. London: Bloomsbury.

Wuilleumier and Audin 1952: Pierre Wuilleumier and Amable Audin, *Les médaillons d'applique gallo-romains de la vallée du Rhône* (Annales de l'Université de Lyon 3.22). Paris: Les Belles Lettres.

Wünsch 1903: Richardus Wünsch (ed.), *Ioannis Lydi de magistratibus populi Romani liber*. Leipzig: Teubner.

Zahlhaas 1975: Gisela Zahlhaas, *Römische Reliefspiegel* (Kataloge der Prähistorischen Staatssammlung München 17). Munich: Lassleben.

Zanker and Ewald 2012: Paul Zanker and Björn C. Ewald, *Living with Myths: The Imagery of Roman Sarcophagi*. Oxford: Oxford University Press.

Zetzel 2018: James E.G. Zetzel, *Critics, Compilers, and Commentators: An Introduction to Roman Philology, 200 BCE–800 CE*. New York: Oxford University Press.

Zevi 2014: Fausto Zevi, 'Demaratus and the "Corinthian" Kings of Rome', in James H. Richardson and Federico Santangelo (eds), *The Roman Historical Tradition: Regal and Republican Rome* (Oxford: Oxford University Press): 53–82.

Ziółkowski 1992: Adam Ziółkowski, *The Temples of Mid-Republican Rome and their Historical and Topographical Context* (Saggi di Storia Antica 4). Rome: 'L'Erma' di Bretschneider.

Ziółkowski 1996: Adam Ziółkowski, 'Of Streets and Crossroads: The Location of the Carinae', *Memoirs of the American Academy in Rome* 41: 121–51.

Ziółkowski 2004: Adam Ziółkowski, *Sacra Via Twenty Years After* (Journal of Juristic Papyrology, Supplement 3). Warsaw: Raphael Taubenschlag Foundation.

Ziółkowski 2019: Adam Ziółkowski, *From* Roma quadrata *to* la grande Roma dei Tarquini*: A Study of the Literary Tradition on Rome's Territorial Growth under the Kings* (Potsdamer Altertumswissenschaftliche Beiträge 70). Stuttgart: Franz Steiner.

Zwierlein 1966: Otto Zwierlein, *Die Rezitationsdramen Senecas* (Beiträge zur klassischen Philologie 20). Meisenheim am Glan: Hain.

GENERAL INDEX

INDEX LOCORUM

A NOTE ON THE TYPE

THIS BOOK has been composed in Miller, a Scotch Roman typeface designed by Matthew Carter and first released by Font Bureau in 1997. It resembles Monticello, the typeface developed for The Papers of Thomas Jefferson in the 1940s by C. H. Griffith and P. J. Conkwright and reinterpreted in digital form by Carter in 2003.

Pleasant Jefferson ("P. J.") Conkwright (1905–1986) was Typographer at Princeton University Press from 1939 to 1970. He was an acclaimed book designer and AIGA Medalist.

The ornament used throughout this book was designed by Pierre Simon Fournier (1712–1768) and was a favorite of Conkwright's, used in his design of the *Princeton University Library Chronicle.*